Land degradation is fast becoming recognized as a key issue for world conservation as we approach the end of the twentieth century. The complex relationship between human development and the environment is explored, with particular emphasis on the causes of land degradation processes. Written as an introduction to the topic, this book provides a clear and timely synthesis of our current understanding of the phenomenon of land degradation.

LAND DEGRADATION
Development and Breakdown
of Terrestrial Environments

LAND DEGRADATION

Development and Breakdown of Terrestrial Environments

C. J. BARROW

Centre for Development Studies
University College of Swansea
University of Wales

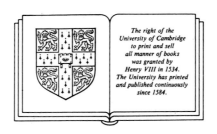

The right of the
University of Cambridge
to print and sell
all manner of books
was granted by
Henry VIII in 1534.
The University has printed
and published continuously
since 1584.

CAMBRIDGE UNIVERSITY PRESS
Cambridge
New York   Port Chester
Melbourne   Sydney

Published by the Press Syndicate of the University of Cambridge
The Pitt Building, Trumpington Street, Cambridge CB2 1RP
40 West 20th Street, New York, NY 10011-4211, USA
10 Stamford Road, Oakleigh, Melbourne 3166, Australia

First published 1991

Printed in Great Britain at the University Press, Cambridge

British Library cataloguing in publication data

Barrow, Christopher J. (Christopher John) *1950–*
Land degradation: development and breakdown of terrestrial environments.
1. Soils. degradation
1. Title
333.73

Library of Congress cataloguing in publication data

Barrow, Christopher J.
Land degradation: development and breakdown of terrestrial environments /
C.J. Barrow
p.   cm.
Includes bibliographical references (p.   ) and index.
ISBN 0-521-35333-5 (hardback)
1. Soil degradation. 2. Polution–Environmental aspects.
3. Soil conservation. 4. Man–Influence on nature. I. Title.
S623.B326   1991
628.5′5–dc20   90–2534 CIP

ISBN 0 521 35333 5 hardback

To Anne and Anna

Contents

Preface

When I began writing this book in 1986 I felt there was a need for a synthesis of the growing literature on land degradation. My hope was to consider both environmental and human factors without falling into the trap of using the 'man and environment' clichés that find their way into many works. In the main I wanted to give the reader an idea of 'where we stood', with the emphasis on why, where, and to what degree, degradation was occurring, rather than on avoidance or cures.

Quite a number of works on the 'greenhouse effect', ozone depletion, deforestation, desertification, etc, have appeared since 1986. If my synthesis has been 'eclipsed' then I am delighted, for I set out to make the problem of land degradation better known. My hope is that this book provides a broad introduction, one which might encourage people to pursue some aspect of land degradation – better still prevention or rehabilitation – more fully.

C. J. Barrow

University College of Swansea,
University of Wales,
Swansea, UK

March 1990

Acknowledgements

It would have been impossible to write this book were it not for the patience shown by my wife and daughter during the evenings and weekends when I worked on the preparation and typing of the manuscript.

   I would like to thank the staff of the Main and Natural Sciences Libraries, University College of Swansea, particularly those in the Inter-Library Loans Department.

1 *Land degradation: an overview*

INTRODUCTION

MUCH OF THE EARTH is degraded, is being degraded or is at risk of degradation. Marine, freshwater, atmospheric, near-space (upper atmosphere: *c.* 15 km altitude to geostationary orbit: *c.* 40,000 km altitude) and terrestrial environments have suffered and continue to suffer degradation. This book focuses on terrestrial degradation, that is, damaged lands, land being the interface between the Earth's solid surface and the atmosphere. Land is subject to a complex of influences, namely atmospheric, geological, solar radiation, and, in all but the coldest, driest, or otherwise inhospitable environments, organic activity. The approach adopted in this book is to progress from the global-scale down through environments and ecosystems that are increasingly more controlled or disrupted and degraded by the activities of Man.

If it were possible to ask the bulk of Mankind their views about land, the chances are that individuals would more often than not recognize three categories: 1. land being utilized, 2. that with potential utility, and 3. that which appears useless, at least in the foreseeable future. Utility, may be said to be the capability of something to meet people's perceived needs/wants. It has been defined in a more formal economic sense as '. . . a measure of self-perceived well-being and depends on the value of goods and services enjoyed' (Lowe & Lewis, 1980: 7). In practice, both economic goods (things measurable in monetary units) and non-economic goods (things not easily measurable in economic units – such as aesthetic quality or a moral responsibility to conserve species) determine utility, but the former tend to dominate.

What is land degradation?

Land degradation may be defined as the loss of utility or potential utility or the reduction, loss or change of features or organisms which cannot be replaced. A precise definition is impossible, given the many factors which may be responsible. In general, land degradation implies a reduction in rank or status, for example, a degradation and/or loss of soil, or a change to a simpler floral/faunal composition or a substitution of one organic form for a lower organic form. Blaikie & Brookfield (1987: 6–7) suggested land is degraded when '. . . it suffers a loss of intrinsic qualities or a decline in its capabilities . . . (it) . . . is therefore best viewed not as a one-way street, but as a result of forces, or the product of an equation, in which both human and natural forces find a place'; that equation being:

Net degradation =
| natural degrading | | natural reproduction + |
| processes + | − | restorative management | $\quad$ (1)
| human interference |

(Blaikie & Brookfield, 1987: 7)

Chartres (in Chisholm & Dumsday, 1987: 7) suggested land degradation was something that can result from any causative factor or combination of factors, which reduces the physical, chemical or biological status of the land and which may restrict the land's productive capacity.

Not infrequently, land degradation results at the end of a 'chain of causation' and is an un-anticipated consequence of what may be far-removed human and/or natural cause(s). The onset of the problem may therefore be difficult to forecast. Some land degradation is due to natural (bio-geophysical) causes, some is due to human causes and some to a combination of causes.

Once land has been degraded, it is often possible to rehabilitate it and thus restore it to a level of utility, possibly not as good as its original state but better than it was in its damaged state. Given satisfactory perception of the threat, funding, technology, and organization, degradation, whatever the cause, would be reduced. Land restoration implies the rehabilitation of degraded land to a standard matching that which it originally had. The one form of degradation which is permanent is the extinction of living species.

In practice, when cost–benefits and other limitations are weighed up, only a portion of degraded land can be satisfactorily rehabilitated. Some degraded land may remain abandoned and neglected for a long time. This derelict land may then be rehabilitated to some sort of utility, quite possibly not its original state, when techniques, funds and motivation permit (Fig. 1.1).

Perception of land degradation

The willingness that people, organizations, governments, etc have to utilize, and perhaps to protect, an environment or a resource depends mainly upon their perception of utility which is influenced by both their attitude and plight. The value attached to an ecosystem or resource can be measured by the amount of money or other utilities foregone in order to obtain some of that resource or to make use of it (Cottrell, 1978: 1). An area of land may have a range of perceived values. For example: a forest may provide timber, serve as a conservation area, support recreation, protect a watershed from erosion and possibly have aesthetic or religious significance. These perceptions are not static, they may vary over time, and, at any one point in time, different

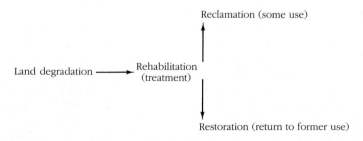

Fig. 1.1. Land degradation terminology.

groups of people may make different demands on the same land. Demands on land can also vary from locality to locality (Immler, 1986: 45). Not all members of a population are likely to enjoy the utility of the land to the same degree and it is common for some people to bear all, or most of, the costs of land development, yet get little benefit from it.

The utility of land can be due to complex factors: climate, communications, law and order, moral and cultural and many other considerations, e.g. a locality or a resource may even be valued purely as a consequence of belief and historical accident (Doxiadis, 1977: 11). Utility of land or a resource often reflects the amount of labour involved in its exploitation, for example, coal has utility in itself as a fuel or raw material for chemicals, etc, it also generates mining, transport, and other employment.

Resource economists since Adam Smith and David Ricardo have argued that the value of a resource or ecosystem is largely governed by the cost of production/realization, particularly labour input costs. Land degradation can adversely affect the yield of labour in terms of production '. . . Other things being equal, the product of work on degraded land is less than the same land without degradation' (Blaikie & Brookfield, 1987: 1). Given that the productive capacity (utility) of land or a resource is, at least in part, Man-made, it is possible for such inputs to come, not from the locality being exploited or valued, but from a distant area, e.g. the value of land in the Caribbean for banana production depends upon the demand for and the ability to transport and market the fruit in Europe. To summarize, land, labour and capital are not always separable in practice, and a resource generally has utility because of inputs of labour and capital.

Investment in enhancement of land utility has been termed landesque capital (Simon, 1981: 86). Landesque capital is capital that can be depleted or added to. Alteration in input of labour or materials, technological innovation, altered natural conditions, changed attitudes towards the land or its produce can lead to land improvement or land degradation. There are land uses that can cause little deterioration in the value of the land, for example, carefully managed tourism or well-managed extraction of water or geothermal energy. There are land uses which cause severe land degradation (e.g. nuclear weapons testing).

To establish whether land degradation has, has not occurred, is occurring, will or will not occur, demands that the past, present and future utility of the land be established. The present is seldom well documented, and, where it is, it may not be an accurate 'baseline'. Information on the past and forecasts of the future are likely to be missing or at best inaccurate. 'Natural landscape' is often the result of long-forgotten human activity, like the degraded *maquis*-type biomes of the Mediterranean – the land at present does not give a true indication of the potential that it once had. The opposite can hold; much of what is now rich Dutch farmland was once relatively unproductive saltmarsh or shallow sea which has been enhanced in utility by Man.

Land degradation studies are frequently hindered by reliance on received information and insufficient, objective and accurate data. For example, it is not unusual for the people of the Himalayas or the Andes to be charged with causing severe land degradation, which, in turn, is seen to be the cause of siltation and flooding in lowlands. The evidence that the situation in the Himalayas and Andes has significantly deteriorated due to Man, and the proof linking siltation and flooding with activity in the uplands is mainly circumstantial and often speculative (Ives & Pitt, 1988: 139, 191; Blaikie, 1989: 23).

To get a useful 'baseline', planners and managers should not overlook the contribution of the palaeoecologist, archaeologist, historian and local people, not only to show past capabilities of the land, but also to indicate if there have been problems or catastrophes which might recur and if there were strategies developed by past peoples to exploit the land that modern land users may be unaware of, and which might prove valuable.

Short-term studies which attempt to explain changes in an ecosystem may be ineffective, especially if dealing with organisms like trees which may live and regenerate only over a period of hundreds of years. In the last ten years, improved knowledge of the structure and function of ecosystems, remote sensing and advances in information storage and retrieval has made it easier to establish baseline data from which to monitor land degradation. However, degradation monitoring is not a precise science and difficulties may not be forecast or recognized even with the best studies.

One reason for delay in recognizing land degradation may be that many people have been conditioned to looking at economic indicators of development, and only when environmental/resource depletion translate into economic difficulties do they really 'notice'. People are more likely to react to more visible forms of land degradation: dust storms, deep gullies, land slides, etc, yet, much land degradation is insidious. Gradual loss of topsoil is one of the major threats to human well-being, but it is not readily apparent, at least not in its early stages. Even when degradation becomes obvious, people may not wish to acknowledge it: to admit he has a soil erosion problem a farmer may feel is admission to bad husbandry; to admit an irrigation project is silting up or suffering salinization may embarrass a government or agency.

Some people, particularly the poor and powerless, may react to problems, including land degradation, in a fatalistic way. They may be perfectly aware of the problem and the long-term implications, but are unable or unwilling to do more than practise what they know to simply scratch a living. It is also common for those in authority to be sufficiently removed from the land that they do not see degradation as a problem nor the efforts to counter it as worthwhile.

Even the most enlightened government or agency is going to weigh the readily apparent short-term labour/economic costs and/or foregone benefits against possible future long-term benefits from degradation control efforts (Chisholm & Dumsday, 1987: 196). There may also be the dilemma for the would-be investor in degradation control: that the money and effort might give better returns if used in some other way; it may make economic sense to degrade and abandon some lands.

Agreement that land degradation is taking place and requires attention is sometimes difficult to achieve, at least in part, because the perception of utility varies: an increase in utility for one affected group may mean a decrease in utility for another group or groups. For example, the replacement of forest by savanna may be welcomed by herders or farmers; their livelihoods can be followed in the area. As a result, a conservationist or forest-dwelling aboriginal people may not be so pleased.

Special interest groups and sometimes governments may discourage recognition/reaction to degradation: it is not uncommon for a government to have decreed an inappropriate land use or activity and then to adhere to it in spite of the damage it causes in order not to have to counter the 'official line' (Blaikie & Brookfield, 1987: 4). In the USA, in the 1930s, writers like Steinbeck, folk-singers like Woody Guthrie, and a number of contemporary environmental activists, strove to publicize the causes and need for control

4

of the 'Dustbowl' conditions in the mid-west (see Chapter 8). Their activities were at the time widely regarded as 'un-American' and subversive.

Perceived solutions to land degradation may not be appropriate; for example, a widespread response in the West has been to apply artificial fertilizers to land that is suffering topsoil erosion and/or decline in fertility – this is a treatment of 'symptoms' not an attempt to cure the causes, it may even delay the breakdown of production – at which point the problems are recognized – and real solutions are difficult.

Development and concern for land degradation

Land degradation is often seen as a consequence or 'side-effect' of development. Concise, generally acceptable definitions of development are not easy to come by, and those that are express wishful thinking rather than realities involved. The IUCN *et al.* (1980) suggested that development was . . . the modification of the biosphere and non-living resources to satisfy human needs and improve the quality of life . . .' The UN General Assembly Resolution 2626 (XXV) of 24th October, 1970, suggested that 'The ultimate objective of development must be to bring about a sustained improvement in the well-being of the individual and bestow benefits on all' (Ghosh, 1984: *vii*). To sustain development its demands must be within the support capabilities of the land, and the environment in general, otherwise degradation will take place.

Land degradation is not a new phenomenon, nor is concern for it a recent development (Roberts, 1989: 182; Bunney, 1990). Greek and Roman writers commented on soil erosion, deforestation, and other problems, and environmental concern was incorporated into Confucianism in China. In medieval Europe, St Francis of Assisi urged more concern for nature, and in the first half of the seventeenth century Francis Bacon penned the maxim: 'We cannot command nature except by obeying her' (translation from Latin – *Essays*, Everyman edn, 1939. London: Dent and Sons). In the late eighteenth century Benjamin Franklin noted '. . . whenever we attempt to amend the Scheme of Providence, and interfere with the govenance of the world, we had need to be very circumspect less we do more harm than good' (Silverman, 1986).

Few decision-makers or the public at large gave much heed to environmental concern before the 1960s. It has been argued that, after the English Reformation (i.e. by the early eighteenth century), a 'Protestant ethic' had emerged in Europe. Those who support the idea of a Protestant ethic hold that the West's religious and moral outlook was compatible with the development of science, technology and capitalism, and that it has moulded Western attitudes towards land and nature. It is claimed by some that it led to Westerners stressing the goodness of hard work, the need to tame and exploit nature and an abhorrence of disorder – attitudes that have not always helped to protect the land (Tawney, 1954; Weber, 1958; Caldwell, 1977; Dawson & Doornkamp, 1973: 249–75).

After the mid eighteenth century. Europe had growing industrialization and rising birth rates. It was, however, possible for people to migrate to the Americas, and to various other colonies, and, increasingly, produce was coming from these lands back to Western Europe, particularly to the UK. By the late eighteenth century/early nineteenth century, it was apparent that the 'frontier would some day close' – in 1798 and 1803 Thomas Malthus published his *Essays on Principles of Population*, examining the interrelationships between population and resources. Drawing on ideas initially spread by French *Philosophs* like Condorcet, Malthus's essays were opposed to utopianism and anarchy and effectively said that as Man could not change nature and the supply of most resources, little could be done to counter poverty (and ultimately land degradation).

In the second half of the nineteenth century 'romantic' poets like Wordsworth, William Blake and Emerson expressed interest in the environment, in that they saw 'industrial man' as a corrupter of nature. In Victorian Britain reformers like Chadwick, anti-establishment intellectuals like William Morris and Robert Owen, and, in Europe, Kropotkin and Marcuse, concerned at what they saw as a decline in public health and morals as a consequence of industrialization and urbanization, were, by the 1860s, preaching 'utilitarian environmentalism'. At this time there was considerable activity in the natural sciences (in the UK, Darwin and in France, Teillhard de Chardin). In the USA, George Perkins Marsh (1864) and others began to promote conservation, and at that time there was an active conservation lobby in S. Africa (Cape Province) (Anderson & Grove, 1987: 21; Grove, 1990). Some have argued that Marsh's book *Man and Nature* (1864) began modern discussion of environmental issues.

Between the 1860s and the 1930s development and environment thinking became clouded by over-crude environmental determinism promoted by writers like Huntington (1915). Brookes (1926), Markham (1944) and Friedrich Ratzel (Simon & Kahn, 1984: 2; Redclift, 1984). Environmental determinism was discredited by the 1940s, but a reaction to it might explain why it was not until the 1960s that there was anything but patchy interest in environmental dimensions of development. A paternalistic attitude toward development flowered in this 1860s' to 1940s' period; the view tended to be that Westerners best knew how to solve environmental, social and economic problems and should command rather than learn from other peoples.

A review of the environment/development literature from the 1960s to the present suggests that attempts to explain why environmental damage occurs can be split into several broad categories (Table 1.1).

From the 1950s (Thomas *et al.*, 1956) and particularly from the early 1970s worries were voiced about an impending 'environmental crisis'.

Endowed with a 'Messianic fervour' (Rees, 1985: 2), many of the activists of the 1960s' to 1970s' 'ecology/environmental movement' (e.g. Hardin, 1968; Ehrlich *et al.*, 1970; Brubaker, 1972; Meadows *et al.*, 1972; Ward & Dubos, 1972) were given derogatory titles by politicians and the press: 'profits of doom', 'Neo-Mathusians', etc. On the whole, the 'movement', which included many environmental and conservation non-governmental organizations, e.g. Friends of the Earth, Environmental Defence Fund, Sierra Club, Council for the Preservation of Rural England, and many others, was interested in conservation and control of human population increase and there was little entry into politics (O'Riordan, 1976; Sandbach, 1980; Clark & Munn, 1986: 8–12).

In 1971, UNESCO launched the Man and Biosphere Programme (MAB), which helped expand awareness of the structure and function of the world's environments and the manner in which Man interacted with nature. By the early 1980s environmental 'stocktaking' provided a foundation for environmental policy advocacy. The International Union for the Conservation of Nature and Natural Resources (IUCN) published the *World Conservation Strategy* (IUCN *et al.*, 1980). Concerned to build 'the social factor' into their environmental recommendations, most environmentalists of the 1970s and 1980s failed to identify either the agency, without which nothing can be achieved, or the mechanism, with which environmental policies could be

Table 1.1. *Explanations of why environmental degradation occurs (from the environment/development literature 1960–1989).*

Category	Explanation	Sources
Neo-Malthusian	Argues demographic pressure leads to overuse or misuse of land, especially marginal land[a]. Criticized for being too simplistic by failing to look at population increase in its social and historical context. Also overlooked the fact that *c.* one-third of the world's people use most resources and consume about six times the energy of the other two-thirds in developing countries.	A, B
Limits to growth or Ghandian approach	Similar to A above	C, D
Economic perspective: (i) tragedy-of the- commons school	Irrational land/resource use causes degradation and can be understood through analysis of issues associated with the economics of production – in particular, faulty property relationships and difficulty in managing common resources[b].	E, F G
(ii) externalities school	Argues that population increase leads to destruction of common resources as individuals acting to maximize their benefit harm society as a whole.	
	In Africa it has been suggested that increased state ownership has reduced community control yet failed to replace it with effective state control. Individuals react by taking what they can from common land before anyone else does[c].	H
	Neo-Malthusian analysis widened to consider externalities as well as population increase. In particular, weaknesses of capital accumulation which lead to accelerated exploitation of land/resources to the point of degradation, profits are then invested elsewhere.	
Dependency perspective	External factors affect population and land use in developing countries, leading to environmental degradation. The external degradation. The external factors include: inappropriate technology transfer, promotion of inappropriate agricultural strategy, trade and aid relationships.	I, J K
Economics thinking	Faulty economics thinking has influenced decision-making – economists tend to see Earth's resources as limitless and have been willing to pursue a 'Faustian bargain', whereby short-term benefits are traded for long-term, unknown, unforeseen costs.	L, M
Neo-Marxist	Wealth of the more advanced countries has been achieved by transfer of resources from the world's poor countries. In so doing poor countries are impoverished and this leads to land degradation.	M

Table 1.1. (*cont.*)

Category	Explanation	Sources
Ethical stance	Man has seen himself as above nature and separate from it (especially in the West), in control, but not obliged to manage it (i.e. act as a steward). In practice, all individuals, regardless of ethics, will tend to be biassed toward short-term gain (see Table 1.2)[d].	N

Notes: [a] Marginal land – for a definition see Chapter 2.
[b] Common resource – communally owned, public property. On which, for example, privately owned livestock are grazed. The consequence is that individuals acting to maximize their benefit harm society as a whole.
[c] It is worth noting that in Australia and the USA, where there is serious land degradation, livestock and land are privately owned.
[d] Various authors point out how 'in-tune' primitive peoples are with their environment. However, this is not always the case (if it ever is). For example, the Maoris made short work of the moas, and inhabitants of Easter Island completely destroyed native palm forests long before contact with Europeans.

implemented (Redclift, 1984: 44). The 1972 UN Conference on the Human Environment (Fournex) and the 1973 UN Conference on the Human Environment (Stockholm) were instrumental in bringing countries together to consider the future of the Earth. The United Nations Environment Programme (UNEP) was established, but the environmental movement waned between about 1975 and 1987. There had nevertheless been a tremendous impact on development thinking and development-related institutions; for example, before 1972 fewer than ten of the world's governments had environmental agencies, by 1987 140 had them (Myers, 1986a).

It is likely that the 1973/4 OPEC oil price rises, which caused widespread concern for energy supplies, diverted attention from environmental worries. OPEC also helped to reduce the funds available in developed, and particularly developing countries for environmental protection. Nevertheless, between 1973 and 1985, there were a number of works expressing environmental/development concern (IUCN, 1975a), notably: the *World Conservation Strategy*; the *Global 2000 Report* (Council on Environmental Quality & Department of State (1982); the *'Brandt Report'* (Independent Commission on International Development Issues, 1980) and the writings of Riddell (1981) and Tolba (1982). From roughly 1985, interest in the social and political issues involved in environment/development problems increased; much of this interest was from people in developed countries (Brown *et al.*, 1984; Myers, 1985a; Bartelmus, 1986).

In the late 1980s, the World Commission on Environment and Development, was asked to formulate a global agenda for change. Its publication of the 'Brundtland Report' (World Commission on Environment and Development, 1987a) marked a shift toward more pragmatic consideration of environment/development. Within a few years of this Report, there was a new interest and, by the late 1980s, a concern for 'green issues' had risen to a level unknown previously (Porritt, 1988).

During the mid to late 1980s the 'Gaia hypothesis', first proposed in the early 1970s, attracted attention as empirical and theoretical work on global bio-geophysical function gathered information on the role of oceanic, atmospheric and organic processes in controlling climate (Goldsmith, 1989).

Table 1.2. *Attitudes towards environment and development.*

1. *Environmental determinism* Essentially, the idea that environmental factors are all-powerful and determine what happens. Man thus has little choice, regardless of what he may think.
2. *Mild environmentalism* View that nature is all-powerful: Man can choose, but at his peril. If environmental rules/limits are disregarded, there will be trouble.
3. *Environmental possibilism* The recognition of possibilities and limitations set by the environment.
4. *Environmental probabilism* Developer attempts to predict typical reaction to a given milieu.
5. *Cognitive behaviouralism* People react to a given milieu in light of previous experience(s).

Source: Based in part on Saarinen, 1966: 26.

Table 1.3. *Approximate global land areas/land use (1977 situation).*

Land use	Area (million ha)
Arable	1,462
Grassland	3,058
Forest	4,077
Other land	4,476
Permanent ice cover	1,400
Total	14,473 → Of this, estimates suggest: 849 is moderately productive and 477 is highly productive agricultural land.

Source: Wolman & Fournier, 1987: 9–10, 13.

HOW SIGNIFICANT A PROBLEM IS LAND DEGRADATION?

To establish the significance of land degradation requires an assessment of how widespread it is, how severe the damage is, and whether or not it is practically controllable or reversible. Measurement is difficult. One complication is that it is possible for degradation to proceed in broadly the same way and at a similar pace in two areas which differ in some aspect of soil, flora, etc, in which case the effects may be quite different. For example, where soil is deep, erosion which would soon affect a shallow soil may have no effect on vegetation cover or fertility for hundreds of years. (Harlin & Berardi, 1987: 151–72). Land degradation has not been easy to measure; before the late 1970s there was little in the way of accurate data on the world's ecosystems (Table 1.3 gives an approximate breakdown of global land use.) Economists of the 1970s tended to dismiss environmental matters as 'intangibles' and so there was little serious assessment unless a problem had developed (Eyre, 1978: 6; Immler, 1986: 45).

One cannot assume that present day social, economic, cultural and environmental conditions are the same as they were in the past, nor that they will remain constant in the future – this can make prediction of rates and seriousness of land degradation difficult. An area cleared of forest may suffer severe erosion until crops or regrowth are established and erosion may then decline to close to original levels until there is some future change in land use.

Land degradation is widespread in the USA, Europe, the USSR and the Third World: all countries, rich or poor, arid or humid, cool or tropical suffer it. It is not only a problem where there are high populations, for, in Australia or Amazonia, where population is sparse and sedentary settlement is a relatively recent phenomenon, there is land degradation. The effects of land degradation may be felt both in the locality where land is damaged and elsewhere. For example, deforestation may drive the price of fuelwood beyond the reach of distant townsfolk; erosion which damages farms in an upland may also cause siltation that ruins irrigated land or possibly causes floods well away in lowlands.

While the causes of land degradation are diverse and often complex, there are some clear trends. One is that land is being lost from productive use at an alarming rate. Over the last 7000 or so years, since most people have come to depend on sedentary agriculture, one estimate suggests 430 million ha of cropland and grazing land have been severely degraded. There can be little doubt that there has been, and continues to be, extinctions of flora and fauna at a disturbing rate (World Commission on Environment and Development, 1987b).

Even if the amount of land available/potentially available to feed mankind, is adequate for the near future, using present agricultural strategies, there is an uneven distribution of land in relation to population (Ghosh, 1984: 75). There is also a risk that some parts of the globe are more prone to environmental change than others. Ultimately there is a limit to availability of land, and demand upon it increases due to rising population, increasing expectations and loss by degradation. In AD 2110, world population is likely to reach 10.5 billion, 9.1 billion of whom will be in the poorer, probably more degraded, developing countries (Wolman & Fournier, 1987: 9). Impressive improvements in crop production since the Second World War will be difficult to sustain if degradation is not controlled, in some cases the production increase may be transient and modernized high-yield production is, at least partly, the reason for land degradation. There is a risk that short-term gains in agricultural production or growth of gross national product create an illusion of progress while land degradation develops largely unheeded until the problem is severe.

Is there an 'environmental crisis'?

Some have talked of an 'environmental crisis' since the 1960s. However, it was really from about 1981 that the fear has been widely articulated. Now it has become a cliché, with little real proof (Thirgood, 1981: 163; Johnston & Taylor, 1986: 1–11; Wolman & Fournier, 1987: 39; Watts, 1989). In the 1970s environmental degradation tended to be regarded mainly as a problem restricted to richer nations, a view widely voiced at the 1972 Stockholm Conference on the Human Environment. In the early 1980s many disagreed that there was a serious environmental problem (Simon, 1981; Simon & Kahn, 1984). Today, some talk of a global environmental crisis, others of the South's environmental crisis.

There are undoubtedly serious environmental problems. Whether there is a global crisis situation, in the sense that it is now a turning point, a last chance to act before world degradation has taken place to the degree that control will be impossible, is more difficult to answer. Some of the global bio-geochemical and bio-geophysical cycles, vital for maintaining climate, atmospheric gases, soil fertility, etc, might be close to breaking point. Certainly, threats to the environment have been growing faster than the willingness or ability to control them.

Some developing countries appear to be trapped in a 'downward spiral' of interlinked ecological and economic decline (World Commission on Environment and Development, 1987a: *xi*). Land degradation has more impact on people when they have no opportunity for alternative livelihoods and/or dwelling sites.

SubSaharan Africa is often singled out as particularly cursed with environmental/development problems (Harrison, 1987a: 27, 41: Onimode, 1988; Mortimore, 1989). There were, in 1975, an estimated 400 million people in Africa south of the Sahara, about 300 million of whom practised subsistence agriculture. For a variety of reasons, for many of these, traditional farming and grazing strategies are breaking down (DeVos, 1975: 125). Whether these problems constitute a crisis is debated (Anderson & Grove, 1987: 81–101).

What are the costs of land degradation?

It is difficult to establish the costs of so complex a phenomenon as land degradation; it involves external costs and benefits (costs incurred offsite, well away from where degradation occurs) as well as the onsite costs. The opportunity cost of land degradation is equal to the income from production on degraded land, less the costs of repairing and preventing land degradation. To an economist, the optimum level of land degradation repair/prevention is likely to be the point at which the marginal cost of repair/prevention is equal to the marginal benefit from repair/prevention.

One can recognize four reference points in studying the economics of land degradation:

1. *zero rate* of land degradation (no land degradation);
2. *natural rate* of land degradation (rate in the absence of human activity);
3. *actual rate* of land degradation (rate given current land management);
4. *optimal rate* of land degradation (corresponding to socially optimal resource allocation and management).

According to Chisholm & Dumsday (1987: 226), an 'economic' solution to land degradation would be one which attained a socially optimal level of land conservation/degradation both now and over the long term, at least social cost. To an economist, the efficient level of land degradation and conservation is where the sum of the total damages (onsite and offsite) plus the costs of abatement are at a minimum. This could well mean degradation greater than natural rates of land degradation.

What forms of land degradation give greatest cause for concern?

Despite their grand scale, some global bio-geochemical and bio-geophysical cycles are vulnerable and could become degraded enough to have disastrous effects. Global levels of carbon dioxide and the Earth's atmospheric ozone levels already give cause for concern. Loss of genetic resources, as species become extinct, is serious and accelerating. The effects of toxic chemicals, heavy metals and other pollutants are significant and increasing. There has been nuclear fall-out, mainly from civil accident and weapons testing, but there is the risk of catastrophic nuclear warfare. Genetic engineering might result in an uncontrolled release of some new form of organism with serious consequences on virtually any of the world's important organic process, organisms or bio-geochemical/bio-geophysical cycles. The HIV (AIDS) virus already shows the potential to debilitate sufficient rural labour to cause neglect of farmland in some regions.

Doubtless, as understanding of the structure and function of the world's ecosystems increases, and as monitoring of their degree of degradation improves, new worries will arise. Since 1973, the 'oil-crisis' has attracted attention, yet the potentially much more serious problem of soil-loss has generated far less interest in spite of the problems it caused in the mid-west of the USA in the 1930s (Brown, 1977: 18; 1978).

Different processes of degradation could act synergistically and some have a cumulative effect, so recognition of the degree of threat may not be easy. The management of land degradation is therefore an art, with a huge palette of responses or avoidance procedures, the application of which involves value judgements, wisdom and scientific skill.

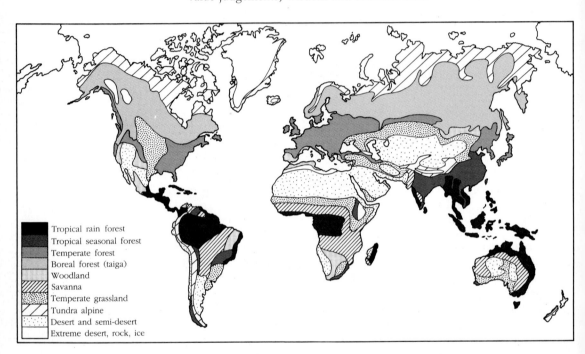

Tropical rain forest
Tropical seasonal forest
Temperate forest
Boreal forest (taiga)
Woodland
Savanna
Temperate grassland
Tundra alpine
Desert and semi-desert
Extreme desert, rock, ice

Fig. 1.2. Global distribution of ecosystems (generalized). Source: *compiled by author from various sources.*

2 Why is land degradation occurring?

CAUSE AND PROCESS

LAND DEGRADATION is commonly blamed on 'acts of God' or 'acts of the peasantry', and there is typically little attempt to assess the real causes. Another approach is to argue that, as land degradation is widespread in environments exploited by Man, then human actions must be the main cause. A wide range of human activities can trigger or exacerbate land degradation; there are also environments which are very vulnerable to degradation, and natural catastrophes from time to time degrade virtually all environments. Also, it would be rash to assume that human activity always has a negative effect on rate of erosion, species survival, etc.

Sometimes the process of land degradation can be followed, but the cause(s) may be obscure. Commonly, a chain-of-causation stretches away in space and/or time from the site where land degradation is manifest (see Fig. 2.1) (Eckholm, 1976; Darkoh, 1987: 25; Blaikie & Brookfield, 1987: 4).

Sometimes causes are local and relatively simple, sometimes land degradation results from, possibly complex, global changes some of which are at least partly caused by human activity. While the scale of global processes may be vast, they may be in a state of dynamic equilibrium, easily upset by human actions. Chadwick & Goodman (1975: 4) recognized three types of bio-geochemical cycle: natural; perturbed (upset by Man) and recycling, i.e. managed by Man to be sustainable. The second type is increasingly common, the last type is often elusive.

Land is a 'stage' within, upon, or above, which, a number of resources may be exploited. Where there is exploitation of more than one resource, this may be mutually compatible, or there may be damaging interactions. Resources vary in character and some are more difficult to manage than others (Ramade, 1984). The following classification of types of resource is generally accepted and gives some indication of 'manageability':

1. *Continuous resources* include: solar energy, wind, gravity, tidal energy, geothermal energy. These continue to be available, and, with the possible exception of solar energy, the receipt of which could be affected by atmospheric pollution, cannot be degraded, even with gross mismanagement.
2. *Renewable resources* (flow resources) include: clean water, flora, fauna, soil, clean air. Rees (1985: 224), defined renewable resources as '. . . those capable of natural regeneration into useful "products" within a timespan relevant to man.' These resources are potentially renewable and could be indefinitely available, provided their capacity to regenerate is not

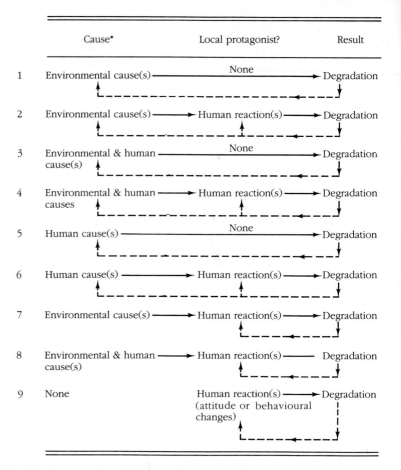

	Cause*	Local protagonist?	Result
1	Environmental cause(s)	None	Degradation
2	Environmental cause(s)	Human reaction(s)	Degradation
3	Environmental & human cause(s)	None	Degradation
4	Environmental & human causes	Human reaction(s)	Degradation
5	Human cause(s)	None	Degradation
6	Human cause(s)	Human reaction(s)	Degradation
7	Environmental cause(s)	Human reaction(s)	Degradation
8	Environmental & human cause(s)	Human reaction(s)	Degradation
9	None	Human reaction(s) (attitude or behavioural changes)	Degradation

Fig. 2.1. Causes and combinations of causes resulting in land degradation. Notes: ————= cause → effect; —————→ = possible feedback (may act to exacerbate degradation or may tend to diminish cause–effect relationships or may have no significant effect. * Causes can be local, external (possibly global) or a combination of both. Environmental=bio-geophysical or bio-geochemical; human= social, economic, cultural, political. Source: author.

damaged by natural catastrophe or human activities. Once degraded beyond a certain critical point, a renewable resource may never recover.

3. *Non-renewable resources* (stock resources) include: many minerals and some groundwaters. These are available only in finite quantities, or else the rate of renewal is so slow that they must be regarded as available only in fixed quantities.

4. *Extrinsic resources* include: human skills, institutions, management abilities, etc. They can be fickle and prone to breakdown or degradation, yet can be continuous resources if well managed (Riddell, 1981: 23).

In categorization of resources, one should not lose sight of the fact that non-renewable resources and continuous resources are opposite ends of the same continuum and that the above classes overlap. The demand for a resource can vary because attitudes, tastes, willingness or ability of people to use or purchase the resource alter, or because a substitute has been found. Technological advances and altered world circumstances affect resource demand, people: '... live and act at a local level, but their alternatives and opportunities are shaped significantly by events at the regional, national and international levels' (Dorner & El-Shafie, 1980: 8).

Table 2.1. *Groupings of theses which seeks to explain why land degradation takes place.*

1. *Natural disaster theses* – blame degradation on bio-geophysical causes or 'acts of God'.
2. *Population change (Neo-Malthusian) theses* – argue degradation occurs when population growth exceeds critical environmental parameters (and possibly in some cases when population decreases).
3. *Underdevelopment theses* – argue resources are exploited to benefit the world economy or developed countries, leaving little profit to manage or restore the degraded environment.
4. *Internationalist theses* – suggest that taxation and other forces interfere with the market and trigger over exploitation.
5. *Legacy of colonialism theses* – argues that trade links, communications, rural–urban linkages, etc, 'hang-overs' from the past, promote poorly managed resource exploitation.
6. *Inappropriate technology and advice theses* – argue that the wrong strategies and techniques are promoted resulting in land degradation.
7. *Ignorance theses* – blame lack of knowledge for degradation, e.g. the use of CFCs and their effect on the ozone layer.
9. *Attitude theses* – blame people's/institution's attitudes for degradation.

Land must be described as a non-renewable (fixed stock) resource, although it has a renewable capacity to support most forms of biological life (Rees, 1985: 224). Exploitation of the world's land has been described by some as conforming to a 'lollipop model', in that, with each 'lick', there is less for the future (Chisholm & Dumsday, 1987: 354). On the other hand, with good management, it might be possible to sustain indefinite usage of land, even improve its utility.

Alternative ways of classifying Earth resources include:

1. a division into – those that can be safely 'stretched' by Man;
   – those that can be safely 'stretched' only if carefully managed;
   – those that cannot/should not be 'stretched.
2. a division into – resources with actual value;
   – resources with option value (possible use perceived);
   – resources with intrinsic value (no obvious practical value, but there is a will to maintain it).

The processes of land and other environmental degradation are not adequately understood, so predictive models are mainly poorly developed (Chisholm & Dumsday, 1987: 322).Table 2.1 groups various theses which seek to explain why land degradation takes place and Figure 2.1 shows causes or combinations of causes that may result in land degradation.

Natural hazards as a cause of land degradation

There are few, if any, regions so blessed that they will not at some point experience a natural disaster. However, some environments are less stable than others or are more likely to suffer disruptions. Areas predisposed to disaster include:

– steeply sloping areas;
– easily damaged soils;
– drylands and localities where soils drain fast;

– lowlands close to the sea, particularly on exposed coasts and in areas
  prone to glacier 'calving', submarine eruption or submarine
  mudlslides;
– regions where rainfall is intense;
– drought-risk areas where rainfall is mainly due to airmass movements
  which can be fickle ('monsoon' rainfall);
– parts of the Earth where hurricanes or similar storms occur;
– areas prone to sudden frost or cold winds;
– areas of earthquake or volcanic activity;
– areas subject to periodic invasion by destructive insects.

There is evidence of periodic natural catastrophes (infrequent on the
human time-scale, but not if judged by the geological time-scale) which
caused widespread and severe land degradation. A number of scientists
argue that massive extinctions of organisms at the end of the Permian and
Cretaceous Periods reflect such catastrophes. Huggett (1988, 1989) provided
a fascinating study of catastrophic tsunamis, arguing that huge waves have
been quite common. The UK he suggested has been, and probably will be,
struck every 0.8 to 1.4 million years by 13 to 130 m tsunamis. Worse, there
are indications of waves *several hundred* metres in height caused in the past by
meteorite/comet strike, eruptions or other Earth processes. There is
evidence of climatic disruption, sufficient to seriously affect human affairs
following the Hekla-3 volcanic eruption (Iceland *c.* 1120 BC) and the
Santorini volcanic eruption (Crete *c.* 1645 BC).

Storms, cyclones and hurricanes are common causes of land degradation.
For example, in 1986, Guadalcanal in the S. Pacific was devastated by
Cyclone Namu, and in 1988 the Atlantic coastlands of Nicaragua were struck
by Hurricane Joan destroying around 7000 km² of tropical forest (*The Times*,
29/11/88: 24). In the short term, these events cause degradation, but, over
the longer term, without such damage, the natural regeneration of some
tropical forests would be upset, for there would be no clearings and less
chance for fresh growth.

The onset and/or severity of a natural disaster may owe something to
human activity – Man may have 'triggered' the disaster or may have
'sensitized' the environment. If development has exceeded environmental
limits, a natural disaster might speed up what may otherwise have been a
virtually inevitable decline. Progress sometimes comes out of adversity – in
reacting to a disaster Man may develop new strategies for using land or
resources which may be less degrading; indeed, much development has been
spurred on by natural and human disasters; notably scientific advances in
times of war.

The worst possible scenario is for Man to practise a land use which makes
land liable to degradation in an area prone to disasters on land that is
especially vulnerable. At the other extreme, there is good management of
land that is not vulnerable in a region seldom subject to disasters. It should
be possible to map natural hazard risk and so be prepared for, or to avoid,
some disasters.

Population change as a cause of land degradation

Population increase has been one of the most frequently cited causes of land
degradation since Malthus drew attention to it. The Malthusian, or more
recently Neo-Malthusian, view is that increasing demographic pressure
results in overuse of reasonable quality land and/or the misuse of marginal,
often easily degraded land. If population increase has that effect, the impact is

double edged: a simultaneous increase in demand made upon the environment in order to support growing numbers of people, and a destruction of the resource base (Clark & Munn, 1986: 8–12).

There is a need to treat the argument that environmental degradation arises whenever population grows, even when it exceeds a region's 'carrying capacity', with caution, for there are areas with large numbers of people and relatively little damage and there are areas with very few people, a short settlement history and much damage. In sensitive areas, or with certain types of exploitation, population need not be high to cause problems. Population stagnation or decline can also be a cause of land degradation.

Globally, human population has shown three periods of relatively rapid increase, if a logarithmic plot is used, followed by periods of relative stability. Arithmetic plotting of the statistics has reinforced the idea that growth has been exponential. There are some who hope that there might be another period of reduced growth in the late twenty-first-century. Whether or not that happens, the world population will have risen above 6000 million by AD 2000. The world today supports roughly three times the human population and roughly 100 times the industrial activity it did a century ago. Although they comprise only about 30% of the world's population, those in developed countries consume roughly five times as much food and commodities as people in developing countries and produce more industrial pollutants.

A number of researchers have tried to establish where population has exceeded the limits of food production (Higgins et al., 1982; Mahar et al., 1985). However, the indications are that population – poverty, and possibly degradation, correlations can be spurious. People, on the whole, have children in response to their economic, political and historical situation – a simplistic Malthusian perspective misses this (Hecht, 1985: 665). Redclift (1987: 30) suggested that it is not so much net global population increase that matters, but the rate of change in population in critical regions.

There has been debate on the relationship between population density, growth rate and agricultural development, particularly the intensity of farming (Boserüp, 1965; Carlstein, 1982). The relationship is by no means a simple one; put crudely it has been claimed that, if a population does not grow enough, or grows too fast for agriculture to respond, then production is likely to remain extensive, and may cause land degradation. If population grows, but not too fast, then intensive agriculture, possibly causing less land degradation, may result.

Marginalization as a cause of land degradation

People may become marginalized – forced or attracted onto poor quality, possibly easily degraded land, because better land is settled; because of unrest; because large landowners monopolize the better land, and possibly make poor use of it; because of the creation of reserves. It is not always unrest or social differentiation which causes people to settle marginal land. The land may be available and people perceive it offers them a chance for a living or a profit (Reining, 1978: 75).

Exploitation of marginal land does not automatically lead to land degradation, nor need the degradation be immediate. Fluctuation in climate, changes in availability and cost of inputs, including labour, outbreak of pests or diseases, altered communications, law and order, new know-how and commercial opportunities, can make land more or less marginal and alter the risk of degradation.

A number of developing countries may be described as almost wholly marginal or even sub-marginal land (Ruddle & Manshard, 1981: 4). Many farmers and herders work marginal land, yet, until relatively recently, little agricultural research or funds were directed to helping them. Rather, efforts concentrated on more-favoured environments and more fortunate agriculturalists.

Poverty as a cause of land degradation

Poor people generally have no choice but to opt for immediate benefit, very often at the expense of long-term sustainability, and they may be quite aware of this. Poverty induces land degradation which, in turn, reinforces poverty leading to further land degradation and so on (UN Center on Transnational Corporations, 1985: 5). Caldwell (1977) argued that '. . . the problems facing the poorer countries are different in kind from those faced by the rich countries a couple of centuries ago . . .', many less-developed countries today are starting with already depleted resource bases in a world where cheap raw materials are a thing of the past.

Land ownership problems as a cause of land degradation

Where land is publicly owned it may be possible to control usage by regulations or by pricing measures and to use public works to counter land degradation. Where land is under private ownership, but there is insecurity, farmers/herders, given the choice, will tend to seek short-term profits rather than risk waiting for uncertain future benefits.

It was once said of tenant farmers in nineteenth-century Ireland, who generally had short, nine-year leases, that the first three years were spent undoing the previous tenant's damage, the next three years in farming well, and the last three years in extracting the maximum from the land regardless of the damage in case the tenure was not renewed.

Where land, or the fuelwood or grazing rights on it, is a common property resource, i.e. is not owned exclusively by any one person or company, but is subject to use by a number of people, degradation is often a problem. In seeking to maximize his/her individual utility, each user of a common resource incrementaly adds to the costs of resource use. What seems a trifling or reasonable demand to an individual, when pursued by many individuals cumulatively, becomes resource degradation. Any attempt by an individual at conservation or rehabilitation would benefit others who have continued to draw full benefit but have made no sacrifice/expended no efforts. To counter common resource-related land degradation, Hardin (1968) suggested population control and privatization of land. Traditionally, control of common resource use has been through social mechanisms, but these can be disrupted by war, changing markets, 'modernization' of people's attitudes, etc.

Political instability and maladministration as causes of land degradation

Harrison (1987a: 52) noted that *c.* 70% of Africa has experienced serious conflict since the mid 1950s, and that Africa, with about 10% of the world's total population, has half the world's total refugees. Unrest, he concluded, must, in large part, be a cause of African land degradation (see also Griffiths & Binns, 1988).

Administrators are often out of touch with the peasantry and their traditional ways of regulating land/resource use. Edicts may be passed which are inappropriate, and/or unsuitable regional or local officers may be appointed which cause rural peoples to abandon satisfactory management, possibly scorn and suspect authority and so resist any innovation that might aid them and counter environmental problems (Mahar *et al.*, 1985: x). Blaikie (1989: 29) cited the eastern clay plains of the Sudan, where laws and state subsidies should ensure satisfactory land management. In practice, the laws are unenforced, the subsidies abused and land degradation is rife. Social change can lead to a breakdown in communications, public order, motivation and the ability of a society to organize: there are numerous examples from history of irrigation systems, grazing strategies, field systems, etc, which have broken down because of social changes. A country, wishing to establish sovereignty over a region, may promote inappropriate settlement, non-viable irrigation projects, and other land uses leading to degradation; examples may be found from the Amazon to the Arctic.

Much, if not most, land/resource degradation could be controlled by the application of technology, but this usually costs money, requires skilled manpower and depends on the socio-cultural and political environment being supportive. Quite a lot of degradation could be controlled with little application of technology, merely better organization and motivation of land users, but this too depends on institutional, political and economic support.

Economic and social causes of land degradation

Many seek to explain resource degradation as a consequence of the economics of production. Private exploitation of land or other resources can cause degradation. Entrepreneurs tend to maximize profits in the short term, possibly incurring degradation, and then invest part or all of the profits elsewhere. Mobility of capital makes it possible for the exploiter to avoid the longer-term economic consequences of resource/land degradation.

External factors acting on the production system can cause or contribute to environmental degradation. Such factors include: world market forces, neo-colonialism, the actions of multinational/transnational corporations (Woddis, 1967: 68, Hecht, 1985: 666). The terms of international trade are seen by many economists as having caused increased economic dependency and indebtedness of developing countries. Geertz (1963) examined the development paths of Japan and Java, both of which in the 1830s had a similar level of development. The former, he noted had, in spite of a poorer endowment of natural resources, developed far more. Java, he suggested, remained underdeveloped, despite a position astride the main trade routes and a good natural resources endowment, because of little reinvestment of profits from resource development.

Many developing countries now spend much of their revenue servicing foreign debts and consequently are less able to afford necessary land management inputs, conservation, etc, and have, in all probability, adopted agricultural strategies which demand them. The result is that the modernized sector of agriculture, which has taken so much of investment in recent years, breaks down, soil conservation is underfunded, and timber, minerals and the land are ruthlessly exploited to try and generate desperately needed foreign exchange.

Developers have come to see technological advance as allowing land to become cheaper and more plentiful by opening up what was marginal land. This is dangerous because it makes it less likely that land will be seen as a finite resource (Chisholm & Dumsday, 1987: 51). Understandably, politicians are more likely to heed the needs and demands of townsfolk than rural peasantry, commonly national food prices are kept low to curry the favour of mainly urban voters, in some cases by importing cheap foreign grain. The result is that farmers have little incentive to farm well, because profits are so low, added to which, the country has little to spend on countering land degradation because it has used funds to buy foreign grain.

Farmers who embark on modern farming involving the input of seeds, fertilizers, pesticides, etc, may find themselves on a 'treadmill of production' – if prices for their produce fall they must react by increasing their production efforts, they then have less time, money and energy to adopt practices that avoid or reduce land degradation. As the costs of production rise, land and labour may become exhausted, together or separately (Blaikie, 1989: 28).

Laissez-faire development, it is claimed, has seldom resulted in control of land degradation (Bain, 1973: 9–38). Even if the problem is perceived, political inertia and individual land-user's blindness are likely to frustrate mitigation/avoidance efforts (Higgins, 1980: 18).

Health problems as a cause of land degradation

Outbreaks of disease often accompany or follow clearance of land, particularly in rainforest areas (Barrow, 1987a: 288, 306). In various countries, land has been developed, only to be neglected, at least in part, because of disease outbreak. Had yellow-fever transmission not been discovered in the late nineteenth century, the Panama Canal would probably never have been completed.

In Africa, large areas are effectively protected from potentially damaging exploitation by the presence of tse tse flies which spread trypanosomiasis. Any control of this disease or the vectors could lay open large areas of land to overgrazing (Linear, 1985). Where diseases or disease vectors have spread to new areas, pastoralists or settlers may be forced to abandon land; it is likely that considerable areas of West Africa which were once farmed or grazed have been abandoned and have become scrub or savanna woodland because of the spread of tse tse or rinderpest. The decline of the feudal open-field system in England and parts of Western Europe, and the consequent loss of many settlements, abandonment of land and changes in farming practices, have been attributed to labour shortages following the Medieval 'Black Death' (plague).

Debilitation as a result of malaria or schistosomiasis probably contributes to poor land management in many parts of the Third World, and the incidence of both may increase considerably where perennial irrigation replaces rain-fed cropping or seasonal irrigation. It is too soon to assess what impact the spread of AIDS may have on rural labour. Debilitation and increased mortality may well deplete peasant labour in some countries leading to land degradation.

Seasonal poverty, malnutrition and seasonal disease outbreaks are widespread. When drought, AIDS or other diseases exacerbate seasonal debilitation, a feedback spiral may begin: the debilitated farm badly, the next harvest is poor, debilitation increases and the decline is exacerbated (Chambers *et al.*, 1981).

Inappropriate agriculture as a cause of land degradation

There has been a tendency of Western attitudes and technology to replace established, often successful, Third World agricultural practices – sometimes with catastrophic results (Baker, 1984). In Australia, the New World and the Eurasian steppes, European agriculture expanded during the nineteenth century. In a large proportion of these lands degradation has been at least an intermittent problem.

The application of 'modern' Western, temperate environment, attitudes and technology to tropical and subtropical conditions has often been unsatisfactory, with crops and methods of farming failing to 'fit' the physical or socioeconomic conditions (Detwyler, 1971: 23). A further complication is that farming has tended to become more dependent upon petroleum, for energy, fertilizers, pesticides, etc. The increased price of petroleum after 1973 drastically altered the costs of inputs.

HOW SENSITIVE IS LAND TO DEGRADATION? HOW STABLE ARE ENVIRONMENTS?

Ecosystem stability, sensitivity and resilience

Ecosystems and bio-geochemical/bio-geophysical cycles tend to resist change and are, on the whole, capable of self-regulation and self-maintenance, within limits. Ecosystem stability is largely a function of two things: sensitivity and resilience to change. Sensitivity may be defined as: the degree to which a given environment undergoes change due to natural forces or human action or a combination of both. Resilience refers to the way in which the ecosystem can withstand use. Some ecosystems are sufficiently resilient to restore themselves if left alone, sometimes Man can restore them if nature does not, sometimes restoration is practically or totally impossible (Holling, 1973: 11). Referring to sensitivity and resilience. Blaikie & Brookfield (1987: 11) suggested a simple classification of land.

1. *Land of low sensitivity/high resilience* Only suffers degradation under conditions of very poor management. This is generally the easiest land on which to 'stretch' production of food or other crops.
2. *Land of high sensitivity/high resilience* Suffers land degradation easily but responds well to good land management/rehabilitation efforts.
3. *Land of low sensitivity/low resilience* Initially resists land degradation but, once the 'threshold' is passed, it is very difficult for any management effort to restore it.
4. *Land of high sensitivity/low resilience* Degrades easily, does not readily respond to management/rehabilitation efforts. This is a not uncommon quality of many tropical and subtropical lands, which are probably best either left alone or radically changed, e.g. from forest to paddy-field rather than forest to rainfed plantation crops.

It would be misleading to move on giving the impression that these concepts of stability and resilience are straightforward and clearly defined. In reality, the concept of ecosystem stability is complex, may be applied at a local, or a global scale, has an inadequate terminology (see Table 2.2), and is by no means established without question (Holling, 1973; Hill, 1987). The term stability is often applied in reference to the response of an ecosystem to disturbance, not just to the question of 'natural' stability. The imprecision of the term stability is unfortunate, for it is difficult to discuss ecosystem disturbance/degradation without reference to it.

The concept of ecosystem stability/ecological stability has much in common with thermodynamics, i.e. that a system may, or may not, have an

Table 2.2. *Terminology used in the analysis of ecosystem stability.*

Characteristics	Definition
General descriptive terms	
1. Constancy	Lack of variation in some property of a system
2. Persistence	The survival time of a system or some component of it[a]
3. Fragility[b]	Implies permanent destruction
Terms used to evaluate system response to disturbance	
(a) Resistance	The ability of a system to resist displacement from its initial state following a disturbance
(b) Resilience[c]	The ability to recover to the initial state after a disturbance[c]
(i) Elasticity	The speed of recovery to the initial state after disturbance
(ii) Amplitude	The zone from which the system will return to the initial state
(iii) Hysteresis	The extent to which the pattern of recovery differs from the path of degradation
(iv) Malleability	The degree to which the new permanent state established after disturbance differs from the initial state

Notes: [a] Response of system may be slow if organisms are long lived, it may take centuries to see if trees are or are not re-establishing well.
[b] Mortimore (1988) is critical of the use of this term.
[c] Some use to indicate ability to resist change.
Source: Hill, 1987: 317; Mortimore, 1988.

ability to remain at, or near, or to return to, a state after disturbance (Pimm, 1984; Hill, 1987: 317). Much of the interest in ecosystem stability was generated by those interested in the question of whether stability was related to biological diversity, i.e. whether the more variety an ecosystem had in terms of different organisms, the more stable it would be. Stability can also be related to biomass production, retention of essential nutrients, etc. There is a recent tendency to use constancy rather than stability and initial state might well be an even better term – indicating a starting point without implying equilibrium exists.

Not everyone espouses the idea of equilibrium, some adopt a 'neo-Catastrophist', rather than Darwinian-evolutionary, viewpoint. Timmerman (1986: 435–454) suggested that the equilibrium concept, because it reflects the Darwinian-evolutionary viewpoint might be a dangerous assumption for it may be the 'norm' which is anomalous, and the best survival strategies of organisms may be worthless against unpredicted large-scale environmental perturbations. If the non-Darwinian, 'neo-Catastrophist' viewpoint is true, evolution would be a process of responses, mistakes, good luck, substantial failures, dead-ends and useless victories on many scales, and the world as we see it becomes a unique historical artefact and much less easy to predict.

Ecologists studying ecosystems have recognized two aspects of response to disturbance: 1. the ability of an ecosystem to resist displacement from its initial state after disturbance; 2. the ability to recover to the initial state after disturbance. Various terms have been applied to these two. For the first, some have used inertia, others use resistance, the latter is probably better. For the second, some have used resilience, some use elasticity, and others stability Mortimore (1988: 62) used the latter to mean the ability of a system to return to an 'equilibrium'. Resilience is sometimes used to refer to the

speed of recovery and occasionally it has been used to indicate how many
times a system can recover after disturbance (Westman, 1985: 480; Singh *et
al.*, 1985: 73). Resilience is probably best used as a measure of the ability of a
system to absorb external disturbance, resistance to perturbation – measured
by the speed of return to the initial state.

It should be noted that natural systems may be able to absorb a given
degree of disturbance if it is suffered slowly, but, if exposed to the same
degree of disturbance rapidly, breakdown may occur.

Following ecosystem disturbance, an environmental manager or re-
searcher is likely to want to know:

1. whether the system will re-establish its initial state?
2. will the system change to a new state?
3. if 1. how rapid is the recovery and how complete?
4. what is the path of recovery after disturbance?
5. how often can recovery occur?
6. will the same path of recovery always be taken?
7. will successive disturbances have different effects?
8. will there be change in the absence of disturbance?
9. is the path of recovery predictable?

Mortimore (1988: 62) examined resilience and stability of semi-arid
ecosystems and concluded that, in areas subjected to extreme climatic
conditions, the faunal populations fluctuate widely but have a high capability
of absorbing periodic extremes of fluctuation (Ludwig, 1987). They are
therefore unstable, using the term to refer to ability to return to an
equilibrium, but are highly resilient: 'The concept of resilience ... accords
well with the realities of human survival in arid or semi-arid ecosystems,
more closely than ideas of equilibrium and stability imported from less
extreme climatic zones.' (Mortimore, 1988: 63). The implication is that it
makes more sense to lose pastoral production in bad years than waste chance
of production in good years if land use is managed to stay within 'carrying
capacity' (See Chapter 8).

Some favour the concept of dynamic equilibrium, whereby individual
parts of an ecosystem change, although overall activity/function remains
stable. In effect, rather than assuming plant/animal populations exist mostly
at, or near, environmental carrying capacity they prefer to believe that
organisms are subject to disturbance and exist in a state of constant or
frequent flux. There are several variants of such 'non-equilibrium' hypotheses (see Davidson *et al.*, 1985: 43). If that is true, competition for resources
may not have time to work to exclude poorer competitors from a community
before conditions change and other, possibly 'fitter', organisms are
disadvantaged. There is a strong chance that, at least some ecosystems adjust
to slow-acting disturbance(s), but may suddenly be overcome by
'catastrophic' change. In effect the 'elasticity' of the ecosystem has been
overstretched. With that in mind, some have explored the application of
catastrophe theory to the equilibrium concept. Figure 2.2 illustrates the
postulated behaviour of an ecosystem under the influence of three variables.
A catastrophic 'jump' takes place at cusps where the factor combination
exceeds the elasticity of the system. An example of this in practice would be
the sudden collapse of a forest ecosystem under stress from the slow build-up
of the effects of pollution, ageing and climatic variation. In ecology, the idea
that balance is achieved in an ecosystem by long-term evolution has been
held by many. If this is the case, a balance or self-replacing climax stage is
achieved, where ther is no disturbance or between disturbances, after a

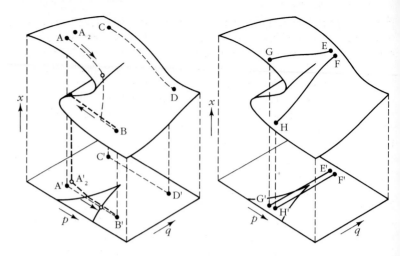

Fig. 2.2. Hypothetical behaviour of an ecosystem under the influence of three variables, according to catastrophe theory. Explanation: *The complex response surface, with an oblique cusp fold, represents the reaction of a forest ecosystem (it could be virtually any other type of ecosystem or other system) to the combined effect of slow-acting variables (p and q) and a fast-acting variable (x). The devlopment from A with changing p and x leads to the edge beyond which, with further change of x, the system cannot follow the surface, but jumps vertically down to the lower surface and then proceeds to B. With change of x and p in reverse the system does not develop back to A, but jumps up at the inner surface of the oblique fold and reaches A.*

C–D is the development at equal change of p but without cusp 'catastrophe' caused by changes of x because q is static at a different value. The diverging development from two very similar states of the system E and F to two very different states G and H is the result of mutual interactions of x and p on q. If the effects of only p and q are observed, the divergence is masked and not recognizable in the two-dimensional projection (G' and H'). The arrows indicate the directions of change. The circles show the jumping points and their projection on the p/q plane. Source: *Davidson et al., 1985: 22 – Fig. 5.3.*

process of succession (Westman, 1985: 480; Rosenberg & Freedman, 1984). According to the concept of succession, an ecosystem returns to a climax state via a series of successional stages – which are equilibrium points reached after disturbance. In effect, succession is a variation of a biological community in space–time.

Concepts of succession have a long history and are often taken for granted. Initially, they were largely based on rangeland studies (Clements, 1916; Holland, 1986; Joss *et al.*, 1986). Many range managers have made use of the concept of succession yet, it has been much criticized, for, in practice, an ecosystem's changes after disturbance may not be as predictable as some would hope. Joss *et al.* (1986: 21–2), gave an example of the deficiency of the concept: in some semi-arid savannas, prolonged heavy grazing could cause a thickening-up of shrubs, which, if grazing is reduced, would then be expected to cease and return to less shrubby climax state if the concept is correct – in practice, the shrub increase may continue.

The gradual breakdown of ecosystem integrity, resulting in a move toward lower life-forms, is termed retrogression. This is approximately the reverse of succession (Holdgate & Woodman, 1976: 123–7; Westman, 1985: 480), pressure on land results in degradation and a new equilibrium (via regression) at a lower level than the original, in terms of type of life-form, species diversity, production, etc. It is likely that each further disturbance will result in retrogression and equilibrium at successively lower levels.

The question of environmental stability at the global level has recently generated considerable interest and often heated disagreement. It may be that the Earth and its biota operate to achieve homoeostatic control over climate and the chemical composition of the environment via various 'feedback controls'. In effect, a steady-state favourable to life is maintained by life, and thus evolution of the species is not independent of evolution of environment and vice versa. Life is not simply adapting to environment, as evolutionists have generally believed, but actively regulates environment (Rambler et al., 1989). This 'Gaia hypothesis' (global biochemical homoeostasis hypothesis) was first put forward in the early 1970s by Lovelock (Lovelock, 1979; Clark & Munn, 1986: 293 Pearce, 1988a; Lovelock & Whitefield, 1982; Lovelock, 1990).

Unfortunately, even if Gaia feedback mechanisms exist, it is unlikely that Man will be saved by Nature from environmental degradation because many of the Earth's functions, regardless of their enormous scale, are finely tuned and Man has upset or is upsetting the tuning. From a Gaian viewpoint: '. . . all attempts to rationalize a subjugated biosphere with man in charge are doomed to failure as the similar concept of benevolent colonialism . . .' (Lovelock, 1979: 145). The Gaia hypothesis is, in many ways, diametrically opposed to mainstream social theory (Jones, 1990).

What are the limits beyond which land degradation occurs?

Ecologists have proposed a range of concepts/parameters which are commonly used by those working in land management. The first is primary productivity, which may be defined as: the rate at which organic matter is created by photosynthesis, and in some very rare cases by other processes, for example, around some deep oceanic fumeroles by utilization of sulphur compounds plus geothermal warmth. The second is maximum sustainable yield, which may be defined as: that fraction of (net) primary productivity, i.e. the amount of CO_2 in organic matter in excess of what is used in metabolism, that it is feasible to remove on an ongoing basis without destroying the primary productivity.

It is theoretically, and sometimes practically possible, to sustain yield of a renewable resource like land by controlling levels of exploitation (see Fig. 2.3(d)). Typically this yield is less than primary productivity, possible only about 70% of it (Reining, 1978: 35). The third concept, carrying capacity, has received a lot of attention, in spite of which, it is still defined in various, often imprecise, ways and is occasionally misused. Definitions include:

- the maximum number of individuals, animal or human, that can be supported in a given environment (generally expressed in kg live weight km²) (Simmons, 1974: 22–24; Ehrlich et al., 1970: 99; Rees, 1985: 28).
- the amount of biological matter the system can yield, for consumption by animals or humans, over a given period of time without impairing its ability to continue producing, or the number of animals it can support without being degraded (Gorse & Steeds, 1987: 12).
- the maximum population of a given species that can be supported indefinitely, in a particular region, allowing for seasonal and random changes, without any degradation of the natural resource base that would diminish the maximum population in the future (Mahar et al., 1985: 45).
- the maximum intensity of use an area will continuously support under a management programme without inducing a permanent change in the biotic environment (Mitchell, 1979: 178).

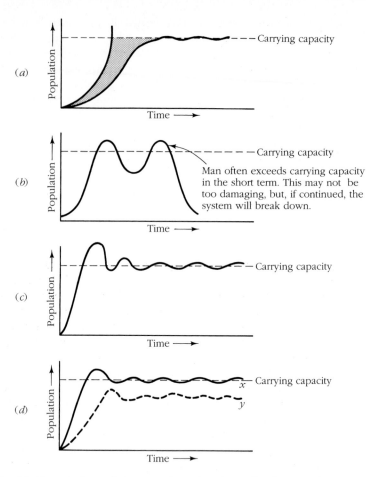

Fig. 2.3. Curves of population growth against time related to carrying capacity. Notes: Fig. (a) theoretical 'sigmoidal' growth; a more likely situation is that of (b) or (c), both of which are somewhat idealized; (d) represents the human situation: a choice of level at anything from luxury, to optimum level (y) or bare survival for maximum numbers (x). To maintain y-level will require management of human numbers and environment. Source: compilation by author.

Some confusion arises because it is possible to have a series of carrying capacities for a given plot of land. Each carrying capacity might reflect an intensity of use, for example: low-intensity (y persons per km²); medium-intensity use ($2y$ persons per km²); high-intensity use ($10y$ persons per km²). The value in parenthesis marks the level at which more intensive use leads to a change of environmental quality, in practice, there may be no step-wise change, just a trend. Also, type of use may be more important than intensity of use.

Natural populations of animals tend to fluctuate about a characteristic carrying capacity (see Fig. 2.4), determined by the scarcest vital resource, which could be water, food or space. It is often claimed that certain tribal cultures are/were adept at living within their environment's carrying capacity; in practice, this is largely unproven (Dasman, 1985: 211). The notion of carrying capacity is attractive to development economists, conservationists and politicians, because it provides a quantifiable index – it seems to allow one to answer the vital land use questions: what is? – what can be? – what should be?

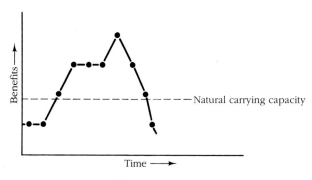

Fig. 2.4 Benefits from technology, e.g. fertilizer use, are likely to diminish after a certain point. Source: *author.*

Caution must be exercised when using this concept. There may be a bio-geophysical carrying capacity that differs from the behavioural carrying capacity. People or animals may cease to co-exist harmoniously well before the bio-geophysical carrying capacity is reached, and fickle attitudes may well affect behavioural carrying capacity. For example, tourists may feel a wilderness area has become 'crowded' if they see even a handful of people.

Man 'stretches' natural carrying capacity through technology, trade (which may reduce carrying capacity of another region or regions), or off-farm activity such as tourism. Indeed, much of Man's labour is designed to 'stretch' bio-geophysical carrying capacity. It should be noted that, while technology may enable Man to stretch carrying capacity, there are likely to be diminishing returns after a certain point (Fig. 2.4).

Wildlife may adapt to availability of resources in an erratic way, with cycles of morbidity or fertility, migration or hibernation, so short-term fluctuations of organism numbers should not be seen as a firm indication that long-term carrying capacity has been exceeded (Mahar *et al.*, 1985: 19). For example, overgrazing can cause a temporary increase in productivity and then a permanent erosion of carrying capacity only if level of usage is not reduced. Such temporary exceeding of carrying capacity may be recovered from in some circumstances, sometimes it may not be possible (Warren, 1986).

Natural fluctuations, in, say, rainfall, may make it difficult to establish what the true long-term carrying capacity is. The application of carrying capacity to semi-arid environments to arrive at satisfactory livestock stocking rates is unlikely to make best use of available natural resources (Spooner & Mann, 1982: 63; Homewood & Rodgers, 1987: 115). Nomadic pastoralists have traditionally taken a different approach, allowing stock numbers to fluctuate with environmental conditions – which, in the long run, makes better use of the land (Horowitz & Little, 1987: 69–71). The pastoralist takes risks, increases herds in good times and tries to survive in bad times. If a country or region had no trade, no chance of improving agricultural production and, no way of slowing population increase, then heeding a carrying capacity model might make sense – but in reality little of the real world is like that.

It is possible for food prices to change leading to famine without any alteration of production or population. In such cases carrying capacity is not very useful. The key point is: how fast can a country or region side-step constraints on production, i.e. yield?

SUSTAINABILITY AND SUSTAINABLE DEVELOPMENT

Clark & Munn (1986: 5) noted: 'A major challenge in the coming decades is to learn how longterm, large-scale interactions between environment and development can be better managed to increase the prospects for ecologically sustainable improvements in human wellbeing' Fig. 2.5).

In Figure 2.5, which could represent yield of livestock, game animals, crops or fisheries: OX = maximum annual yield; OY = annual effort required to maximize sustainable yield. Typically, the rise between O and maximum sustainable yield is due to some decrease in competition for food or some other reason for increase in growth rate, e.g. improved climate. Seldom is there a clear 'critical point', it is more likely there will be a less clearly defined critical zone – a point or general level at which land, aquifer, fishstock, etc, reaches a point of no return. A similar type of curve could be constructed for an ecosystem's absorptive capacity, i.e. showing how, if rates of pollutant discharge exceed the capacity of the ecosystem to satisfactorily break them down, or if the pollutant is non-biodegradable, a 'critical point' is reached and any further pollution would result in more or less total loss of absorptive capacity (Rees, 1985: 27–8).

Sustainable yield is not a costless strategy, it involves forgoing consumption in the short term, as a sort of investment in the future, that investment has to be evaluated against other potential investments. Some argue that there are circumstances where use of a renewable resource beyond its critical point, is a rational development decision. This may be true where, say, a groundwater is overexploited to pay for industrial development/ infrastructure that provides sustained long-term employment.

It is theoretically possible to achieve environmentally and socially sustainable development, but achieving it in practice involves many challenges (Clark & Munn, 1986; Barbier, 1987; Rees, 1990). There will be no single, simple route to meeting the needs and aspirations of many different peoples, but one thing is clear: steps towards achieving such development in many regions must be taken now, or very soon, or the opportunity will be lost (World Commission on Environment and Development, 1987a: 40).

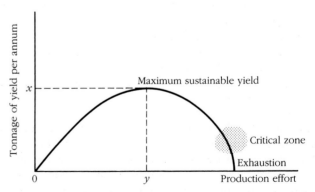

$0x$ = Maximum annual yield consistent with sustainability
$0y$ = Annual effort required to maximize sustainable yield

Fig. 2.5. The sustainable yield curve. Source: Dregne, H. (1985). *Environment,* 27(8), 16–33.

Conway (1985), writing on agricultural systems suggested four properties
were important:

- *productivity* (measured by yield or net income);
- *stability* of yield or net income;
- *sustainability* of yield or income;
- *equitability* of yield or income distribution.

Referring to these properties, it is possible to have a very productive but vulnerable, unstable, possibly unsustainable agricultural strategy. It is possible to have a less productive but more stable and sustainable strategy, and, perhaps beyond realistic hope, a highly productive, highly stable and highly sustainable strategy. Until quite recently the focus of agricultural development has been mainly on the very productive but vulnerable agricultural strategy (Tisdell, 1988: 375).

When stable production has not been achieved, there may be a relatively slow decline in productivity/breakdown or degradation of the environment or, at the other extreme, it may become apparent suddenly and markedly with little or no warning.

Something may render an agricultural strategy unsustainable from within, e.g. soil erosion, or from without, e.g. climatic change.

The concept of sustainable development

'Sustainable development is a vague concept, but it is as powerful as many other vague concepts such as liberty, equality and justice.' (Timberlake, 1988: 61).

The call for those involved in development to encompass consideration of environment is not new (Caldwell, 1984: 299; Dasman, 1985: 215). The concept of ecologically sustainable development seems to have been first voiced in 1972, possibly 1968. The *World Conservation Strategy* (IUCN *et al.*, 1980) and more recently: the *'Brundtland Report'* (World Commission on Environment and Development, 1987a) and the *'Pearce Report'* (Pearce *et al.*, 1989), gave the concept publicity. There is a strong anthropomorphic bias in much of what has been said/written on sustainable development, for people worry about nature primarily in terms of what nature offers their own welfare.

Sustainable development implies an anticipate-and-avoid, rather than a react-and-cure approach to development; it demands that the question be asked: '. . . is it ever acceptable to engage in actions that reduce the potential of future generations to meet their needs?' Sustainable development could be defined as any activity that raises social welfare with the maximum amount of resource conservation and the minimum amount of environmental degradation allowable within given economic, social and technical constraints (Barbier, 1987: 105; *Futures*, 1988; Munn, 1988). (A recent review of the meaning of sustainable development may be found in Pearce *et al.*, 1989: 28–50.)

Distinction has been drawn between sustainable development and sustainable exploitation, whereby the latter is taken to mean a dynamic equilibrium between natural production and offtake, a steady-state which can be graphically expressed by a horizontal line. Sustainable development is linked more to economic growth; this is expressed as a percentage increase, an upward trend, an exponential curve if graphically represented (*IUCN Bulletin*, 1989, 20: 28; MacNeill, 1989).

There are those who feel that sustainable development involves contradictory goals (Warren, 1986: 90; Redclift, 1987; Munn, 1988: 2; Anon,

1987a), but in spite of this, it has come to be generally accepted that 'real' development cannot take place unless the strategies are environmentally sustainable and consistent with social values and institutions. Development might be defined, at least by the non-Marxist, as a process whereby the real per capita income of a country increases over time, subject to the stipulation that the number of people below the 'poverty line' does not increase, and that the distribution of income does not become more unequal. It has been claimed that sustainable development should ensure the poor have access to secure livelihoods. To do that it is necessary to maximize goals across three systems: 1. the biological system, the goal being to sustain biological diversity and productivity; 2. the economic system, the goal being to satisfy basic need, enhance equity, improve useful goods and services; 3. the social system, the goal being to sustain institutions, social justice, and participation.

Sustainable development, if it is to be achieved, will require politically effective strategies for its implementation. Also, environmental studies, economics and politics will have to operate on the same 'wavelength' (Pearce *et al.*, 1989: 4; Rees, 1990). Those in power will have to have incentives to pursue, or be convinced of the need for, long-term solutions/strategies which forego short-term gains. Scientists will have to concern themselves with the 'messy', unpredictable world of human beings (Caldwell, 1984; Timberlake, 1988: 6). Without stable patterns of economic exchange and political and social structures, sustainable development will be elusive.

There are many ways in which pursuit of sustainable development could help mankind avoid land degradation.

1. Temporary, unsustained development could support population growth, hardship and land degradation may ensue if production failed.
2. In developing countries, if development in an area fails, people may have difficulty moving/finding alternative livelihood/adapting to a new area – all of which can trigger land degradation.
3. Incomes near the subsistence level give their recipients little margin to weather-out failures and setbacks – this can lead to land degradation.
4. Lack of adequate social services in developing countries means there is little incentive to control population, for children serve as 'security' for parents, and little support if production fails.
5. People in developing countries are likely to be more directly dependent on the environment for survival than those in developed countries.
6. In the developing countries, alternative strategies/technologies are often untried or unavailable.

3 Land degradation through global pollution: the 'greenhouse effect'

A RANGE OF POLLUTION-RELATED THREATS are presently apparent, although some have yet to be confirmed as real. These include: industrial pollution, unwanted side-effects of agrochemical use, nuclear warfare, disturbance of crucial bio-geophysical or bio-geochemical cycles and problems resulting from 'genetic engineering'. The consequences of some of these threats are sufficiently terrible that, and until fears prove to be unfounded, governments would be wise to make contingency plans and not risk waiting for proof (Gleick, 1989). Some of the problems stem from industrial activity and consumption patterns in richer nations, some from activities in developing countries, particularly forest clearing and burning. The scale of these problems is global, and any chance of alleviating them lies first in understanding the structure and function of the Earths' bio-geochemical cycles and of how Man is interfering with these. Land will suffer degradation because of these pollution-related threats, even though there may be no change in the way it is being used, and even if it is conserved or protected.

WHAT IS THE 'GREENHOUSE EFFECT'?

In 1863 John Tyndall published a paper suggesting water vapour played a role in regulating the Earth's atmospheric temperature; these ideas were taken a stage further by Arrhenius and Chamberlain in the 1890s, who suggested carbon dioxide (CO_2) played a role in controlling global temperatures. The understanding today is that the atmosphere keeps the Earth's surface roughly 33 °C warmer than it would otherwise be. It should also be noted that, if there were CO_2 levels in the Earth's atmosphere as high as those on Venus, our average surface temperatures might rise to well over 100 °C.

The maintenance of the Earth's temperature regime is achieved in the following manner. Solar energy from the Sun passes through the atmosphere with virtually no absorption taking place, although some solar radiation is reflected back to space by clouds. Some of this incoming solar radiation in the shorter wavelengths (ultra-violet) helps to maintain an ozone layer in the upper atmosphere, the stratosphere – c. 22–28 km altitude. The Earth's land and sea surface is warmed by incoming solar radiation and re-radiates, but at longer wavelengths. Some of the re-radiated energy, roughly 30%, is absorbed by water vapour in the atmosphere; some is absorbed by CO_2, the absorption being mainly in the longer wavelengths, particularly in the infra-red, the rest escapes into space. Most of the trapping of re-radiated energy takes place in the lower atmosphere, the troposphere – $c.$ 0–14 km altitude (Gribbin, 1988f). A change in the relative concentration of atmospheric gases and/or a change in amounts of water vapour in the atmosphere, and/or a change in the nature of cloud cover could alter climate.

'Greenhouse gases'

The so-called 'greenhouse gases' which play a role in maintaining the temperature of the Earth's atmosphere and surface are: water vapour; CO_2; nitrous oxide (N_2O); methane (CH_4); hydrogen sulphide (H_2S), a range of chlorofluorocarbon gases (CFCs) and related compounds like halons, and low-altitude (tropospheric) ozone (O_3).

These gases are increasing in relation to the non-'greenhouse gases'; it is frequently claimed that this increase has already caused, and will in future cause further change, in the Earth's surface/atmospheric temperatures. There is no unanimous agreement, some authorities feel it is premature to claim the reality of 'greenhouse warming'; some suggest there is warming, but that it is due to natural fluctuations such as solar radiation change, while others support 'greenhouse warming' (Bryson, 1989; Roberts, 1989). Before it can be proved that there really is 'greenhouse warming', the following questions have to be answered:

1. Ignoring the effects of 'greenhouse gases', is the Earth's surface/atmospheric temperature steady, may there perhaps be change due to periodic variation in solar radiation emission, perturbations in the Earth's orbit, etc?
2. Might changes in concentration of one 'greenhouse gas' cancel out or amplify changes due to changed concentration of another/others?
3. Are there natural or anthropogenic processes that could counter or amplify the effects of change in concentration of 'greenhouse gases'; might man-made dust or volcanic dust/gases or gases generated by organisms like plankton have effects on global temperatures; just how much excess 'greenhouse gas' can be neutralized by 'sinks' like forests or marine plankton?
4. Global pollution is affecting the Earth's stratospheric ozone layer, CFCs, CH_4 and N_2O are active in this, as well as affecting absorption of re-radiated solar radiation. Alteration of the ozone layer will change incoming solar radiation; this could directly cause land degradation effects, due to raised ultra-violet radiation striking plants and animals and soil; this may counter or reinforce changes due to 'greenhouse gases'; the latter is more likely. Figure 3.1 gives a summary of the main 'greenhouse gases'.

Man is clearly upsetting the natural 'cocktail' of atmospheric gases. The possibility that this might be a problem was first voiced in the 1940s and warnings were given by the Scripps Institute of Oceanography in 1957. Since the International Geophysical Year (from about 1959–60), changes in global atmospheric CO_2 have been logged, notably by an observatory on Mt Mauna Loa, Hawaii. There is also evidence in the form of atmospheric gas bubbles trapped in ice caps. Antarctic and Greenland ice cores have been analysed to give records of fluctuation in various atmospheric gases, notably CO_2, going as far back as 60,000 BC or earlier.

More details are given later in this chapter, but, in general, atmospheric CO_2 has increased exponentially from a 'pre-industrial' level of roughly 270 to 280 parts per million by volume (ppmv) in around AD 1750 to about 346

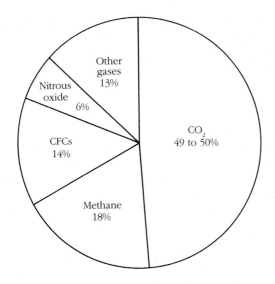

Fig. 3.1. The main 'greenhouse gases' – relative contributions to the 'greenhouse effect' in the mid 1980s. Source: based on Boyle & Ardill, 1989: 27 (Fig. 5); Pearce, 1989b: 38.

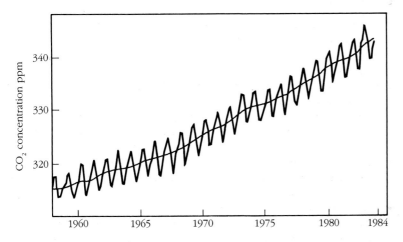

Fig. 3.2. The build-up of CO_2 in the atmosphere, recorded at Mauna Loa, Hawaii. Source: Gribbin, 1988f: 3 (no Fig. number).

ppmv in 1985 and to about 350 ppmv in 1989 (Boyle & Ardill, 1989: 25). There are fears that, by AD 2000, the level could be 560 ppmv or more (Barbier, 1989b: 20). Houghton & Woodwell (1989: 19) suggest that, since AD 1860, the average global temperature has increased by 0.5 °C to 0.7 °C, and the warming trend is likely to accelerate. This is presently hotly debated (Bryson, 1989). In 1988, the ex-Prime Minister of Sweden, Mr Ullsten, noted: 'Humanity is conducting an unintended, uncontrolled experiment, whose ultimate consequences could be second only to global nuclear war' (Jones, 1988).

Evidence from Antarctic and Greenland ice cores show that, at the peak chill of the last 'Ice Age', the most recent major cool period (glacial): between about 20,000 and 15,000 BP, atmospheric concentration of CO_2 was around 190 ppmv. The global mean temperature would have been roughly 4 °C cooler than now (Boyle & Ardill, 1989: 25). During interglacial periods, the last from *c*. 120,000 to 60,000 BP, atmospheric concentration of CO_2 was as high as, or slightly higher than, present-day levels – around 350 ppmv, and temperatures in mid-latitudes were probably 1 °C to 3 °C above today's. Interglacial sea levels were higher than now, probably by at least 6 m, and possibly even 80 m in one of the early interglacials (Fifield, 1988; Lloyd, 1988).

Attention has focused on CO_2, but other 'greenhouse gases' are already affecting climate and it has been suggested that by AD 2030 their effect will probably exceed that of CO_2 (Bolin *et al.*, 1986: *xxi*; Gribbin, 1988f: 3).

Carbon dioxide

The records from Mauna Loa, which is away from larger sources of pollution, show an annual rhythm with a rising trend (see Fig. 3.2). The annual fluctuation is associated with seasonal land vegetation changes; most land is in the Northern Hemisphere, so the pattern reflects northern seasons. The long-term rise is generally believed to reflect human activity, especially combustion of various fuels.

Concentration of CO_2 in the atmosphere appears to control temperature, and, in turn, sea level. From about 10,000 BP to around AD 1750, CO_2 concentrations were between 250 and 290 ppmv. Making some allowances for the effects of other 'greenhouse gases', there is likely to be the equivalent of twice the pre-industrial (pre-1750) concentration of CO_2 by AD 2030 (Anon, 1987d; Skiba & Cresser, 1988: 43; Wellburn, 1988: 165). There are claims that CO_2 concentrations were significantly higher in the Jurassic Period (*c*. 213 to 144 million years BP) than they are now (Rind, 1984: 49). In spite of much uncertainty, global warming seems likely.

Most of the 'anthropogenic CO_2' results from combustion of hydrocarbons, especially coal. The burning of forest and woodlands probably accounts for roughly one-quarter of all CO_2 build-up (Bolin *et al.*, 1986). Use of limestone for smelting and making slaked-lime also releases CO_2. According to Gribbin (1988f: 2), about half the CO_2 produced by Man is absorbed by some natural 'sink' and effectively taken out of the temperature-affecting system. These 'CO_2 sinks' include: fixation as soil organic carbon; incorporation into calcareous skeletal materials by marine plankton (this is the major sink); fixation and incorporation into plant tissue by terrestrial vegetation, not only forests and woodlands, tropical grasslands probably fix as much at least as tropical forest (DeGroot, 1990); absorption and precipitation as carbonate sediments by seawater. The 'sinks' are not well understood. For example, marine plankton may not fix in a steady constant manner, there will be seasonal variations and possibly fluctuation as populations of various organisms rise and fall in response to global warming or cooling, predation, availability of nutrients and so on. Because sunlight is required, most fixation of CO_2 by plankton takes place only in the upper few metres of the oceans, any warming of climate, oceanic pollution, altered supply of nutrients like phosphorus or increased solar radiation might have a feedback effect, so that changing conditions could affect plankton near the surface and so would change rates of fixation. Lovelock (1979; 1990) discussed the possibility that marine plankton might play a controlling role in maintaining global CO_2 levels/climate through a mechanism involving the release of dimethyl sylphide and methyl iodide.

There is some debate as to whether a feedback exists, whereby, as sea surface temperatures rise, more warming occurs with each successive increment of greenhouse gases. This is because greenhouse warming of the sea releases more water vapour which in turn warms the atmosphere.

Boyle & Ardill (1989: 33) offered estimates of where the Man-made CO_2 emissions were coming from, as a rough percentage of total emissions: N. America contributed 27% (the USA 24% of that); E. Europe 25%; W. Europe 15%; China 9%; Pacific countries 6%; the 72 less-developed countries 5%; remaining nations 14%, of which 3% came from the UK.

When vegetation is cleared and burnt, there is a double impact: CO_2 is immediately released, and the long-term benefit of CO_2 fixation by that vegetation is lost. If the burning of forest in Latin America, particularly in Amazonia, continues to accelerate in the way it was up to 1989 its contribution to global CO_2 increase will become about 70% of estimates of likely fossil fuel combustion emissions in the not too distant future (Boyle & Ardill, 1989: 34).

To fix about 3000 million tonnes of CO_2 a year, which would be enough to mitigate the 'greenhouse effect', would require an end to deforestation and the planting of an estimated 3,118,800 million km² of forest, or would require some way of boosting marine plankton activity. Enough land for planting is apparently available in wastelands, areas in need of replanting and so on. The cost would be roughly US$ 120,000 million, spread over perhaps ten years, much less than the costs of trying to rectify likely consequences of the 'greenhouse effect', and probably easier to pursue than taxes on CO_2 emissions (Myers, N. 1989 Letter: 'Forest Exploitation', *The Times*, 25/4/89: 17).

Methane

Like CO_2, methane (CH_4) absorbs infra-red radiation re-radiated from the Earth's surface, but is between six times and 25 times more effective in raising the temperature of the lower atmosphere than CO_2 (Pearce, 1989c: 37). It is clear that CH_4 levels have been rising ever since the Industrial Revolution. Before the nineteenth century, levels seem to have been more or less stable; measurement began in the 1960s, monitoring of global levels in 1978, but ice-core data allows earlier levels to be established. The rise since early Victorian times seems largely due to human activities. Estimates vary, but one is that, over the last 150 to 200 years, global atmospheric CH_4 levels have risen, from 0.65 ppmv to 1.5 to 1.7 ppmv and are increasing at between 1% and 2% per annum (Rambler *et al.*, 1989: 65). By AD 2050, levels will probably be about 2.5 ppmv (MacKenzie, 1984: *iii*; Gee, 1988a; Boyle & Ardill, 1989: 29).

Fears have been voiced that, as global temperatures rise, peatlands in the high latitudes could begin to release large amounts of methane and cause a 'run-away' climatic warming (Pearce, 1989d).

Methane emissions also affect the rate of ozone formation in the lower atmosphere; the effect is to increase ozone at low altitude. If more methane gets into the upper atmosphere, the effect is to decrease ozone levels there (Anon., 1988e).

Methane is produced through biological decomposition by micro-organisms under anaerobic conditions, such as exist in swamps, and particularly in paddy-fields which have expanded in area and are now an important source; peaty soils; the guts of livestock: a typical western domestic cow generates around 200 grams day^{-1} of CH_4, and globally there may be over 1300 million cattle; human sewage; landfill refuse disposal sites (Pearce, 1989c). Bouwman, 1990 suggested that paddy-fields might account for 20% of the global increase in methane. Methane is also released in the Tropics by termites. This is believed by some to be a significant emission source; by industry, coal mining, oil-well drilling and waste of unburnt natural gas. Asphalt on roads and buildings also releases methane. About one-third of methane emissions is due to inefficient combustion of hydrocarbon fuels (Bolin *et al.*, 1986: 161–3).

Little is known about methane sinks. Soil bacteria fix some (what effect acid deposition and use of nitrogenous fertilizers may have on this is uncertain). A little known, but potentially serious risk is that, as the climate warms, methane hydrates in deep oceans could suddenly release huge amounts of methane and hydrocarbons, suddenly accelerating the 'greenhouse effect'.

Control of methane levels might be sought by burning off as much as possible emitted from refuse and sewage, taking more care with fertilizer application and, as far as possible, avoiding agricultural practices that lead to anaerobic soil conditions.

Chlorofluorocarbons

Chlorofluorocarbons (CFCs), halons and related compounds are generally held responsible for 'ozone holes'; they are also very effective 'greenhouse gases' – one molecule of either of the two more common types of CFC ($CFCl_3$ or CFC-11 and CF_2, Cl_2 CFC-12) has about the same effect as 10,000 molecules of CO_2 (Gribbin, 1988f: 3). The sources of CFCs are discussed later in this chapter.

Carbon monoxide

CO is the second most abundant 'greenhouse gas' after CO_2. Levels are highest in winter months at high latitude where there is incomplete combustion of hydrocarbon fuels to heat buildings. Incomplete combustion of motor vehicle fuel is another major source. The emissions are probably increasing at between 1% and 5% per annum (Rambler *et al.*, 1989: 69).

Nitrous oxide

Nitrous oxide (N_2O) is effective as a 'greenhouse gas' and contributes to the formulation of tropospheric ozone. N_2O is released naturally by forests, especially tropical rainforests, and grasslands, it is also formed by lightning. Man-made emissions result from: use of artificial nitrogenous fertilizers, the combustion of hydrocarbon fuel and the combustion of biomass. There is also some emission from animal wastes and human sewage. There are signs that N_2O may be liberated by oceanic plankton and these releases could play a part in regulating global temperature.

It would seem that the pre-industrial level of N_2O was about 285 ppbv (parts per billion by volume); by 1989 it had risen to 305 ppbv. Globally, N_2O is increasing above natural levels by about 0.2% to 0.3% a year (Boyle & Ardill, 1989: 30; Rambler *et al.*, 1989: 70).

Hydrogen sulphide

According to Wellburn (1988: 182) over 90% emissions of H_2S are accountable to Man, the rest results from decay processes and releases from living vegetation.

Sulphur dioxide

Sulphur dioxide (SO_2) is not strictly a 'greenhouse gas', in fact it might be the opposite. Volcanic emission of SO_2 is erratic and unpredictable: at times it could be considerable. There are indications that Man-made SO_2 emissions have increased ten-fold over the last century, and cause an increase in cloud cover. This has been especially apparent over the Northern Hemisphere. The effect might be to counter the 'greenhouse effect'. If this is the case, then control of 'greenhouse gas' emissions should be cautious in case the SO_2 cooling effect 'takes over' especially if volcanoes suddenly outgassed a lot (*Nature, London*, vol. 339: p. 365). To complicate matters, SO_2 might be quite easily and rapidly controlled, before other 'greenhouse gases'; in order to reduce acid pollution, the situation might then arise that the 'greenhouse effect' accelerates.

What land degradation will the 'greenhouse effect' cause?

Modelling and forecasts could prove wrong and land users could suddenly face new constraints and risks. The impact of 'greenhouse effects' depends on the speed at which the change occurs as well as the severity. Organisms, societies and economies can possibly adapt to relativley slow change; sudden change may prove catastrophic.

Natural events such as volcanic eruption could suddenly alter predictions. Not all volcanic eruptions cause global cooling, Mt St. Helens (USA) in 1980 did not. However, there is evidence that the Tambora eruption (Indonesia, 1815) caused a $0.5\,°C$ to $1.0\,°C$ lowering of global temperatures between 1815 and 1817, and El Chichon (Mexico, 1982) probably cooled the Northern Hemisphere in 1983 and 1984.

At present, decision-makers and the public have been alerted that there are likely to be changes. A gradual steady response, starting counter-measures soon may overcome most likely difficulties; delay may save money *if* predictions are over-pessimistic, but, if the predictions are not overpessimistic, inaction will cost far more (Anon, 1988d).

Climatic impacts

The climatic consequences of the 'greenhouse effect' probably lag; in which case we have not yet really experienced the effects of changes since say 1940 (Wellburn, 1988: 166). The World Meteorological Organization drew up the World Climate Programme after a Geneva conference in 1979. This Programme focuses on climatic change and the risks these may pose, and aims to improve: data collection, exchange of information, monitoring and warning to governments and the public. Much of the prediction being made is based on computer modelling. The state-of-the-art is far from perfection, so forecasts are not accurate and differ widely.

With the foregoing caveats in mind, the predictions are that there will be an increase in global mean equilibrium surface temperature over that of 1986 of between $0.5\,°C$ and $5.5\,°C$ by AD 2030. Barbier (1989b: 21) suggested the 'best guess' for AD 2030 is $1.0\,°C$ to $2.1\,°C$ warmer than today, and, because of a lag effect due to the thermal inertia of the oceans, the eventual change, if pollution rose no more after AD 2030, would be between $1.5\,°C$ and $3.1\,°C$ warmer than 1989. Gribbin (1988f: 3) suggested that, until a clearer pictures emerges, a reasonable estimate is probably a global mean equilibrium surface temperature of about $+2\,°C$ by AD 2030. None of these predictions allow for factors such as volcanic eruptions, fluctuation in solar radiation or unforeseen effects that might arise as some pollutants are controlled and others continue to be emitted.

The effects of warming are likely to be uneven: at the Equator increases may be 0.5 °C to 1 °C or less, at higher latitudes the rise may be greater. Some suggest 2 °C to 3 °C, others suggest not more than 1 °C; polar latitudes might have the greatest warming. There is more or less agreement over the pattern, but not over the level of change. Northern high-latitude autumn and winter may become warmer by as much as 6°C, although W. Europe might get more easterlies and therefore more snow and colder winters as a result (*The Times*, 28/11/89: 4). There is reasonable agreement that there will be changes in prevailing winds and in the distribution of precipitation around the world, but much divergence over details. It seems likely that continental interiors will tend to become drier (Rind, 1984; Anon. 1988c; Parry, 1988a; 1989b). Annual mean precipitation may increase in mid to high latitudes, probably more markedly in the Northern Hemisphere, where summers may also become drier. Barbier (1989: 22) suggested there might be enhanced winter rainfall in latitudes between 60° N and 90° N, and reduced summer rain in latitudes between 30° N and 60° N.

There have been fears voiced that rainfalls will decrease in much of the USA, Europe, the USSR and Japan, but other sources predict Japan could benefit from warming sufficiently to improve crop production. Within these areas are some of the world's most crucial food-producing regions. Crops like maize in the USA are already quite close to their tolerance limits. India, North Africa and the Middle East might have better rainfalls by AD 2030, and, in the humid Tropics, rainfall might increase (Bolin *et al.*, 1986: *xxi*). The pattern of storms may alter and possibly their severity will increase in many regions. Some have suggested that 'greenhouse effect'-related climatic change is already apparent in the Sahelian–Sudanic Zone of Africa (see Chapter 8). There would be considerable effect on West and Northwest European land use if, as some fear, climatic warming causes a shift in the track of the Gulf Stream. However far-fetched this risk may seem, it is believed the N. Atlantic has already warmed by around 1°C over the last century. Two predictions of the situation by AD 2030 are given in Fig. 3.3.

Rapid change might severely affect forested areas, regeneration could be upset and mature trees might die, as well as irrigated agriculture in semi-arid regions. There may also be significant changes in fuelwood availability if rainfall patterns change.

Sea level changes

During the Last Interglacial, sea levels were between probably about 6.0 m, possibly as much as 30 m above present; during the glacials sea level stood as much as 120 m below present (Tooley & Shennon, 1987). That sea levels are rising is not debated, but what level will be reached by say AD 2030 is debated. There is also uncertainty over pace of change: a gradual, expected sea level change has very different implications than a sudden or erratic change. Barbier (1989b: 29) feared the change is more likely to be quite sudden than slow and gradual. Estimates of sea level rise over the next 100 years vary between 0.4 and 2.0 m, assuming that there is no sudden massive break-up and melting of the West Antarctic ice sheet (Hekstra, 1989). It should be noted that as global mean temperatures rise oceans will expand, adding to other causes of rising sea levels. If the West Antarctic break-up and melt were to happen, sea levels would probably quickly rise more than 4.0 m

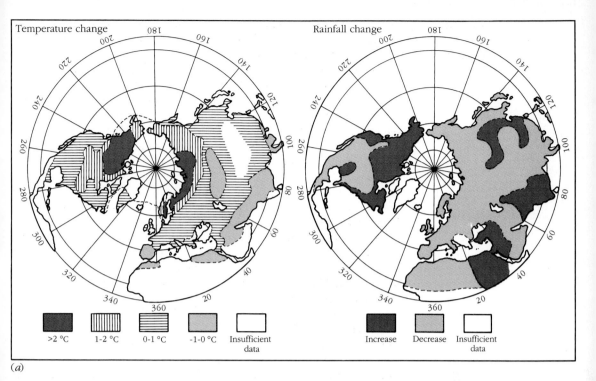

Temperature change

>2 °C 1-2 °C 0-1 °C -1-0 °C Insufficient data

Rainfall change

Increase Decrease Insufficient data

(a)

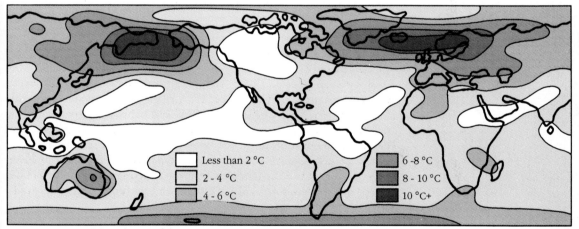

Less than 2 °C   6 -8 °C
2 - 4 °C   8 - 10 °C
4 - 6 °C   10 °C+

One computer model prediction of the coming greenhouse warming (the effects will not be uniform)

(b)

Fig. 3.3. Two predictions of likely climatic impacts of the 'greenhouse effect'.
Sources: (a) *Gribbin, 1988f: 4;* (b) *Gribbin, 1988b: 31.*

above present levels (Milliman *et al.*, 1989). Many researchers feel that break-up of the West Antarctic ice sheet is unlikely before the late twenty-first century, but from then on is quite likely. Estimates of the likely rise by AD 2030 range from 15 to 30 cm to 3.5 m with many favouring 65 cm (Tooley, 1987: 295; Wells & Edwards, 1989).

Even a modest sea level rise of 30 to 65 cm could have dire consequences; there are many regions where storms already cause severe damage or threaten to. Some countries may be able to find the funds and/or labour to build and maintain coastal defences, others may be able to develop

Table 3.1. *Regions vulnerable to moderate (0.5 to 1.5 m) sea level rise.*

*Coastal areas bordering the North Sea: Holland, parts of Eastern UK including
London, Hamburg and lower Elbe Floodplain.
*Lowlands around the Baltic.
*Deltaic lowlands of Mediterranean, particularly the Nile Delta, Po Estuary,
Rhone Delta, Lac Ichkeul (Tunisia), N. Agean, Venice. The Nile Delta
(including Port Said and Alexandria) is already in trouble due to subsidence
and increased coastal erosion since the Aswan Dam reduced silt carried down
the Nile[a].
*Ebro Delta/Estuary, Gulf of Cadiz (Iberian Peninsular).
*Mississippi Delta/Louisiana (exacerbated due to subsidence)[bd].
*Bangladesh: Ganges–Brahmaputra–Meghna Delta, exacerbated due to
mangrove removal[c]. Potentially huge numbers of people to be relocated.
*Eastern Seaboard of USA: New Jersey to Mexican Border is vulnerable,
especially the islands off New Jersey, Boston at risk if rise is over 50 cm.
*Maldives (Indian Ocean). Little land above 2 m altitude, virtually none above
2.5 m – a rise of 0.5 m, and as many as 177,000 people – the 1989 population –
would probably need evacuation[a].
*Parts of Florida.
*Kirabati, Tuvalu, Tonga, and the Marshall Is. (Pacific Ocean).
*Coastal Lowlands of China[b].
*Huanghe River Delta (China)[b].
Guyana, Amazon Basin.
Singapore (over 20 cm would flood reclaimed areas).

Note: *indicates impact could be severe.
Sources: [a] Bird, 1985; Tooley & Shennan, 1987
     [b] Tooley, 1987: 295
     [c] Barbier, 1989 a, b: 28
     [d] DeLaune *et al.*, 1987.

alternative land areas and evacuate people, but some will not. Hekstra (1989)
feared that 'greenhouse effect'-related sea level rise could render as much as
one-fifth of the world's cropland useless. There need not be actual
permanent inundation to cause land degradation; in East Anglia (UK) in
1953, 300 people were killed by sea flooding, and in the late 1980s over
20,234 ha of the same region were believed to be in immediate danger (*The
Times*, 4/9/88: A4). Even a slight rise in sea level will increase the danger
from storm surges and extra high tides. The danger is increasing in the UK as
many of the coastal defences are over 30 years old and are in need of
improvement even without the threat of rising sea level. There will be
considerable variation in impact of sea level rises, due to local tidal
conditions and storm exposure UNEP, 1987). Bangladesh and the Nile
Delta are especially vulnerable because they are low lying and are suffering
subsidence which compounds the problem (Milliman *et al.*, 1989).

There will be considerable indirect effects of sea level rise. Those
evacuated, or who have resettled themselves from vulnerable coastal
lowlands, will add to pressures on land suitable for cultivation/pasture; these
environments will probably already be under stress because of 'greenhouse
effect'-related climatic change. Salt intrusion into aquifers and salt contamination of estuarine or deltaic farmlands will increase. Some islands might lose
fresh groundwater supplies and have to be abandoned even if not actually
inundated. Table 3.1 lists some of the regions vulnerable to even a quite
slight rise in sea level. If nations are forced to spend money on improving
coastal defences, then there will be less to spend on environmental

management or conservation. Barbier (1989b: 29) speculated that sea level rise will result in greater changes of the world's economic systems and standards of living than at any time since the Industrial Revolution. A rise of 1.4 m would certainly affect many major cities, and a lot of the world's better agricultural land is close to sea level. Important inshore and estuarine fisheries might also be affected – possibly one-fifth of the world's people could suffer directly (Bolin *et al.*, 1986: *xxviii*). There would also be considerable political stress, possibly leading to armed conflicts.

Bangladesh is roughly four-fifths delta lands. In 1970, roughly 300,000 people died when a single cyclonic storm raised waves. A sea level rise of, say, 1.0 m would cover roughly 11.5% to 17% of Bangladeshi territory (Titus, 1990: 140). At present, such land would have about 9% of the total population. Assuming a doubling of population by AD 2030, which is likely, at least 112 million people might need evacuation. As events in 1970 proved, storms can flood large areas that are normally above sea level, and 112 million could be a gross underestimate (Boyle & Ardil, 1989: 71, 112). Much of Egypt's fertile delta lands are less than 2.0 m above sea level, and have a population of around 50 million (the city of Alexandria is particularly vulnerable). A 50.0 cm rise could displace 3.3 million people (Boyle & Ardill, 1989: 71).

Improvements to sea defences in the UK to meet the likely threat by AD 2030 will probably cost between £5000 and £8000 million (at 1988 prices). Figure 3.3 shows the approximate areas of the UK likely to suffer from sea level rises. Already The Netherlands has calculated the costs of a 1.0 m sea level rise, assuming a sea defence response rather than a retreat to high ground, as roughly US$ 5000 to US$ 6000 million over the next 50 to 100 years (Hekstra, 1986; 1989: 9). A 2.0 m rise might cost The Netherlands up to US$ 8800 million (Barbier, 1989b: 29). The Dutch take the risks of sea level rise seriously: in 1953, a 4.0 m tidal surge killed many, and flooded vast areas. Since then, the Dutch have planned to withstand a 5.0 m surge. In 1990, the defences to meet that aim will be completed having taken the best part of 40 years to build. To raise the defences a further 50.0 cm will cost roughly US$ 2.2 billion, spread over a 20-year period (Boyle & Ardill, 1989: 74).

America's eastern seaboard and it's offshore islands plus the states bordering the Gulf of Mexico will suffer badly if there is even a quite moderate sea levels rise (Hecht, 1988). Barbier (1989b: 28) suggested that a 1.0 m sea level rise would cost the USA US$ 10,000 to US$ 100,000 million to meet the threat along only its eastern coast. Hekstra (1989) estimated possible world costs of sea level rise; however, any such prediction must, at this stage, be highly speculative. It is more useful to note the time that defences take to build, even in richer nations. Sea level rise will disrupt sewage disposal systems, wetland drainage and coastal vegetation. It may be more sensible in some situations not to try to protect coastlands, but to allow the land to flood in the hope that saltmarshes, mangroves and other swamps form and lead to natural accretion which will, in the long term, give better, cheaper defences.

Nuclear power stations have been built within a few metres of present sea level. In the UK, there are plans to expand Hinkley Point which is already near enough to sea level to cause concern (see *The Ecologist*, 19(1): 14). Unless procedures and resources for de-commissioning improve, these sites are likely to require onsite safe containment of old reactors for very long periods of time. Over such a time-scale, sea level is quite likely to rise enough to be a threat to safe containment. Any breach of containment could result in serious land degradation.

Fig. 3.4. Map of areas of the UK (shaded) which are less than 5 m altitude. Effects of rising sea level will be felt mainly within these areas. Notes: *The Severn, Thames and Humber estuaries are especially at risk.* Source: *Davenport & Young, 1988; Anon, 1988* New Scientist, *123 (1671), p. 38.*

Hydrological Impacts

Table 3.2 gives some expected flows for major river systems as a consequence of 'greenhouse effect'-related climatic change. The world's largest system is not included, however, there are indications that the Amazon Basin had much drier conditions several thousand years ago, during glacial periods, and a different cover of vegetation. The 'greenhouse effect' could upset Amazonian hydrology enough to have serious consequences on a vegetation that might have long enjoyed conditions of very little change in temperature or rainfall/soil moisture (not all would agree on

Table 3.2. *Expected flow changes in major river systems affected by CO₂-induced climatic change.*

A Rivers experiencing decreases in flows

River system	Location
Hwang Ho	China
Amu Darya	Soviet Union
Ayr Darya	Soviet Union
Tigris-Euphrates	Turkey, Syria, Iraq
Zambezi	Zimbabwe, Zambia
Sao Francisco	Brazil

B Rivers experiencing some flow and storage loss

River system	Location
Congo	Central Africa
Rhone	Western Europe
Po	Western Europe
Danube	Eastern Europe
Yangtze	China
Rio Grande	United States
	Mexico

C Rivers experiencing increases in flows

River system	Location
Niger	Africa
Chari	Africa
Senegal	Africa
Volta	Africa
Blue Nile	Africa
Mekong	Indochina
Brahmaputra	South Asia

Source: Barbier, 1989b: 24 (Table 2).

this point). As far as possible, reserves and conservation areas should be selected so as to have as much hydrological stability as possible. If they are to conserve over the coming centuries. They should also be linked together or linked to additional, different environments wherever possible by 'corridors' or 'stepping-stone' conservation areas so that species could retreat and survive.

A mere 2 °C warming above present conditions could cause marked reduction in run-off in western and mid-western USA, cutting flows in rivers such as the Colorado, Rio Grande, and Missouri. Areas that depend on winter rain and snow-melt to supply spring and summer water could be disadvantaged, e.g. California. Groundwaters would also tend to fall in the west and mid-west of the USA. The combined effect of reduced streamflows and reduced groundwater would severely affect agriculture and urban water supplies. There will doubtless be similar threats in other world regions, especially those between 30° N and 60° N (Barbier, 1989b: 24).

Reservoirs might suffer increased evaporation losses causing their water to become more saline, and some may no longer provide adequate supplies to cities, irrigation or hydropower turbines.

The impact of warming on the mid latitudes of the Northern Hemisphere is not clear. Potential productivity losses, due to decreased rainfall and

increased evaporation, might be offset by increased photosynthesis, resulting in better water use efficiency; and warmer conditions might allow the
growing season to be extended into wetter parts of the year. There could
even be increases in rain-fed agriculture.

Impacts on plants and animals

Tropical forests, already under stress through deforestation, will probably
be subject to added pressures from 'greenhouse effect'-related climatic
change. There have been considerable changes in climate before Man began
to affect natural systems. In the future, however, the change is likely to be
faster than natural climatic changes have been in the past. Wildlife is
nowadays less able to adapt to environmental change by moving because
development has blocked the escape routes. It is inevitable that some wild
species and some crop varieties will be unable to withstand the change (Pain,
1988; Parsons, 1989).

At high latitude, tundra 'meadows' will probably be affected, and, in all
probability, the tree line will move north and uphill in highlands. Some of
the wild or plantation tree varieties presently growing in Europe and North
America require a cool winter and may not flourish or set seed if conditions
warm (e.g. Sitka spruce). The impact on vegetation could be considerable if
climatic change is sudden. Given the time it takes trees to mature, it is
important to start identifying and planting suitable replacements soon.
Northern Hemisphere crop and tree varities will have to be bred to
withstand warming, and possibly storm or rainfall patterns and levels of
disease/insect attack will be quite different from those of today. Storms like
the very destructive UK gales of 1987 and 1990 might become more
common-place. Agricultural practices in the Northern Hemisphere will
probably have to be adapted. For example, winter wheat may be less
practical. Breeding new crop or livestock varieties and developing suitable
management techniques takes time; development efforts should start now.

There are hopes that rising CO_2 levels will enhance photosynthetic
efficiency of crops, and compensate for unfavourable environmental change,
but there are many unanswered questions.

1. Will the result, if enhancement occurs, be more, poorer quality, plant
   material and thus an illusory gain, or will it be beneficial (Idso, 1985: 31)?
2. Will better photosynthetic efficiency mean less demand for water?
3. Which crops/trees, will best respond?
4. Will conditions mean more variation in yields from year to year?

Efforts have started to try and predict the effects of rising CO_2 on
agriculture (Parry et al., 1988a, b). Rising CO_2 can have direct effects on plant
metabolism, and indirect effects through environmental changes. A number
of researchers have used controlled-environment chambers, in which
growth conditions, including the composition of the atmosphere, can be
exactly controlled to assess the effects of increased CO_2. Commercial growers
have long known that certain levels of CO_2 boost glasshouse crops, and
some deliberately raise CO_2 concentration around their crops by about 1000
ppmv. Above that level, further increase might have little beneficial effect.
There has been an attempt to compare records of the yields of Australian
wheat from 1958 to 1977 with the known rate of CO_2 increase (Skiba &
Cresser, 1988).

All higher plants fall into two broad groups with different photosynthetic
metabolic pathways: C3 and C4. The former includes: wheat, soya, rice,
barley, oats, cotton, many tree fruits and forest trees (Wellburn, 1988: 170;

Skiba & Cresser, 1988: 144). C4 plants include: maize, sugar cane, sorghum, and most tropical crops.

C3 and C4 plants vary in their response to rising CO_2 levels. At present, plants with C4-type metabolism are more efficient at fixing CO_2 to form biomass and are often more economical in moisture demands. The moisture savings arise because the C4-type plants tend to have fewer stomata (without which metabolism would cease, but through which moisture escapes) and/or tend to close these 'leaf pores', opening them to admit CO_2 mainly at night or in dull weather (Barrow, 1987a: 159). Rising CO_2 levels might cause C4-type plants to partially close their stomata more of the time. The saving in transpiration losses could have significant effects on demand for irrigation water by C4 plants. Both C4 and C3 plants will possibly require less water. Consequently increased run-off, waterlogging and salinity problems will result in some regions, and there is also a chance that the effects of pollution might be reduced if plants have their pores closed more during daylight.

Rising temperatures and CO_2, at least until the gas is about 10% above present levels, might boost C3 yields. The increased photosynthesis might also help reduce the CO_2 rise. If CO_2 levels rise more than 10%, the effects are uncertain. It is possible that C3 plants would benefit more from CO_2 increase if it exceeds 10%. In theory, a doubling of CO_2 would significantly increase C3 yields. It is possible that the effects of rising CO_2 will be unevenly spread, with the Third World worst affected because it relies more on C4 crops.

Prediction is difficult when questions like plant metabolism and climatic change are involved. It seems possible that, at first, C4 and then C3 plants would show enhanced growth. Trees may increase their growth rates, and, in the longer term, C3 crops may improve. Bolin *et al.* (1986: *xxix*) speculated that, in mid-latitudes, by the mid twenty-first century, there might be depressed wheat and maize yields. Much will depend on how well crop breeders manage to adapt existing varieties and produce new ones. There is also the problem of pest/crop response to environmental change: a C3 crop with C4 weeds could give very different results to a C4 crop with C3 weeds at a given level of CO_2. The same is true of natural forest/woodland and plantations, where some components of the vegetation (many weeds are C3 plants) may gain an advantage at the epense of others.

It is clear that there is the potential for great change: change which could upset food reserves, food prices, and alter the pattern of land use. The change is unlikely to strike evenly; some regions/countries will suffer more, some may gain more. Those concerned with long-range planning might be advised to allow for between 3% and 17% reduction in the average yields of crops which at present we depend upon. It is possible that the limits of cereal production in mid-latitude N. America and the USSR will shift north (Warrick, 1988). In addition to shifts in regional patterns of agriculture, there might well be expansion of irrigated cultivation in the USA and possibly elsewhere (Adams *et al.*, 1990). Rainfall changes may cancel out or may reinforce the effects of temperature and CO_2 levels. In temperate countries such as the UK it might become possible to economically produce crops like sunflower, maize, soya and navy beans. Wheat and barley yields might also improve in the temperate lands.

There will be changes in flora and fauna if climate alters. Some of these alterations will be welcome, while some will cause problems. Wildlife may suffer as new species colonize, e.g. in the UK at present the African clawed toad (*Xenopus xenopus*) has become established in Wales (UK), and there are fears that warmer conditions could allow it to displace native amphibians.

Pest and health problems

Some weed species might benefit more from climatic change and increased CO_2 levels than the crops with which they compete. It is too soon to make detailed predictions of the effect on animal pests. There have, however, been suggestions that warmer than average winters have already led to an unusually high rate of increase of rodents in Europe. If winter frosts in temperate regions are light, then there also tends to be greater survival of insects like aphids which carry virus diseases of plants very effectively. There could be devastation of crops. The impact of the 'greenhouse effect' on the activity of soil organisms and micro-organisms is unknown. It might be that nematode worms, which damage many crops, become more widespread. Changed rainfall and wind patterns could well cause alterations in the incidence of locust damage.

Human health problems can affect land use: areas recognized to have a disease risk may be avoided or abandoned, and people debilitated by illness have a reduced capacity for labour. In parts of the Tropics, seasonal drought- or disease-related debilitation could degenerate into a vicious cycle of reduced labour leading to reduced crops, to malnutrition, to further impaired health, to reduced labour to . . . . Diseases which might spread, even to parts of developed countries, if temperatures rise include: malaria, schistosomiasis and hookworm infections (Pain, 1988: 39). Strains of malaria were, or are still, present in Western Europe and N. America but nowadays seldom get transmitted to humans. Climatic change might favour insect vectors and trigger outbreaks. The effect of rising temperatures and CO_2 levels on livestock diseases is uncertain.

Health impacts will not be confined to middle latitudes. It takes little variation in tropical environments to change insect disease vector patterns. For example, in the Malagasy Republic in 1988, a particularly bad malaria outbreak killed thousands of people. Apparently this occurred when above-average temperatures favoured a particular mosquito vector (Boyle & Ardill, 1989: 78).

Impacts on soil

It seems possible that, even ignoring the increasingly widespread effects of acid pollution, there will be a greater risk of increased soil acidity due to temperature rises affecting the activity of soil micro-organisms and the breakdown of organic material and agrochemicals (Skiba & Cresser, 1988). As with pollution-related acidification, the problem will not be uniform: some areas will suffer more than others, for example, those with already acidic or neutral soils. Changed rainfall, altered storm incidence, increased incidence of forest fires and raised summer temperatures/drought could all lead to more soil erosion. It is common practice, in temperate countries, to plough at the end of winter, or in early autumn. This may no longer be possible, and the demand for lime, fertilizers and so on will probably change.

Dust and climatic change

Airborne dust and non-'greenhouse' gases like sulphur dioxide could reinforce or counter the 'greenhouse effect'. There are two dust sources: natural and Man-made.

Volcanic eruptions can eject large quantities of dust, water vapour and some of the 'greenhouse gases' high into the atmosphere. Particularly 'dusty' eruptions have been: Krakatoa (Indonesia, 1883); Agung (Bali, 1970); Mt St

Helens (USA, 1980). Such emissions might cause a series of especially cold winters and depressed summer temperatures in high latitudes. The problem is deciding whether it is the dust or something else erupted with the dust, like sulphur dioxide or sulphur compounds, causing the bulk of the cooling (Anon. 1988f; 1988g). Soot, generated by large forest fires, may also raise sufficient particulate matter into the atmosphere to cause cooling. There are signs of large fires during the Cretaceous (144–65 million years BP) that might have had a global cooling effect (Goldberg, 1985). Forest fires in Kalimantan (N. Borneo) between 1982 and 1983 (see Chapter 5) raised vast quantities of soot (Malingreau *et al.*, 1985). Amazonian soils have charcoal layers which suggest there have been very large fires in the past.

Man-made dust, including soot and ash, is generated through burning vegetation and combustion of hydrocarbon fuels, by vehicles, power stations, factories and homes. One potential Man-made source of vast amounts of soot and dust is warfare. Hopefully, the possibility that Man could cause a 'nuclear winter' will never be put to the test (see Chapter 11).

During droughts, large amounts of dust can be raised by winds, grazing animals and cultivation. This may have at least a regional impact on meteorology. A phenomenon recently recognized is the 'Arctic haze'. Observed mainly in March–April and August over the Arctic, this is probably due to combustion of hydrocarbon fuels in mid and high latitudes generating soot and graphite dust (Pearce, 1988b). If such pollution gets worse, it might have an effect on stratospheric ozone. There is also a possibility that deposition will lead to 'dirty snow' that will melt faster in spring and pollute tundra areas.

REACTIONS TO THE 'GREENHOUSE EFFECT'

Conflicts have to be faced when reacting to the 'greenhouse effect'; one that also applies to other environmental difficulties, is that only speculation or incomplete evidence is available, but there is so little time, and the potential threats are so great, that to wait for research to provide 'adequate' facts would be foolhardy.

There are a number of possible 'greenhouse effect' scenarios.

1. Emissions continue to grow and/or various feedbacks result in escalation of effects.
2. Emissions are slow and the effects remain more or less constant.
3. There is a considerable cut in emissions, and effects stay at roughly the present level.
4. The wrong gases are cut too much/too soon and the other 'greenhouse gases' cause problems.

Schneider (1989) pointed out that there are three ways in which Man can respond to the 'greenhouse effect': mitigation, adaption, prevention.

Control of emissions

In 1988, widespread agreement was reached at Toronto that there was a serious problem and a need to act. The UNEP and WMO are to convene an International Convention on Climatic Change in 1992 to try and promote suitable responses to the threat. To control 'greenhouse gases', there are a number of issues that need attention:

 – climatic monitoring and modelling must be improved;
 – research must be increased to improve understanding of changes and effects;

47

– policies must be agreed and developed to reduce greenhouse gases;
– strategies must be adopted to reduce damage and cope with the problems.

There are a number of theoretically practical measures to control 'greenhouse gas' levels, for example:

– Conserve energy through building insulation, improve public transport to reduce numbers of private cars, waste heat recovery, improved motor vehicle engines, improved boilers, use of hydrogen as a fuel, alternatives to air conditioning, etc. These seem the most promising routes (Pearce, 1989a). In Canada, power companies offer rebates to consumers if they trade in old, inefficient appliances for newer, more efficient ones.
– Reduce combustion of hydrocarbon fuel. Alternatives include: nuclear power generation (expensive, some risk and likely to be increasingly opposed by the public), wind, wave, geothermal or solar energy (use may have promise if they can be made cost-effective).
– Tax CO_2 and other 'greenhouse gas' generation (difficult to impose and enforce). Emission control by law is a possibility. The Montreal Protocol on CFCs is a possible model for managing such emission control.
– Use more biofuel like alcohol or fuelwood. Burning these fuels releases some CO_2. However, less fossil hydrocarbons would be released into the world ecosystem, and the growing fuel would fix some carbon, i.e a net decrease of CO_2 might take place.
– Plant more trees, possibly establish lagoons containing algae or aquatic weeds; there may be some risks that algae would themselves release unwanted 'greenhouse' gases.

If fast-growing forests were planted, as CO_2 sinks, an area of forest the size of W. Europe would be needed to soak up 15 to 20% of 1989 emissions, assuming there was no forest clearing to counter the planting, which is unlikely to be the case (Boyle & Ardill, 1989: 154). Reduction of 'greenhouse gas' emissions is vital, but it will not have an immediate effect. As a consequence of emissions so far, the world is committed to change.

Adapting to the 'greenhouse effect'

There are a range of measures for reducing the impacts of the 'greenhouse effect', for example:

1. Reduce development in areas vulnerable to sea level rise or climatic change. There may be a need for relocation of many people.
2. Start developing appropriate crops, livestock and agricultural techniques/strategies as soon as possible.
3. Improve monitoring of the situation as it develops.
4. Respond with appropriate inputs, soil protection, conservation areas/reserves, coastal defences, etc.

Recognizing possible controls and responses is one thing, funding and organizing the controls and responses is another. A major part of the challenge will be institutional development. Technological development and agricultural research will not be enough.

4 *Land degradation through global pollution: stratospheric ozone depletion, acid deposition and tropospheric ozone increase*

STRATOSPHERIC OZONE DEPLETION

AN OZONE LAYER is maintained by natural process in the stratosphere between roughly 18 and 50 km altitude. Human activity is upsetting the maintenance of this ozone layer (Gribbin, 1988d: 3; 1988e). Near the Earth's surface in the troposphere, solar radiation acts on pollutants formed mainly by partial combustion of hydrocarbon fuel to create a photochemical smog rich in O_3. This low-altitude tropospheric ozone can damage plants and animals and acts as a 'greenhouse gas' (in order to reduce confusion between stratospheric and tropospheric ozone, these are separated by coverage of acid deposition).

Stratospheric ozone (O_3) is formed as oxygen filtering up from the troposphere to the stratosphere is acted upon by sunlight. This photodissociation of oxygen to form O_3 is greater above the Tropics, where solar radiation is stronger. However, high altitude winds transport the gas toward the Poles and help maintain a global 'layer' particularly between 20 and 30 km altitude. There is little O_3 formation over whichever pole happens to be in polar 'night', so there has always been some variation in quantity of O_3 between high and low latitudes and from season to season, but as far as is known no actual gaps occur naturally.

Since the mid-1980s an unusual degree of thinning or gaps have been observed, particularly over the Antarctic. What land degradation effect these thinnings and gaps will have is uncertain. Terrestrial and marine plant productivity might be significantly affected, and there may be climatic effects, especially in polar and high latitudes.

What is depleting the ozone?

Natural variations in ozone formation occur, if solar radiation receipts vary, but it is widely accepted that it is human activity that is presently damaging the ozone layer. The problem arises partly because conditions over the Poles are so cold during winters that O_3-'scavenging' compounds can accumulate in stratospheric clouds for some months with little breakdown. When the Sun returns, photochemical reactions release active chlorine which attacks the already depleted O_3. Volcanic eruptions may also attack the stratospheric ozone layer by liberating chlorine or fluorine compounds (Anon, 1988g; Joyce, 1988b) (details of the reactions are given by Dütsch, 1987).

Various reactions destroy O_3, for example, largely Man-made oxides of nitrogen such as nitrous oxide (N_2O) can act as a catalyst to convert O_3 and

O_2 into molecular oxygen. Each molecule of N_2O can 'scavenge' very many molecules of O_3. The source of the N_2O is mainly hydrocarbon fuel-burning vehicle exhausts. There have been fears in the past that high-flying commercial supersonic aircraft would deliver enough N_2O in the upper atmosphere to cause problems, but so far there are too few to have much effect. Methane gas can 'scavenge' O_3. Bromine and halons, used in fire extinguishers and for industrial uses, can break down O_3, as can carbon tetrachloride and methyl chloroform; use of these compounds has been increasing in recent years. Chlorine (Cl_2) is another very effective 'scavenger' of O_3. There are many sources of the Cl_2 reaching the upper atmosphere. However, the main one is a group of gases known as chlorofluorocarbons (CFCs). For a list, with indication of relative ability to 'scavange' ozone, see Boyle & Ardill (1989: 266). CFCs appear to have been the main culprits for ozone depletion.

The first warning on the possibility that CFCs might affect the O_3 was made by Lovelock (1979: 104, 115–16). Lovelock proposed a Gaia hypothesis in which he suggested the possibility that organisms had control over their physical environment to the extent that they maintained what was to them a suitable atmospheric gas mix, global temperature regime and radiation receipts. Several Gaian processes were suggested by Lovelock: one is that algae, especially marine algae, could produce methyl chloride, dimethyl sulphide and sulphonic acid which, like CFCs, act as O_3 'scavengers'. Too little solar radiation would encourage algae to produce methyl chloride, which would reduce O_3 in the atmosphere, allow in more radiation which would reduce algal output of methyl chloride and allow O_3 to rise, and so on. In effect, the Earth's biota would regulate radiation receipts to maintain a sort of environmental 'steady-state'. CO_2 levels may affect the liberation of these compounds, not only radiation receipts. Other vegetation might have a similar 'ploy', for example: tropical rainforest releases gases including nitrous oxide (N_2O), methane and isoprene. The latter is a hydrocarbon gas which very effectively 'scavenges' O_3 (*The Times*, 29/3/88: 12).

CFCs are widely used as refrigerants, as aerosol can propellants, as agents to blow (form or foam) certain plastics and as de-greasing/cleaning agents in the electronics industry. Some types have been increasing in the atmosphere by around 7% a year. Those CFCs which are efficient at 'scavenging' O_3 are very slow to break down; they therefore pose a real threat to the Earth's stratospheric ozone layer. Such CFCs like 'freon-11' (CFC-11) and 'freon-12' (CFC-12) have been used for about 60 years as cheaper, and until recently what was believed to be safe, more effective and non-toxic substitutes for ammonia refrigerant. Aerosol cans are a mainly post-1950s development, and propellants are now being changed to avoid CFCs.

Ozone 'holes'

Between 1925 and 1942, at about which time use of CFCs began to increase, atmospheric O_3 increased by between 2% and 3% but, between 1960 and 1981 it fell 1% to 2% (Bolin *et al.*, 1986: 176–9; MacKenzie, 1988b). The depletion at the Poles may be of the order of 3% over the last 20 years (Anon, 1988c; *The Times*, 18/10/88: 6). The risk of O_3 depletion was noted in the early 1980s, but was felt unlikely to be a problem before the twenty-first century (Tolba, 1987b: 16).

In 1984, an 'ozone hole' was noted over the Antarctic; it was reported in 1985 and mapped in 1986 (Farman *et al.*, 1985). In spring, 1987 at 18 km

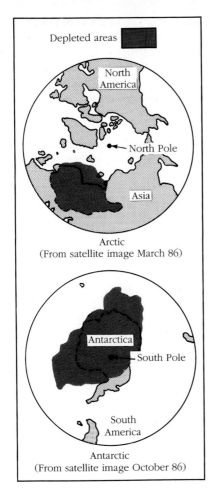

Depleted areas

North America

North Pole

Asia

Arctic
(From satellite image March 86)

Antarctica

South Pole

South America

Antarctic
(From satellite image October 86)

Fig. 4.1. Antarctic and Arctic ozone 'holes'; areas where thinning of stratospheric O_3 had occurred in October, 1986 and March, 1986 respectively. Source: Based on various sources, including The Daily Telegraph, 4/10/88: 2.

above the Antarctic about half the usual O_3 was missing. By 1989, the Antarctic 'hole' was more or less continent sized and had 95% loss of O_3 in some areas; in early 1990 the hole appeared to be getting larger and more persistent. Australia and New Zealand have voiced concern that the ozone depletion might significantly affect them (Farman, 1987; Clover, 1988; Gribbin, 1988e: *viii*; Pearce & Anderson, 1989).

Since March 1986 there has been debate about the possible existence of a 'hole' over the Arctic. Certainly, there has been a decrease in ozone in the Northern Hemisphere, with marked thinning over the Arctic and, in 1988, a reduction of O_3 by as much as 6% was noted as far south as Nottingham, UK (Dayton, 1988; Gribbin, 1988e: 122–6; Pearce, 1988b).

Where O_3 concentration is reduced, more ultra-violet radiation, particularly UV-B, will reach the Earth's surface. Increased exposure to UV-B might have the following effects.

1. Reduced plant metabolism could affect oceanic plankton, leading to increased 'greenhouse effect'. It could also depress terrestrial crop yields;
2. increased mutagenesis in plants and animals;

3. increased incidence of skin cancers and eye cataracts of animals and Man (Russel Jones & Wigley, 1989);
4. possibly changes to wind patterns/weather circulation;
5. possible impact on nitrogen fixation by bacteria/algae in rice paddies, resulting in lowered rice crops and reduced sustainability;
6. as more UV-B gets through to lower atmosphere, it might cause more photochemical reaction and so *increase* tropospheric ozone and other pollutants like PANs;
7. increased UV-B will damage paint, plastics, wood, rubber, textiles – resulting in degradation of infrastructure, such as: canal linings, pipes, farm equipment, etc.

Impacts 1. and 4. could greatly disrupt world food and commodity crop production and fisheries, 2. might also have this effect.

Some crops are known to be especially sensitive to UV-B. These include: tobacco, soya and grapes (Skarby & Selden, 1984). A 25% increase in exposure to UV-B might well lead to a 25% fall in soya yields, according to Gribbin (1988f: 4). Areas most likely to be affected are those at higher latitudes, especially higher altitude vegetation. Alpine and boreal or austral forests and pastures may well be affected more than other regions. Upland tree die-back would result in more avalanche and landslide damage. There is a likely increase in occurrence of 'sports', mutations that might have value. Crop plants and tree 'sports' might be beneficial, but it is also possible that lower organisms, because they have more generations in a given time, will undergo more mutagenasis than higher organisms. The result might be more variation of existing plant and animal diseases, change in pest insects and other nuisance invertebrates that make their control more difficult, and possibly give rise to new forms of virus, bacteria, etc. Animal immune systems may become less resistant to disease as UV-B increases.

Responses to ozone depletion

Given the persistence of CFCs, and that vast amounts of these gases have dispersed, there is little that can be done to immediately reduce O_3 depletion. However, it is vital that further damage be controlled. The key to this is to act to reduce releases of CFCs and other O_3-'scavenging' gases. Use of CFCs can be reduced by finding alternative working fluids for refrigerators and air conditioning and non-CFC or halon propellants for aerosol cans and fire extinguishers, and other compounds for foaming plastics or cleaning electronics. Rewards for safe disposal would help reduce emissions. Better engineering, servicing and recycling of refrigeration/air-conditioning equipment would help.

There has been progress with finding substitute propellants for aerosol cans. The USA banned CFCs as aerosol can propellants in 1978. Canada and Scandinavia followed by 1987 (Gribbin, 1979: 474; Rowland, 1988: 101). In 1987, the Montreal Protocol, the first global treaty agreement aimed at reducing CFC emissions, was signed by 27 nations (Boyle & Ardill, 1989: 143, 258 gave a listing of signatories). The agreement of those nations was to aim for a reduction of emissions to 50% of the 1986 level by 1999. In 1988, the USA called on all nations to ratify the Montreal Protocol.

Even if the Montreal Protocol's reduction goals were achieved now, CFC scavenger compounds would probably reach about twice the 1988 levels. It would probably need an 85% or greater reduction in emissions to stabilize O_3 at the 1988 levels (Anon. 1988c; Jones, 1988: 58; Roan, 1989).

In 1989, delegates from 124 nations at a conference on CFCs in London called for a 100% reduction in CFC emissions by 1999. Even if the various pledges, innovations and controls took effect by 1999, loss of O_3 would probably not start to decline for more than 20 years, because already released CFCs will continue to work their way to the stratosphere. While there has been progress in establishing protocols and in finding chlorine-free alternatives to the worst CFCs, there are potentially vast numbers of first-time buyers of refrigerators in countries like China, India, Brazil. These countries are, or will be, manufacturing their own refrigerators and are likely to seek to use cheap, established CFC technology. If substitues are more expensive and/or less easy to manufacture, then they will tend not to be adopted. It might be necessary for richer nations to subsidize CFC alternatives to encourage their use.

At the time of writing, CFC-12, one of the most effective scavengers, and CFC-11 had been banned virtually worldwide. Already in Europe some manufacturers are selling CFC-'friendly' refrigerators and at least one supermarket chain is sponsoring a CFC-recovery scheme to deal with old ones. There are also signs that corporate industry has begun to respond to the ozone threat (Boyle & Ardill, 1989: 234).

ACID DEPOSITION

Pollutants can be deposited gradually or suddenly, close to the source of pollution or much further afield. Some are removed from the air in rain, snow or mist, as 'wet deposition', some simply settle out as 'dry deposition'. Pollutants acidify the moisture that has trapped them, and/or the ground or water they are deposited on.

'Acid rain' is a blanket term that has gained widespread use. The term was first used by Robert Angus Smith in Manchester in 1872 in a report to the Chief Alkali Inspector. Unfortunately, it is a misleading term, for acid deposition can be 'wet': rain, snow, mist, cloud droplets, hail or 'dry': gas, dust/particulate matter, fine aerosols, smog. Acid deposition is a better term than acid rain. The effect of acid deposition is acidification, a change towards more acid conditions, i.e. a lower pH (Hicks, 1984; McCormick, 1988).

Acid deposition can degrade land in a number of ways. These are:

1. damage to plants and/or animals;
2. direct alteration of soil chemistry/structure;
3. alteration of plant metabolism;
4. alteration of metabolism or species diversity of soil micro-organisms leading to change in fertility/soil chemistry.

On a local scale, acid deposition has been recognized as a problem in some localities of the UK for centuries (McCormick, 1988). From the 1750s, until as recently as 1952, domestic and industrial use of coal as fuel led to severe smog which damaged buildings, people's health and vegetation within several kilometres of cities or industrial sites: it is no accident that the poor, working class settlements are generally on the eastern, downwind, side of UK industrial towns.

In 1952, smog killed over 4000 people and hospitalized over 2000 in London. The causes were a combination of domestic coal fires, carbon industry and power generation (which also burnt coal) plus winter fog conditions. In 1984, at least 500 people were hospitalized in Athens and there were many deaths due to smog caused by motor vehicles pollution during a period of high air temperatures and little wind (Elsworth, 1984: 3). The response to smog-pollution in the UK, and many other countries since the 1950s, has been to discourage the use of untreated domestic fuel and to encourage the consumption of electricity generated by large coal- or oil-fuelled power stations sited outside urban centres and equipped with high smoke stacks. Vehicular pollution is now being dealt with. Occasional severe air pollution within, and 'downwind' of, industrial areas and cities has been reduced, but at the cost of causing much more widespread, lower-level, more constant, acid deposition problems.

In the 1960s, Scandinavian scientists began to link pollution blown from the UK and Europe with acidification of lakes and streams. Sweden voiced concern about this at the 1972 Stockholm Conference on the Human Environment. In subsequent years, debate has given way to acceptance that acidification is real, and there has been the realization that not only lakes and streams are affected. A number of countries well away from industrial areas now face sufficient acid deposition to affect soils, plant growth, animal and human health. (In this section little attention is given to impacts on lakes, streams or marine waters like the Baltic. These are, however, serious.)

Uncontaminated rain is slightly acid, typically about pH 5.6 because it has reacted with CO_2 in the atmosphere to form weak carbonic acid (Park, 1987: 1; Pearce, 1986a: 1). It has become an accepted definition that acid deposition is occurring if the precipitate has a pH of less than 5.1 (Elsworth, 1984: 5). It should be noted that the pH-scale is not arithmetic: a slight change in pH means many times greater or lesser acidity, e.g. pH 4 is 10,000 times more acid than pH 8). So far attention has focused on acid precipitation in Europe and North America, especially in E. USA, but the threat is becoming much more widespread, so much so that Park (1987: *xii*) was moved to comment: '. . .acid pollution is one of the most serious problems in developing countries.'

In Central Europe today, rain of pH 4.1 and pH 3.0 is common. Even in the western fringes of Europe, in Eire and in Portugal, storms have yielded rain with pH 3.0, and fog or mist can be even lower. In the UK, rain has been recorded with a pH of 2.4, worse than vinegar. Elsworth (1984: 5) suggested the UK's rainfall was between, roughly, 10 and 70 times normal acidity. It was probably more acid still over parts of Europe (Pearce, 1987b: 1).

Causes of acid deposition

Sulphur dioxide (SO_2) emissions are a major cause of acid deposition. There are various natural sources: sea spray; bacteria in anaerobic conditions may release SO_2; volcanoes sometimes emit SO_2; weathering of gypsum compounds and, in the Canadian Arctic, natural underground fires in bituminous shales release SO_2 (Perry et al., 1987). Vegetation can produce SO_2, N_2O and hydrogen sulphide (H_2S), while growing and when burnt. Joyce (1988b) suggested that Amazonian rainforest produced enough N_2O to acidify precipitation downwind. Man-made emissions are produced mainly by: burning hydrocarbon fuels; copper smelting; and burning off vegetation (Gorham, 1989; Wellburn, 1988: 23).

Volcanic releases of SO_2 are not constant. For example, the Mount St Helens eruption (USA 1980) raised atmospheric SO_2 levels to roughly twice the normal (Park, 1987: 33), but, in an average year, volcanoes vent a little less than UK power stations did in 1987 (Pearce, 1987b: 22). Three UK thermal power stations: Drax, Eggborough and Ferrybridge were reckoned to produce about one-fifth of the UK's sulphur emissions, and the Sudbury nickel and copper smelter (USA) apparently produced more SO_2 between

1969 and 1979 than all volcanoes throughout Earth history (McCormick, 1988: 10). Clearly, human actions distort nature, and control of the emissions from even a few installations can have significant effect.

Combustion of coal, especially high sulphur content coal, in power stations is probably the largest artificial SO_2 source. In 1989, natural and Man-made emissions were roughly the same, but the distribution of the Man-made SO_2 was uneven. Over Europe and the USA, around 90% of SO_2 would be Man-made, because those are the land areas where there is most polluting industry (Rodhe & Herrera, 1988: 11).

The effects of SO_2 are almost certainly 'enhanced' by other Man-made pollutants, notably, nitric oxide (NO) and nitrous oxide (N_2O) (these are often abbreviated to the not very satisfactory: 'NOX'); metal particles from industrial activity; ozone produced by motor vehicle pollution undergoing photochemical reactions while in the air; ammonia – given off by sewage, livestock and some types of artificial fertilizer (Pearce, 1986a, b). Artificial, nitrate-type fertilizers contribute to NOX in the atmosphere when they undergo denitrification by soil microbial action (Wellburn, 1988: 64). In developed countries, around 30% of oxides of nitrogen are produced by road vehicles, roughly 45% by power stations and roughly 25% by industrial and domestic sources (Wellburn, 1988: 68).

N_2O can persist for over 20 years; it tends to concentrate in the stratosphere, where, with sunlight and other compounds, it plays a part in the reduction of ozone. Much N_2O is produced by soil micro-organisms, especially in waterlogged and/or compacted soils. Irrigation development thus increase N_2O emissions. Hydrocarbon-fuelled power stations and vehicles give off NO_2 and NO.

Cores taken through Greenland ice sheets well away from areas of industrial activity show a two- to three-fold increase in sulphate and nitrate deposition over the last century (Park, 1987: 35). At certain times of year, NOX levels in the Northern Hemisphere are five to ten times natural levels.

Peroxyacetyl nitrates or 'PANs' ($CH_3CO_2NO_2$), although short-lived, are very toxic to plants and animals, along with ozone, which is also very damaging to organisms when present in sufficient concentrations. At low altitude, they are formed when air, polluted with NOX from vehicle exhausts and power stations, is exposed to sunlight. This is more likely to take place in urban areas when conditions are warm. Los Angeles (USA) and São Paulo (Brazil) have infamous 'photochemical smogs' in which PANs and ozone are made from a NOX and SO_2-rich 'cocktail'. As global warming takes place, and ozone depletion allows through more sunlight, PANs and low altitude ozone damage may increase at higher latitudes.

Below roughly 12 km altitude, tropospheric ozone is involved in the transformation of NO_2 into HNO_3. This then helps to transform sulphur, mainly from SO_2, into H_2SO_4 (Mohnen, 1988: 14). SO_2 in the air reacts with moisture and some is oxidized. This then reacts with the hydrogen present to form sulphuric acid (H_2SO_4). In dry air, the process of H_2SO_4 formation is slower and less efficient. If moisture is scarce for long enough, then SO_2 may disperse without being converted to H_2SO_4. To summarize, reactions involving SO_2 are directly, or indirectly, catalysed by 'NOX', ozone, metallic particles and ammonia (Pearce, 1987b: 2). SO_2 also reacts with ammonia in the atmosphere or in soil, where ammonia-forming fertilizer or microbial activity has made ammonium sulphate. In the soil, the SO_2 and ammonium sulphate will probably be converted to nitric acid (HNO_3). NO in the atmosphere is converted to NO_2, which is then oxidized to form HNO_3 (Pearce, 1987b: 2). Under some conditions, these processes might be beneficial and improve fertility, but, especially where soils are already slightly acid, degradation is more likely.

It is apparent that terrestrial organisms are affected by pollutant gases in the atmosphere in a number of ways, often with more than one process operating at the same time. A soil may have H_2SO_4 forming within it as 'dry' acid deposition products are broken down, and, at the same time, there may be an input of 'wet' 'acid rain'. It is difficult to keep account of cause and effect. In a crude way, Elsworth (1984: 6) attempted this, suggesting that roughly 70% of acid deposition/pollution was due to SO_2 emissions, much of that due to combustion of coal, and roughly 30% due to nitrogen compounds.

The extent of the problem

Cloud and mist can carry pollutants considerable distances. Dust and gases can also blow a long way on winds. Vegetation can intercept dust, gases, mist and cloud driven by the wind, and so accumulate pollutants. The plant cover of exposed, high ground is particularly vulnerable because wind exposure helps it collect efficiently, and because, at moderate to high altitude, the harsh environment puts vegetation under stress, weakening it before any pollution receipt. Temperature inversions may hold down pollution and lead to locally higher contamination, and storms of acid rain may give localities higher than average pollution. Prediction of effects of acid deposition on the land are therefore difficult, even if there is a modern monitoring network. Even in remote regions like the North Slope of Alaska

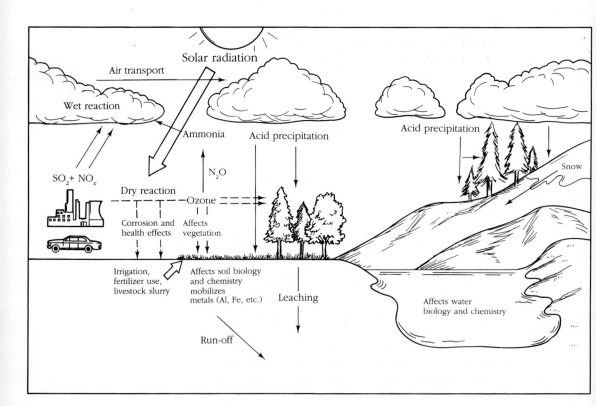

Fig. 4.2. Simplified illustration of acid pollution pathways. Source: *McCormick, 1988: 14.*

or northern USSR, vegetation is now trapping quite high levels of acid
pollution. The deposition may not be steady, but episodic, as the Chernobyl
fall-out over Europe proved.

The effects of pollution when it arrives will vary. For example, if it is
winter, and broad-leaved trees have few leaves, little may be intercepted; if it
is spring, and there are delicate shoots and leaves, more is intercepted and
damage may be great. The efficiency of interception by conifers and broad-
leaved trees also differs. Broad-leaved trees in temperate environments lose
leaves annually and rid themselves of non-soil pollution more effectively
than do conifers. Broad-leaved trees may sometimes shed leaves and regrow
new ones after a severe pollution episode. If deposition is moderate to high,
the point will come where leaf-shedding makes little difference because acid
deposition has affected the soil. It might be possible that different soil micro-
organisms in broad-leaved and coniferous forests vary in ability to counter
acidity build-up if deposition is slight to moderate.

The northern polar regions, including the high Arctic, receive acid
deposition in the northern spring, as polluted air moves into the region. This
is manifest as 'Arctic haze' and as soot and graphite particles in the snow. In
summer, frontal systems tend to prevent such airmass movements. Environments which have winter snowfalls may get a spring flush of acid pollution as
the snow melts releasing several months' accumulation of pollutants in a
short period which could cause considerable damage to the soil and to soil
organisms.

Dry and wet acid deposition take place at different rates. Rates of dry
deposition (D_d) depend upon the pollution concentration velocity (C_a) and
deposition velocity (V_d) which, in turn, depend upon the nature of the
uptake or receiving surfaces. In contrast, rates of wet deposition (D_w) do not
depend on the underlying surface characteristics but on the precipitation rate
(P), the wash-out-ratio (W), i.e. the concentration of dissolved pollutants
per unit mass of cloudwater or rainwater divided by the concentration of the
pollutant or precursor per unit mass of air, and the ambient air concentration
(C_a).

Thus:
$$D_d = C_a V_d$$
$$D_w = W P C_a \qquad (2)$$

(Wellburn, 1988: 108)

Increased use of electricity in most of Western Europe has resulted in
large power stations which, in much of Western Europe, burn coal or oil.
France, due to greater use of nuclear generation, burns less hydrocarbon
fuel. These thermal power stations discharge pollutants from high smoke
stacks. About 50% of this pollution falls as dust within a few kilometres,
30% is rained out within a few kilometres, but 20% or so can stay aloft for
three or even four days, and, if winds are favourable, can travel 2000 or more
kilometres. The problem tends to be worst when there are slow-moving
high pressure areas with low advective and dispersal rates (Wellburn, 1988:
108).

Things are getting better, at least in Western Europe, and emissions of
SO_2 probably peaked between 1975 and 1978. From 1985, they have shown a
slight decline due to domestic emission controls, and, possibly in countries
like the UK, the effects of recession on industrial fuel use. In Eastern
European countries like Poland, where much high sulphur content brown
coal is burnt, the picture may be less promising.

Figure 4.3 indicates the general distribution of sulphur compounds over
Europe in the late 1980s, Figure 4.4 gives a global picture for the early 1980s

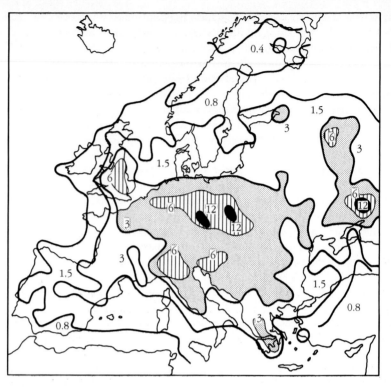

Fig. 4.3. Total fall-out of sulphur over Europe (late 1980s) (in g m² y⁻¹). Source: Pearce, 1987b: 23 (no Fig. no. in text).

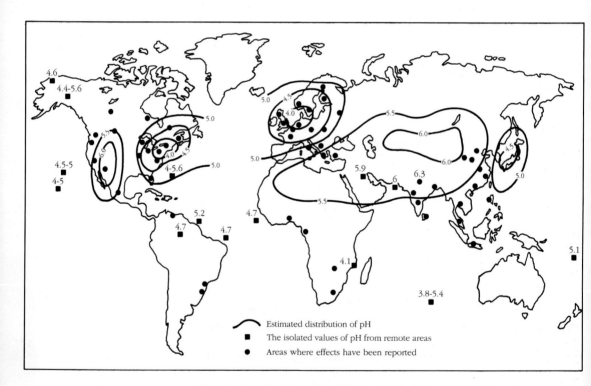

Fig. 4.4. Global pattern of acid deposition in the early 1980s. Sources: Park, 1987: Fig. 1.1; McCormick, 1988: p. 4.

Table 4.1. *Acid and alkaline substances observed in the atmosphere and their effect on terrestrial and aquatic systems.*

Substance	Effect
H_2S, SO_2, H_2SO_4	+
NO_x, HNO_3	+,o
HCl, HF	+
Organic acids	+,o
NH_3	+,o,−
Ammonium salts	+
Alkaline dust	−

Key: + acidifying − neutralizing o no significant effect.
Source: Rodhe & Herrera, 1988: 6 (Table 1.1).

Table 4.2. *Areas reported to have acid pollution problems by 1988.*
Source of data indicated by superscript number (key follows Table)

Location	Biome/damage	Rain/cloud pH
Arctic (Barrow, Alaska)		
Australia (Katherine, Jabiru)		3.9–5.4[1]
Australia (around Sydney)		* [2]
Austria	Forest damage reported	
Brazil (São Paulo, Rio, São Jose dos Campos, Santos, Cubatão[A])	Soils[B] C D	3
Chile (esp. Criciuma region[E] and Ventanas)[F]		
China (esp. S. and SW. China: Luizhang, Sechuan, Guishow, Keyang, Shisun Provinces)[G H]		4.6–4.7 [14, 4]
Czechoslovakia (esp. Ergebirg Mtns.)		5
Denmark	quite common to get	<4.0 [6]
France	forest damage reported	
Germany. W.	*c.* half of all forests affected	
Germany. E. (Bohemia badly affected)	Severe forest damage by 1980	
Hong Kong	Mainly related to traffic	
Indian (Pune) [I]		6.3–8.0 [7]
Ivory Coast	Forest damage noted	4.2–5.0 [8]
Japan [J]		
Kenya (Nairobi region)	Traffic-related	
Malaysia [K]		
Mexico (esp. Mexico City) [L]		
Netherlands	Forest damage reported	
Nigeria [M]		5.2–5.9 [9, 14, 15]
Philippines Metro. Manilla esp.)		
Poland [N]	Severe forest/soil damage	10
Peru [O]		
Spain		11
S. Africa [P]	Forest damage	
Sweden		

Table 4.2. (*cont.*)

Location	Biome/damage	Rain/cloud pH
Switzerland	Forest damage	
Turkey		
Thailand (Bangkok)	Traffic and industry	
UK	Forest damage widespread	
USSR[Q]	Forest damage/soil problems[12]	
USA (many regions in east and west)	Forest damage	
Venezuela[R]	Forest damage	3.0–6.7[13]
Yugoslavia	Forest damage	
Zambia (esp. Copper Belt)		

Key: Sp = spring Su = summer W = winter
* = level not ascertained but significant
A Reputedly, world's worst-polluted area, very high acid deposition.
B Amazonian soils are vulnerable to acidification because they are naturally acid and have high aluminium content. Metal smelting near Belém could cause problems.
C Some acid deposition due to smoke and gases from burning of forests.
D S. E. Brazil burns a lot of coal.
E Coal burning.
F Copper smelting.
G Heavy dependence on coal (*c.* 70% energy needs), many small domestic fires.
H Sichuan Province especially badly polluted McCormick (1988: 6–12) suggests China is world's third greatest emitter of acid pollutants, much due to combustion of high sulphur-content coal. In regions south of the Gobi Desert, calcareous dust counters acid deposition.
I Calcutta, Bombay, Delhi are badly affected. Sources are industrial and domestic use of coal, over 65% of India's electricity is from coal-fired power stations.
J Osaka and Tokyo are especially bad regions. Source is use of high-sulphur content oil from Middle East for electricity generation.
K Bad around Kuala Lumpur (Klang Valley esp.) and east of Penang (Pinang). Industrial and power generation and road traffic sources.
L Mexico City one of the world's worst-polluted, source road traffic and industrial. Yucatan Peninsula is affected. Some Mexican soil is very vulnerable because it is already acidic and high in aluminium.
M Lagos and Ibadan esp. Oil refining, oil-fuelled power stations and metal smelting.
N Krakow, Katowice, Nowa Huta, Gdansk and Warsaw regions badly affected. Brown coal burnt for power generation and domestic heating.
O Mining and smelting cause pollution.
P Use of coal for power, SASOL coal–oil/petrol plants. E. Transvaal, Johannesburg/Witwatersrand badly affected.
Q Donbas Coalfield region badly affected, forest damage widespread. Gets much of Europe's pollution. USSR itself reputed to be one of the biggest producers of SO_2.
R Has areas of very sensitive soil, like Brazil, and probably other tropical American states. Urban pollution and oil processing sources. Caracas and Cuidad Guayana badly affected.
Data source:
 1 Rodhe & Herrera, 1988: 20.
 2 Rodhe & Herrera, 1988: 347.
 3 Rodhe & Herrera, 1988: 11, 197; Elsworth, 1984; Wellburn, 1988: 109.
 4 Rodhe & Herrera, 1988: 20; Perry *et al.*, 1987; Elsworth, 1984; Dianwu Zhao & Bozen Sun, 1986: 2–6.
 5 Pearce, 1987b.
 6 Welburn, 1988: 109.
 7 Rodhe & Herrera, 1988: 20.
 8 Perry *et al.*, 1987: 264; Elsworth, 1984; Lacaux *et al.*, 1987.
 9 Rodhe & Herrera, 1988: 20, 297.
10 Glenny, 1987.
11 Parry *et al.*, 1988a, b: 49.
12 McCormick, 1988: 113.
13 Rodhe & Herrera, 1988: 20, 211.
14 Rodhe, 1989: 156–7.
15 *Ambio, XV(1)*, p. 47.

Table 4.3. *Acid deposition impacts on land.*

Direct
Damage to soil.
Injury to crops or forests.
Damage to terrestrial fauna: amphibians and possibly songbirds are vulnerable.

Secondary
Reduction of amphibia/songbirds, etc, reduces predation of insect pests.
Health of farm labourers suffers due to acidity of water and/or toxic compounds
mobilized and accumulated in crops.
Capacity for labour declines.
Damage to soil micro-organisms: loss of mycorrhizal fungi,
Reduction of beneficial bacteria, earthworms, etc.
Increased corrosion of farm equipment/buildings, increases chances of
breakdowns and raises costs.
Acidification of ground and surface waters may damage crops if used to irrigate
or may injure livestock.
Acid deposition kills trees in highlands, avalanche and landslide risks increase.
Pollination of crops reduced: maize is apparently vulnerable.

Cumulative
acid deposition mobilizes compounds which stress vegetation and make it
vulnerable to frost, drought, disease, etc.

(NOX deposition patterns were similar). Taken with Table 4.2, it is clear that many regions well away from industrial development or large urban areas have at least occasional acid deposition.

Impacts of acid deposition

Acid deposition can have direct, secondary or cumulative effects (see Table 4.3). By the time there are obvious signs of acid deposition, much damage has already been done to the ecosystem. There are likely to be 'thresholds': levels of acid deposition, which, once exceeded, result in severe effects, although there is little apparent problem before that level is reached.

Damage to vegetation

Natural acid deposition can damage vegetation, for example, in Nicaragua in the 1950s, volcanic emissions caused quite widespread forest damage (Rodhe & Herrera, 1988: 126). Until relatively recently, acid pollution damage was either related to industrial or urban areas. Non-ferrous metal smelting plants have a particularly bad record. The Trail Copper Smelter (British Columbia), Anaconda Aluminium Smelter (Montana, USA) and Sudbury Copper Smelter (Ontario) have caused considerable forest damage (Detwyler, 1971: 526; Park 1987: 96).

Lichens can be good indicators of air quality because they rely on dissolved solids in rainwater for nutrients – they are directly affected by any increase in acidity. Plants growing in the soil are likely to enjoy more 'buffering' from chemicals in the soil which may counter the acid deposition. In general, lichen species diversity decreases as SO_2 and acid deposition levels increase. Even in the non-industrial areas of the UK, acid-tolerant lichens are increasing and acid-intolerant ones are decreasing (Park, 1987: 97). Epiphytes like *Bromeliad* spp. or orchids are important in the Tropics

and, like lichens, are probably vulnerable to acid deposition (Roche &
Herrera, 1988: 127).

The symptoms of acid damage may be difficult to recognize and may vary
even from plant to plant of the same species. Injury may be in the form of
visible canopy damage to plant structures, there may be a decline in
productivity or ability to reproduce, or there may be increased vulnerability
to some other difficulty: frost, insect damage, drought, other pollution, etc.
Plants may not be damaged directly; it may be that symbiotic bacteria or
fungi are affected and a plant then has less support in its quest for nutrients
(Jansen & VanDobben, 1987).

Forest die-back syndrome (USA) or *waldschäden* ('forest death') (Germany), was noted first with fir trees in the late 1960s in the Black Forest,
Bavaria (Germany), and in the 1970s in mountain regions of W. Germany
and the Alps, although real media attention began after 1981 (Park, 1987: 3;
Hutchinson & Meema, 1987). German tree-ring studies suggest that the
problem has increased over the 25 years up to 1985 (Anon. 1985a;
McCormick, 1988: 5; *Geojournal*, 1988).

The vulnerability of vegetation seems to depend on many factors which
include: position, altitude, soil, moisture availability, i.e. the effects of die-
back are synergistic (Hinrichsen, 1986; Cowling, 1989). Die-back was first
noted in Germany in stands of silver fir (*Abies alba*), then Norway spruce
(*Picea abies*). Subsequently, other conifers, for example, Scots pine (*Pinus
sylvestris*). Broad-leaved trees have so far been less susceptible. However,
these are increasingly showing signs of die-back in many areas. In Europe,
beech (*Fraxinus* spp.) and oaks (*Quercus* spp.) are generally the first broad-
leaved trees to show signs of damage (Wellburn, 1988: 206). In N. America,
the eastern hemlock (*Tsuga canadensis*), and red spruce (*Picea rubra*) appear to
be vulnerable conifers and the sugar maple (*Acer saccharum*) and birch (*Betula*
spp.) are broad-leaf species which suffer (Freedman, 1989: 125).

Possibly conifers have suffered more because they grow in exposed
positions and have 'needles' which collect pollution well (Usher &
Thompson, 1988: 151). There are also indications that afforestation with
conifers can cause soil acidification. There seems to be some correlation
between die-back and recent increase in the corrosion of glass in European
churches. However, Park (1987: 110) observed that, in some areas, trees
suffering die-back had SO_2-sensitive lichens still growing on them. There
must be some doubt for there have been cases of die-back where pollution
seems low, and there is evidence of extensive stands of trees, for example:
Metasidros polymorpha in Hawaii that suffer die-back due to ageing or root
infection (Freedman, 1989: 126).

It is difficult to assess the cost of forest die-back; the process is under way
in many areas without having yet manifest itself and acid deposition is
increasing. Also, the process of die-back may take up to 30 years to complete.
Forests in Europe, the USA, especially Vermont and Maine, and in the
USSR have already been widely affected and, in Germany, Finland, Sweden,
France, the costs in terms of lost timber and need for replanting are already
considerable. In 1988, the cost of acid deposition to Scottish foresters was
estimated to be roughly £25 million (Milne, 1988b: 56). Elsworth (1984: 18)
estimated that over half of Germany's coniferous forests were showing signs
of die-back, and about 560,000 ha were 'devastated'. By 1985, the damage
was probably costing W. Germany roughly US$ 300 million a year
(McCormick, 1988: 27). In 1984, about half of the EEC's agricultural land
was under forest. In 1989, about 22% of the UK's conifers were moderately
affected by die-back and 5% were severely affected (*The Times*, 9/11/89: 22).
Already, signs of die-back are apparent in forests of developing countries.

Table 4.4. *Hypotheses suggested to explain die-back.*

There are two broad types of hypothesis for die-back: 'top-down': pollution affects leaves and leads to die-back; 'bottom-up': pollution affects soil/roots and leads to die-back.
* Indicates process that might, rather than be the sole cause of damage, debilitate and lead to die-back from a range of factors like drought, frost or disease.

Hypothesis	General features
1. Leaf damage*	Leaf damage affects availability of magnesium, roots cannot make up deficiency. Evergreens suffer more because needles trap more pollution and leaves are shed less often than broad-leaved trees.
2. Bad practice*	Bad forestry practices: use of foreign species that require certain conditions (monocultures with little genetic range). Trees may cause acidification on some soils as needles accumulate. Fertilizers used cause increased hydrogen ions (> pH).
3. Acid rain/soil	Mainly due to 'wet' deposition. Leaching*. Soils are leached of essential nutrients/minerals, especially magnesium. Toxic ions, like aluminium, increase and upset soil micro-organisms, especially mycorrhizal fungi-tree root associations.
4. Disruption	Acid deposition hinders photosynthesis*. Halocarbons and other pollutants render plants vulnerable to UV damage disrupting photosynthesis.
5. Ozone/photochemical	Sunlight produces 'low-altitude' tropospheric ozone• PANs, SO_2, hydrogen peroxide, etc, then play a part in attacking vegetation. Wax coating on conifer needles may be vulnerable. Europe 1976 had high levels of low altitude ozone.
6. Pollution-enhanced stress*	Droughts or unusually cold winters or enhanced levels of disease/pests together with atmospheric pollution, cause demise of sensitive, weaker, exposed and older trees.
7. Excess nitrogen or ammonium deposition*	Forests/vegetation gets more nitrogen ('wet' and 'dry' deposition), growth is stimulated and is too fast, vegetation then vulnerable to stress/parasite attack. An excess of nitrates in soil might cause plants which have evolved to cope with limited amounts to suffer reduced 'cold hardening'. The excess nitrogen might result in a failure to reduce water in leaves ready to face frosts.
8. SO_2 pollution*	SO_2 suppresses plant growth, debilitation increases vulnerability to pests, diseases, frost, drought, etc.
9. Alternatives	Wide range of possibilities, e.g. tetra-ethyl lead additive to motor fuel may play a role.
10. Synergism*	Any of above acting together, with or without other factors.

• Tropospheric ozone formation is discussed later in this chapter.
Sources: Geojournal (1988) special issue 17(2); Hinrichsen, 1986; Klein & Perkins, 1987: 91–2; McCormick, 1988: 31; Mohnen, 1988; Pearce, 1987b: 107; Wellburn, 1988: 213).

Damage to soils (acidification)

Soil acidification can occur naturally, for example, when a newly deposited glacial soil weathers. Where land is under agricultural use, repeated harvesting of biomass can remove enough bases to acidify the soil, and agrochemical use can lower pH. Recently, air pollution-related acidification, i.e. due to acid deposition has been increasing to the extent that many fear that, if it is not checked, vast areas of soil may suffer degradation that could seriously affect agriculture and wildlife. Some soil scientists believe that, in general, natural soil processes and agricultural management practices play a more important role in acidification than does atmospheric pollution. Even if that is the case, acid deposition is one more unwelcome pressure on the environment.

Soil acidification may be defined as the decrease in acid neutralization capacity of the soil. In most soils, particularly in those with a greater mineral content, cations weather to neutralize acidity. Soil acidification begins when rate of acid input exceeds the rate of neutralization resulting from weathering. Acid pollution of soil tends to have the following effects. 1. Increasing acidity slows down breakdown of litter, in the soil or on the surface, by soil organisms. 2. Increasing acidity interferes with plant roots' absorption of soluble material, moisture and nutrients. 3. Cations (K^+, Ca^{2+}, Mg^{2+} and Na^+) get leached out of the soil to be replaced by hydrogen and aluminium ions, and toxic heavy metals are likely to be mobilized.

Soils are generally less vulnerable to acidification than streams or lakes, because they are more likely to be able to buffer the acidity. Soils vary a great deal in their buffering capacity. In temperate and in colder environments, soils over slow-weathering, non-alkaline bedrocks like granite, weathered glacial deposits, or sandy material are more likely to be badly affected (McCormick, 1988: 23; Park, 1987: 3). It is possible that, in a few localities, excessively alkaline soils might be made more useful by acidification. Sulphur deposition might also improve those soils deficient in that element (Park, 1987: 2).

Tropical/subtropical lateritic soils are vulnerable. Large areas of the Tropics, and some non-tropical regions, have soils that could be raised by acid deposition to pH levels high enough to result in excessive mobilization of aluminium. If the pH exceeds 6.0, it could lead to aluminium crust or layer formation, and plant growth is upset below that level (Rodhe & Herrera, 1988: 24; Tabatabai, 1985). Moran (1987) warned that large areas of South America have soils that are already quite acidic and have a high aluminium content. These soils become degraded if acid deposition takes place.

The more alkaline a soil is, the more resistant to acidification it is likely to be. Deeper soils and soils with high organic content also tend to be more resistant. Some regions receive wind-blown dust that is sufficiently alkaline to counter acidification, for example, areas around the Gobi Desert. Application of artificial fertilizers may increase the chances of soil acidification. Rodhe & Herrera (1988) examined the vulnerability of soils to acid deposition (see Figure 4.5). Their conclusion was that soils of lowland S. America and Cambisols of Europe, the USA and S. China are especially vulnerable.

The effect of acid deposition on peatlands is still uncertain. The South Pennines (UK) blanket peats have been heavily polluted with sulphur/acid deposition since the Industrial Revolution. One effect has been the decrease of the plants vital for peat formation, notably *Sphagnum* spp. The number of *Sphagnum* spp. has generally declined in the Pennines, and as a consequence

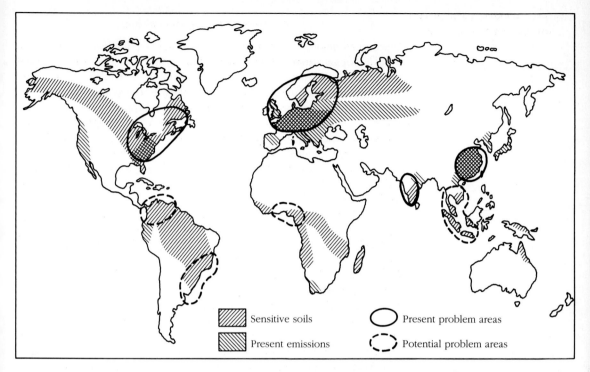

Fig. 4.5. Schematic map showing regions that currently have acidification problems, and regions, where, based on soil characteristics and expected acid emission patterns, acidification might become severe in the future. Source: Rodhe & Herrera, 1988: 27 Fig. 1.8.

there has been widespread erosion, also due in part to trampling by Man and livestock and to occasional fires. The increased acidity of these UK uplands has led to severe reduction in species diversity and the domination of the vegetation by two species: *Eriophorum vaginatum* and *Vaccinium myrtilius* (Lighttowlers, 1988; Perry *et al.*, 1987: 554–61; Usher & Thompson, 1988: 355).

Damage to crops

Separating crop damage due to acidification of soil, direct acid deposition damage, low altitude ozone damage, and a multiplicity of plant diseases, pest activity and environmental factors, such as drought, is difficult. It may well be that acid deposition has made a crop more vulnerable to other things, but proving this to be the case is difficult. There are nitrophilic plants which like acid soils. It is also possible that high acidity and atmospheric sulphur could, as many urban UK rose growers are aware, discourage crop pests like aphids and fungal diseases. Wellburn (1988: 52) reported that cereals and grasses might benefit from slight acid deposition, but, once levels rose above 60 ppmv, SO_2, species like the European grass *Lollium perenne* L began to suffer. Some crops are particularly vulnerable to acid deposition, including rye, salad vegetables, barley, oats, wheat, tomatoes, apples and pears (Elsworth, 1984).

Elsworth (1984: 48) and McCormick (1988: 5) have made crude estimates of the value of crop losses due to acid deposition; the latter suggested it was costing Europe US$ 500 million a year (in 1985).

Responses to acid deposition

Once emission of acid pollutants/precursors of pollution has taken place, the gases/particles disperse, there can be little further control and the response must be palliative.

Pollution control involves costs and/or the foregoing of presently enjoyed benefits, at least in the short term. But there may also be by-products or benefits, in addition to reduced pollution, which may help to compensate, and might even more than pay for the process. There are four ways by which emissions can be decreased.

1. Burn less hydrocarbon fuel. To do so requires conservation of energy, improved furnaces/boilers and motors and use of alternative sources of heat and power.
2. Use less-polluting fuel, or treat the fuel in order to reduce its capacity to pollute.
3. Burn fuel in such a way that emissions are reduced.
4. Remove pollutants after burning from exhaust gases.

Burn less fuel

Fuel consumption can be reduced by: improving efficiency of energy use, either by cutting energy losses, insulating homes and other buildings, recovering waste heat, improving efficiency of burn to get less waste, and/or cutting energy demand (people adapt demands in response to change in attitudes, taxation or legislation).

Alternative energy

Avoid hydrocarbon fuel, use: hydropower, nuclear power, tidal power, wind power, geothermal energy, harness differences in ocean temperatures and/or solar energy.

Use less-polluting fuel

Methane, hydrogen, alcohol and 'smokeless' coal-substitutes may be used in place of coal or fuel oil. Both coal and oil can be treated to remove some of their sulphur content; coal may have as much as 5% sulphur and oils up to 3%. Sometimes, simply crushing and washing coal with water is enough to considerably reduce pollution, because there may be less ash produced and a better burn. This may be quite cost-effective. Sulphur can be removed from oil using solvents (this is done in Japan).

Burn fuel so as to produce less pollution

There are a number of new designs for furnaces burning coal or oil to ensure better combustion; the fluidized-bed combustion furnace is one form. It is also possible to inject crushed lime with the fuel to reduce pollution.

Car engines may be of the 'lean-burn' type, in which a sparse fuel mixture is more fully burnt. It is also possible to fit internal combustion engines with effective pollution control devices such as three-way catalytic converters. Certainly, better control of fuel–air mixtures in vehicle engines and furnaces can markedly reduce pollution by preventing incomplete combustion.

Remove pollutants after burning

To reduce vehicle emissions, air can be injected into the hot vehicle exhaust gases to ensure fuller combustion and/or the gas stream can be passed through a catalytic converter. To use a catalytic converter, fuel must be free of tetra-ethyl lead 'anti-knock' additive (lead-free petrol). Furnaces, power stations, heating plants, smelting plants, waste incinerations, etc, may have their flue gases 'wet scrubbed' using a spray of water, lime or chemicals to remove pollution from the flue gases and collect it as a slurry for disposal, hopefully where there will be no land degradation. Some such scrubbing produces gypsum which can be sold to the construction industry, or used to treat acid-sulphate soils. 'Dry scrubbing' – the use of ammonia sprays to remove pollution – produces a by-product that can be used as fertilizer. Flue gases may also have pollutants removed using electrostatic precipitators. Pollution control technology has long been available, Battersea Power Station (London) had flue gas desulphurization facilities that were up to 90% efficient in 1929.

Post-deposition measures

There may be situations where it is cost effective to apply alkaline material, e.g. agricultural lime or magnesium salts to the land to counter acidification. It may be possible to adapt land use to acidification by selecting crops and tree species that resist acid soils, high aluminium levels, etc.

Emission control agreements and regulation

As with other environmental agreements, there must be 'teeth', means of enforcement, and standards with which to judge each situation by a common yardstick. Without these, efforts are likely to be in vain. In the UK, legislation since the 1950s has largely cured local acid deposition. To cure regional and international acid deposition demands co-operation between nations and this has been slow coming. Table 4.5, though not a complete list, indicates the relatively slow and unsteady progress toward controls, even when a threat is apparent and when there is relatively little sacrifice required to reduce the threat.

The main problem in controlling acid deposition has been that of cost. Future power stations in the UK will have better pollution control equipment that may well reduce emissions by over 90%. Unfortunately, there are many old power stations in Europe, and, in countries suffering from recession, like Poland, there are few resources to spend on pollution control. Having available the technology, perhaps the costs should be borne by more than one nation?

Some environmentalists have proposed a 'carbon tax' be introduced, whereby fuels would be taxed according to their capacity to generate carbon dioxide, or possibly other pollutants. While such a tax could discourage pollution and might generate funds for environmental management, getting worldwide adoption and enforcement would probably be difficult.

LOW-ALTITUDE (TROPOSPHERIC) OZONE POLLUTION

The formation of low altitude ozone has already been discussed. Levels have been increasing globally at about 0.25% a year, but, locally, the levels may

Table 4.5. *Acid pollution control developments 1972–1989.*

Year	Statement/measure/agreement	Source
1866	Ibsen commented on UK soot reaching Norway in his play *Brand*.	
1972	Sweden reported over 9000 acidified lakes.	
1975	Canada reports acidification.	
1975	Initiative on Acid Pollution (President Carter), USA.	
1979	International Convention on Long Range Transboundary Air Pollution (W. Germany not very supportive).	
1979–80	Convention on Long-Range Transboundary Air Pollution, Geneva (Norway and Sweden active in organization: 32 countries sign, including USA and the EEC).	
1980	Canada and USA sign Memorandum of Intent on Transboundary Air Pollution (a commitment to joint research).	
1980	OECD give independent confirmation of Scandinavian charges.	
1982	Sweden reports over 18,000 acidified lakes.	
1982	Multilateral Conference on Acidification of the Environment (Stockholm). recognized pollution and noted that there were solutions available – proposed '30% Club' (supported by Canada, Austria, Switzerland, W. Germany, Sweden, Denmark, Norway and France).	
1983	W. Germany tries to get the EEC to insist on catalytic converters on all cars built after 1986 and introduction of unleaded petrol.	
1983	UNEP published *The State of the Environment* with a chapter on 'Acid Rain'	
1983	Co-operative Program for Monitoring and Evaluation of the Long Range Transmission of Air Pollution in Europe (EMEP). Signatories undertake to develop, without delay, policies and strategies to reduce pollution.	
1984	Ottawa Conference – the '30% Club' formed (members pledged to reduce SO_2 emissions to at least 30% of their 1980 levels by 1993).	
1985	Helsinki–UK, Greece, Eire, USA, Poland, France refuse to join '30% Club' (for a range of reasons).	
1985	UK, biggest emitter of SO_2 in W. Europe (McCormick, 1988: 86).	
1985	'30% Club' has 21 signatories (in 1982 32 had expressed support)[1]	
1988	May – only four USA states: Mass., Wisconsin., Minnesota and New York, have actually passed laws to reduce power station emissions.[5]	
1988	EEC *proposal* for two-stage conversion to lead-free petrol by 1989 for all new, and by 1991 for all vehicles and to adopt USA Emission Control standards in 1995.	
1989	Widespread signs of broad-leaved tree die-back reported in southern, lowland UK according to NGO Greenpeace.[2]	
1989	UK Central Electricity Generating Board announces it will renew a joint research initiative with British Coal to develop cleaner-burn power stations.[3]	
1989	UK announces £1.8 billion programme to reduce power station emissions.[4]	

Proposals made by 1989

1994	All new cars of over 1400 cc in EEC to have a catalytic converter.	
1994	All cars of under 1400 cc to have lean-burn engines.	

Notes: [1] For details see Anon, 1986; Alcamo *et al.*, 1987.
[2] *The Times*, 14/11/88: 8.
[3] *The Times*, 12/2/89: A3.
[4] *The Sunday Times*, 19/2/89: A3.
[5] *New Scientist*, 18(1611): 30.

well be higher at certain times of the year. Parts of W. Germany have
recorded levels that have risen 60% between 1967 and 1980. Worldwide, this
ozone is cited as a cause of vegetation damage. In California, grapes and
tobacco have been found to be vulnerable to low-altitude ozone pollution. In
the UK, in the summer of 1983, ozone levels in some regions were high
enough to damage peas and beans (Skarby & Seldon, 1984). (For a recent
review of tropospheric ozone increase impact on crops and forest productivity, see Botkin *et al.*, 1989: 106–10.)

5 Degradation of tropical rainforests, tropical/subtropical seasonally dry and tropical/subtropical upland forests, woodlands and scrublands

THE NATURE OF THE PROBLEM

THE LOSS OF FOREST, woodland and scrubland is by no means new, but the degradation has reached a point where it threatens the extinction of many organisms and the long-term well-being of Mankind. When forest degeneration becomes serious, there may be little time to act to aid recovery. If action is not taken, the loss may well be total and permanent, and in many countries the situation is already critical or has passed that point (Myers, 1988: 217).

There is a vast range of forest, woodland and scrubland formations; some have clear boundaries and can be easily mapped, others grade almost imperceptibly into different formations. Vegetation may have been altered by past disturbance, which may not be easily recognized, or there may be a fringe of disturbance, variable in width and degree of degradation around a formation. Disturbance can develop so fast that the record of vegetation cover can soon be misleading (Bruenig, 1987). Grouping various formations is virtually unavoidable, although, at best, arbitrary (see Table 5.1), for what are apparently comparable formations in different regions may in reality be quite different and subject to dissimilar patterns of exploitation. Great caution is thus needed when mapping and assessing the degradation of forest, woodland or scrubland. One must not lose sight of the fact that forests/woodlands/scrublands are dynamic systems, subject to a complex range of influences. Degradation may be necessary for long-term survival of a forest/woodland/scrubland. Without periodic storm, disease or fire damage, clearings would be rare and regeneration would take place after vegetation aged and died, resulting in a different cover, at least for a time.

Deforestation is a much-used, ill-defined and imprecise term, that tends to be used to imply quantitative loss of woody vegetation. There can also be qualitative changes, from say, species-diverse tropical forest to single-species eucalyptus or pine plantation, or to less species-rich secondary (regrowth) forest. Each year, around 4.0 million ha of virgin tropical forests are converted to secondary forests. The damage caused by thinning vegetation depends on how this was done: was it mechanized, was it well managed, was it by felling or burning or chemical defoliation, was it extensive or as small clearances? There is little distinction in most of the literature between vegetation loss that will 'heal' and that which will not.

There are varying degrees of forest/woodland/scrubland degradation, ranging from almost imperceptible reductions in vigour and/or species diversity or a decline in regeneration which may be a spread over decades or even centuries, making their recognition difficult, to clearly apparent changes: changed species diversity, thinning, altered regeneration or resistance to pests/diseases and invasion of undesirable 'exotic' species. Forest degradation does not simply mean the loss of a vegetation cover; it can mean altered local or regional hydrology, altered climate and serious offsite impacts such as: flood damage and siltation.

Temperate closed forests have suffered the greatest cumulative losses: 32% to 35% has been destroyed; subtropical woody savannas and deciduous forests have fared next worse, 24% to 25% destroyed. So far, moist tropical forests have been 4% to 6% destroyed (Repetto & Gillis, 1988: 2). Between roughly 7000 BP and 1988, the total loss of the world's forested area has been about one-fifth: 4 to 5 billion ha. Forests still cover roughly two-fifths of the Earth's land surface, about 3.5 times the area occupied by crops. Just over half of the remaining closed and more open forests and woodlands are in the developing countries where, since 1945, deforestation has been accelerating. For example, between 1958 and 1968, Central America lost 38% of its forest/woodland and Africa 24% (for a recent country-by-country listing of deforestation between 1981 and 1985, see Repetto & Gillis, 1988: 6–9).

TROPICAL RAINFOREST DEGRADATION

Humid tropical closed forest

There is tremendous diversity of humid tropical forest. For convenience, this chapter uses the loose term: rainforest. Predominently, evergreen, mainly broad-leaved and closed (i.e. the tree canopy coves at least 20% of the ground when viewed from above). Such forests occurred below roughly 1000 m altitude virtually everywhere temperatures were relatively constant

Table 5.1. *Distribution of the world's forests and woodlands (million ha) in the middle 1980s.*

Region	Land area	A Closed forest Area	% land area	B Other wooded areas Total area	Open woodland	Forest fallow[c]	(A+B) Total Forest + woodlands Area	%
Tropical	4,815	1,202	25	1,144	734	410	2,346	49
Africa	2,190	217(190)	10	652(640)	486	166	869	40
Asia & Pacific	945	306(410)	32	104(100)	31	73	410	43
Latin America	1,680	679(680)	40	388(280)	217	170	1,067	64
Temperate	6,417	1,590	25	563	na	—	2,153	34
N. America[a]	1,835	459(470)	25	275(176)	na	—	734	40
Europe	472	145(138)	31	35(37)	na	—	181	38
USSR	2,227	792(680)	36	138(240)	na	—	930	42
Other countries[b]	1,883	194	10	115	na	—	309	16
World	13,077	2,792	21	1,707	734	410	4,499	34

Notes: [a] = Canada and USA.
  [b] = Australia + China + Israel + Japan + New Zealand + S. Africa.
  [c] = Wooded regrowth areas cleared in last 20 years.
  / = not applicable.
  na = not available.
  ( ) = Figs in parenthesis – source Eckholm 1979: 11 (mid-1970s values)
Sources: Eckholm 1979: 11; World Resources Institute, World Bank, UNEP 1985: 70.

at around 24 °C; there were no frosts, and precipitation was above 1500 mm
y⁻¹ or, more usually, 4000 to 10,000 mm y⁻¹ (Parsons, 1975; Caufield, 1982,
1985).

Even within a limited area, rainforest vegetation cover varies as a result of differences in soil: drainage, aspect, altitude, history of disturbance. Locally, broad-leaved trees may give way to bamboo or conifers even in the low altitude Tropics. Soils below rainforest are usually, but not always, poor, for example, there may be rich volcanic soils. Rainforest vegetation is adapted to survive on infertile soil, so crops or pasture established after forest removal often prove less able to flourish.

Rainforests are not changeless; a forest may be in a natural 'steady-state' comprising a mosaic of aging trees, clearings caused by storm, landslip, lightning, or human activity with regeneration seedlings and areas of mature or immature trees. Storm or fire damage is not always localized, hurricanes can devastate large areas, and coastal lowland forests in Chile, Japan and Hawaii have suffered tsunami damage in historical times (Dudley & Min Lee, 1988). Past climatic fluctuations caused significant changes in the distribution of rainforest, and in some areas the vegetation may still be responding to such changes (Douglas & Spencer, 1985: 36).

Rainforests differ from other forests in that they tend to be more dependent on animals than wind for pollination and seed dispersal; they are genetically far more diverse, typically with 50 to 200 or even more species per ha, in a temperate forest there are seldom more than 10 per ha. The consequence is that, if an area of rainforest is disturbed, there is a risk that complex chains, and webs of interdependence controlling regeneration can be cut, especially if a large area is affected or if a crucial species or locality that harbours pollinators/seed dispersers is disturbed. For example, the South East Asian rainforest fruit: *rambutan* (*Nephelium* spp.) depends on gibbons for seed dispersal. A consequence of high genetic diversity is that the density of individuals of any one plant species is likely to be low; therefore to maintain a breeding population that is viable in the long term will probably demand conserving quite a large area of rainforest (see Chapter 12).

Probably over half the world's genetic resources are to be found in rainforests; it is possible for a single volcanic peak in Indonesia to have more plant species on its flanks than there are in the whole of the USA (Hadley & Lanly, 1983). South East Asia, with only 0.5% of the Earth's total land area probably has 10% of all plant species and the Malagasy Republic, already badly deforested, has at least five times as many tree species as North America (Davidson *et al.*, 1985: 5–7; *The Environmentalist*, 1985). In general, the richest species diversity will be found in low altitude rainforest, especially where soils are rich (see inset map Fig. 5.1).

Extent of rainforest

Often unreliable and/or out-of-date 'guesstimates', rather than recent and reliable statistics, are cited. Some of the best statistics are those released by the FAO, the UNDP, and the UNEP. The UNEP Global Resources Information Database attempts to provide regularly updated, reliable data, but even some of these may be based on inaccurate national estimates. Myers (1980) gave a detailed country-by-country appraisal of extent, rate of loss and cause of loss (see also Williams, 1989). Remote sensing has greatly helped assessment of forest cover (Myers, 1988). Figure 5.1 gives a relatively recent map of general extent of rainforest. In 1988, closed forests probably covered about 29 million km², roughly 21% of the Earth's land surface and

66% of the tropical land area, of this roughly 43% was closed tropical forest, and about 90% of this was tropical rainforest (World Resources Institute *et al.*, 1988: 70). Open forests/woodlands in drier regions probably comprises about 21% of the world's total forest/woodland cover; scrubland roughly 13%, forest fallow (land recovering from clearance) about 1.0% and conifers, mainly in plantation forests, about 0.4% (Independent Commission on International Humanitarian Issues, 1986b: 42; World Bank, 1988).

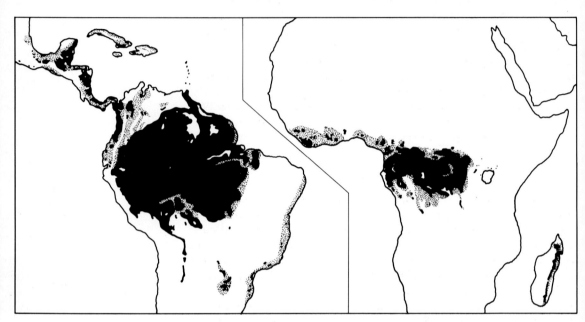

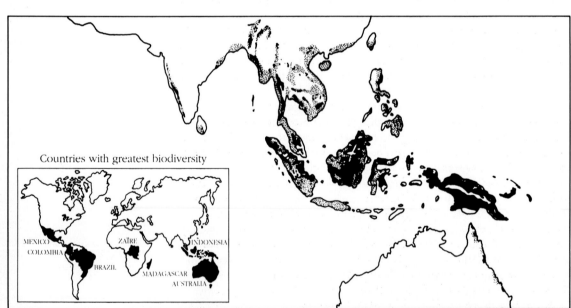

Fig. 5.1. World distribution of humid tropical forest. Key: *solid approx. extent 1986; stippled area probably forested before clearance.* Source: *World Resources Institute et al., 1988: 74 p. 5.1; Lewis & Berry, 1988: 114 (Fig. 4.1). Countries with greatest biodiversity:* Source: *Compiled by author.*

According to Caufield (1982: *v*) tropical rainforest probably covered something like 900 million ha in 1982. There were in addition, roughly 300 million ha of closed tropical forest but not rainforest. Taking the total of rainforest, plus other tropical forests of around 1200 million ha, about 38 million ha of those were under 'sustained management' in 1982, i.e. at least in theory, were managed to ensure regeneration of some sort or were replanted when cut (Steinlin, 1982: 6).

Estimates vary, but it is likely that about 140 million people live in and around, or are dependent upon, the 1200 million ha of closed tropical forests, only 1% to 2% of these were tribal peoples with a culture likely to be adapted to forest-dwelling. Forest degradation has tended to be accompanied by drastic reduction of aboriginal peoples and expansion of settlers. Brazil, in AD 1500, probably had 6 to 9 million forest-dwelling Indians, now there are probably less than 200,000 (Caufield, 1982: *iii*; Independent Commission on International Humanitarian Issues, 1986b; 16).

Brazil has the greatest remaining area of rainforest, virtually all in Amazonia. At around 331 million ha, this is three times that left in the countries with the next greatest area: Indonesia and Zaïre.

Extent of damage

Unfortunately, there is little account in statistics on deforestation or degradation of standing trees, i.e. loss of limbs, removal of foliage for fodder, etc, nor does reduction of species diversity or thinning of cover show up. A major problem is that deforestation, some prefer the term conversion, can range from marginal modification of cover to fundamental transformation, and statistics seldom indicates the degree (Myers, 1980: 7).

To summarize, by 1982, roughly half of the original cover of tropical rainforest had been destroyed (Caufield, 1982: 5). Williams (1989: 177) put the original cover at 12.7 million km², and that remaining in 1989 as 12.29 million km². Roughly 25% of remaining tropical rainforest was in tropical Asia (mainly South East Asia); roughly 57% was in tropical America (mainly Amazonia), and roughly 18% in tropical Africa, mainly in Zaïre and Gabon (Aubréville, 1985; Lewis & Berry, 1988: 114). Brazil alone had over 31% of the world's remaining tropical rainforest (Gradwohl & Greenberg, 1988: 34).

The global situation is bad, and in some countries, for example, Haiti, Malagasy, the Philippines, E. Australia, Java and Sumatra, deforestation is very worrying. There are a few regions where the situation has improved, for example, areas where there was plantation agriculture in the eighteenth century which has since been abandoned, and now there is a greater forest/woodland cover (Eyre, 1987). Parts of Panama were badly deforested during canal construction in the nineteenth century and have regained some forest cover. Also parts of Africa may have had a lower population in the last two centuries than previously; consequently scrub and woodland has increased (DeVos, 1975). Though only about 1% of tropical forest was/is coniferous, this has been especially badly hit, particularly the cedar (*Podocarpus* spp.) and Parana pine (*Araucaria* spp.) of tropical Latin America, because these woods are much in demand in the USA and Europe.

Between 1976 and 1980, the estimated global loss of tropical rainforest was about 6.5 million ha y^{-1}, roughly 0.6% of the 1980 total extent (Hadley & Lanly, 1983: 12). This seems a reasonable estimate, but others have put the rate as high as 20 million ha y^{-1} (Johnstone, 1987) or as low as 5.6 million ha y^{-1} (Caufield, 1982: iii). Between 1981 and 1985, the rate was put at around

Table 5.2. *Tropical forest/woodland deforestation rates (early 1980s).*

Region	Remaining undisturbed tropical forest/woodland (thousand km²)	% loss p/a
Central America		
Costa Rica	16	4.0
El Salvador	1	3.3
Belize	14	0.7
Panama	42	0.7
South America		
Brazil	3575	0.4
Colombia	464	1.8
Ecuador	142	2.4
Suriname	148	0.4
Africa		
Cameroon	180	0.5
Ghana	17	1.3
Nigeria	60	5.0
Zaïre	1056	0.2
SE Asia		
Indonesia	1139	0.5
Malaysia	201	1.2
Papua New Guinea	342	0.6
Thailand	83	2.9

Source: Lanly, 1982 (Table 1); Sinclair, L. (1985) *Ambio, XIV*(6), 352; World Resources Institute, *et al.,* 1988: 71.

7.1 million ha y^{-1}, with a further 4.4 million ha y^{-1} 'degraded' (World Resources Institue *et al.,* 1985: I − v; Lal *et al.,* 1986: *ix*; Bowander, 1987: 248; Repetto, 1987: 94). By 1988, tropical rainforest losses plus significant degradation was probably around 100,000 km² y^{-1} (globally), something like a loss of just over 2.0% of the total each year (Myers, 1988: 217). Cross (1988) put the loss at 0.6% of the total extent per year, but this was felt by the World Wildlife Fund to be too conservative.

There are already regions, once forested, where today there is virtually no rainforest left. By 1985, countries like Nigeria, Thailand and Mexico, which have been, or still are, exporters of timber, had begun to import timber, wood products and pulp. It seems likely that by AD 2000 the present 33 tropical timber exporting countries will have shrunk to ten. In Nigeria's case, in 1985 such imports cost about US$ 210 million, a sum similar to that spent on food imports (World Resources Institute *et al.,* 1986: I − 10). Table 5.2 gives estimates of cover and rates of loss. Some have suggested that, by AD 2035, virtually all lowland tropical rainforest will have gone (Cartwright, 1989: 116).

PROBLEM REGIONS

Africa

It has been estimated that tropical Africa is being deforested at a rate of 0.6% per year (Independent Commission on International Humanitarian Issues, 1986b: 42). Most of West Africa's forests have gone, or are going, fast.

Harrison, (1987c: 54) put the rate of loss for West Africa at about 4.0% per
year. The Ivory Coast probably has the world's highest rate of loss. Only
about 22% of the 1957 cover remained in 1987, at which time annual losses
had accelerated to about 7% per annum (Bourke, 1987; Repetto, 1987: 94).
Country-by-country details of extent, rate of loss and causes of loss may be
found in Myers, 1980: 151–67 and Lewis & Berry, 1988: 115. Zaïre, Gabon,
the Mt Kenya region and parts of Uganda, Tanzania, Rwanda and Ethiopia
have most of the remaining forests. Repetto & Gillis (1988) gives case
studies of deforestation in Liberia, Ghana, Gabon and the Ivory Coast.

The Malagasy Republic (Madagascar) has lost much of its once rich flora
and fauna, a high proportion of which were endemic, in the 1500 to 2500
years since Man arrived there. The Island's humid tropical rainforests have
suffered along with drier forests and woodlands; by 1972 roughly 80% of the
Island was degraded savanna grassland carrying over 10 million cattle. In
1972, an estimate suggested between 12,500,000 and 16,700,000 ha of
rainforest remained, of which 4,300,000 ha was 'degraded' (Battistini &
Richard-Vindard, 1972: 191, 311; *The Times*, 11/8/88: 13). By 1986, forest
cover seems to have declined to about 15% of the Island's land area
surviving mainly on steeper slopes, with a loss of 150,000 ha y^{-1} (Chown,
1986). A more recent figure is that only 10% of Madagascar's forest remains
(Botkin, *et al.*, 1989: 92).

Latin America

According to Parsons (1975: 28) two-thirds of Central American rainforest
had gone by the mid 1970s. One estimate put the rate of deforestation of
tropical America at about 0.64% per annum in the early 1980s (Independent
Commission on International Humanitarian Issues, 1986b: 42). Forests on
the lower eastern slopes of the Andes of Peru, Ecuador and Colombia have
suffered. Brazil has lost much of the forest outside Amazonia since the
seventeenth century; in 1989 only about 2% of the once extensive Atlantic
forests remained (Botkin, *et al.*, 1989: 92). Brazil has the world's largest
expanse of rainforest in its Amazon territory. This began to come under
pressure after the 1920s, and more so after the road construction began in the
late 1960s/early 1970s; it is now beginning to be dissected into blocks. About
10% of the original Brazilian Amazonian forest has been cleared and
something like 63% of the remaining is officially allocated to development
projects, scheduled to be flooded by hydroelectric projects or disrupted by
mining (Malingreau & Tucker, 1988). Roughly 3.4% has protected status as
parks, reserves, etc (Dawnay, 1989). Satellite data for 1984–5 and for 1986
suggested that there has been a marked increase in squatter settlement and
clearing, so estimates may be over-conservative. Barbier (1989a: 124)
reckoned that about 9% of non-Brazilian Amazon forests (*c*. 403,000 km²)
had been deforested or degraded. Fearnside (1989) estimated 35,000 km² of
dense Brazilian Amazon rainforest were lost in 1987 alone, and that losses by
1988 comprised about 12% of the original cover. In 1960, Costa Rica was
roughly 60% forested, much of this rainforest. By 1986 an estimate put the
cover at 30% (Myers, 1986a).

The Caribbean

Deforestation is the rule on most Caribbean islands: Barbados, Jamaica,
Cuba and Haiti have lost much of their forest cover. On the latter island, the
situation has degenerated to the point where fuelwood is scarce and soil

erosion is chronic. In 1950, about 80% of Haiti was forested, some of this by rainforest, by 1985 this had fallen to around 10% (Ferguson, 1988; World Resources Institute *et al.*, 1985: II; Lewis & Coffey, 1985). Now probably only Cuba, Puerto Rico and Dominica have much forest (Myers, 1980: 68).

Asia

In China, deforestation was well under way by 4000 BP. Recent claims that the Indian subcontinent is 23% forested seem unlikely (*The Economist*, 6/12/86: 93), and remote sensing suggests that, in the mid 1980s, 10% or less of India was still forested. The distinction between rainforest and other forest cover was not made (Shyamsunder & Parameswarappa, 1987; Myers, 1988: 216). The present situation is that little unspoilt lowland rainforest exists outside of reserves, and that even some of the protected areas are deteriorating. Highland areas have tended to escape logging and settlement a little longer. However, their forests are not lowland tropical forests, and lack the same species diversity. The Chittagong Hills (Bangladesh) may still have about 6000 km², but in parts this is severely degraded (Myers, 1980: 68).

In 1950, Sri Lanka had between 50% and 65% forest cover. By the 1980s, this had dropped to around 26% (Myers, 1980: 102). Simple areal statistics need to be treated with care. As an example: the Peoples' Republic of China had the world's sixth greatest area of forest in 1981, *c.* 115 million ha. However, if this is weighed against the total land area of the country, the forest covers only about 12% and the per capita area of forest is pitifully small (Repetto & Gillis, 1988: 205).

South East Asia

It seems likely that South East Asia is being deforested faster than any other world region. Since AD 1800 over 100 million ha of lowland rainforest has been lost (Lal *et al.*, 1986: 189). In 1980, there were probably about 180 million ha of undisturbed South East Asian rainforest, 45% of which was in Papua New Guinea, Sulawesi, Maluku, Irian Jaya and Brunei, only about 6% of those 180 million ha were reserves or national parks (IUCN, 1975b; Davidson *et al.*, 1985: 13). Averaged out, the rate of clearing for the whole of South East Asia was roughly 0.6% per annum in the mid 1980s (Davidson, *et al.*, 1985: 14). However, on the national scale the range of variation is considerable, for example, Thailand's losses were around 3.0% per annum and Papua New Guinea's around 0.1% per annum.

In 1985, 43% of Peninsular Malaysia still had a cover of rainforest, 50% of which was Forest Reserve and 6% National Park, but the Reserves are often subject to controlled cutting. The remaining 44% was principally what was left after the more diverse lowland forest had been cleared, so only about half Peninsular Malaysian forest was undisturbed in the mid 1980s and this was mainly the less diverse upland forest (Davidson *et al.*, 1985). Indonesia's rainforest cover declined from roughly 65 million ha in 1960 to roughly 20 million ha in 1987 (Johnstone, 1987). Burma still had about 52% forest cover in 1980, but earns a considerable part of its foreign earnings from exports of forest products/timber (Myers, 1980: 62).

In 1960, the Philippines had roughly 16 million ha of rainforest; in 1987 this had fallen to 1.0 million ha according to Johnstone (1987). Other sources suggest that, from a cover of around 75% of the total land area in 1948, it had fallen to between 25 and 30% 'reasonably dense' forest by (1988 (MacKenzie, 1988a).

In 1978, about 25% of Thailand's total forest would have been rainforest; the rest, mainly 'monsoonal deciduous forest' (Myers, 1988: 216). In the last ten years Thailand has lost about 25% of its forest (Hirsch, 1987), and, by 1980, had ceased to export teak (*Tectonia* spp.), leaving Burma as the world's main source.

Papua New Guinea still had about 86% forest cover in 1980, but only about 44% of that tropical moist forest was at altitudes lower than 300 m, the rest was upland forest, not really 'true lowland rainforest' (Myers, 1980: 91).

Australia and the Pacific

Australia's tropical rainforest remains mainly as a fragmented cover along the eastern seaboard from Cape York to Queensland where there is 6000 to 7000 km² – roughly 0.3% of the total land area. Rainforest further south, into Tasmania, is subtropical or temperate (Aikin & Leigh, 1987). Little of the rainforest has not been logged at some point since the Europeans arrived, although it may look natural (Myers, 1980: 63).

European settlers have probably cleared 50% (*c.* 40 million ha) of the original forest cover and about one-third (*c.* 63 million ha) of the original woodland and scrub – in about the last 150 years (Campbell, 1990).

Reasons for tropical rainforest degradation

Sinclair (1985: 353) suggested: '. . . poverty, skewed land distribution . . .' due to historical patterns of land settlement and commercial agricultural development, and low agricultural productivity were the main causes of rainforest loss. Not all deforestation happens because of poverty and/or underdevelopment; developed countries must share some of the blame for Third World deforestation. A recent bibliography listing causes of deforestation may be found in Allen & Barnes (1985).

Population increase

In some regions, rising human population does seem to lead to rainforest degradation. It lies at the end of a 'chain-of-causation, whereby rising population leads to increased demand for fuelwood, land or forest products. In 1988, probably in the region of 500 million people lived in forested regions, many being recent squatters (Repetto & Gillis, 1988: 12).

Improved communications

Road, power transmission line, railway, and canal construction cause deforestation, directly, and by enabling settlers to gain access, or by providing routes for the ingress of plants and animals which may damage forests and by facilitating the removal of timber and other products. Caufield (1982) suggested that over 25% of Brazilian Amazon deforestation was a result of road construction which allowed settlers in. In Peru, Colombia and Ecuador, roads have been driven across the Andes and into the rainforests of the eastern slopes by oil companies, providing access for government-supported settlers and squatters. Before 1914, the Belém–Bragança railway opened large areas of Pará to settlers. Within 20 years (1883–1908) this land had become the infamous, ruined 'Bragantina Zone'. In Gabon, rapid forest loss occurred after the trans-Gabon Railway opened the interior to settlers. In Amazonia, Brazil there has been a vast road-building programme, allowing settlers to spread into Acré, Rondônia, Matto Grosso and Pará (Branford & Glock, 1985; Malingreau & Tucker, 1988: 54). One road in Rondônia attracted over 500,000 settlers within a few years (Gradwohl & Greenberg, 1988: 41).

Large dams

Hydroelectric, and other impoundments, have a marked effect on rainforests. The areas flooded by such projects are likely to include some of the best, most diverse lowland forest, since the soils of a river valley are likely to be richer than those of higher ground and, in drier areas, groundwater and flooding help maintain forest diversity.

Smallholder agriculture

Steinlin (1982: 7) suggested expansion of small-scale agriculture was the main cause of loss of rainforest. Much of the blame is laid against shifting cultivators. Fernando (1989) described shifting cultivation as the '. . .single greatest threat to the conservation of the biological diversity of the tropical forests of Asia'. In Africa, Steinlin (1982: 7) suggested roughly 70% of rainforest loss was through shifting cultivation, and Hadley & Lanly (1983) suggested it had accounted for roughly 50% of Asian deforestation and roughly 35% of Latin America's. In many regions, shifting cultivation did little long-term damage to rainforest, until land use degenerated because of 'development pressure', e.g. population increase or warfare. Shifting cultivation is a generic term: it is misleading to compare the shifting cultivation of disillusioned, disorientated, poverty-stricken settlers with that practised by tribal peoples (Adriawan & Moniaga, 1986: 269; Davidson et al., 1985: 120). Shifting cultivation may thus be part of a process leading to deforestation.

In the Malagasy Republic, much forest loss is due to pastoralists burning grasslands to improve grazing. Every year the burn encroaches on the remaining forest and the cattle prevent regeneration. This pattern is common wherever cattle are pastured close to forest.

There are probably in excess of 500 million small-scale cultivators in humid tropical forest environments. What these people need are intensive, sustainable land use strategies. Myers (1987a: 323) calculated that, if a typical (six-person) peasant family could subsist on roughly 2 ha of land (in some case families do so on as little as 0.5 ha in a humid tropical environment), then the land deforested since 1950, he calculated 3 million km², should have been enough to support almost twice the present subsistence cultivator population worldwide. The message is that cultivators have not been very effective land users, and that there might be grounds for future optimism.

Large-scale commercial agriculture

In Central America, clearing to provide pasture for large ranches, may have caused around 38% of forest losses between 1966 and 1975 (Independent Commission on International Humanitarian Issues, 1986b: 50). Since 1945 the demand for lean, grass-fed beef has increased considerably. Import of such meat from Latin America to the USA has been able to under-cut costs of Montana or Texas beef, typically by as much as 50%. The market opportunities generated by this 'hamburger connection' has stimulated deforestation in countries like Honduras (Myers, 1986a, b).

In Amazonian Brazil, deforestation to create large ranches has been provoked by different forces (Branford & Glock, 1985; Repetto & Gillis, 1988: 28, 247–94). Investors in Amazonia may offset costs against tax on operations elsewhere in Brazil; this and land speculation lies at the root of clearance. More is to be made from acquiring, and simply holding on to, pasture than through efficient, sustained cattle production. In the words of Hecht (1985: 680): 'Acquisition of land is the vehicle for capturing direct and indirect state subsidies.' Whatever the causes, ranching-related clearing has probably accounted for about 72% of deforestation in Brazilian Amazonia (Repetto, 1987: 98; Little & Horowitz, 1987: 47).

Large areas of Nigeria, and other West African states, Malaysia, Papua New Guinea, Indonesia, Brazil, Hawaii and Latin American have been cleared to grow export crops like coffee, tea (generally at higher altitude), cocoa, coffee, bananas, tobacco, oil-palm, rubber, kola nut, etc. In N. Thailand there has been recent deforestation to grow cassava for export to Europe as animal feedstock (Hirsch, 1987). In Brazil and the Caribbean, sugar production was a major reason for deforestation from the mid-seventeenth to late-nineteenth centuries, both to provide plantation land and to provide fuelwood to process the cane. Much of Peninsular Malaysia's lowland rainforest has been converted to either oil-palm or rubber plantation since the 1950s.

In Brazil, land is increasingly used for crops to produce alcohol fuel for vehicles, or feedstock for industry. Future demand on forest/woodland for land to grow alcohol-producing crops, produce charcoal or cellulose, will probably increase. Farmers displaced by fuel/industrial feedstock production will turn to easily degraded marginal land.

In Peru and Colombia, *coca* (*Erythroxzyllum coca*), the raw material for cocaine is grown in clearings, mainly by squatters. In the Peruvian Amazon, in 1973, there were an estimated 2228 ha of *coca*. In 1980 there were believed to be over 30,000 ha; 1 ha was worth roughly US$ 30,000 per annum to the grower by 1987. Control of such cropping and clearance by persuasion of farmers is difficult (Little & Horowitz, 1987: 291).

Failure to assist the poor

Poverty and deforestation are commonly directly or indirectly related: '. . . Tragically it is the rural poor themselves who are the primary agents of destruction as they clear forests for agricultural land, fuelwood, and other necessities. Lacking other means to meet their daily survival needs, rural people are forced to steadily erode the capacity of the natural environment to support them.' (World Resources Institute *et al.*, 1985: 1).

In many parts of the world, but especially in Latin America, land is concentrated in the hands of a few people, the poor are denied access to such land, and often with high rates of population increase, have little choice but to open up forest or migrate to urban slums to seek employment (Gradwohl & Greenberg, 1988: 42). In the early 1980s, roughly 93% of Latin America's arable land was in the hands of 7% of the landowners; 70% of Brazil's population were landless and 85% of Java's people were landless. In Honduras, two-thirds of the fertile land was in the hands of 5% of landowners in the late 1980s; in Colombia, although only 0.7% of farms exceed 800 ha they cover 41% of the country (Gradwohl & Greenberg, 1988: 41). In Brazilian Amazonia, between 1960 and 1982, two size classes of landholding increased dramatically: those over 25,000 ha and those under 10 ha: the large ranches and the squatters respectively (Caufield, 1982: 25).

A question yet to be solved by those studying Indian deforestation is how rural people become shifted from a 'constructive dependence' on forest, practising shifting cultivation and gathering forest products to a 'destructive dependence', whereby they cut trees and degrade the land. The role of women in deforestation and the role of indebtness also deserve more attention (Fernandes *et al.*, 1988).

Demand for timber, woodchips, pulp and forest products

Between 1950 and 1982, developing countries increased their export of tropical hardwoods about 16-fold (Repetto, 1987: 95). Logging has probably been more of a cause of deforestation in South East Asia than in other world regions (Davidson *et al.*, 1985: 15). Between 1979 and 1982, timber sales were the major foreign exchange earner for the Philippines (Reppeto, 1987: 95). East Malaysia is now reputed to be the main supplier of Japan's tropical hardwoods (Johnstone, 1987). The Ivory Coast has granted favourable tax concessions to timber companies, logging progressed rapidly and, once opened up, the forest was prevented from regenerating by smallholders growing crops like cocoa (Bourke, 1987). In spite of the increased exploitation, a relatively small proportion of timber revenue comes to developing countries, Repetto (1987: 95) suggested Indonesia has had less than 50% of the value of her tropical timber exports. Anderson (1989: 166) cited 1983 figures showing that in one case in Sarawak the companies made gross earnings of M$ 300 per tonne, the concessionaries made around M$ 10 per tonne and the government made about M$ 24 per tonne royalty. The local people got no direct reward for the damage to their customary lands. Timber is often logged and exported illegally. For example, Myers (1987b) reported claims that more than half the logs exported from the Philippines were 'poached' by 'cronies' of the former President Marcos.

Tropical timber can be exported as roundwood (logs or poles), as sawnwood (planks, veneers, etc), as chips or pulp. The trend is likely to be toward more export of sawnwood, chips and pulp. This gives a better return to the exporter but is resisted by purchasing nations. Industrial countries have typically set tariff barriers to discourage inputs of processed wood probably to protect their own wood manufacturing industries. In 1982, *c.* 32% of tropical timber went to Europe, *c.* 53% to Japan, which was the world's largest importer of tropical timber in 1987 (Johnstone, 1987) and *c.* 15% to the USA (Caufield, 1982: 29). In 1982, six nations produced 70% of tropical hardwood exports: Indonesia, Malaysia, the Philippines, Papua New Guinea, Brazil and the Ivory Coast; eight others: Colombia, Ecuador, Gabon, Ghana, Nigeria, Costa Rica, Burma and Thailand a further 20%. The trade is very selective. Relatively few species are exported; many others, a large proportion of which are probably useful, are just wasted getting at the commercially attractive material. Roughly 25% of world trade in tropical hardwoods is in Dipterocarp species, e.g. *meranti* (*Shorea* spp.). The UK imported around £30 million worth of Brazilian mahogany (*Swietonia macrophylla*) in 1987 (Branford, 1988).

There are two general forms of timber extraction: clear felling and selective logging. In theory, the latter permits forest regeneration, if well managed so as to leave enough cover undisturbed for reseeding and no further disturbance occurs. In a recent review, Anderson (1989) doubted there were more than a very few examples of sustained timber extraction from rainforests. Good management is difficult, the very process of selection can lead to genetic erosion, whereby the best trees are removed and the poor specimens are left to regenerate. Also, removal of the selected timber almost always involves considerable damage to other species and disturbance of the ground: log-hauling trails, forest roads, etc. Typically, removal of 10% of standing timber would damage 55% or more of the remainder. A recent estimate was that, for every m³ of timber extracted from West Africa's rainforests, 4.5 m³ were destroyed (Independent Commission on International Humanitarian Issues, 1986b: 50). In Ghana, selective logging of 'mahogany' (*meranti*) and *afforamosa* (*Pericopsis elata*) opened up rainforest land to settlers, resulting in complete and permanent forest loss. It is not unknown for a logging interest to return to a logged-over area after some years for an illegal second cut which greatly reduces chances of satisfactory forest regeneration.

Although a lot of rainforest gets cleared, very little of it is used. In many cases the timber is simply burnt or left to rot, on a global scale, perhaps 2% of the standing timber gets exported (Bruenig, 1987: 70). In their haste to get badly needed foreign currency, developing countries tend to offer multinational or privately owned timber companies concessions that generally mean the 'host' country recovers little of the profit. This tends to encourage a 'cut-and-run' pattern of exploitation. According to Parsons (1975: 35), Granada was quickly stripped of rainforest by American timber interests by the mid 1970s. Increasingly, the rainforest that is left is in remote, rugged or swampy terrain or existing reserves. This is often relatively poor-quality rainforest in terms of genetic resources. Repetto (1987: 95), claimed that, in 1983, Indonesia granted more timber concession than the actual area remaining under forest. Another, more conservative estimate suggested that over 40% of Indonesian forest was leased to timber companies by 1985.

Roughly 7% of the world supply of paper pulp came from rainforest sources in 1982 (Caufield, 1982: 30). There is a rising demand for pulp and for woodchips, the latter for paper pulp, compression-board, rayon and other cellulose-derived products. The trend has been to exploit areas like mangrove forests for these products. An American, D. Ludwig, explored the possibility of producing paper pulp by growing exotic pine, eucalyptus and *Gmelina arborea* trees on land cleared from Amazonian rainforest. The Jarí Project, established by Ludwig's company, but since sold to a Brazilian consortium, was producing good-quality paper pulp by the mid 1980s, some from the plantation trees, some from rainforest cutting.

The list of forest products is huge; the more important include: Brazil nut, rattan, bamboo, chicle, quinine, rosewood oil and timber, sasparilla, ipecacuanha, coco, greenheart, and various waxes. Collection of forest products has led to some tropical deforestation. For example, Brazil wood (*Caesalpinea* spp.), a prized dyestuff in pre-industrial Europe, attracted the Portuguese to Brazil, gave the country its name, and was partly responsible for the loss of rainforest along the Atlantic coasts. Until the 1920s, when plantations came into production in the Far East, and artificial substitutes were developed, natural rubber (*Hevea brasiliensis*) came only from wild trees in Brazilian Amazonia, and the cities of Belém, Manaus and Santarém were founded on profits from its collection. Since the First World War, large areas of what is now Malaysia and Indonesia have been cleared to plant rubber and oil-palm plantations.

There is growing demand for rattan; export earnings from rattan products are second after tropical hardwood: the world market for rattan products in 1988 was worth about £1500 million. There are some 600 species of these wild climbing palms in South East Asia which are used to construct furniture and woven goods. About 25 species are commercially exploited (e.g. *Daemonorops hystrix* or *Korthulsia ferox*) but they are almost 100% gathered from the wild and tend to grow in little-disturbed rainforest. This attracts exploiters to the areas most in need to protection, and rattan is even being cut in national parks, such is the demand. Obviously, there is an urgent need to cultivate rattan species (Caldecott, 1988; MacKensie, 1988b; Ives & Pitt, 1988: 79).

It has been estimated that pharmaceutical companies extracted about US$ 100 million worth of material from tropical rainforests in 1984 alone (Ives & Pitt, 1988: 79). This sum little reflects what pharmaceutical value there is in unexploited rainforest. Without doubt, a great deal could be exploited as sources of new drugs, new crops, new commodities. For example, a recently discovered rainforest plant, the rosy periwinkle (*Catharanthus roseus*), an increasingly rare native of Madagascar, provides an important anti-cancer drug.

Administrative causes

While not strictly a rainforest area, deforestation in Nepal was hastened by 1957 government legislation which nationalized forests. Similar processes could operate in rainforests elsewhere (Little & Horowitz, 1987: 373). Nepalese peasants, fearing nationalization, converted as much private forest as possible to agricultural or grazing land before the laws came into force. Later, the government realized their error and repealed the legislation (Sattaur, 1987). Lax licensing laws which fail to control logging, and the offer of tax concessions to timber, help to encourage loss of forest. The Peruvian–Amazon Rural Development Law, designed to increase coloniz-ation, has led to considerable forest clearing. Opponents argue that it is founded on the mistaken belief that the Amazon is limitless and under-populated (*The Times*, 19/7/89: 9).

The failure to encourage wood-processing and the export of finished or semi-finished wood products rather than unsawn timber, has meant that developing countries get less profit and exercises less control than they might over logging (Hurst, 1989). Repetto & Gillis (1988) document how government policies affecting taxation, credit, and timber concessions, contribute towards deforestation.

Land settlement schemes

Between the early 1960s and 1985 the Malaysian Federal Land Development Agency (FELDA) settled over 64,000 families on land cleared from the lowland tropical rainforest of Peninsular Malaysia and has had one of the best records of keeping settlers on the land they are allocated. Elsewhere, settlers tend to drift into shifting cultivation which destroys large areas of forest (Davidson *et al.*, 1985: 38). In Brazil, the Programa Integraçao Nacional (PIN) settled vast numbers of peasants, mainly from north eastern Brazil along the roads constructed through the Amazon between the mid 1960s and late 1970s. Government-supported settlement of Brazilian Amazonia continues under the auspices of the Instituto Nacional de Colonizaçao e Reforma Agrária (INCRA), settlement now being mainly in western and north western Amazonia Rondônia, Acré and Roraima) rather than in eastern Amazonia (Pára). Peru, Columbia, Bolivia and Ecuador have also settled people in their Amazon rainforest territories. Peru, for example, settled 15,000 poor families from Lima in 1980 on the Pichis–Palcazu Special Project (Independent Commission on International Humanitarian Issues, 1986b: 32).

By far the greatest programme of relocation, with roughly 80% of resettlement since 1986 being in rainforest environments, is Indonesia's Transmigration Programme. In 1982, c. 70% of Indonesia's population, roughly 150 million, lived in Java, Bali and Madura, areas which comprise less than 10% of the land area of Indonesia. Since the start of the twentieth century, there has been spontaneous movement of people, mainly the landless, from these 'Inner Islands' to settle the more lightly populated 'Outer Islands': mainly in Sumatra and Kalimantan. In future this is likely to shift to central Sulawesi, Timor Maluku and Irian Jaya. The Transmigration Programme began in 1978 with the goal of resettling 500,000 families between then and 1983, and 1.2 million between 1983 and 1988. The ultimate, speculative, goal is to resettle about 15 million people by AD 2000) (Repetto & Gillis, 1988: 77). It seems likely that, in the 1970s, almost 1,000,000 were moved (Repetto, 1986; Lal *et al.*, 1986: 119; Repetto & Gillis, 1988: 33).

About 80% of transmigration settlement sites are in unspoilt primary forest much of which is in coastal lowlands where there are often potentially acid sulphate soils that are difficult to cultivate, and where, if sea level were to rise, the settlers would be forced to relocate (Repetto & Gillis, 1988: 77). The Transmigration Programme settlement has probably led to the clearance of c. 48 million ha of rainforest, much of which is now degraded and agriculturally of little value, with E. Kalimantan particularly badly affected (Kartawinata *et al.*, 1981). The Programme is expensive: in 1982, each resettled family cost US$ 5000 (Lal *et al.*, 1986: 124), by 1986, this had risen to US$ 12,000 per family. Much of the funding has come from international aid, and would probably have been better spent on more useful things than a costly transfer of people to environments where they commonly fail to sustain agriculture, particularly as the numbers resettled come nowhere near keeping pace with the rate of population increase on the 'Inner Islands' (Myers, 1980: 73; Gradwohl & Greenberg, 1988: 40).

The role of fire

Fire damage is more common in drier forests and woodlands than in rainforests. However, there is palaeoecological evidence of extensive natural fires in rainforests (carbon fragments in the soils) and cultivators burn large areas during a dry spells, even in the most humid environments. With low numbers of shifting cultivators, rainforest is maintained as a constantly changing mosaic of burnt, regenerating and untouched patches which ensure some degree of equilibrium. As well as being burnt from within, rainforests are 'nibbled at' from the edges by natural fires or by those set by Man in drier fringing woodlands or grassland. The latter is common in Costa Rica, the Malagasy Republic, Brazil and many other countries.

Drought can affect rainforest and, especially if it has been disturbed, it may then be set alight on a large scale by cultivators or natural causes. An esimated 200,000 ha of Brazilian Amazonia were destroyed by fires set by cultivators in 1987 (*The Times*, 13/10/88: 28). There have recently been extensive fires in rainforests in Haiti, and, in 1983, a fire in the Central Highlands of the Dominican Republic destroyed over 3000 ha of rainforest in spite of humid conditions and effective fire fighting (Independent Commission on International Humanitarian Issues, 1986b: 36). In 1989, a large area of tropical moist forest was destroyed around Cancun (Mexico) by a fire lasting over 5 months. Indonesia suffered huge fires between 1982 and early 1984, when over 35,000 km^2 of Eastern Kalimantan (Borneo) rainforest were destroyed. Malingreau *et al.* (1985: 315–20) suggested that drought, possibly related to the ENSO phenomenon (see Chapter 8), made these forests vulnerable. In 1982, rainfall seems to have been *c.* 60% below the norm (a drier than average year in 1971 did not allow extensive fires to develop). Either the 1982–3 drought was especially severe or, more likely, the region had been opened by logging and settled which rendered even areas of swamp forest vulnerable (Adriawan & Moniaga, 1986).

Fuelwood collection

It is difficult to separate rainforest from drier forest/woodland data relating to fuelwood consumption. In rainforest areas, once settled, the demand for fuel will certainly lead to some deforestation. However, it is in drier environments, cooler environments and upland environments where fuel-wood collection is likely to be more of a problem (Mather, 1987; Morgan & Moss, 1988), because these tend to be environments where tree growth is slower, where vegetation may be more sparse and, where, in the upland and drier environments, there may be greater demand for heating as well as for cooking fuel.

Much of the deforestation of Haiti is said to be due to fuelwood collection (Ferguson, 1988): Stevenson (1989) was more specific, blaming fuelwood collection as the main cause, and agricultural clearance by smallholders as a secondary cause. Stevenson suggested the dynamics are as follows: in Haiti, land is in the hands of many smallholders who find it profitable (and often have no choice) to sell trees for fuel – the causes of deforestation are thus: 1. local property rights; 2. lack of rural employment, which forces the smallholders to sell wood. If this is the case, a tax on charcoal might help slow fuelwood collection.

The degradation of the Sahelian–Sudanic Zone (some authorities prefer Sudano–Sahelian Zone) (SSZ) also might, at least in part, been due to fuelwood collection (see Chapter 8). However, Leach & Mearns (1989: 9–16) argue that fuelwood collection is seldom a major cause of rainforest loss.

UPLAND TROPICAL FOREST DEGRADATION

According to Ives & Pitt (1988: *xi*), as much as half of the world's upland forests are already significantly degraded. Quantitative data is not easy to come by, however. There are also a lot of clichés and untested claims made about upland deforestation. Without good records and adequate monitor-ing, it is difficult to get an accurate picture of extent, rate and effect of deforestation. For example, Ives & Pitt (1988: 55) discuss the common speculation that 50% of Nepal's forests have gone in the last 30 years; others suggest the loss is nearer 75%. However, such estimates are largely unconfirmed (Repetto, 1987: 109).

In the Tropics and subtropics, forest above 1,000 m altitude may be termed sub-montane broad-leaved evergreen forest. Above 3000 m, con-ditions hinder closed broad-leaved forest. However, there is much variation due to aspect, altitude, soil, wind exposure, gradient, etc, so that it is difficult to draw up useful categories. It is usual for species diversity to decline with altitude, for species composition to change and, for conifers like *Podocarpus* spp. to appear. Some upland forest is of considerable value for genetic conservation, even though it may lack the species diversity of tropical lowland forest. Much is still unknown about the role of upland areas in the long-term survival of lowland floras and faunas. Ideally some rainforest reserves will include areas of upland. There are uplands where the forest cover is more or less unique: it may be the remnants of once-extensive lower altitude vegetation, and such areas represent a last chance for conservation. In Somalia and Ethiopia, for example, there are 'relict' areas of *Juniperus procera* 'forest' which elsewhere has been burnt or grazed out of existence (DeVos, 1975: 71).

Some uplands have had marked human population increase: in some Andean countries, around 2.5% per annum over the last 30 years (Brush, 1987: 271). The pattern of settlement/clearance is uneven: of the Andean countries, Peru has problems, some others do not. Where there has been migration to other regions, such rates of increase may have had little effect.

6 Degradation of seasonally dry tropical/subtropical and Mediterranean woodlands and scrublands, temperate and high-latitude forests

SEASONALLY DRY TROPICAL/SUBTROPICAL FOREST, WOODLAND AND SCRUBLAND DEGRADATION

WHEREVER TROPICAL and subtropical soils lose sufficient moisture for long enough to hinder plant growth, or if there are: infertile soils or poor drainage, the presence of hard layers, excessive salts or other toxic compounds, there will be a reduction in species diversity and possibly a thinning of the canopy, compared with rainforest. The range of forms such forests/woodlands may take is so diverse that it is difficult to allocate them to anything but broad categories. In many regions, the forests/woodlands lose their leaves during dry periods and might be called 'rain-green' forest/woodland. With drier conditions and/or less favourable soils, tree cover becomes more and more 'open' permitting a more or less continuous herb/grass groundcover. Transition between types of forest/woodland may be gradual or abrupt. At some point where trees become more and more scattered and the grass/herb layer more developed, the flora is likely to be given the generic term: savanna. Savanna may thus be dry, closed woodland, dry, open woodland or a grassy 'parkland' of scattered trees/shrubs.

There has been debate about the origins of savannas, particularly the role of fire in their formation and whether they have been more or less extensive as a consequence of Pleistocene climatic changes (Balek, 1977: 50; Boutier, 1983; Franke & Chasin, 1980: 126; Harris, 1980; Furley & Newey, 1983: 292; Cole, 1986: 11–25). While there are still many unresolved questions, it seems likely that Man has extended, and is extending, such areas in many parts of the world, especially in Africa (Lewis & Berry, 1988: 202). It is not uncommon for relict areas of more species-rich forest to remain in a region of mainly grass savanna or relatively low diversity forest/woodland, in ravines, on steep slopes or wherever there is protection from fire, grazing and woodcutting.

Precise estimates of seasonally dry forests are difficult to come by, but it seems likely that savannas cover around 23 million km², roughly 20% of the Earth's land surface, or: 50 to 65% of Africa, 60% of Australia; 45% of Latin America and 10% of India and South East Asia (Cole, 1986: 1; Lal et al., 1986: 69). One of the problems with statistics is that 'open' is seldom defined and may vary from source to source. Steinlin (1982) noted that there were 734 million ha of open tropical 'tree formations'. 480 million ha of which were in Africa, 217 million ha were in tropical America and 35 million were in Asia. Open, seasonally dry woodland in Africa, Asia and Australia tend to be dominated by *Acacia* spp.; in Latin and North America, Leguminosae and Mimoseaceae take the place of the Acacias.

Open, seasonally dry woodland covers large parts of: Zimbabwe, Malawi, Zambia, Mozambique, Angola, S. Zaïre and S. Tanzania – where the rainfall is less than 1000 mm y^{-1}, and the dry season less than 6 months. Two formations are often distinguished: *miombo* and *mopane* – the former dominated by *Brachstegia* spp., *Berlinia, Copaifera* spp. and *Julbernadia* spp.; the latter by *Colophospernum mopane* and *Terminalia* spp. (DeVos, 1975: 77). The *mopane* woodlands are generally found in drier areas than the *miombo*; to what extent these formations are natural, or derived from a more closed forest before the arrival of Europeans, is uncertain. In Australia, seasonally dry woodlands such as the *mulga*, dominated by *Acacia aneura*, are the approximate equivalent of the *mopane* and *miombo*.

Large parts of the SSZ have a cover of open woodland dominated by species such as: Acacias, *Commiphora* spp., and *Bouhinia refescens* (DeVos, 1975: 49). It is likely that large parts of Central Africa were once more populous, and that open woodlands have replaced once grazed or farmed land, so today's vegetation is not the direct result of degradation of natural vegetation cover.

Brazil has around 83,000 km² of deciduous woodland/scrub, mainly in the North East. The Brazilian *caatinga* is a deciduous (6- to 11-month dry season) shrub/tree woodland, open enough to have a grass/herb groundcover. The Brazilian *cerrado* is a more closed cover woodland/scrub. The *sertão* is more thorny and arid than the *cerrado* or *caatinga*. These associations are prone to droughts and bushfires, may be subject to heavy goat grazing and are easily degraded (Smith & Baillie, 1985; Joss *et al.*, 1986: 243). Seasonally dry forest/woodlands are often regions of great human poverty and severe environmental degradation; they therefore deserve more attention. Not all of these areas have poor soil fertility; some have considerable agricultural potential; yet at present less than 1% of the world's savannas/seasonally dry forests/woodlands are cropped (according to Garlick & Keay, 1970: 60). Development pressures on such areas are therefore likely to increase.

Rate of loss of seasonally dry tropical/subtropical forest, woodland and scrublands

Concern for the loss of tropical rainforests tends to eclipse concern for loss of other types of forest, although this is considerable and of great consequence to human welfare. Steinlin (1982: 6) suggested that around 3.8 million ha y^{-1} were being lost between 1981 and 1985. FAO estimates suggested that Africa's open woodlands were being lost at around 2.3 million ha y^{-1} in the mid 1980s (Weber & Stoney, 1989: *vii*). Since 1940, Ethiopia has probably lost at least 40% of its drier forest (Harrison, 1987c: 54).

MEDITERRANEAN AND MEDITERRANEAN-TYPE FOREST, WOODLAND AND SCRUB DEGRADATION

The distinction between scrubland and woodland is not always clear-cut; some of the plant formations already discussed, like the *caatinga*, might be classed either as scrubland or open woodland. In the Mediterranean-type environments, growth is mainly during a moist, cooler winter and spring and less in the hot, dry summer. Vegetation is likely to be scrub or open woodland. In most regions, a long history of overgrazing, fire and wood-cutting, means that the present-day cover is no 'baseline' from which to judge natural productivity. In the Mediterranean proper, various scrub formations replaced forests and woodlands long ago, in some cases before 9000 BP – the question is, where was there once forest and where was there always scrub or grassland?

In the Mediterranean proper, there are names for different scrub/woodland formations. *Maquis* is a widely used term for a low, dense evergreen scrub/woodland (in Italy *macchia*, in Greece *xerovuni*). *Maquis* may degrade to a more species-poor, low-scrub-dominated formation, rich in aromatic and fire-resistant herbs often called *garrigue*. In some areas, *garrigue* may degrade to form a sort of desert-steppe (*batha*) (DeVos, 1975: 62; Thirgood, 1981: 11, 21–6). In Mediterranean-type regions, various similar formations may be recognized.

Extent and rate of loss

Historical records show that Medemia palms (*Medemia argun*) were once common in parts of Egypt; 3000 years later they have survived cutting in only two remote and uninhabited oases. The dry steppelands of N. Africa once probably had a cover of *Pinus halepensis*, *Juniperus phoenicea* and/or *Tetreclinis articulata*. The northern slopes of the Atlas Mountains probably had extensive forests of oaks, especially *Quercus ilex*, sweet chestnut and pines. Syria and Egypt had much greater areas of Acacia woodland before about 4000 BP than they now have. The Levant began to lose forest from about 300 BC and Morocco's forests were lost during the last *c.* 3000 years (DeVos, 1975: 62; Thirgood, 1981: 21–6).

The degradation of Mediterranean-type environments in Chile, California (the *chaporral* scrub), S. Africa (*fynbos* scrub) and Australia (*mallee* scrub) has been going on for, at most, a few centuries, but the effects are marked. In some Mediterranean areas the land may have been degraded in prehistoric/historic times and attained a post-disturbance 'steady-state' but is now changing to yet another, probably lower-grade steady-state due to new pressures such as increased tourism (Ruddle & Manshard, 1981: 191–3).

While Mediterranean-type regions show clearly the impact of human activity, the problem is that available data are generally insufficient to estimate degree or rate of change in vegetation, though historical records and palaeoecology can help to fill in gaps in knowledge.

CAUSES OF DEGRADATION OF SEASONALLY-DRY AND MEDITERRANEAN-TYPE FORESTS, WOODLANDS AND SCRUB

As woody cover thins, and grass/herb cover increases, the pattern of degradation becomes one familiar in regions suffering desertification. Indeed, there is an unbroken transition.

Fire

Fire is one of the main factors determining vegetation cover in regions with dry seasons. Soils and faunas are also directly and indirectly affected by fire. For a while after a bushfire there is likely to be increased run-off and erosion. This decreases as grass and herbs develop, and may even fall below what there was when there was a cover of brush or forest with little understorey, because transpiration losses have grown with the re-vegetation. The damage following a fire depends on the season in which it struck, the severity of the burn, and the time since the last one. If fire strikes too soon in the growing season, plants may find it difficult to regenerate, as they have not set seed nor gained strength in their below-ground structures. Fire after the growing season will have less long-term effect because the vegetation has had a chance to scatter seed, form tubers, etc. Fire followed by heavy rains will tend to lead to erosion; light rains soon after a fire may encourage re-vegetation enough to reduce wind and rain erosion when heavier storms occur. The severity of burn depends on how much above-ground dry matter has accumulated; the more of this there is the hotter the fire will tend to be and the more damage it will do to flora, fauna and soil (De Booysen & Tainton, 1984).

Frequency of natural fires is variable, ranging from one every five years to one every 100 years or so (Joss *et al.*, 1986: 573). Because frequent, relatively cool and fast-moving fires are less damaging than hotter, slower, less-frequent ones, attempts to prevent fires may be a mistake, for, when one does occur, it will have plenty of fuel and will do more damage. It is possible for a region to have above-average rainfall which causes growth and accumulation of dry matter, a fire breaks out and the burn will be fierce and may do considerable damage. This was the situation in Australia in 1973/4 and 1974/5, when about one-sixth of the land was affected by such fires (Vines, 1987). The removal of grazing may have a similar effect, vegetation accumulates and more than usually severe fires follows.

In some regions, for example, in parts of southwestern USA, vegetation is fire adapted and depends on bushfires to maintain itself. Mid-western and southwestern USA grasslands tend to be invaded by scrub (especially *mesquite*), which reduces the grazing value if there are not frequent bushfires. (Kozlowski & Ahlgren, 1974: 172, 390). Now restricted to a few limited areas of Sierra Nevada (California) the giant redwood (*Sequoiadendron giganteum*) cannot regenerate unless fire sweeps through the stands of trees and triggers the release of seeds (i.e. it has a serotinous character).

Douglas fir (*Pseudotsuga menziesii*) forests of Pacific northwest USA are maintained by infrequent fire. Without full sunlight, Douglas fir cannot colonize or regenerate, cedars and hemlock gradually take over, and no seed would be set unless fire opens up clearings; yet, once established, the Douglas fir does not like *frequent* burning. In the USA Great Lakes region, mixed hardwoods and jackpines (*Pinus banksiana*) have been opened up during the last 200 years by logging; once opened, fire is more frequent. The jackpines have seeds which survive fire and the result is increasingly widespread pure stands of jackpine of even age. In southwestern USA Ponderosa pine (*Pinus paulustris*) withstands regular gentle fires, but is destroyed by infrequent intense fires (Cooper, 1974: 294).

A cosmopolitan species which tends to be favoured by frequent burning is the bracken (*Pteridium* spp.); it may poison livestock, offers little grazing and may have carcinogenic properties if its spores are regularly inhaled or absorbed from contaminated water supplies.

In 1987, a large fire destroyed roughly one million ha of forests in N.E. China. China is reputed to have some of the worst forest fires in the world, and is estimated to have lost 8.6 million ha of forests/woodlands between 1964 and 1989, an area roughly equivalent to one-third of all plantings made in that period (Forestier, 1989: 52).

In Europe, perhaps 200,000 ha y^{-1} are burnt in an average year (Calabri, 1983; Jackson *et al.*, 1984: 190). However, not all of that should be seen as 'degradation', for some land has long been a fire-modified scrub/heathland and regular burning is used to maintain the vegetation cover or grazing. In S. Europe, 1989 was a bad year for fires, the Côte d'Azure (France), Sardinia, Corsica and parts of the Iberian Peninsula were badly hit.

Records show that there were unusually severe fires in Wisconsin, Michigan, Minnesota and in the adjoining Canadian Prairies in 1871; in southeast USA in 1988; in New South Wales, Australia in 1939, 1983 and 1987. Man's occasional use of fire to clear vegetation or drive game may have begun as long as 1.5 million years ago (*The Times*, 2/12/88: 5), and probably dates back several millenia in many parts of the world (Clark & McLoughlan, 1986; Vines, 1987). In recent years, tourism has helped to increase the frequency of fires in many areas. Fire used to clear cultivation plots, improve pasturage or to kill ticks and other pests can get out of hand and encroach on woodlands (Gee, 1988b).

Overgrazing

Where drier forest/woodland is penetrable, pigs, goats and, to a lesser extent, cattle may remove seedlings and browse trees; goats have some ability to climb trees. There is also a chance that new plant species may be introduced in animal droppings or as seeds adhering to the livestock, and these might upset the natural vegetation. Often herders prune trees and shrubs for animals that could never reach the material, or transport it to livestock being stall-fed elsewhere.

Large areas of open dryland woodland and savanna in Africa are more or less protected from livestock grazing by the presence of tse tse fly and the risk from the cattle and human disease it carries. A cheap, effective control of tse tse fly, or the trypanosomiasis it carries, would probably mean quite considerable areas of Africa would come under pressure from livestock grazing (Dregne, 1983: 129; Linear, 1985).

Pigs played a major role in the deforestation of the Mediterranean and in reducing Europe's temperate forests. They also do considerable damage in parts of Papua New Guinea, Northern Australia and a number of Pacific and other oceanic islands. However, it is the goat that receives the blame for a great deal of forest/woodland damage. The deforestation of a number of oceanic islands is blamed on goats released within the last 300 years. Whether this reputation is deserved or not is debated. Dunbar (1984), argued that goats prefer to graze the brush layer, rather than groundcover, so they open up scrub vegetation and favour grass and herbs which should tend to reduce soil erosion and bushfire damage and so would not be particularly damaging in scrubland.

Goats are prolific breeders; if confined to a locality/island, then they might damage vegetation (Joss *et al.*, 1986: 132). Probably, goats need the assistance of woodcutters, cattle or fire to change forest or woodland to scrub. As they are the animal of the poorest people, and are likely to be found in the more marginal habitats, the goat may be damned by association, i.e. it is found where there is degradation, but might not be the main cause, or it may deliver the *coup de grâce* (Thirgood, 1981: 68).

Fuelwood collection

Fuelwood is the major source of energy in most of the Third World; it is often the only affordable means of cooking, domestic heating, etc. When fuelwood supplies fail, people gather crop residues or dung which is almost certainly the start of a catastrophic decline in soil fertility. A debated question is: just to what extent is fuelwood collection a cause of forest/woodland loss? The issue is complicated because there may be commercial demand for fuelwood or wood to make charcoal for distant, even export, markets and/or industrial use. In the 1970s, Kenya exported large quantities of charcoal to Saudi Arabia, this has now been officially banned (Lewis & Berry, 1988: 241).

There is a growing literature of the role of fuelwood/charcoal collection in deforestation/desertification, some of which, but not all, suggests it is an important cause (e.g. Bowander, 1987; Little & Horowitz, 1987: 120; Eckholm et al., 1984; Moss & Morgan, 1981). There has been questioning of what are seen to be mistaken or simplistic analyses of the situation. Leach & Mearns (1989: 6–9) are critical of the common practice of looking at fuelwood use estimates, checking these with assessments of standing wood stock and annual tree growth, and relating the results with projected population growth. This, they argue, tends to give a picture of shortfall of yield, which they feel is sometimes, at least, incorrect because, in their view, consumption does not automatically exceed renewable supplies, since people adjust their fuel usage. Leach & Mearns (1989: 9) suggest fuelwood is often provided by agricultural clearance, i.e. it is a by-product, rather than a direct cause of deforestation. A similar view was voiced by Foley et al. (1984: 11), citing a region with 3% per annum population growth and an average family holding of about 3 ha, consuming $3 \ t \ y^{-1}$ fuelwood and with nearby forests/woods producing $300 \ t \ ha \ y^{-1}$ biomass (a reasonably realistic scenario for much of the world's seasonally dry woodlands/savannas). As the frontier of clearance expands due to population increase, the area of land cleared for farming would be roughly 100 times the area of woodland lost to meet fuel needs. In short, land hunger may exceed fuelwood collection as a cause of deforestation over large parts of the Third World. The foregoing estimates are probably conservative, but it should be noted that there have been few accurate estimates of year-round fuelwood use in the Third World; also that consumption is likely to be quite variable.

Tables of possible fuelwood consumption in the Third World are given by Agarwal (1986: 6–9). These indicate considerable spatial and temporal variation in use. As women and children often gather much of the supply, keeping track of what is collected is not easy.

When fuelwood and substitutes become scarce, the people have a problem, for few tropical crops are palatable or safe unless cooked. That forest/woodland reserves are raided for fuel by poor people is hardly surprising. When fuelwood runs short, prices escalate. In Orissa State (India) in 1987, one tonne of fuelwood retailed at between Rs 300 and 350 (roughly US$ 23 to 27), a lot of money compared with the average wage (Anon, 1987c: 6.3). In many parts of the Tropics, fuelwood and charcoal come from coastal mangrove forests.

Some Third World cities are supplied with fuelwood/charcoal from quite a large area. If they have access to road transport, gangs may cut timber from as far away as 300 km. This was the situation around Dakar, Senegal in 1984. The impact of commercial gathering is especially severe when trees are scattered, as is the case in drier regions. Witney (in Little & Horowitz, 1987: 131) describes the situation in South Kordofan province (Sudan), where a settlement requires a fuelwood 'catchment' of about 2800 km² to ensure a supply, assuming that, when part of the area was depleted of trees, more could regenerate. A settlement of 250 people would probably need 47 km², and one of 100,000 people 28,160 km². If dryland forest/woodland is cleared, there will probably be a reduction in nitrogen fixation resulting in soil deterioration. Without some mature trees, regeneration is difficult and pests which damage tree seedlings may increase.

Logging

The loss of palm groves from Egypt, millenia ago, and the loss of other Mediterranean forests/woodlands, is documented in historical records. There is Biblical evidence and references from classical Egypt, until the nineteenth century, of the difficulty in obtaining timber for building construction and shipbuilding (Thirgood, 1981: **9**, 36–40).

Clearing for agriculture

There are numerous strategies for bringing areas of savanna, woodland or scrubland into production. For example, there are agro-sylvipastoral systems whereby Acacia trees yielding gum-arabic or shea-butter trees provide a saleable crop, and grain and livestock are obtained in their shade. There are bush-fallow systems which depend upon the gathering of grass or branches from scattered trees into heaps where they are burnt, or broken down by termites. The heaps are planted with subsistence crops just before rains. In parts of Africa, particularly in Zambia and N. Zimbabwe variants of this strategy are known as *chitamene* (Allan, 1965). In the past, the strategy had probably reached an equilibrium with the environment, but, in recent decades, population growth and other factors have led to excessive *chitamene*, and trees and soil have begun to suffer.

Mechanization has permitted large-scale cultivation of seasonally dry regions. Bulldozers with blades, or pairs of bulldozers dragging chains between them are used to grub up trees and shrubs, mechanized ploughing then breaks up heavy grassland that would have been impossible for earlier generations of farmers to use. Great, caution is required: if ploughing is mis-timed, soil may blow away; there may be weed invasion problems and a host of other difficulties. Such clearance makes future woodland regeneration unlikely.

Other causes

In some African savanna woodlands, people try to attract honey bees by making holes in trees. This, plus the damage during honey collection, can kill quite a lot of timber (Ezealor, 1987).

HIGH-LATITUDE FOREST AND WOODLAND DEGRADATION

Vast areas of high-latitude cold temperate, mainly coniferous, boreal forests form a belt from Alaska/W. USA to E. Siberia, between about 45° N and 70° N, which probably exceeds 1500 million ha area (Gamlin, 1988) (Fig. 6.1). However, it is the temperate, mainly broad-leaved or mixed broad-leaved/conifer forests south of the boreal forests that have suffered considerable degradation in Europe, and, to a slightly lesser extent, in the New World. There is a growing trend in Scandinavia, N. America and the USSR to fell mixed conifer forest and replant with single species: *Pinus contorta*, *P. sylvestris* and *Picea abies* being common choices (Barr & Braden, 1988).

Forest Clearance in Europe was under way by the Mesolithic, and accelerated after arable farming arrived, depending on location, anywhere from 7000 to 1000 BP. What remained in Europe by Medieval times, after millenia of slash-and-burn agriculture, was subjected to the demands of swine herding, monastic clearance, metal smelting, ship-building, and further increases in farming pressures from the seventeenth century AD. By the nineteenth century such pressures had largely destroyed the lowland mixed oak forests of W. Europe. Away from the western lowlands, in Germany, Austria, Scandinavia, lower populations and harsher conditions helped preserve the forest although, in the UK, the Caledonian pine forests of Scotland had come under attack by the eighteenth century. The UK, up to the Mesolithic, had probably been largely covered by forests; this cover had shrunk to about 10% by the 1980s (Milne, 1988a: 45). Iceland, settled in the ninth century AD, once had extensive thickets of dwarf birch and localized birch forest; by 1976 about 1% remained.

It seems likely that at least a portion of the treeless heathlands and wet moorlands in northwest Europe result from the degradation of an original forest/woodland cover as a result of human activities before the Iron Age. Once the tree cover had been disturbed, soils became leached and often formed iron-pans and, in higher wetter localities, peat blankets 'Holdgate & Woodman, 1976: 129–44; Hawkes, 1978: 3–16).

Between 1850 and 1980, N. America lost an estimated 3% of its forest and woodland, and the USSR lost roughly 12% in this period (Repetto & Gillis, 1988: 3). Once coal and then oil/natural gas had supplemented or replaced wood as a fuel, forest depletion in Europe and N. America saw some respite although pulp, building timber and woodchip demands are increasing. Mainly since the First World War, there has been some extension of forest/woodland compared with the situation at the start of the twentieth century. But, throughout the temperate and sub-tropical regions, the pattern has been one of replacement of natural, generally broad-leaved forests, with

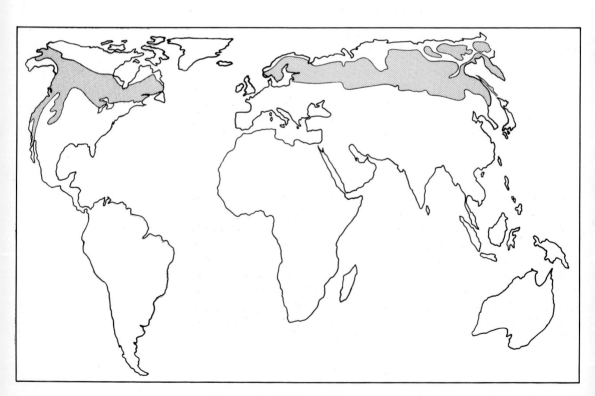

Fig. 6.1. *Northern High-latitude Temperate closed forest and woodland.* Source: *Modified from Gamlin (1988: 41–7 Fig. on pp. 46–7).*

plantations of exotic conifers, poplars or eucalyptus. Thus, while areal decline has been reduced, qualitative changes have been marked. In the UK, there has actually been an increase in area of woodland since Victorian times: in 1871 there were 531,875 ha in England alone; in 1967 this had increased to 890,049 ha. Virtually all of the UK expansion has been due to the planting of exotic conifer plantations on less-productive agricultural land or heathland/moorland. The pattern is similar in Europe, N. America, China, S. Korea and in many other regions. An outbreak of Dutch Elm Disease in the 1970s has thinned many UK broad-leaved woodlands.

The austral broad-leaved forests of Chile, Southern Australia/Tasmania and New Zeland have suffered from logging, clearing for agriculture and introduction of damaging exotic plants and animals. In New Zealand and Chile, southern beech (*Nothofagus* spp.) have been extensively logged, and in some regions have been replaced with faster-growing conifers, especially in Chile. A thousand years ago, New Zealand was about 75% broad-leaved forest; by 1979 this was reduced to roughly 22%. The loss has been especially severe in the lowlands, where, in 1979, only about 7% of the indigenous forest remained (Sage, 1979a).

Although the boreal forests probably play little part in the global carbon dioxide budget, the trees and the soil beneath store huge amounts: possibly one-sixth of the world total above-ground carbon dioxide, and one-fifth of the world total below-ground carbon dioxide. If the boreal forests were to die, possibly because of climatic change or acidification, there could be massive release of carbon dioxide with serious climatic consequences (IIASA, 1989: 8).

Causes of degradation

Timber and pulp demand

The boreal forests provide a large proportion of the developed countries' timber and paper pulp. In 1984, about one-third of the world's commercial roundwood came from such forests, especially those of the USSR (Bruenig, 1987: 70). The rayon and nylon industries depend on cellulose, much of which comes from these forests, although Japanese factories are more likely to use cellulose from South East Asian mangrove forests (see Chapter 7).

Acid deposition and other pollution

Although Sweden, Norway, Finland, Germany, Canada, the UK and the USA lead the world in forestry management, there are signs of deterioration of their forests. A major cause is acid deposition, coupled in some regions with the effects of industrial pollution, motor vehicle emissions and related low-altitude ozone production (see Chapter 4). Coniferous forests seem especially vulnerable to such pollution, but there are increasing signs that the problem is spreading to broad-leaved trees. Rising levels of CO_2 in the Earth's atmosphere may alter climate in the high latitudes enough to affect presently grown conifer species, some of which originate from regions like British Colombia and require a cold winter to flourish.

Fire

Fire is less of a problem in high-latitude forests than tropical or subtropical, but it is still significant. Canada loses 3 million ha a year of its boreal forest to natural fires (Freedman, 1989: 6). Western Tasmania's *Nothofagus* forests have recently been badly damaged by fires (Wolman & Fournier, 1987: 59). A SCOPE study (SCOPE, 1983) examined the problem in the Northern Hemisphere high latitudes.

TEMPERATE HEDGEROW DEGRADATION

In the UK, hedgerows have become valuable conservation areas for flora and fauna (in general, the older the hedge the richer the wildlife it harbours). But, in recent years, UK hedges have suffered: many kilometres have been grubbed up to create larger fields that are more suited to mechanized cereal cultivation and many remaining hedges are no longer laid by hand in the traditional manner, rather, they are close-trimmed mechanically several times a year which reduces species diversity and prevents the development of tall 'emergent' trees. Hedges are also disappearing or losing their species diversity because of urban expansion and road widening, the use of road salt, pesticides and traffic pollution. Hedgerows in eastern England, especially in East Anglia, have suffered most.

Since 1945, an estimated 8046 km y^{-1} have been lost (Hawkes, 1978: 89; Pollard *et al.*, 1974). A Countryside Commission estimate suggested that, in England and Wales, of the *c.* 795,000 km of hedgerows in 1947, about 175,000 km had been lost by 1985. Brittany (France) has also lost quite a lot of hedgerow. The UK Government has recently introduced grants to encourage hedge planting; ten years ago grants were available for the opposite. However, these seem to have had less incentive than the desire by farmers to ease use of machinery (*The Times*, 5/7/89: 5). Apart from loss of valuable wildlife conservation habitats, hedgerow loss can render an area more vulnerable to wind erosion, as has been the case in parts of East Anglia (UK).

THE CONSEQUENCES OF DEFORESTATION

Species loss

The increasingly rapid loss of tropical forest directly and indirectly endangers the survival of a large proportion of the world's wildlife.

Climatic change

Rainforests are like large water bodies: they moderate surrounding climate, reducing temperature fluctuation between day and night, maintaining humidity, at least downwind, and reducing windspeed downwind. Between 50% and 90% of precipitation on rainforest is evaporated or transpired, bare soil in the same location would lose about 30% and grassland about 40% (Independent Commission on International Humanitarian Issues, 1986b: 47). It has been suggested that removal of extensive areas of forest will reduce downwind rainfall by as much as 20% (Anon, 1988a). Possibly removal of large areas of forest could sufficiently alter the albedo to affect regional, and possibly global heat flux, i.e. altered reflection of solar radiation from the area could be enough to change airmass movements (Barbier, 1989a: 128; Molion, 1989; Reynolds & Thompson, 1989). Forests generally get rid of more heat through evapotranspiration from the warming effect of the Sun than do bare soil or grassland.

Small clearings are unlikely to have much effect. However, if clearance is of at least medium size, say more than 100 km², there may well be a downwind effect, for example: Mann (1987) felt there were signs of climatic change in The Gambia after extensive clearing. There have been fears voiced that rainfall south and east of Amazonia's forests may decrease as the forest is destroyed (Salatti et al., 1983). However, there is little detailed record of climatic change after clearance.

There has been debate about the relationship between rising global CO_2 levels and deforestation, particularly of tropical rainforest. It seems likely that mature forest acts only to a limited degree as a sink for excess CO_2 or as a significant means of converting CO_2 to oxygen (Caufield, 1982: 18). However, the destruction of such forest, particularly by fire, has two effects: 1. there is a release of fixed CO_2 that is present in plant tissue and soil, and; 2. there is a reduction in the CO_2 fixation that would have been done by the vegetation destroyed. If new forest were to be established, particularly if largely fast-growing species, then this might help reduce atmospheric CO_2 levels. Lal et al. (1986: 195–202) have tried to quantify the effect of burning tropical forests, and suggested it is responsible for roughly 90% of global release of CO_2 from terrestrial biota to environment.

Impacts on hydrology

Many researchers believe there is likely to be an increase in run-off soon after forest clearance; it seems that return to hydrological conditions similar to those of pre-clearance can sometimes be rapid (Freedman, 1989: 243). To attribute the blame for recent severe floods in, say the Indus Basin, on deforestation of uplands, is common, but it is largely unproven (Independent Commission on International Humanitarian Issues, 1986b: 35). Ives & Pitt (1988: 11) make this point, with respect to deforestation in the foothills of the Himalayas. They argue that, in monsoon/heavy storm rainfall areas, once ground is saturated, even well-forested, undisturbed areas can produce enough run-off for catastrophic floods to occur downstream. To say deforestation causes altered run-off, water quality, etc may well be an oversimplification and floods and/or siltation could occur even without degradation of the catchment. In some forests/woodlands, leaf-litter and groundcover plants reduce or delay run-off. If grazing or fire removes these, even if the tree cover is largely intact, there may be much altered run-off (Ives & Pitt, 1988: 106). It is possible for splash erosion to be greater under certain forest cover, compared with non-forest vegetation, because the forest trees accumulate rain on their leaves and release it as large, erosive drops to the ground far below; the result may be increased silt load in streams (Ives & Pitt, 1988: 105). Thornes (1989) made the same point, and suggested that, in some parts of the Mediterranean, low, continuous scrub gave better soil protection than woodland.

Much of the silt and run-off problems associated with tropical deforestation are the result of logging roads and log skid-trails, i.e. they are because of poor planning of forest roads and/or careless use of machinery. One author mentions that, were logging companies to hire bulldozer crews which had not previously worked on road construction or other civil engineering involving scraping and compaction, there would probably be much less logging impact. Another alternative is to use cable-logging or skylines to pluck out the timber with less damage to remaining vegetation and soil.

The typical claim is that deforestation of watersheds causes increased erosion leading to siltation problems downstream, and this, in turn, may cause flooding due to channel blockage and altered quantity, quality and timing of streamflow. There is no shortage of reference to silted-up reservoirs or irrigation projects; the linkages to deforestation is often not really proven, for example: in Panama it has been claimed there is a link between deforestation and reduced water supply for the Panama Canal (Simons, 1989). However, climatic causes must be ruled out before this can be certain. In some cases, the loss of forest means that less mist, cloud and drizzle is trapped as it blows past and there is a reduction in precipitation receipt; this seems to have occurred in parts of Chile (Barrow, 1987a: 196).

Most controlled watershed experiments have been in temperate regions (El-Swaify et al., 1985: 680–90), so there is probably insufficient testing of the hypothesis that cutting forest/woodland in a seasonal rainfall region leads to increased dry season flow or more stored groundwater. There are situations where altering natural vegetation has raised groundwater and possibly improved streamflow. There are others where the result has been a reduction; apparently it depends on whether the replacement cover evapotranspires more or less and how effective it is at slowing run-off and improving infiltration.

The impact of deforestation depends, in part, on the way in which the vegetation is removed, whether cutting is by hand or bulldozer, and whether the area is burnt after cutting. What replaces the forest/woodland is also important: it might be scrubland regrowth forest, oil palm or rubber plantation or sugar cane, etc. One of the worst replacements for forest/woodland is probably overgrazed pastureland, which will give higher yields of silt, and differs a great deal in its evapotranspiration losses compared with the natural vegetation cover.

Loss of access to forest products

The loss of access to forest affects poor people, who often depend upon game, fruit, medicinal plants, and gathering forest products for sale or barter. In Amazonian Pará (Brazil), there is a lucrative trade in the fruit of palms like the Açai (Euterpe edulis) wild rubber, Brazil nuts (Bertholetia excelsa) and other products. Without these opportunities, many would have no adequate livelihood – the situation is, or was, similar in many other countries. In part, because of loss of access to forest products, in part, because of contact with outsiders, and their diseases and antagonism, forest-dwelling peoples have suffered greatly from Amazonia to Sabah, from the Philippines to Panama. The Amazonian Indian population is believed to have fallen from around 5 million in AD 1500 to roughly 200,000 in 1989. At least 87 Indian groups have become extinct in Brazil alone; in Indonesia, transmigration may have disrupted over 70,000 tribespeople (Friends of the Earth, 1989 Rainforest pamphlet, February, 1989, London).

Health impacts

A number of diseases can afflict humans or livestock when vegetation cover is altered. These include: yellow-fever, scrub typhus, malaria, Chaga's disease, trypanosomiasis/nagana, leishmaniasis and many other mosquito- or fly-borne infections. Outbreaks generally arise because settlers clearing forest come into contact with disease-vector insects which may also increase as a consequence of clearing. In many parts of Latin America, particularly in Amazonia, Chaga's disease (Trypanosomiasis cruzeii) spreads as reduviid bugs which carry it get transported by settlers and cargo, and possibly on house sparrows that spread into cleared areas after roads are built. The character of dwellings in frontier regions favour reduviid bugs and disease transmission to humans.

Two African tse tse fly species (*Glossinia* spp.) carry sleeping sickness and have specific habitat needs. Altering vegetation may favour the fly and trypanosomiasis transmission, or may discourage it. Clearing tree cover to create open tall-grass savanna favours ticks and transmission of encephalitic diseases and scrub typhus.

In N.E. USA, increased human access to open woodland areas and reforestation has led to tick-borne Lyme Disease becoming a growing public health risk in States like Connecticut and New York State. Lyme Disease is present in wooded areas of the UK New Forest and in parts of Europe, but is much less of a problem due to complex environmental reasons. However, parts of Europe have a growing problem with tick-borne meningitis. Opening up woodland and repairing damaged woodland may therefore need careful management to reduce such problems.

Economic impacts

It is impossible to attach a cost to the loss of forests or woodlands: species may become extinct without their potential value being appraised; much of the timber is wasted and no account of this is kept; the loss to people living in, or near, forests is difficult to assess and the effect on watersheds from changed stream silt loads, altered streamflow and erosion rates is difficult to assess. It is unproven, but difficult to dispute that the economic costs of deforestation have probably far exceeded any gain from cleared agricultural land, sales of timber, etc (Eckholm, 1979).

Aesthetic losses

The loss of the rich diversity of tropical forests must leave Mankind poorer in more than just the economic sense. Nations like Brazil have a great deal of national pride in their forest lands. In Germany, forests have an important place in the culture, and fears about the die-back of coniferous forests have been a significant factor in helping to stimulate the formation of the German 'Green Movement'. That, in turn, has played a significant role in stimulating politically active environmentalism.

COUNTERING FOREST AND WOODLAND DEGRADATION

There are ways in which demand for tropical timber could be cut. The consumer in richer countries might be educated to seek alternatives. Taxes and restrictions could be used to reduce trade in timber and provide funds to protect forest or reforest. There could be more conservative use of timber, through use of thin veneers, re-cycling, etc. Poor countries could be assisted to get more profit from timber sales which might mean less cutting. In practice, profit and sovereignty are involved, and these can make solutions difficult.

In developing countries, where the actions of local people are the cause of deforestation, there are two strategies which offer some hope for slowing tropical deforestation which are cheap and fast enough to be worth consideration: 1. involve local people in management and benefits of forestry, this could be through social forestry or community forestry

(Buckman, 1987): 2. 'agroforestry', the planting of trees on croplands and pastures.

In developed countries, grant aid, tax incentives and government or private sector planting programmes have long been used to ensure some replanting and management of forest/woodland. In the developed world, the problems are mainly: 1. stimulating sufficient planting of the right type and in the right places, and, 2. reacting to the threat of die-back of forests/woodlands due to pollution, diseases and possibly climatic changes.

In both developed and developing countries, much could be achieved through an alteration of attitude toward forests – from one of seeing the potential for exploitation to one of seeing the need and desirability to conserve and make exploitation more rational, sustained and less wasteful.

Support for forest conservation is growing; in 1989, over three million people signed a petition delivered to the UN calling for better strategies for forest conservation. Bodies, such as the World Rainforest Movement, have called for a ban on aid for projects in forested areas and a cessation of trade in timber from virgin forest areas (Pearce, 1989b).

Plans to save tropical forests

In 1985, the World Resources Institute, World Bank and UNDP published a *Tropical Forestry Action Plan* (TFAP). This had been prepared over several years through combined efforts of governments, forestry agencies, UN agencies and NGOs. It seeks to provide a flexible strategy that responds to carefully determined needs and, above all, is realistic and practical. It was intended that the TFAP would give a five-year framework for co-ordinated action aimed at establishing 'sustained forestry'. The TFAP is implemented at the request of a tropical country, and administration is under control of the FAO (World Resources Institute *et al.*, 1985 *IUCN Bulletin*, 1989, vol. 20, Nos. 2/3, p. 22). In 1990, the TPAF involved 73 Third World countries and received US$ 1 billion in funding. However, bodies like the World Rainforest Movement have been critical of the Plan and have called for its restructuring.

In late 1988, Brazil's President Sarney ordered the preparation of a plan designed to halt deforestation, particularly in Amazonia (*The Times*, 13/10/88: 28). The plan incorporates a programme of forest monitoring using satellite remote sensing to spot clearance and burning.

Measures that could help reduce or reverse degradation

There are various ways in which forest/woodland areas can be managed:

1. they may be conserved or protected;
2. they may be sustainably managed;
3. they may be non-sustainably used;
4. the land may be developed for cultivation, grazing, roads, reservoirs, housing, etc.

Natural forest may be cut and allowed to regenerate with little assistance; may be cut and helped to regenerate; or may be cut and replaced with plantation stands of trees.

Conservation

The problems associated with tropical forest conservation: e.g. minimum size of long-term viable reserves, shape and pattern of reserves, is discussed in

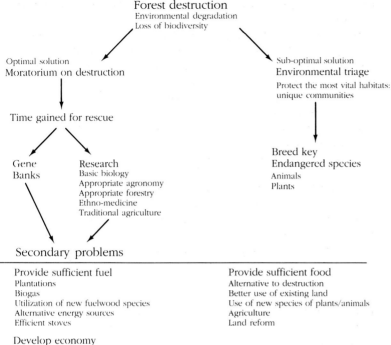

Forest destruction
Environmental degradation
Loss of biodiversity

Optimal solution
Moratorium on destruction

Sub-optimal solution
Environmental triage
Protect the most vital habitats:
unique communities

Time gained for rescue

Gene
Banks

Research
Basic biology
Appropriate agronomy
Appropriate forestry
Ethno-medicine
Traditional agriculture

Breed key
Endangered species
Animals
Plants

Secondary problems

Provide sufficient fuel
Plantations
Biogas
Utilization of new fuelwood species
Alternative energy sources
Efficient stoves

Provide sufficient food
Alternative to destruction
Better use of existing land
Use of new species of plants/animals
Agriculture
Land reform

Develop economy
non-destructively

New relations with developed world, reforestation
particularly aid programmes,
rational exploitation

Fig. 6.2. Optimal and sub-optimal solutions to forest destruction. Notes:
Triage = conserve only that which is unspoilt, abandon the already degraded to its
fate.

Chapter 12. With forest destruction progressing at a very rapid rate, and
with developing countries desperately short of funding, there is unlikely to
be careful, monitored and optimal conservation unless there are massive
increases in international aid and a change in attitude of national policy-
makers. As with reforestation and afforestation, conservation/protection
requires funding. There are basically two routes available (see Fig. 6.2): the
sub-optimal route is likely to be more frequently followed.

The means of taking pressure off remaining forests/woodlands are to:

1. prohibit/strictly license forest use;
2. reforest degraded areas, plant unforested, unfarmed land with trees;
3. encourage substitution of forest products/provide alternative energy
   sources;
4. alter the demands from developed countries which 'drive' the tropical
   hardwood/forest products trade (NGOs in rich nations may help encourage
   such changes).

The World Resources Institute *et al.* (1985) examined 56 countries seriously
affected by deforestation and estimated that US$ 8 billion would be needed
between 1985 and AD 2000 to make any real impact on tropical deforestation.
This is a sum roughly twice the total foreign aid those 56 countries received
for all purposes in 1985. In late 1989 it seemed that over US$ 800 million
would be available each year to aid tropical forest conservation (Pearce,
1989b).

Managed forests

It is difficult to get an overall picture of the managed forest situation. Management strategies may be sufficiently good to ensure some sustainable production of timber and forest products. However, forests are often 'managed' only on paper. In tropical Africa, there was probably more managed forest during colonial times than now. Recent estimates suggested that the continent has only about 2 million ha today: roughly: 1,167,000 ha in Ghana, 442,000 ha in Uganda, 70,000 ha in Kenya, 50,000 ha in the Sudan and 5000 ha in Zambia (World Resources Institute *et al.*, 1985: 23). In tropical America and in the Caribbean, there are managed forests in Honduras, Nicaragua, Cuba, Trinidad and Tobago, Costa Rica, El Salvador, Surinam, Colombia and Brazil (much of which is coniferous or eucalyptus). Most of the lowland forest remaining in Peninsular Malaysia and Thailand is managed on a long-term cycle of cutting and protected regrowth. Tropical Asia: Burma, Bangladesh, India and Pakistan has some managed forest. India alone had 32 million ha in the mid 1980s and over 100 years of expertise in management (World Resources Institute *et al.* 1985: 23). Excluding the Indian subcontinent, only about 2% to 3% of tropical Asia's cleared forests are now under management.

Too often, selective logging strategies allow excessive damage to surrounding timber, fail to prevent damaging repeat cutting within a few years of the first cut, and do not enforce minimum girth requirements or set these so low that immature trees are taken.

When plantations replace natural forest, in addition to aesthetic impacts, there may be changes in regional hydrology, water quality and survival of wildlife. Establishing a plantation may involve land drainage, use of fertilizers and pesticide. Drainage speeds the flow of water to streams, which may be polluted and, in turn, may damage wetlands. In Europe and in the USA, there are signs that conifer plantations trap more pollutants from the air than natural forests. The increased trapping may damage soil and/or reach streams and so affect wetlands. Wildlife impacts may be reduced by the provision of suitable nesting boxes and careful management of groundcover to try and compensate for the uniformity of most plantation cover.

Better control of fire

There are various ways in which forest/woodland/savanna fires can be controlled:

1. prohibit all fires;
2. control burning by authorities;
3. restrict burning to certain times of year/environmental conditions;
4. remove excessive amounts of brush from time to time;
5. create fire-breaks of at least 15 m width;
6. alter vegetation to a form that is less vulnerable to fire.

In regions where winds are predictable, it is possible to construct fire-breaks in advance to aid control of fires. These must be at 90° to the likely direction of wind-blown fire, must be sufficiently wide and kept clear of flammable debris.

Help natural forests regenerate

It is not going to be practical to reforest all damaged forests, even if the money and the will is available. There may be changes set in motion by clearing which make regeneration and regrowth impossible or difficult. For example, in Panama, large areas were deforested between 1904 and 1915 when the Canal was being constructed, some areas have regrown, but some became grassland and now are virtually impossible to reforest (Gradwohl & Greenberg, 1988). Natural regeneration demands forest close enough to supply seeds to the cleared area, as tropical forest tree species tend to have seeds that survive poorly in soil and there is thus little useful growth from seeds left in the soil after clearing. There are other problems associated with clearing:

- soils may lose nutrients or develop crusts;
- mycorrhizal fungi without which many trees could not survive, may be lost on clearing;
- the local/regional climate alters enough to prevent re-establishment of forest;
- complex webs of pollinators, seed dispersal organism and flora are broken on clearing and may not be re-established;
- weed species/pest animals spread into cleared area and this regrowth prevents other species getting re-established;
- once opened, the area can be grazed, burnt more easily or picked over by firewood collectors, preventing regeneration.

It may be helpful in some situations to manage cleared areas to prevent regrowth of aggressive 'weed' species which might encroach on remaining forest. In effect, a zone of plantation forestry or agriculture may be preferable to regrowth around an unspoilt area or a conservation area.

Reforestation and afforestation

In some areas natural forest may be replaced with a tree cover, more-or-less approximating to it in species composition. In some areas, land with ltitle or no tree cover, at least in recent times, may be planted with trees or shrubs (afforestation).

There is little point in replanting if local people then misuse the trees. The involvement of local people in tree planting offers advantages: they are likely to be cheaper than labour brought in from outside; they may have useful local knowledge; they will probably take better care of trees which they have planted, provided they understand the value of planting and provided they benefit in some way(s) from the planting.

There is a large and growing literature on the methods of reforestation/afforestation, and on suitable species, especially for afforest-ation in humid and dryland environments from the Tropics to cool temperate environments. There is no shortage of, at least, general knowledge about how to reforest/afforest. What is less well established, and what is crucial, are management strategies and institutional development strategies, for, without these, the chances of success are limited.

Planting may take the following forms:

1. replacement areas;
2. small patches (in corners of paddocks/fields);
3. strips (windbreaks and hedges possibly as part of an agroforestry system, for stabilization of banks, roadsides, hillsides, etc);
4. buffer zones/belts between conservation areas and possibly incompatible land use;
5. large- or medium-sized plantations.

Planting and replanting may be classified into the following types:

1. mixtures of native species;
2. pure stands of one, or a few, native species;

3. mixture of native, and exotic, species;
4. pure stands of one, or a few, exotic species.

An alternative classification could be based on type of tree: softwoods (mainly confiers); native hardwoods; exotic hardwoods; whether the environment is tropical, subtropical or cooler.

Plantation forestry is not new; teak has been grown in this manner since AD 1680 in Sri Lanka. According to Kuusela (1987) there were only around 100 million ha of tree plantations worldwide; another source suggested 11.5 million ha in the Tropics (World Resources Institute et al., 1985).

The greatest area of tropical forest plantations has been established in Brazil. In 1980, Brazil had over 25,000 km², less than 1000 km² of which was in Amazonia, most was broad-leaved non-rainforest trees, especially eucalyptus, grown for paper pulp (Myers, 1980: 42). Between 1984 and 1985, Brazil planted over 4 million ha of pines and eucalyptus.

In Africa, plantations are added to at a rate of about 126,000 ha year – something like one-thirtieth of the rate of forest loss (Harrison, 1987c: 54). Until recently, plantations were more likely to be large-scale privately owned or state-run. However, there has recently been much interest in smaller-scale community-managed forestry. By 1983, Zambia had planted over 450,000 ha of pines and eucalyptus (World Resources Institute et al., 1987: 31).

Asia has replaced lost forest/woodlands with plantations at a higher rate than any other major region of the Third World; in 1983, there was 1 ha planted for every 4 or 5 ha lost. The rate in Africa would have been about 1:29 and in tropical America about 1:10 (Hadley & Lanly, 1983: 14).

Outside the Tropics, Chile had planted 320,000 ha of Monterey pine (*Pinus radiata*) mainly between 1974 and 1978. By 1984, Chile had planted over 1.1 million ha of pines (the natural forest cover at that time was about 20 million ha), largely thanks to state-supported private-owned forestry with tax incentives for planters (World Resources Institute et al., 1985: 27). New Zealand has also planted a lot of *P. radiata*; in 1986 there were 9390 km²: 3.5% of New Zealand's total land area (Roberts, 1987).

For plantation forestry to succeed, certain problems have to be overcome and this is especially difficult in poor tropical nations:

1. there has to be an adequate rate of return on investment. For example, in Amazonia 15% may not be enough to pay for transport, etc;
2. there should be personnel with technical knowledge/management knowledge;
3. human pressures that might lead to damage to plantations have to be alleviated;
4. there has to be a political commitment to establish plantations.

Austria and Sweden have been exploring the use of dense-planted, fast-growing willow (*Salix* spp.) as a source of fuel. There are trees that provide either feedstock for fuel production, or products like waxes, latex, tannin, cellulose, etc. In Malaysia, and in some other countries, rubber is widely grown as a plantation crop. In the future, it seems likely that fuel, plastics, etc, will be produced from tree plantations. How widespread this becomes depends largely on the cost and availability of petroleum.

Fuelwood plantations and woodlots

Fuelwood plantations and woodlots should be established in regions where the population have stripped the available supplies of wood, or are doing so. Without managed fuelwood supplies, remaining forests and woodlands will be plundered, probably even if they are reserves, and land degradation will

Table 6.1. *Some commonly used plantation trees.*

Tree/shrub	Environment	rainfall needs (mm)	Value
Eucalyptus spp. [B]	Temp.–trop.	>800	T,F,S,P,C,H
Grevillea spp.[B]	Trop.–subtrop.	>800	T,F,S,SM,H
Araucaria spp.[C]	Trop. uplands–subtrop.	–	T,S
Cedrela spp.[C]	Subtrop.	–	T,S
Tectonia grandis[B2]	Trop.	1500	T
Terminalia ivorensis	Trop.	–	T
Pinus spp.[C]	Trop.–cool	–	T,S,P,C
Cypressus spp.[C]	Subtrop.	–	T,S,P,C
Acacia spp.[B]	Trop.–subtrop.	–	F,FD,S,GA,EC,H
Guiera senegalensis[B]	Trop.	>800	F,FD,S,EC
Combretum spp.[B]	Trop.	>800	F,FD,S,EC
Anacardium occidentalis[B1]	Trop.	>600	N,FR
Tamarix spp.	Trop.–subtrop.	–	EC,S,F
Casurina spp.[C]	Trop.	–	S,EC,F
Sesbania sesban	Trop.	>800	T,F,SM,FD
Populus spp.[B]	Temp.	–	T,S
Leucaena leucocephala[B]	Trop.	>800	F,S,SM,FD,CH, P,EC,T
Acacia auriculiformus[B]	Trop.	–	reclaim mine spoil, H
Calliandra spp.[B]	Trop.	–	F,H
Swietenia mahogani[B]	Trop.	–	T
Gmelina arbora[B]	Trop.	–	P,T
Prosopis spp.[B]	Trop.–subtrop.	–	F,FD,S,SM,FD,FR, EC,HC
Azadirachta indica,[B]	Trop.–subtrop.	>600	S,SM,FD,F
Dichrostachys cinerea[B]	Trop.	–	F

Bamboos: much potential, research needed, some development in China.
Rattans: much potential, research needed, should be domesticated.
Palms: much potential, research into new plantation spp. needed.

Notes: [B] = broad-leaved T = timber F = fuelwood S = shelter P = pulp.
[C] = conifer C = cellulose GA = gum-arabic CH = charcoal EC = erosion control
SM = soil mulch (improves soil fertility) FD = fodder N = nuts FR = fruit
H = supports honey production.
[1] In some parts of Africa, cashew nut would be an ideal plantation crop, but people refuse it because it is believed to attract ghosts. Similar taboos exist in parts of India with respect to tamarind (*Tamarindus indica*).
[2] Teak is intolerant of close spacing and allows little groundcover vegetation, consequently there is often quite severe erosion and/or duricrust formation beneath plantations.
* Weber & Stoney (1989: 47, 53) gives an extensive list of African tree species suitable for plantations in arid and semiarid tropics. Also details of precipitation needs of various plantation species.
* Agarwal (1986: 55) gives an extensive list of potential fuelwood species.
* Salt-tolerant and dryland potential species, see Barrow (1987a: 162–4, 217–18).
* Honey production support see *Unasylva*, 1982: vol. 34, p. 38.

set in as the people turn to burning crop residue and dung. As natural wood supplies dwindle, gathering wood becomes more and more difficult. Women and children, who tend to be the collectors, suffer most at first then, as they expend more and more time and energy collecting, farming efforts decline, and cooking may be restricted, resulting in health problems which, in turn, hinder farming. There are three basic questions to answer if effective fuelwood production is to be achieved.

1. Where and in what form is the fuelwood to be grown?
2. What type of wood should be grown?
3. How is the planting management to be organized/managed?

Answering question 2 is probably the easiest. The tree or shrub must fit the environmental constraints, it must have burning qualities acceptable to people, it must provide a sustained crop; if possible it should have useful non-fuel qualities. Also there should be no taboo or dislike of growing it. There are indications that fast-growing exotics, including eucalyptus, may burn too fast, leave too few cooking embers and so on. Speed of growth should not be the only criteria for choosing fuelwood plantation and woodlot species (Vietmeyer, 1979; Prior & Tuohy, 1987).

It is possible to sustain production of fuel and fodder from trees in a number of ways. Those with considerable promise for developing countries are: coppicing, pollarding, lopping and pruning (Fig. 6.3). Foley & Barnard, 1984: 37).

It is possible to grow non-tree sources of fuel: rushes and reeds or aquatic plants like water hyacinth (*Eichhornia crassipes*). These may be used directly or as a source of charcoal and could offer a way of utilizing salty land, swamps or even sewage disposal lagoons. These plants together with bamboo, which is generally underutilized outside the People's Republic of China, could take the pressure off trees. Bamboo is very fast-growing: 20 m in 12 weeks is possible, and it can give twice the yield of most other forms of timber/fuelwood. Bamboo can be used as hedges, and small woodlots of bamboo could easily be fitted into spare patches of land around villages. There is also the advantage that it is close-growing and has strong roots, making it ideal for erosion control. It can also be used for construction and as a food source.

In 1971, Ghana embarked on a programme to reforest degraded land covered in useless regrowth to form plantations of fast-growing exotic trees that could yield fuel and pulp. Initially, the land was burnt to clear it and settlers did a lot of damage to planted seedlings. In 1974, the Ghanian Government ceased burning the land and, with UNDP aid, began to convert the unwanted timber cleared before replanting into charcoal. Any useful trees were left. The settlers were encouraged to crop around the trees that were left and to care for planted saplings. The result was less erosion because burning ceased, the settlers still got some crops, the saplings were given the better protection from weeds and from disgruntled settlers, and there were profits from charcoal where, previously, timber had been burnt and wasted.

Problems with plantations

While exotic species may have some advantages over indigenous species: they can be fast-growing, and subject to fewer pests/diseases, etc, there may also be problems: for example, the risk that the plant may become a nuisance – as has been the case with salt cedar (*Tamarugo* spp.) in the southwest USA (see Chapter 11). Some of the 500 or so species of eucalyptus have been widely adopted for plantations from the equatorial Tropics to areas where plants must have frost tolerance, most are fast-growing and some of the genus can flourish in drylands where few other trees will grow (FAO, 1981).

Eucalyptus wood is now a major source of cellulose for paper, and rayon and is increasingly planted for local timber, fuelwood and as shelter-belts. By 1986, about 12% of Portugal's forests were exotic eucalyptus plantations. Ethiopia is very dependent on eucalyptus for urban fuelwood supplies and

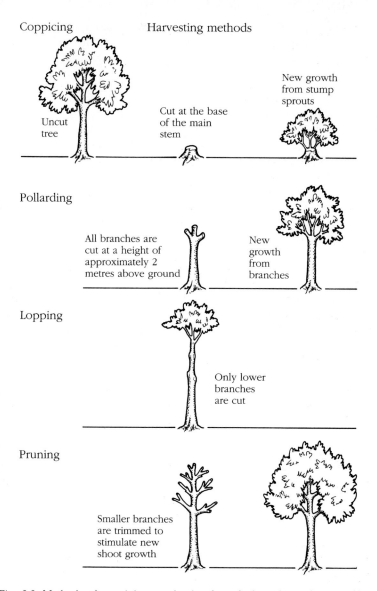

Harvesting methods

Coppicing

Uncut tree

Cut at the base of the main stem

New growth from stump sprouts

Pollarding

All branches are cut at a height of approximately 2 metres above ground

New growth from branches

Lopping

Only lower branches are cut

Pruning

Smaller branches are trimmed to stimulate new shoot growth

Fig. 6.3. Methods of sustaining production from fuelwood supply trees. Notes: Trees may be grown in a hedge/windbreak in plantation or woodlot, scattered amongst crops or across pasture. Broad-leaved trees, such as: Grevillea robusta and Azadirachta indica (the neem), Leucaena spp. (ipil ipil or subabul) and eucalyptus spp. can generally be pollarded or coppiced, only a few conifers can (one is Sequoia semperverens). Source: Roughly based on Weber & Stoney, 1989 p. 169 (no Fig. number).

construction. Some of the Brazilian steel industry depends quite heavily on eucalyptus plantations to provide charcoal for smelting. However, there are critics, and, in some areas, farmers are now rejecting 'gum trees', and have even been felling plantations.

It has been claimed that eucalyptus removes too much moisture and nutrients from the ground and releases toxins that affect nearby crops. In some situations, the effect of planting has been to dry springs, wells and streams. The degree to which this is a problem seems to depend mainly on which species is grown and on where the eucalyptus is grown, i.e., it may be more of a problem in land capability assessment (Eckholm *et al.*, 1984; 66–9).

Little grows beneath eucalyptus, there can therefore be considerable erosion of the planted area, and there is little habitat for wildlife (Joyce, 1988a). There may also be a greater risk of fire with eucalyptus plantations than with native forests.

It is also argued by some that eucalyptus can be 'socially inappropriate', in that it can provide a means for richer landholders to profit at the expense of the poor. In Portugal, some have called eucalyptus the 'fascist tree', because it seems to impoverish the soil and the people. One problem is that it may replace vines and oaks which give more employment. It is also favoured by larger landowners (Kardell *et al.*, 1986). In Thailand, the poor displaced from common lands by eucalyptus plantations, encroach on the remaining forests exacerbating deforestation (Lohmann, 1990). In parts of India, eucalyptus plantations can be profitably grown on what is otherwise marginal land, for sale to the pulp industry or as timber. The poor are driven off this land and possibly their own holdings and may end up as part-time labour for the plantation owners. One account of eucalyptus plantations in Uttar Pradesh (India) reports that a single seedling cost Rs 7 or 8 in 1986 and that 1500 trees could be grown on one ha, the best 1000 of which would fetch Rs 50 each when mature (which might be within 15 years). A farmer without irrigation might easily make Rs 6000 ha year, better than any other possible crop (*The Economist*, 6/12/86: 93). That is fine, provided smallholders are not displaced and food production is not neglected or driven into marginal, easily degraded land. Lohmann (1990) cites a recent study which suggests 100 ha of eucalyptus plantation will provide jobs for only two or three people. He goes on to argue that eucalyptus plantations are *not* forests – they are cut every five or six years. Also, the tree is a means for exploiting 'under-utilized' resources (which may include common land, forests, etc).

Agroforestry

Agroforestry is the deliberate association of trees and shrubs with crops, livestock or other production factors like honey production. It is felt by many to hold great promise. However, there can be problems in adopting it, one of which is that farmers may need new land (Foley & Bernard, 1984: 128; Winterbottom & Hazlewood, 1987). Agroforestry is not new, one form, the *taungya* system, was developed by German foresters in Burma in the 1850s as a means of sustaining teak production (Eckholm *et al.*, 1984: 78–9). Agroforestry encompasses a wide range of traditional land use strategies and more recently developed approaches to agricultural production, many 'invented' by technicians working with local farmers or pastoralists, a recent bibliography of forms of agroforestry may be found in Weber & Stoney (1989: Appendix E).

Because agroforestry produces sustained supplies of forage and fuelwood and mulch for the cropland, there is great potential for reducing the pressures on uncleared land, for reducing dung collection and for reducing fuelwood collection. Under agroforestry, these products, and possibly others are produced 'on-farm'. Farmers using agroforestry should enjoy a secure, diversified, more sustainable, production system and there may be opportunities for improving soil fertility and for making better use of limited soil moisture (Barrow, 1987a: 157). Alley-cropping is one form of agroforestry involving the cultivation of lines of trees or shrubs, e.g. *Leucaena* or *Sesbania rostrata* to form the walls of cropped 'alleys', the tree/shrub walls give shade/shelter, provide mulch to maintain soil fertility, provide fuelwood by clipping or pollarding and can provide fodder. There are various forms of 'dispersed tree' system. Trees like acacia are spaced out with crops and/or grazing between and beneath. The trees give: fuel, timber, fodder, shade, gum-arabic, hive sites and flowers for honey production and help fix nitrogen for soil fertility maintenance.

Community forestry, farm and village woodlots and cash crop tree farming

There tends to be some overlapping usage of the terms social forestry and community forestry. Both embrace the idea that it is vital is to involve the farmer and local people in forestry designed to meet household and community needs (Arnold, 1987). If local people are fully involved, then they are more likely to enjoy the benefits of reforestation, rather than some 'outsider', and should have more commitment to planting, protecting and caring for trees (Westoby, 1987). The farmer, family or community may require assistance to organize, finance and manage tree plantings. There may be a need for aiding access to seeds or seedlings, there may be special conditions, e.g. when barely adequate moisture requires assistance with terrace or microcatchment construction.

In Haiti, a community afforestation development initiative: the Agro-forestry Outreach Project, funded by USAID, has had some success. Massive fuelwood collection had caused severe erosion/drought problems. In 1981, a feasibility study led to an effort between 1982 and 1986, involving 170 voluntary agencies and 110,000 farmers in tree and shrub planting: as hedgerows, woodlots and as alley-cropping schemes. The aim was to cut erosion and to grow fuel and cash-crops. At a cost of US$ 8 million, over 13 million seedlings were planted between 1982 and 1984, twice the target (World Resources Institute *et al.*, 1985; Repetto, 1987; Winterbottom & Hazlewood, 1987: 108; Ferguson, 1988).

In West Bengal (India), a Social Forestry Project was launched in 1981 with World Bank assistance. The aim was to increase wood and fodder production in the State. Various approaches were tried involving 51,000 farmers, and, by the start of 1985, 24,000 ha of trees had been established at a total cost of US$ 43.5 million. Most of the farmers involved owned less than 2 ha mainly planted with *Eucalyptus* spp. and *Acacia auriculiformis*. An interesting aspect of this Project has been the effort to involve landless people. These people were given deeds to plots of unused, poor-quality degraded land, but no right to sell, and right to all benefits of using the land. Eight years after planting, the land began to give profits of roughly US$ 1600 to US$ 3200 per ha (1985 values) (World Resources Institute *et al.*, 1985: II p. 5). The organizers assisted the participants in the Project by providing seedlings to them at a cost of US$ 63 per ha – the poorest were given free seedlings, fertilizer and insecticide to combat termite attack, and, for the first three years, an incentive payment to encourage planting. This was later dropped when the trees were seen by all to be profitable and so no incentive was required.

Korea launched a Village Fuelwood Programme in 1973 to meet fuelwood demands through woodlots/plantations. Local community participation was organized through Village Forestry Associations, which, in effect, operated as village co-operative groups supplying seedlings and fertilizer at subsidized prices. The cost from 1973–78 was US$ 600 million. In addition to this planting, the Korean Government has prohibited the sale of fuelwood to city residents and has stepped up rural electrification. As a consequence of these activities, fuelwood consumption fell from 55% to 19% of total energy consumption between 1966 and 1979 (World Resources

Institute, *et al.*, 1985: II, p. 7). This National Forest Plan was so successful that it met its targets five years ahead of schedule in 1977.

The Smallholder Tree Farming Project of the Philippines was begun in 1972, financed by the Development Bank of the Philippines. It has since been copied elsewhere in the Islands. Farmers with at least 10 ha, which by many countries standards is hardly a smallholding, signed agreements to sell wood to the Paper Industry Corporation of the Philippines. Each then got a loan, with a grace period and then low interest to cover the costs of planting 8 ha with *Albizzia falcatoria* over a period of eight years. The Development Bank and the Paper Industry Corporation provided supervision and assistance. Success was such, that, in 1974, the Project was expanded, with farmers paying 25% of costs of planting. Obviously the benefits were apparent by this time, and the minimum size of holdings for participants was reduced to 5 ha. In spite of various setbacks, there has been considerable planting and results are described as reasonable (World Resources Institute *et al.*, 1985: II, p. 29).

In Gujarat (India), the State Forestry Department began a social forestry programme in the early 1970s, aimed at getting farmers to plant marginal or unused land with crops or eucalyptus seedlings. After five years, the total return to each farmer was found to be about US$ 5900 per ha, mainly from sale of coppiced eucalyptus poles. A common practice was to intercrop cotton with the eucalyptus. Farmers got 10,000 seedlings free, the cost of which was about US$ 2.0 per hundred. By 1983 about 150,000 ha had been planted, about 35% of the planters had landholdings of less than 2 ha. Costs were kept down by using schools and some private farmers to supply the seedlings with a buy-back arrangement to guarantee a certain return (World Resources Institute, 1985: II, p. 3).

In Gujarat, there have been some successes in settling shifting cultivators on degraded land and using them to reforest. Each family is given 37.5 ha to be planted with trees at the rate of 2.5 ha year, the land being prepared by the Forestry Department. The family must protect and manage the plantings and in return get paid for 25 days' labour per month. The Forestry Department takes 80% of profits made and the families keep the remaining 20% – by 1982 18,000 ha of degraded land had been settled and planted.

In the Sudan, Ethiopia and in parts of the W. African SSZ, there is a tradition of cropping and grazing savanna with scattered acacia trees. Typically, the land is ploughed around the trees and a rain-fed grain crop is obtained. The land is left fallow to recover, during which time acacia seedlings grow up, regular production of gum-arabic is obtained from the mature acacia, and some livestock grazing may take place. This may continue for up to 9 years, by which time the seedling acacias are ready to tap for gum. Gum-arabic provides a high proportion of the Sudan's export earnings. At about the twelfth year, the land is again cleared and a grain crop is obtained. The trees give shade, help prevent soil erosion, provide wood and fodder. In recent years, the system has broken down in many areas. The reasons for the breakdown seem to be increased demand for fuelwood and demand for more grazing. The fallows are shortened, the acacias are overexploited, fail to regenerate, and the soil degenerates and erodes.

The governments of the Sudan and the Netherlands have funded a three-year afforestation programme in Kordofan Province (Sudan) to reverse this type of agro-sylvipastoral system decline. Roughly US$ 1.5 million was spent on planting *Acacia senegal*, using improved seeds. In spite of a range of problems, the planting targets were exceeded, roughly 15,000 ha being planted in three years (World Resources Institute *et al.*, 1985: II, p. 11).

Funding reforestation, afforestation and forest conservation

A major problem with reforestation, afforestation and forest conservation is funding. The World Resources Institute *et al.* (1985: I) estimated that at least US$ 8 billion would be needed between 1985 and AD 2000 to make any real impact on tropical deforestation.

Costa Rica, with one of the world's worst records of deforestation, has made some progress with what has come to be termed 'debt swap for nature' (see Chapter 12). Through this strategy, a small country with a large, relative to the size of the country, National Debt of over US$ 1.5 billion in 1988 has got government, private concerns and overseas banks to work together to protect forests and pay for replanting of damaged land. The developments are promising, and are already being followed elsewhere. The Costa Rican debt swap works in the following manner: one donor US$ buys *c.* 3 US$ of international debt. Provided that each donor dollar is used for conservation, the Central Bank of Costa Rica returns US$ 3.75 to the donor for each US$ dollar donated, as a bond giving *c.* 20% interest over three to five years. The donor thus gets a return on the investment/aid, and the foreign banks get some debt money back. If the bank holding the debt is a USA bank, then it can write off some of the debt to USA taxes. Costa Rica is given money for conservation/reforestation, repays a little of its foreign debt and retains control of the management of conservation/reforestation (Simons, 1988a).

For roughly 30 years, the People's Republic of China has reforested and afforested; the amount probably works out at about 0.13 ha per head of population, an expansion of forest area from about 8.6% of total land area in 1949 to 12.7% in 1979 (World Resources Institute *et al.*, 1985: II, p. 8). This would equate to an area of roughly ten times the size of England since 1949. However, possibly as little as 26 million ha has actually survived. This is too little if set against the fact that China once had roughly 11% of its territory forested (the USA, the USSR and Japan had: approx. 33%, 35% and 66% respectively). In AD 2000, China's forested area will have fallen to 8% or less (Forestier, 1989: 52).

Citizen action to counter deforestation

The Chipko Movement is a 'people's ecology movement' in which women have been especially active. It professes (Ghandian-style) non-violent, non-co-operation and has been active in protecting forest and woodland in the Indian subcontinent. The roots of the movement lie in 1972 when the Indian State Forestry Department cleared village woodlots in the Gharwal region of Uttar Pradesh. Resistance to state and private clearance spread to Himchal Pradesh, Kashmir, Arunachal Pradesh, Karnataka, Rajasthan, Bihar and Vindhyas (Central India). In 1973, women successfully used passive resistance to repel forest developers seeking to supply sports goods' manufacturers with wood. There was already several years history of local opposition to this logging. Following some years of lobbying and resistance, the hillwomen got an official ban on commercial tree felling above 1000 m altitude and on slopes of over 30 degrees. The Chipko, and the similar Appiko, movements have reportedly replanted a large area of forest, possibly more than 30 million ha (Agarwal, 1986: 123, 138; Shiva & Bandyopadhyay, 1986; 1988).

In the Philippines, NGOs and the Catholic Church have been active in supporting and promoting citizen groups seeking to protect existing and to plant new forests. In England, from Medieval times, a few forests which were under considerable pressure, for example, from woodcutters, swine and peasant agriculture, have been effectively protected by appointed or elected citizen groups or officers with legal backing, for example: the 'Verderers' of the New Forest and similar officers in the Forest of Dean, Exmoor and Dartmoor.

In 1989, in Açre State, Brazilian Amazonia, Chico Mendes was murdered for organizing rubber tappers to resist forest clearance, mainly by cattle ranchers. Mendes has become a new kind of 'saint', an 'eco-martyr'. His activities and untimely death has sparked off a growing forest conservation movement in Amazonia and elsewhere. Unfortunately, such men are rare.

THE NEED TO REDUCE WASTE OF TIMBER AND IMPROVE CONTROL OF LOGGING AND THE TIMBER TRADE

Wherever possible, developing countries would be advised to export processed timber products: veneer, sawn planks, plywood, doors, door/window frames, furniture, etc, not uncut logs. By so doing, the maximum profit is obtained and this may mean less forest is cut and local people would be given work (James, 1989). Typically a 4-tonne *sapele* log in Zaïre would bring villagers around £40; if cut into veneer it would fetch about £500, as door/window frames it would give about £1200 (James, 1989). Unfortunately, import duties on finished wood products imposed by developed countries hinder this; additionally the expertise, equipment and funds to set up such timber industries in developing countries are not always easy to come by; logging concerns may play a part in discouraging such transfer of technology. Increasingly, NGOs in developed countries and some 'green parties' are beginning to encourage such policies and actively discourage the public from buying certain types of tropical wood products.

Recently, the Friends of the Earth (an NGO) have been lobbying developed countries to establish a Code of Conduct for Tropical Timber Traders. This would include provisions for forcing labelling of timber products to show the source: indicating if wood is not from a sustainable plantation or managed forest. Timber from undesirable sources should, under such a Code, be taxed, outlawed and any revenue generated should go to conservation and replanting work.

There is a lot that could be done to cut the demand for tropical timber. For example, 20% of Japan's timber imports, much of it tropical timber, goes to make plywood that is used in the construction industry for shuttering, i.e. to contain concrete while it cures; it is then thrown away. If re-usable metal or plastic shuttering were adopted, wood imports could be cut (Cross, 1988). Japan also consumes large quantities of disposable chop-sticks, a waste that might be reduced. In virtually all developed countries, there is a lot more that could be done to recycle timber and wood-based products, especially paper products and this might relieve demand for timber.

Only a relatively few of the vast range of tropical timber species are sold in developed country markets; this could be easily remedied by better publicity, plus establishment of better standards/construction research programmes. A use of what is presently wasted would help to take the pressure off species in greatest demand and might help reduce the areas logged. An organization recently established to help control trade in tropical timber is the International Tropical Timber Organization (ITTO). This was set up to run the International Tropical Timber Agreement of 1984, signed by 36 producer and 33 consumer nations, which were involved in 95% of tropical timber trade in 1988 (Cross, 1988). One proposal made by the ITTO was a surcharge, possibly 3%, on all tropical timber arriving in a consumer country, the proceeds of which were to pay for sustainable development/reforestation. In Japan, a major importer of tropical timber, there are signs of increasing NGO activity – for example, the Japan Tropical Forest Action Network.

Reduction of fuelwood demand

Traditional domestic fires, such as the three-stone-type cooking fires of Africa and Asia, are not very efficient and probably supply only 5% to 10% of the heat they generate to the cooking pot. The traditional *jiko* stove of Kenya is better with an efficiency of about 19%: improved versions can achieve up to 30%. There has been a lot of interest in developing improved stoves or fire-places. Unfortunately, much of what is written on the subject is based on sketchy data and sometimes false assumptions (Foley et al., 1984: 12). The goal recently has been to produce a cooking/heating source which is 20% or more efficient at a cost of less than US$ 5. Such a stove might be expected to considerably reduce fuel demand. A typical assumption is that, for a peasant family, the annual reduction would be about equivalent to one-half of the production of a 1 ha woodlot (Folley et al., 1984: 14). Were all the rural folk in countries like Nepal or Kenya to adopt such stoves, then savings in wood use could be huge. However, as Munslow et al. (1988: 11) warned, fuel supply/consumption is not a simple problem and there is unlikely to be a simple, rapid solution – fuelwood use is likely to grow for some years.

In many African countries, notably in Kenya and Burkina Faso, improved versions of traditional *jiko*-type stoves or improved three-stone fires with clay/dung surrounds are spreading fast. The reasons is that the people can see their value. Harrison (1987b: 41) notes that, in Kenya, an improved *jiko* stove pays for itself within 8 weeks in fuel savings, and the Burkina Faso improved fire-place may burn up to 70% less than the traditional version (Harrison, 1987b: 42).

It should not be overlooked that much of the demand for fuelwood is from urban areas; improved rural stoves will have little effect on urban charcoal demand. Also, in some regions at least, fuelwood seems to be a 'by-product' of clearance for agriculture, so adoption of improved stoves may not have much effect on cutting (Agarwal, 1986; Leach & Mearns, 1989: 14).

Interrelationships between fuelwood/charcoal/crop residue and dung trade are often strong and the supply of these fuels may be controlled by an elaborate network of dealers and middlemen. Sale of fuel is often an 'insurance' measure; farmers and peasants turn to it when crops fail or when they need money and are probably aware of the degradation caused but are victims of circumstance. Altering demand/supply of rural fuel supplies can be difficult. Where there is a trade in charcoal, the chances are that traditional conversion of wood is wasteful and might be improved by application of appropriate technology kilns.

It may be possible for the people to adopt alternative cooking/heating/lighting methods. Biogas, kerosene, solar stoves and rural electrification have some potential. Indonesia is a nation which has subsidized domestic kerosene to try and reduce fuelwood demand. However, kerosene tends to be used for lighting and has done little to reduce fuelwood demand (Repetto & Gillis, 1988: 82). There have probably been over one million family-sized biogas units installed per year in China since 1975, and they appear to have been quite successful. Elsewhere, including

India, where there has been interest in promoting biogas, adoption and success in use has been less promising. China's success may reflect a rather unique mix of household refuse, sewage and livestock manure available as biogas reactor feedstock. Alternatives to fuelwood involve cost and changed habits; these may be difficult to overcome.

Reduction of demand for pulp and woodchips

There could be much more recycling of paper products and a reduction of wastage through excessive packaging. Electronic media should have helped to reduce the demand for paper but, in practice, may have actually increased it as photocopying and printing become easier. There is hope for meeting pulp and woodchip demand from plantation trees rather than mangrove forests or natural forests. Mangroves are at present under great pressure to supply woodchip and paper pulp (see Chapter 7). Perhaps the most promising routes to relieve pressure on forests to meet pulp demand are the use of field crops to produce paper –*kenaf* (*Hibiscus cannabinus*) and straw hold great promise (some countries like the UK may use straw for most of their paper needs by the end of the decade).

Kenaf is fast growing and tolerates salty irrigation water. There are already commercial organizations preparing to produce newsprint from it in Texas, USA (Anon, 1990).

7 The degradation of wetlands, tundra, uplands and islands

DEGRADATION OF WETLANDS

WETLAND CAN BE APPLIED to a broad range of ecosystems, probably the best definition is that of Maltby (1986): '. . . a collective term for ecosystems whose formation has been dominated by water, and whose processes and characteristics are largely controlled by water . . . a place wet enough for long enough to develop a specially adapted vegetation and other organisms.' Wetlands include: marshes, fens, bogs, peatlands, swamps, mangrove forests, coastal saltmarshes, Man-made paddy-fields and irrigated fields (Table 7.1). About 6% of the Earth's land surface is wetland and some countries have very extensive areas of wetland, for example, over 25% of Indonesia is swampland (Maltby, 1986: 41). Some wetlands are densely populated, for example, the Bangladesh deltalands have over 100 million inhabitants.

Wetlands are not wastelands; they are often vital breeding and feeding areas for river or marine fish and other creatures. For this reason, and because some have been difficult for Man to settle and despoil, they are important for wildlife conservation. Wetlands often play a vital role in moderating river flows, and in helping to cleanse streamflows. Wetlands are generally very productive; the world's most productive ecosystems are probably reedswamps. For example, an unfertilized papyrus (*Cyperus papyrus*) swamp can yield as much vegetable matter (biomass), naturally, without addition of fertilizer, as a well-fertilized maize field (Maltby, 1986: 12). Wetlands may well be ecosystems more able to sustain crop production than drier environments. This is because inflow of water brings dissolved nutrients and suspended sediments which help renew fertility. Algae and bacteria that fix nitrogen which aids plant growth are mainly responsible for the productivity of rice paddy-fields. Because wetlands tend to occur where gradients are gentle, and where there is much aquatic vegetation, they are more likely to be areas of sediment accumulation than loss.

A wetland crop, rice, feeds roughly half the world's population. The sago palm (*Metroxylon sagu*) is the staple of about one-quarter of the people of Papua New Guinea and of large parts of Indonesia. Sago production seems to have little impact on swamp environments. Were it a more nutritious food, or if it could be processed to improve its food value, it might make sense to harvest sago rather than clear swamps for rice cultivation.

In many parts of the world, reeds (*Phragmites* spp.), rushes (*Juncus* spp.) and willows (*Salix* spp.) are used for thatch, house construction, boat building and basket construction. They also have great potential as sources

Table 7.1. *Types of wetland.*

Marshes[a]:
  (i) tidal marshes: (a) saltmarshes (b) mangrove swamps
  (ii) tidal freshwater marshes, the result of freshwater backed up by tides – for
      example: the *várzeas* of E. Amazonia[b]
  (iii) freshwater marshes[c]
  (iv) seasonally flooded lowlands – for example, the *dambos* of parts of Africa

Fens:
Differ from (iii) above, in that these accumulate peat, and are non-acidic.

Water meadows:
Artificially created. Common in England before 1939 and parts of Europe.
Lowlands were flooded in winter by means of weirs and ditches. The flooding
raised the spring-time soil temperature and improved nitrogen fixation, giving
better grazing and hay yields.

Swamps:
Causes of waterlogging vary. In general non-acidic. In the Tropics, swamps
are generally dominated by papyrus (*Cyperus papyrus*) or *Typha* spp; in cooler
regions *Phragmites* spp. take their place.

Mires and peatlands:
Attempts have been made to classify mires by their nutrient status (nutrient-rich,
nutrient-poor, intermediate) (peats are less widespread in the Tropics, where
they are likely to occur mainly in mangrove swamps, river cut-offs and delta
areas). Mire peats can form in hollows, above the ground surface, having grown
up from a hollow, and, if precipitation is sufficiently in excess of
evapotranspiration, may form raised bogs (ombromorphic mires) on level
ground or gentle slopes or blanket peat sometimes on steeper slopes.

Note: [a] Some use this term to denote wetlands with mainly mineral soils. Where
soils have a lot of organic matter, mire or peatland is commonly used.
  [b] *Várzeas* of E. Amazonia flood as tides back-up river flows, those in W.
Amazonia are inundated by periodic high river levels caused by rainfall (Barrow,
1987c).
  [c] Some swamps may form as a consequence of wildlife activity – in N.
America (at least in the past) the beaver (*Castor* spp.) probably started many
wetlands by damming streams.
Sources: Maltby, 1986: 34; Moore & Bellamy, 1974; Etherington, 1983.

of pulp to make paper as fuel or a feedstock from which to distil alcohol fuel.
In Europe, there are plans in some countries (e.g. Austria) for quite large-
scale generation of electricity supplies from willows grown in wetlands.
Many wetlands provide important seasonal or permanent grazing for
livestock (DeVos, 1975: 155). Coastal swamps and mangrove forests are a
source of many products vital for the survival of poor rural people, for
example, mangrove wood may be used for building or charcoal.

Worldwide, there are extensive areas of wetland forest and seasonal or
permanent swamps (see Table 7.2). It is likely that new highly productive
and sustainable agricultural systems which rely on wetlands and wetland
species could be developed. For example, there has been some success in the
USA in growing the wetland tree, bald cyprus (*Taxodium distichum*) in ponds
which also serve for aquaculture of prawns or fish. There are a number of
aquatic animals with potential for integration in wetland crop or timber
production, such as the capybara (*Hydrochaerus hydrochaerus*), turtles, and
water buffalo. Maltby (1986: 24) describes a shrimp/*Tilapia*/duck/crocodile
production system tried in Jamaica.

Table 7.2. *Major wetlands of the world.*

Wetland	Extent	
Tropical		
Várzeas (Amazon Basin)	?64,000–128,000 km²	F
USA wetland forest (especially Louisiana)	> 30 million ha	F
Sudd (Sudan/Egypt)	11,000 km²	F
Sundarbans (Bangladesh)	–	D
Niger 'Inland Delta' (Mali)	–	F
Mekong Delta (Vietnam)	4 million ha	F*
Okavango Swamps (Botswana)	–	F
Great Lake/Tonle Sap (Kampuchea)	> 1.5 million ha	F
Congo Basin (Central Africa)	–	F
Gran Pantanal (Paraná R., Brazil)	–	F
Tana R. 'Delta' (Kenya)	–	F
Indus Delta (Pakistan)	–	D
Irawaddy Delta (Burma)	3.5 million ha	D
Ganges/Brahmaputra Floodplain (India)	> 5 million ha	F
Fly River Floodplain (Papua New Guinea)	over 4.5 million ha	F
Black River Morasses (Jamaica)	–	F
Kafue Flats (Zambia)	–	F
Mid-Senegal R. (Senegal)	–	F
Subtropical		
Mississippi Floodlands (USA)	–	F
Everglades (Florida, USA)	–	F
Nile Delta (Egypt)	–	D
Temperate		
Danube Delta (Romania)	–	D/F
Somerset Levels (UK)	–	F
Camargue (France)	–	F

Notes: F = periodic flooding. D = delta area.
*IUCN 1989 *A Directory of Asia's and SE Asia's Wetlands.*
Sources: Barrow, 1985: 114; Maltby, 1986: 15; Maltby, 1986: 23.

Freshwater aquaculture has tremendous potential for improvement. But a very real risk is that the pollution of rivers and wetlands, especially by agricultural chemicals, will mean that some, or even most, of this potential might be lost before there is even a chance to appraise its value (this is a particular threat in Amazonia, which has a rich freshwater fauna). This would be a double degradation: the wetland would be degraded, and the potential for developing intensive, sustainable food and commodity production strategies, which might help take pressure off other lands, would be wrecked.

Wetlands may be damaged if one or more of the following occur:

- If the supply of water is disrupted.
- If the waterlogged area is drained.
- If there is pollution: agrochemicals, defoliants used in warfare, industrial, sewage, etc.
- If acid deposition takes place.
- If invasive plants or animals are introduced.
- If there is climatic change reducing rainfall or river flows.
- If sea level alters or if there is tectonic movement.
- If the wetland environment is disturbed by excessive human exploitation: timber removal, tourism, etc.

Dams and barrages constructed for hydroelectric generation, flood control or irrigation supply are increasingly altering natural river flows with considerable impact on wetlands, often for hundreds of kilometres downstream. This has been the case with the Kafue Flats (a periodically flooded wetland in Zambia) because dams and agricultural development upstream altered river flows, and similar developments, are beginning in Amazonia (Barrow, 1987b). When large canals, or pipelines, transfer water from river system to river system, often over long distances, it can alter wetlands downstream of the point of water diversion, and downstream of the point of delivery of diverted water. Water transfer not only alters the flow regime and water quality of two or more stream systems, it can enable organisms to disperse and cause problems in areas they may have had difficulty reaching naturally.

Drainage schemes have disrupted many wetlands, either by diverting water inputs, for example, when a stream is channelized and flooding is reduced, or by removing water from the wetland – the Sudd wetlands of the Sudan and Egypt are undergoing such changes as a consequence of the Jonglei Canal (Barrow, 1987a: 286; Howell *et al.*, 1988).

Some countries have drained wetlands on a huge scale, such as the Netherlands, since the sixteenth century or earlier. In the eastern UK, in the seventeenth and eighteenth centuries, extensive drainage owed much to the efforts of Dutch engineers like Morris or Vermuyden. Today, Dutch engineers are still active in many parts of the world. Wetlands are attractive because their soils are often rich when drained and, at least in the short term, can be very productive.

A serious threat is posed in many areas by agrochemicals, sewage, saline return flows from irrigation and industrial pollution. These pollutants can affect wetlands great distances from the point of release. Wetlands tend to be the lowest point and so accumulate polluted water. In Amazonia, there are threats from mining involving the use of mercury to separate gold from ore, and from aluminium and iron processing and large-scale agricultural projects. In Pakistan, the Indus Delta is threatened by pollution from industries sited far upstream, and, in Papua New Guinea, copper mining and processing has led to wetland pollution. In Malaysia and in parts of Central America, pesticides have been used on oil-palm and banana plantations; these compounds soon escape to contaminate wetlands. Processing agricultural commodities like rubber, palm oil, sugar or pineapples can cause serious eutrophication problems if the effluent reaches wetlands. Many wetland species are filter-feeders and so can accumulate poisons, bacteria, etc.

While some wetlands offer the potential for stable, sustained crop production, some are easily damaged. If there is any alteration in input of water or sediment or outflow, then there can be rapid change to wetlands. Winkler (1985: 325) estimated that, globally, there had been a 50% loss of wetlands since AD 1900. Such estimates are, at best, imprecise because mapping has been poor, but certainly the rate of loss in developed countries has been rapid. The USA may have lost 87 million ha of wetlands since European settlement, i.e. 54% of its original total (Mitsch & Gosselink, 1986). The main cause of the loss has been, directly and indirectly, agricultural activity, direct loss from clearing and draining, and indirect loss because of contamination of wetlands with pesticides, fertilizers, salty surplus irrigation water and herbicides. In Europe, fertilizer and sewage pollution has resulted in rapid, weakened reed growth. If there are then harsh weather conditions, the vegetation gets badly damaged and the reedswamp is degraded. The draining of wetlands can have impacts on river systems and their floodlands if the drainage water is rich in FeS or H_2SO_4, as is sometimes the case.

Mangrove swamps

Mangroves are restricted to shallow brackish, and salt waters, in regions which have no frosts between $25°N$ and $25°S$ of the Equator (local conditions may permit mangroves as far north as $32°N$). Mangroves now probably comprise about 0.6% (about 15.8 million ha) of the world's total forest cover. About 41% (roughly 5.4 million ha) is in tropical Asia and N. Australia, fringing the shores or islands of the Indian Ocean, or grows along the East Pacific coasts (Kunstadter et al., 1986: xi). One of the largest

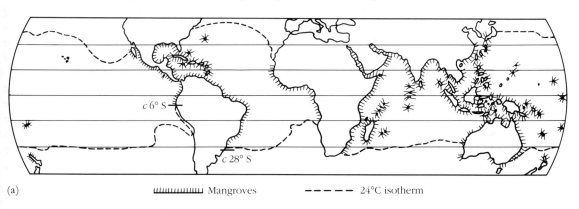

(a)   ⊔⊔⊔⊔⊔⊔⊔⊔⊔⊔ Mangroves   – – – – – 24°C isotherm

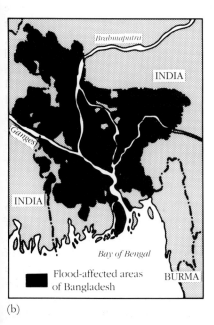

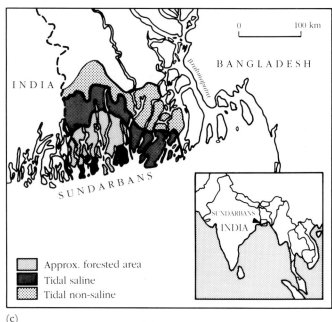

(b)   (c)

Fig. 7.1. (a) *World distribution of mangroves (1980).* Source: *Hutchings & Saenger, 1987: 4 (Fig. 1); Lindén & Jernelöv, 1980: 81.*
(b) *Area of Ganges/Brahmaputra Floodplain and Delta prone to flooding.* Source: World Development UNDP 2(3): page 9. (No Fig. No.). Note: *The above is* not *UK Journal World Development.*
(c) *The Sunderbans (Bangladesh).* Source: *Chapman, 1975: 18; Lindén & Jergelöv, 1980: 81 (Fig. 1); Kunstadter* et al., *1986; Ong, 1982.*

remaining continuous areas is the Sunderbans of the Ganges Delta
Bangladesh), where there are probably over 1 million ha. Any removal of
mangroves from the coasts of this region leaves the land open to even greater
risk than the already high threat of storm surge and high tides (Stoddart &
Pethick, 1984).

There are about 60 common mangrove species, in the Persian Gulf, Sinai
Peninsular, Fiji, S. Japan, S. Australia, and E. South America. *Avicennia* spp.
are the more common; elsewhere *Rhizophora* spp., and *Sonneratia* spp., take
their place Kundstadter *et al.*, 1986; Hutchings & Saenger, 1987: 1).
Mangroves are valuble for coastal protection against waves and storms and
as areas where fish, shellfish an crustaceans: prawns, shrimps, crabs, etc, feed
and breed. They are important refuges for other wildlife, and so have a value
as genetic reserves. Plants in mangrove swamps include salt-resistant species
which may have value if domesticated as crops for areas where there are poor
supplies of fresh water. Mangroves are traditionally exploited for charcoal,
tan-bark, building timber and other products. So far, there has been little, or
no attempt to improve any mangrove species for timber or other
production, and little deliberate planting: their importance is undervalued.

Worldwide mangrove swamps have been under threat or are being
threatened by:

- Silt pollution as a result of developments inland that charge streams
  with silt and sewage pollution – beyond a certain point mangroves
  suffer; at lower levels mangrove swamps can help render sewage safe.
- Oil spill from tankers at sea. This is a particular risk for swamps
  bordering the busy Straits of Malacca (off W. Malaysia and Indonesia).
- Clearcutting or overcutting, to provide woodchips for rayon production especially in Japan. *Avicennia* spp. and *Ceriops* spp. are especially
  in demand for rayon feedstock, and, to a lesser extent, for chipboard
  manufacture and for making paper pulp. There have consequently
  been massive loss of the mangrove forests of South East Asia since the
  1960s. Indonesia was exploiting 2000 km² of mangroves for chip
  production in 1988 (Fortes, 1988: 210), and Malaysia has also been
  badly affected (Ong, 1982).
- Clearing for housing or industrial buildings. Between 1922 and 1987,
  Singapore lost about 9% of its mangroves for building land (Fortes,
  1988: 210).
- Clearing land to make aquaculture ponds. One source has suggested
  that, between 1967 and 1978, over 40% of mangroves in the
  Philippines have been converted to fishponds (Kunstadter *et al.*, 1986:
  6). It is possible that 25% of Malaysia's remaining mangroves will be
  cleared for aquaculture (Burbridge, 1988: 172). Shrimps and prawns
  command a high price on the world market and this makes conversion
  of mangroves to aquaculture ponds attractive.
- Decreased flows of freshwater as a result of stream diversion, dams
  and irrigation use. The salinity change along the coasts may affect
  mangroves.
- Clearance for agriculture. Indonesia cleared an estimated 200,000 ha
  between 1969 and 1974 for agriculture and, between 1974 and 1979, an
  even larger area (Kunstadter *et al.*, 1986: 6). Such clearance can go
  wrong; on being drained, some mangrove swamps develop acid-
  sulphate soils which are infertile and difficult to reclaim (this has
  happened quite frequently in Indonesia).
- Clearance to provide charcoal.

It seems probable that, by 1990, the extent of mangroves worldwide will be about 79% of that in 1979. by AD 2000 this could have fallen to 54% of the 1979 area (Kunstadter *et al.*, 1986: 8). In 1920, the Philippines probably had about 450,000 ha of mangroves, in 1978 there were about 146,000 ha left and losses were running at around 2000 ha a year (Vannucci, 1988: 216). In Vietnam, about 40,000 ha were destroyed by defoliant spraying and the cleared areas have been slow to recover (Maltby, 1986: 46). In Australia, Florida and the Caribbean, the situation gives cause for concern, largely due to losses because of building development.

It should be possible to manage mangrove swamp areas to give a sustained yield of timber, charcoal, etc, and to produce prawns, crabs, fish, etc. At the same time, the vegetation offers effective coastal protection against storms and erosion. Some nations have realized the value of mangroves and have started to protect and even replant. In Bangladesh, where coastal protection is vital, many thousand hectares have been planted in the last decade, and, in the Philippines, a Presidential Decree has been pronounced with the intent, in practice not always successfully achieved, to protect a 40 metre (minimum) width mangrove belt around the coast.

If the world's oceans do rise as a result of the greenhouse effect, then mangroves are likely to become even more valueable: unlike artificial sea defences they are self-repairing, they can keep up with gradual rise in sea level and they are cheaper (Lewis, 1982: 153–71; Hutchings & Saenger, 1987: 309).

Coastal wetlands and saltmarshes

There has been considerable loss of coastal wetlands other than mangrove swamps, worldwide. The USA, Europe, and China have been especially badly affected Lewis (1982: 74) estimated that 30 to 40% of the coastal wetlands of the USA had been lost, 24,200 ha in Florida alone. California has probably lost two-thirds of its coastal marshes, and there have been considerable losses along the Atlantic coast of N. America (Lewis, 1982: 46). Channelization of rivers and removal of wetland timber has led to considerable land degradation in the south of the USA (Templet & Meyer-Arendt, 1988). In Europe, pressures on coastal wetlands are likely to increase as estuarine barrages are built for power generation, flood control and domestic water supply. Worldwide, sea level rises associated with the 'greenhouse effect' will probably have an effect on coastal wetlands where the terrain inland slopes too much to allow, or where coastal defences prevent re-establishment at a higher level.

Peatlands

Worldwide there are at least 500 million ha of peatlands which constitute about 2 to 3% of the Earth's land surface (Maltby, 1986: 50; Hutchinson & Meema, 1987: 513) Fig. 7.2; Table 7.3). Roughly 40% of the world's peatlands are in the USSR, roughly 36% is in Canada. The bulk of this Soviet and Canadian peatland is frozen for about 40 weeks of the year (Taylor & Smith, 1980). Peat is organic matter formed from dead plants. In theory, any plant community can form peat if conditions are suitable, which means that there should be saturated, deoxygenated, acidic conditions at the surface of the ground to prevent normal decay Moore & Bellamy, 1974: 204). Given suitable conditions, peat can accumulate at between 0.2 and 1.6 mm y^{-1} (Maltby, 1986: 50). A layer of peat may build up to a point, which depends on

Table 7.3. *Distribution of peatlands (approximate areas)*

(a) Country	Area (ha)	Country	Area (ha)
Western Europe		China	4,200,000 (0.3)
Austria	22,000	Fiji	4,000
Belgium	18,000	Indonesia	17,000,000 (14)
Denmark	120,000	India	32,000
Finland	10,400,000 (31)	Israel	5,000
France	90,000	Japan	250,000
West Germany	1,110,000 (4.5)	Korea (DPR)	136,000
Great Britain	1,580,000 (7)	Malaysia	2,500,000 (4)
Greece	5,000	Papua New Guinea	—
Iceland	1,000,000 (10)	Philippines	6,000
Ireland (Eire)	1,180,000 (17)	Sri Lanka	2,500
Italy	120,000	Thailand	68,000
Luxembourg	200	Vietnam	183,000
Netherlands	280,000		
Norway	3,000,000 (9)	*Central America & Caribbean*	
Spain	6,000	British Honduras	68,000
Sweden	7,000,000 (16)	Costa Rica	37,000
Switzerland	55,000	Cuba	767,000
		El Salvador	9,000
Eastern Europe		Belize	453,000
Bulgaria	1,000	Jamaica	21,000
Czechoslovakia	30,750	Nicaragua	371,000
East Germany	489,000	Panama	787,000
Hungary	30,000	Puerto Rico	10,000
Poland	1,300,000 (4.5)	Trinidad and Tobago	1,000
Romania	7,000		
USSR	150,000,000 (7)	*South America*	
Yugoslavia	100,000	Argentina	45,000
		Bolivia	900
Africa		Brazil	1,500,000
Angola	—	Chile	1.047,000
Burundi	14,000	Colombia	339,000
Congo	290,000	Falkland Is.	1,151,000
Guinea	525,000	French Guiana	162,000
Ivory Coast	32,000	Guyana	813,880
Lesotho	—	Paraguay	considerable
Liberia	40,000	Surinam	113,000
Malagasy (Republic)	197,000	Uruguay	3,000
Malawi	91,000	Venezuela	1,000,000
Mozambique	—		
Rwanda	80,000	*North America*	
Senegal	1,500	Canada	150,000,000 (19)
Uganda	1,420,000	USA – Alaska	49,400,000 (20)
Zaïre	—	USA – S of 49°N	10,240,000 (1.3)
Zambia	1,106,000		
		The Pacific	
Asia		Australia (esp. Queensland,	
Bangladesh	60,000	Tasmania)	15,000
		New Zealand	150,000 (0.6)

Notes: Figures approximate ha. Figures in ( ) indicate approximate % of land
that is peatland.
Tropical and subtropical peatland extent is probably underestimated.
Sources: Moore & Bellamy, 1974: 187 (Table 9.1); Sjörs, 1980 (Table 1);
Maltby, 1986: 52.

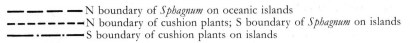

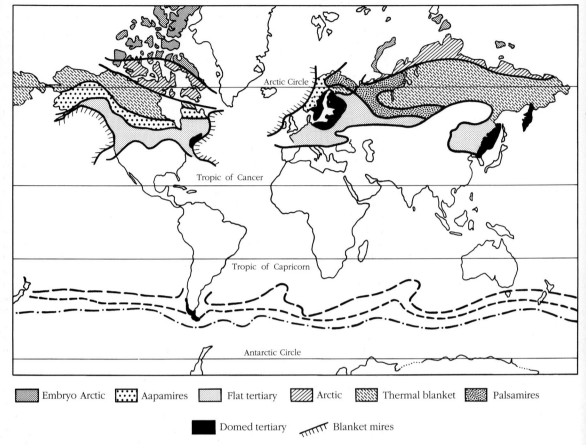

Fig. 7.2. Map of peatlands (showing main types of peat mires). Sources: Based on Moore & Bellamy, 1974: 182 (Fig. 8.1).

terrain and climate, where the accumulation and destruction are in approximate equilibrium. However, in some situations, accumulation outpaces loss and layers as much as 15 m thick can accumulate.

Not all peatlands would have developed without human activity, although they may appear natural to the casual observer. There is an extensive literature which suggests that much of the upland peat of the UK, Eire and other parts of NW Europe and Scandinavia are 'anthropogenic' and formed mainly between 3500 to 4500 years ago as a result, at least in part of forest felling and possibly ploughing (Dimbleby, 1975; Moore, 1975; Roberts, 1989: 183).

Peat is exploited for fuel, horticultural (Table 7.4) and industrial use. Peatlands are also degraded by agricultural development, drainage, pollution and fire.

Use of peat for domestic fuel has a long history; more recently, some countries have turned to it for electricity generation. The USSR and Eire have been the main users of peat for electricity generation; in 1974, the former was harvesting around 80 million tonnes (Moore & Bellamy, 1974: 189). Peat provides roughly 20% of Eire's energy needs (and 40% of

Table 7.4. *Estimated total peat production and exploitation for fuel and horticultural use.*

Country	Fuel peat	Horticultural peat	Total
USSR	32,000	48,600	80,600
Ireland (Eire)	2,255	153	2,408
Finland	1,255	202	1,457
West Germany	101	810	911
China	323	526	849
United States	0	324	324
Canada	0	198	198
Poland	0	113	113
Sweden	0	109	109
Czechoslovakia	0	109	109
East Germany	0	69	69
Great Britain	no data	69	69
France	20	40	60
Denmark	0	44	44
Norway	0.4	33	33.4
New Zealand	0	4	4
Others	41	1,174	1,215
Total	c. 36,000	c. 52,000	c. 88,000

Source: Maltby, 1986: 130.

electricity). Jamaica has developed peat resources of the Black River Basin and the Morass of Negril for electricity generation.

In Scotland, and on some Scottish islands, peat is used to fuel whisky distilleries. Substitutes would be very difficult to find, so cutting must be very well managed to prevent waste and if possible encourage future peat growth. Burundi (Central Africa) has large reserves of peat which could be a useful domestic fuel source if the problem of high ash content is overcome (Anon, 1982; 1983; Board na Mona, 1985).

Where peat is taken from 'raised bogs' on a large scale, as is the case in Eire and in parts of the USSR, it is unlikely that regeneration will take place, because the vegetation has been disturbed and because the removal of the bulk of the peat strata leaves a layer that can be drained, fertilized and profitably converted to agricultural land. There are indications that, with oxidation and tillage, these new farmlands will have a relatively short life and it is not established what will finally remain after peat cutting and a period of agricultural use. When drained, and put to agricultural use, these peatlands are likely to release considerable quantities of CO_2 with the effect of increasing the 'greenhouse effect'. An estimated 30 million tonnes of carbon are being added to the atmosphere each year from use of peat as a fuel (Maltby, 1986: 53).

The drainage of peatlands for conversion to agricultural land has been a worldwide trend for decades. Drainage of peatland generally results in shrinkage and oxidation; some tropical and temperate peats may suffer acid-sulphate problems on drainage. In parts of the UK Fens, drained peatland surfaces have subsided due to shrinkage at over $3.0 \, \mathrm{cm \, y^{-1}}$. In the same region, there are also losses of dried peat through wind erosion. Since their drainage in the seventeenth-century, the black fen soil areas of farmland in

East Anglia have been eroded so much that they are now only about one-twentieth of their original extent (*The Times*, 28/7/89: 14). In the UK, the Somerset Levels and West Sedgemoor, the Halvergate Marshes and areas of Exmoor have been drained and converted to farming, the main impact being the loss of wildlife (Lowe *et al.*, 1986: 187). Once peat has been drained, it can sometimes burn below ground; forest fires in Kalimantan, Indonesia left large areas of peat smouldering for a long time after the bushfires had passed (Briggs & Courtney, 1985).

In the People's Republic of China, large areas of peatland in the Zhujiang (Pearl) River Delta have been drained and converted to agricultural land (Ruddle, 1987: 172; 184). Much of the land being settled by the Indonesian Transmigration Programme is peatland (Ruddle, 1987: 175). There has been a great deal of afforestation on peatlands, notably in Finland and in other Scandinavian countries. The planting is generally with conifers and on a large scale. Plainting takes place after the peatland has been drained and treated with chemical fertilizers. The impact on the peatland wildlife is considerable and there are also likely to be impacts on regional hydrology, streamflow and stream water quality. Worries have been voiced in the UK over threatened continued afforestation of up to 40,000 ha of the Flow Country of Caithness and Sutherland, Northern Scotland, which has been largely prompted by profits and tax benefits to be gained from investing in this type of forestry.

So far, there are few crops which can be grown directly on peats without upsetting the peatbog ecology and releasing CO_2. Cranberry and blueberry growing, which are locally important in North America, are about the only options presently available (Moore & Bellamy, 1974: 202).

Much of the peat cut in Canada is exported to the USA for horticultural use. Eire's horticultural peat exports earnt over US\$ 18 million between 1983 and 1984 (Maltby, 1986: 130). *Sphagnum* and 'fen' peats are under particular pressure for horticultural use. In the UK, removal of horticultural peat from the Somerset Levels near Glastonbury and Thorn Waste, Yorkshire have generated controversy. It has been suggested that lowland UK peat deposits can meet the demand for horticultural peat only for about ten years more (*The Sunday Times*, 6/7/89: A7).

In the uplands of the UK there are areas of the blanket peat and raised bogs where the ecology appears to have been drastically altered over a wide area by acid deposition, particularly in the Pennines (*Sphagnum* spp., important peat-forming plants are very sensitive to acid deposition). In addition to acid deposition, peatlands are sensitive to direct or indirect contamination with fertilizers, detergents, industrial effluents, particles and dusts, pesticides, herbicides and heavy metals. The Chernobyl accident has shown that peatlands may retain radioactive fall-out for long periods. In Scandinavia, reindeer and other grazing animals feeding on peatland and tundra are still affected by Chernobyl fall-out.

Fen, marsh or swamp may be contaminated with sewage, farm waste, effluent from processing agricultural produce excess chemical fertilizer or agricultural lime. This enrichment (eutrophication) means a change in acidity and nutrient status that will affect the wildlife of the peatland, and will alter the quality and rate of accumulation of the peat.

Erosion is a threat in tundra and in upland peatlands, especially where peat overlies permanently frozen ground, and where there is a thin, mobile, ill-drained layer during warmer times of year. Scars caused by cross-country vehicles, walkers, road construction and by mineral exploitation may develop fast and persist for a very long time because plant growth and peat regeneration are restricted to a short summer. In Alaska and W. Siberia, there is the threat of leakage of oil or natural gas pipelines which could contaminate the peatlands.

Peat can be used to produce alcohol, montan wax, a high-value wax, briquettes to substitute for charcoal, fibreboard, kraft paper and cardboard, and other useful products. Improvements to briquette-making machines and automated harvesting may lead to more peat development to fuel railways, electricity generation and to supply domestic fuel, because the briquetting makes drying easier.

Peatlands are a 'carbon sink', they accumulate carbon from the atmosphere and 'lock it up'. In the *short term*, this sink role is probably not that important. However, burning or drainage and oxidation of peatlands will, as well as reducing the removal of CO_2 from the atmosphere, release carbon that has been accumulated possibly over several thousand years. Methane may also be liberated by micro-organisms as peats breakdown. Degradation of peatlands may well significantly increase the 'greenhouse effect'. Organic soils, of which peats are the main form, store roughly 500 times the CO_2 released by burning fossil fuels up to 1986; this assuming an average carbon content of 50% and using generally accepted estimates of the extent of peatlands (Maltby, 1986: 53).

When peatlands are drained, heavy metals that have been held in the peat may be released. These can cause considerable damage if they reach rivers or lakes (Winkler, 1985: 325).

TUNDRA

The tundra biome, which is mainly in the Northern Hemisphere, includes a diverse range of high latitude/high altitude habitats, all of which have in common: cool to extremely low temperatures for part of the year, a more-or-less complete vegetation cover of herbs, grasses, bryophytes, lichens, dwarf trees and shrubs. Soils are variable, some are well drained and some more-or-less waterlogged. While the upper 30 to 75 cm of soil thaw in the summer months, deeper levels remain frozen as permafrost, (Bliss *et al.*, 1981: 8). Tundra areas were more extensive during the Pleistocene glacial periods. Since about 12,000 BP they have shrunk, nevertheless there is still probably between 20 and 25% of the Earth's land surface which could be classed as tundra (of which there are about 20 million km² in the Northern Hemisphere). In general, tundra habitats have relatively few taxa and store a lot of organic carbon below ground (in effect large areas of tundra are 'frozen peatlands'), the risk of carbon dioxide liberation should there be a thaw has already been discussed.

Polar tundra and alpine tundra areas can be easily disturbed, especially in late spring and in summer when the surface layers of the soil have thawed and are saturated above an impermeable ice layer. If there is disturbance of the vegetation, especially where the ground slopes, there is likely to be erosion, and re-vegetation is typically very slow. Depressions and hummocks may form (thermocarst features). Solifluxion is also a problem wherever there is a slope and, with some soils, and, where it is cold enough, frost heaving and other cryoturbation phenomena may take place. Trampling, passage of vehicles, oil spills and overgrazing can degrade tundra.

Damage can be done during the winter in spite of a snow layer. Snow can be compacted by trampling, by skiers and by the passage of skidoos or other vehicles. The compacted snow does not protect the vegetation beneath in the same way as natural snow cover. There are also likely to be changes in melting in the spring which could reduce the growing season, and lead to local concentration of run-off causing local erosion. Passage across a thickness of snow could mean trampling or ski damage to the crowns of plants, where they emerge from, or are close to, the snow surface. Given the slow rate of vegetation growth, this could have serious consequences, particularly on shrub and tree regeneration. Many of these difficulties are associated with alpine ski resort development which is discussed in the next section of this chapter.

The tundras of the USSR have the longest history of human impact, those of N. America have been affected by development since the early nineteenth-century. Although in both Old and New Worlds, Man was active as a hunter-gatherer from prehistoric times to the present, and has probably caused the extinction of several species of large mammal (notably the mammoth and mastodon spp.; in the cast of N. America, 73% of large mammals were lost mainly between 14,000 and 10,000 BP, according to Roberts, 1989: 58) but his numbers have been so low as to cause little land damage. Since the end of the last century, mining activity has increased in tundra regions. Coal has been mined in Spitzbergen (Svalbard), although, as much for politico-strategic reasons as for profit, by the USSR and Norway since the 1940s. There were 'gold rushes' in the Yukon and Klondike of Alaska and the Yellowknife and Whitehorse regions of Canada late in the last, and in the first half of this, century. Gas and oil-fields are worked in Alaska, Canada and the USSR and, in both the New World and the Old World, gas/oil pipelines, service roads and railways have been driven across tundra regions. So far, the pipelines and roads seem to have done little damage, except possibly for disruption to animals through pipeline avoidance and hindered migration. In the USSR, a leak from the West Siberia to Urals natural gas pipeline burnt an area of taiga (high latitude woodland) in 1989.

Mining activity causes land degradation similar to that at lower latitude. However, the pipelines/roads servicing them may be more disruptive in tundra environments. Petroleum, lead, gold, uranium, asbestos, zinc, and other minerals are won from northern USSR, the north of N. America and Greenland. There is a chance that, in the future, breakdown of the Antarctic Treaty might allow more airport construction and mineral exploitation in the subAntarctic islands and Antarctica. In cold environments (as in dryland environments – indeed, cold regions may often be quite arid) recovery of vegetation cover after disturbance can be very slow. The re-vegetation of one gold mine's tailings in a tundra area of the USSR has made little progress after ten years.

The soils and the bryophyte/lichen/herb vegetation of tundra/alpine tundra areas seem to hold radioactive fall-out and other pollutants like heavy metals. Tundra areas in Scandinavia, contaminated by the Chernobyl accident, are still of little use for grazing.

PROTECTION OF WETLANDS AND PEATLANDS

There has been some progress toward better protection of wetlands; unfortunately, even in Europe, the pace of change has been slow. In the 1960s, the International Biological Programme (IBP) initiated Project AQUA and the IUCN began Project MAR. These were (respectively) designed to increase protection of wetlands and to increase awareness of the importance of wetland and peatland ecosystems and the threats to which they were exposed (Maltby, 1986: 93). In 1966, IUCN started Project TELMA the aim of which was to prepare a world list of peatland sites of international significance to science and promote their conservation. Much of the early impetus came from the International Wildfowl Research Bureau (Slimbridge, UK), following a series of conferences and meetings, e.g. the 1974 Heligenhafen Conference on the Conservation of Wetlands, the Bureau and others organized a Convention on Wetlands of International Importance, especially as waterfowl habitats. This is generally known as the Ramsar Convention, after the Iranian town where it was first held. The Ramsar Convention, drawn up in 1971, came into force in 1975, and was one of the world's first international conservation treaties with 45 signatory states. Reports in 1987 suggested that the Convention was short of funds, was breached by some of the signatories and did not include some crucial nations (Pain, 1987). In practice, signatories also apparently tend to ignore the terms to which they are signatory. In late 1989, the IUCN published a wetlands policy statement: *Wetland Conservation and Sustainable Development* (IUCN, 1989).

Wetland protection faces certain problems: a wetland probably cannot be protected effectively unless there is control over the catchment area supplying it with water. Any pollution or drainage in that catchment could affect the wetland. Therefore, wetland protection/conservation, to be effective, may require control of a large area that is probably subject to multiple demands, i.e. wetland management requires watershed management. Peatlands may be less of a problem in this respect if they are in the upper part of a catchment, which is the case with many blanket peats or raised bogs.

A further problem faced by those attempting to protect wetlands and peatlands has been the lack of an adequate database. With inadequate information on extent, structure and function of wetlands and peatlands, effective management is severely hindered. The International Biological Programme (IBP) has done much to improve knowledge of the structure and function of wetlands and peatlands, through programmes like its Tundra Biome studies. The IUCN has established a database on wetlands, and, in 1984/1985, with the World Wildlife Fund, worked on a Wetlands Campaign to raise funds for conservation (Sayer & McNeely, 1984).

DEGRADATION OF UPLANDS

There is no rigid, wholly satisfactory definition of upland or highland. Uplands include mountains, high plateaux and inter-montane basins, moorlands and hilly land, regions which for one or more reasons have a harsh or difficult environment and which may include peatlands and tundra-like environments. The difficulties depend on altitude, aspect and latitude and on whether the region is continental, an island or coastal environment. In higher-latitudes, especially away from the moderating effects of the sea, low temperatures become a problem for plants, livestock and Man at altitudes far below that at which they cause difficulty in the Tropics. At higher-latitudes, it is likely that low temperatures, particularly during winters, will hinder animal and plant life before low atmospheric pressure and/or high incidence of solar radiation, especially UV-B, become a problem. In the Alps of Europe, at mid-latitude, the growing season is shortened by roughly 6 or 7 days per 100 m rise in altitude.

Some uplands have parts, at least, which get more precipitation than lower altitude lands. In such upland, there is likely to be upland rainforest ('cloud forest' or elfin forest), or, if particularly high, exposed or with conditions in some way unfavourable for trees, scrub or moorland with peat deposits may form; much of what has been said in the last section applies to uplands.

Upland floras and faunas are, in part, the product of a history of past climatic change. During the Pleistocene glacial period the firn/frost line and the vegetation zones of uplands were shifted downslope. The shift was not uniform, that on a range or large upland differed from that on isolate peaks due to the Masseherebung effect, and there were differences between north-, south-, east-, and west-facing slopes and those adjacent to warmer seas. In Papua New Guinea, for example, the firn line (the lower limit of permanent snowfields) was depressed by up to about 1000 m, and, consequently, upper limits of the forest were depressed at times by as much as 1600 m (Flenley, 1982). In the event of future climatic change, conservation of upland species will depend on their being able to shift up- or downslope.

In the mountains and high plateaux (*altiplanos*) of the central Andes of Bolivia, Peru, Colombia, Ecuador and Northern Chile and the Himalayas, low atmospheric pressure and radiation do affect plants, animals and Man. There is often strong diurnal and seasonal temperature variation in uplands, and frost is possible at high altitude even in Sri Lanka, Papua New Guinea or Kenya. It is possible to get, at least occasional, frosts, in tropical uplands down to as low as 1500 m altitude (Mani & Giddings, 1980: 5). At high altitude on tropical mountains, e.g. in Ruwenzori or on Mt Kenya, vegetation must withstand high daytime temperature and solar radiation receipts and night-time freezing conditions, plus frequent high winds year-round.

Wind is commonly a problem, both in terms of exposure to prevailing winds and to local up- or down-mountain katabatic winds, Föhn winds, etc. High radiation and wind make many uplands very desiccating environments, to which the flora has to adapt to survive.

Uplands are likely to have areas with steep slopes, where erosion is a problem, where landslides are a risk and where avalanche may be a threat. The Highlands of Papua New Guinea, the Andes, Alps and Himalayas have frequent landslides.

Road communications are difficult in upland areas, soils tend to be thinner and climatic conditions harsher. Consequently, poverty is common, people lack political 'voice', are likely to have poor education and healthcare (Allen *et al.*, 1988). Yet, in the past, there have been civilizations, established at quite high altitudes, that fed their people and maintained road links in spite of the terrain: notably the Incas of the Andes.

Uplands are likely to suffer the effects of pollution more than other environments, because their vegetation cover intercepts wind-blown clouds that carry contaminants and because their plants are under 'stress', growing near to the environmental limits (El-Ashry, 1985). Because agriculture is closer to the 'margins' than at lower altitude, upland areas are likely to be more affected by climatic change.

In many parts of the world, the cool climate, and rugged scenery are an attraction. In India, Africa and Malaysia there are 'hill stations'/resorts where those who can afford to can escape the heat of lowlands and view different scenery and flora. Tropical uplands are free of many of the diseases that plague tropical lowlands. For this reason, and because the tree cover can be easier to clear, people have tended to settle these lands. There is also increasing siting of communications equipment, meteorological and astronomical observatories in uplands which may cause some damage to the environment.

The uplands are not an insignificant part of the Earth's surface, nor are they empty. Between one-quarter and one-third of the world's land surface is 'upland', and roughly one-tenth of all mankind (*c.* 400 million) live in these lands, mainly in Africa, Asia and South America (Müller-Hohenstein, 1975: 5: 19). Writers like Eckholm (1976: 75) have argued that about 40% of the world's population, if not actually living in the uplands, are affected by what people do in uplands, in that they benefit from eroded soil or suffer from floods, possibly caused by upland misuse. There are several large, high altitude cities including Quito, Ecuador; Lima, Peru; La Paz, Bolivia (3658 m above sea level); Lhasa, Tibet (3685 m); Imata, Peru (4404 m); Mexico City, Mexico (2308 m).

In many upland regions, human and livestock populations are increasing rapidly. However, it seems likely that, in Latin America, upland populations, although rapidly increasing in some areas, (Andean countries have averaged a 25% population growth rate for the last 30 years) are presently lower than they have been in the past. This is probably a consequence of the introduction of European diseases during the Conquest and, in countries like Bolivia and Peru, because of out-migration caused in part by feudal landownership patterns. Upland populations are unevenly dispersed, generally heaviest concentrations are inter-montane basins or on plateaux. Peru probably has the worst upland overpopulation. In upland areas of Europe and the UK, out-migration may be a problem, especially in the Massif Central of France, in that it results in a population with distorted age, sex and educational characteristics.

Some countries are virtually all upland, for example: China is roughly 65% mountains, and Nepal, Afghanistan, Tibet, Bolivia, Switzerland and Austria, Iran, Ecuador and Colombia have a high proportion of upland. In Africa, Rwanda and Burundi have over 50% of their territories above 1000 m altitude, Kenya is over 40% upland, and Ethiopia, Tanzania, Zimbabwe, Malawi and Uganda have a lot of high ground. In Venezuela, 16% of the population live in the upland Andean states which comprise a mere 3% of the national territory.

Misuse of an upland environment might not only affect local people; sediment and/or altered streamflow can affect populations and environment even hundreds of kilometres away in lowlands. However, the precise nature of this relationship has not generally been worked out: to blame upland peoples for lowland flooding (this is something of a cliché) is usually based on little more than suspicion (Little & Horowitz, 1987; Ives & Pitt, 1988; Ives & Messerli, 1989).

Deforestation of uplands

In uplands, people are likely to require more fuelwood for heating than at lower altitudes; trees are also likely to be slower growing, as in lower altitude drylands. There is overgrazing in many uplands, but, in Nepal, Turkey and Afghanistan, the situation is particularly bad. It is quite common in uplands worldwide for farmers to cut grass/hay, tree and shrub branches to stall-feed livestock. Where slopes are steep and soils thin, stall-fed cattle are more productive and cause less erosion than free-ranging or tethered beasts; they are also less likely to fall and injure themselves. In spite of widespread stall-feeding, grazing/fodder demands have caused serious deforestation in many uplands, notably in Nepal. Little & Horowitz (1987: 291) observed that, although there was a lot of deforestation on the Peruvian Andes Amazon-side slopes, there was little agricultural development. Many countries now prohibit logging above a certain altitude, but enforcement is often insufficient.

Cultivation and pastoralism in uplands

The uplands of Bolivia are quite densely settled and intensively farmed for tuber crops, including the potato and grain crops of chenopodium species or edible lupin, as high as 3800 to 4000 m around Lake Titicaca. Livestock: llamas and alpaca, may be pastured in summer, as high as 4500 m in the uplands of Bolivia, and, in the Himalayas, yaks may be grazed to a similar altitude. Cattle seldom range above 4000 m. Afghanistan may have as many as 17 million nomads living between 1500 and 3500 m. The Western Hindu Kush is quite densely settled, with cropping to 3500 m and pasturage, at least in summer, to about 4000 m.

In many, if not all, uplands, a seasonal pattern of transhumance has developed. Livestock are taken up-slope in the early summer, and return in autumn. In some regions there is a seasonal in- or out-migration of people seeking employment. Some of the world's best tea and coffee are grown at high altitudes in: Kenya, Jamaica, Papua New Guinea, Sri Lanka, Malaysia and Costa Rica.

Because policing uplands is often difficult, because the climate can be cooler and moister than at lower altitudes, some uplands have been attractive to squatter farmers. In the Cameron Highlands of Malaysia, squatter farmers produce vegetable crops for urban markets on very steep land, cutting terraced fields, in some cases having terraces with a drop of over two metres. The soil erosion from such operations, combined with heavy use of pesticides, can cause considerable damage downslope in wetlands and floodlands. In Latin America, Indochina and Afghanistan/Pakistan illicit drug production, *coca* in the former, opium in the latter two areas, is common. In Bolivia, rising *coca* prices have stimulated squatter settlement of the *altiplano* and the settler's degrade considerable areas with shifting cultivation (Eastwood & Pollard, 1987).

Soil erosion in uplands

Upland soil erosion may be more of a problem in the Tropics and subtropics because the climate is less of a constraint on farming. In Papua New Guinea, crops are grown up to 2800 m altitude (Mt Wilhelm). Ploughing is recorded in the Ethiopian Highlands as high as 4000 m, and regular cropping takes place up to 2000 m. Upland soils tend to be thin and stony and, if the slopes are steep, soon erode.

In some ways, the situation today in uplands like those of Nepal is similar to that in Switzerland in the 1880s. Serious deforestation has led to increased erosion and possibly flood damage downslope. In Switzerland, the response was to pass and enforce forestry laws. It remains to be seen whether passing and enforcing such laws is possible or will work as well in Third World countries.

Tourism impact

In Europe, the Alps have been settled for centuries, and much of these lands are no longer natural; they have been altered and are now, in a state of 'balance' maintained by farming and forestry, but frequently also used for tourism: notably skiing and hillwalking. If, for some reason, farming or forestry are neglected, then degradation may occur and tourism can play a key role in this. In an ideal world, tourism would give an alpine area winter employment in wintersports, woodcarving, hotel management, etc, and would yield funds for environmental management and to bolster up marginal land agriculture.

In practice, tourism depends on forests and the attractive pastures of traditional farming but does not invest in these (Price, 1987). There is a tendency for alpine farmers to neglect farming to earn better money running hotels. Pastures grow too long and forestry is neglected. The scenic value of the region declines, and, with this neglect, there is a growing sprawl of hotels. Winter snow slips off the neglected alpine grasslands more than it would from well-grazed grasslands, because the long grass bends and fails to anchor the snowpack, and because it can ferment and form a lubricating layer, causing avalanche damage and erosion. To compound the problems of Alpine areas, warm winters seem increasingly common and mean reduced tourism revenue to pay for heavy investment in lift equipment, roads, etc.

The best-studied Alpine agricultural community is that of Obergurgl (Austria). Settled from AD 1400, the sunny western valley sides were cleared for pastures, and pastoralism flourished to the degree that, by 1830, marriage was prohibited to control population and younger people out-migrated (Müller-Hohenstein, 1975: 77; Moser & Moser, 1986). In the twentieth century, Obergurgl has attracted tourism. From 1971, the impact of tourism on Obergurgl has been researched under the Man and Biosphere Programme, and a detailed management strategy has been deveolped for the valley.

Hopefully there will be an increasing trend to functional integration of tourism and farming in European uplands, with more of the profits of the former diverted to subsidize and support the latter.

Since the 1960s, there has been a marked increase in skiing. In the Alps, the Sierra Nevada (Spain), Andorra, the Bulgarian Tatras, Norway, Sweden, Poland and Yugoslavia, Colorado (USA), and in parts of Japan, Australia, New Zealand, Chile and Argentina there has been widespread construction of pisted runs and facilities to serve skiers, and, in recent years, increasing use of artificial snow-making equipment. In the Alps alone, there are an estimated 41,000 downhill ski trails, most longer than 1 km. Construction of pisted runs involves disturbance of natural vegetation, often by bulldozer or grader – recovery is generally very slow.

Some pistes are sown with exotic grass species and these exclude native herbs and grasses. The effect is to open up grass areas that were once forested or had a shrub or herb/grass cover. Once opened, these areas tend to have later but more rapid snow-melt and can channel meltwater and summer run-off to lower slopes where gullying or sheet erosion occurs (Price, 1987). If not well sited, or if the runs are not grazed enough in summer, or, if the grass is not cut and removed as hay, there is a risk that winter snow will dislodge from these slopes more easily than from natural pastures and cause avalanche damage (as was the case at St Anton, Austria in 1979). The opening of runs may allow the wind to get into belts of trees and then topple areas of established forest Mosiman, 1985).

During winter, unless the resorts are well managed, skiers may go off-piste and cause damage to shrubs and smaller trees. The overall effect is to hinder and discourage forest and shrub regeneration, which, in turn, reduces avalanche and erosion protection. Artificial snow-making may lead to excessive accumulations of snow and ice and increased run-off; there is also a risk that chemical or biological additives may be mixed with the water used to make the 'snow' (the equipment is also noisy and makes heavy demands on local water supplies).

Price (1985) felt that the impact of skiing was worst on convex slopes where snow cover was thin because the passage of skiers caused compaction and delayed spring melt which reduced the length of the growing season (artificial snow-making may have a similar effect). Increased tourism in uplands inevitably means electricity supply, accommodation, road and sewage disposal facilities.

In Scotland, there has been concern that skiing disturbs wildlife, particularly grouse breeding. The impacts of skiing may be greater in Scotland than in the rest of Europe, because the UK has relatively little alpine/tundra vegetation (Wilson *et al.*, 1970; Bayfield, 1971; Mitchell, 1979: 183; Simons, 1988c). The greatest controversy has been caused by developments and proposed developments in the Cairngorms, particularly at Lurchers Gulley (part of the Northern Corries Site of Special Scientific Interest) and at Lecht and Glen Shee.

If climatic warming takes place, many ski resorts, which have cost a lot to establish, may cease to be profitable, environmental management will probably be neglected, and there will be pressure to develop facilities where there are good snow conditions, possibly in Scandinavia, higher areas of the Alps and in the Rockies.

In uplands, where tourist activity involves walking or climbing, the main problems are: littering with cans, bottles and plastic packaging or discarded equipment, all may take many years to decompose; the wearing of paths, a problem in the Pennines and Lake District of the UK, where, in some areas, special stone or gravel and rubber-membrane paths have had to be constructed; disturbance of wildlife (for example, on Mt Kenya) and increased risk of accidental fire (Mahaney, 1986).

Where upland villages have developed a tourist industry, a problem is satisfactory disposal of sewage and refuse. All too often this has meant the pollution and eutrophication of upland lakes or streams. In the Tropics, there have been extensive, recreational resort, golf course and casino developments in uplands, for example, the Cameron Highlands, Genting Highlands, Frazers Hill and Penang Hill resorts of Malaysia and summer hill resorts in N. India. It seems likely that more countries will turn to harnessing streams for electricity, and this will lead to dams and flooding of upland valleys by reservoirs and the construction of mini-hydroelectric plants. The latter do not actually impound flows and may be preferable to fuelwood use and deforestation in nations like Nepal or Tibet.

Degradation due to mining in uplands

Bolivia and Peru have high altitude mines (copper, lead, zinc, tin). The main problems associated with such mining are: air pollution, especially dust and acid deposition, noise from processing, chemical effluent, spoil-heaps and deforestation to provide props, fuel, etc. If mining pollutes streams with compounds such as mercury or arsenic, then a very large part of the catchment could be affected.

Transport and communications development impact

In recent years, there has been considerable increase in communications across uplands; there are new highways in Tibet (Gerrard, 1988: 240), the Andes and through the Alps. Road and rail routes can cause landslides, and the former, atmospheric pollution especially if there is a lot of lorry transport. In Europe, the proposed Alpine Protection Treaty will probably encourage or force as much heavy transport as possible onto trans-Alpine electric railways in order to cut pollution.

Many uplands now have telecommunications equipment positioned near their summits, and, in Colorado, the Canary Islands, Hawaii and the Snowy Mountains (Australia), there are quite large astronomical and meteorological observatories. Where there has been ski resort development, cable cars, and various forms of lifts have usually been installed; these often make access to the uplands easier in the summer months, leading to increased wear of paths and fellfield or moorland vegetation.

DEGRADATION OF ISLANDS

Islands are often crowded, and thus are prone to all the familiar land degradation of the mainland. In addition, they seem vulnerable to plant and animal species loss (Troumbis, 1987). There is an extensive literature on island biogeography, particularly on species losses, a literature that is of interest to those concerned with mainland conservation areas as well as those concerned with islands, but it is a literature within which many theories are not yet substantiated (Kent, 1987: 91).

Island biogeography: relevance to island degradation

An understanding of the way in which species are lost from islands is of crucial importance for conservation because, in effect, conservation areas are 'islands' in a 'sea' of disturbance/development.

Acording to biogeographers, there are two basic types of island: oceanic and continental shelf islands (see Chapter 11). For a given size of island, these would be expected to differ in species numbers, species retention, and species:area relationships. Macarthur & Wilson (1967: 26–30), suggest that, given time, an island will establish a balance between extinction of its species and immigration by new species (the 'equilibrium theory') such that the number of species will remain roughly constant (see Fig. 7.3). It has been argued that extinction rate depends in part on the size of an island and in part on the habitat, heterogeneity (more diversity of habitats is likely to result in more species). These views are not universally accepted (see Gilbert, 1980), but, if they are true, the implications are that: smaller islands are likely to have less diversity of habitat, and a catastrophe like a drought, fire, storm or eruption will leave less land unaffected, and probably lose more species over time. Miller (1978: 191–2) examined the relationship between species number and island size, and arrived at the following equations:

$$S = CA^z \tag{3}$$

or

$$\log S = \log C + z \log A \tag{4}$$

(to give a linear output)

Where: S = number of species in a given taxon

C = constant giving the number of species when A has a value of 1

A = the area of the island

z = the slope of the regression line relating S and A (i.e. the relationship between species number and island area)

Colonization is believed to depend largely on the distance between the island and a continental landmass or other islands. There can be no precise rules because plants and animals differ in their resistance to extinction and in their ability to disperse and to colonize new territories. The concept of relaxation time (Kent, 1987: 96) implies that, after a new island is formed, or

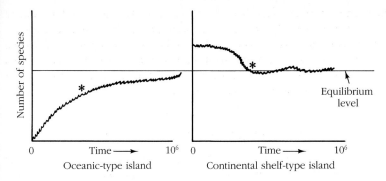

Fig. 7.3. Oceanic and continental shelf-type islands: species numbers over time (assuming both to have originated without plants or animals or to have had these removed by, say, a volcanic eruption). Source: Based on Harris, 1984a: 72 (Fig. 6.1).

when an existing island is disrupted, species take time to reach a new equilibrium.

These concepts have been applied to conservation areas on land, forest reserves, etc, by those wishing to predict how many species a reserve can maintain, what size or shape it should be and how close to other reserves or natural environments it should be (Gorman, 1979: 65) (see Chapter 12). If relaxation time applies to conservation areas on land, such as Amazon rainforest reserves, there is a need for conservation services to exercise caution. The prediction, if relaxation time applies, would be that a reserve might initially hold too many species, which will decline until relaxation time has elapsed. Even very well-managed reserves might thus lose species for some time, and some species present in a new reserve may disappear.

The causes of degradation of island environments

Increasing human populations

There can be little doubt that some island environments have become degraded because of the demands of rising population; for example, Easter Island has been overpopulated at various points in the past and appears to have completely lost, through human activity, a once extensive cover of woodland within the last 1000 years. The palm species that formed those woods is now extinct, not one plant remains on the Island (Flenley & King, 1984; Roberts, 1989: 136).

Historical records show the Madeira Islands once had an extensive tree cover; their name reflects this. Not long after their discovery by the Portuguese in the fifteenth century, the forests were destroyed (Roberts, 1989: 157).

Introductions and 'invasions' of new species

The deliberate or accidental introduction, or natural dispersal, of plants and animals to islands, especially more remote oceanic islands, has caused tremendous loss of species (Sage, 1979b). There is a large literature on the problems faced by the Hawaiian islands. Another island group suffering from invasion and introductions are the Galapagos. A shrubby tree, first introduced in 1946 – the red quinine (*Chinchona succirubra*) has recently begun to seriously threaten the native flora and fauna over large parts of the Galapagos (Macdonald *et al.*, 1988).

Overgrazing, fire, felling and hunting

The list of islands where Man, either aboriginal settlers, European colonists or seafarers (and their feral or tended livestock) have destroyed tree cover and wildlife is a long one, and one which includes: Madagascar (loss of the *Aepyornis* spp., *Hippopotamus lemerti*, and many other animals), New Zealand (loss of the *Diornis* spp. – the moas and many other species) and Mauritius (the loss of the dodo). Once widespread in the Caribbean and Central America, hardwood trees like the mahogany and greenheart are now, at best, uncommon.

Throughout the literature on island degradation, the introduction of goats, pigs and, to a lesser extent, cattle are cited as the cause of problems. For example, Saint Helena has lost most of its, once extensive, woodland: the blame has been levelled at goats released in 1513 (Coblentz, 1978; Gall, 1981; Dunbar, 1984). In cooler latitudes, introduced sheep, rabbits and in a few cases (e.g. on S. Georgia and Kerguelen Is.) reindeer, have done great damage to island tussock grasses, and to upland tussock grasses in New Zealand, in the New Zealand islands, islands of the southern oceans and South Atlantic. On Tristan da Cunha (S. Atlantic) the tree *Phylica arborea* was common before grazing livestock and fuelwood collection began in the nineteenth century, and now it is close to extinction. On the Ile Amsterdam (S. Indian Ocean) a *Phylica* spp. related to that on Tristan da Cunha is suffering a similar fate. Rabbit damage has been especially bad on the Iles Kerguelen and Macquarie Island.

Island degradation due to altered market conditions, fashions and technological change

The present state of many Caribbean islands owes much to the demands from Europe, during the eighteenth, nineteenth and twentieth centuries, for mahogany, sugar, coffee and, more recently, bananas and tourism (Watts, 1966, 1987). The production of latter commodity, and the associated clearing of natural forest for plantations, began only after suitable steam shipping and refrigeration made transport to market possible.

In the Mediterranean, some islands have seen a reduced demand for their dried fruits, mainly due to the spread of refrigeration since the 1950s, plus altered consumer demands. Consequently, olive, fig, almond and plum orchards and terraced fields have been neglected (Margaris, 1987: 133). In the Aegean, there has been a trend toward neglecting 'extensive' olive production in favour of intensive' sunflower and maize-oil production, which is seen as more profitable. Unfortunately, the 'intensive' production is much less suited to the environment, and soil erosion is increasing. Also in the Aegean islands, acorns were once used for tanning and people encouraged oak trees. Now chemicals are used for tanning and there is no longer an incentive to nurture and plant oaks. The same is true of pines, which were much used in the past for pine-nut and resin production. Resin is now chemically synthesized and interest in encouraging/managing pine trees has diminished (Margaris, 1987: 135).

Military activity and mining

Over the centuries, islands have suffered damage from warfare, because they were of strategic value for controlling ocean communications or as coaling ports or harbours, because they offered easy provisions or fuelwood

supplies, or because they were defensible positions and were besieged. More
recently, islands have been used for airstrips, to test destructive weapons, or
as sites for communications and surveillance stations. During the 1940s,
islands like Guam, the Bonnins, Iwo Jima and Eniwetok suffered tremendous damage due to high explosive bombardment. From the 1950s, a
number of oceanic islands have been badly blast damaged and contaminated
by fall-out or have been virtually destroyed by nuclear testing (see Chapter
11).

Mining, particularly for phosphates, has done great damage to some
oceanic islands. Barnaba in the Pacific has suffered to the extent that its
inhabitants have had to abandon it. Nauru (Central Pacific) is also being
badly degraded and islands of the W. Indian Ocean share a similar fate
(Fosberg, 1972).

Island degradation as a consequence of damage to coral reefs and/or mangroves

Where waters are warm (above 20 °C), shallow and silty mangroves may
grow and protect the land from storm waves. Throughout the Tropics,
island and mainland shores are suffering erosion following the loss of
mangroves (the problem of mangroves degradation is discussed earlier in
this chapter).

Warm, clear waters may develop coral reefs. Such reefs break up waves
before they can reach the shore and thus offer considerable storm protection,
expecially for oceanic islands. Some atolls are, at least in part, formed by the
growth of coral. Worldwide, there are an estimated 115,000 km² of coral
atolls and there are an estimated 617,000 km² of fringing reefs protecting
island and mainland coastlines (Pain, 1990).

Coral is being damaged worldwide by: the products of terrestrial erosion
brought down by streams to silt up clear coastal waters; by sewage and
industrial effluent; by the removal of coral for building-stone or cement-
making, or for sale to tourists; by dragging anchors and by the crown-of-
thorns starfish (*Acanthaster planci*) which has spread in recent years. A survey
of the status of coral reefs is provided by the UNEP & IUCN (1988). There
are some grounds for optimism *if* reef damage can be controlled, for the
indications are that the 'greenhouse effect' might encourage reef growth,
especially the fringing reefs (Pain, 1990).

8 Land degradation in drylands

DRYLANDS

DRYLANDS may be defined as environments where there is permanent, seasonal or periodic significant moisture deficiency. Such conditions are to be found in tropical, subtropical, temperate and polar latitudes. Even in Amazonia, if soils are free-draining, periods of soil moisture deficiency are possible (Cloudsley–Thompson, 1975). One may subdivide using a wide range of parameters, for example, mean annual rainfall; length of dry or wet seasons; monthly precipitation; vegetation characteristics (Heathcote, 1983: 12–20; Barrow, 1987a: 24–7; Beaumont, 1989: 3), but the lack of precise, widely used definitions hinders mapping and discussion of dryland degradation.

In 1951, UNESCO launched an Arid Zone Research Programme, One of its tasks was to provide an acceptable definition of aridity – the result the Meigs Index (1953) which relates available rainfall to potential evapotranspiration. Subsequently revised, it has been widely accepted for subdividing the world's drylands (UN, 1977; Adams *et al.*, 1978: 15; Hall *et al.*, 1979: 73). Using Meigs' Index, drylands can be subdivided into: semi-arid lands (Index − 20 to − 40); arid lands (− 40 to − 57) and extremely arid lands (− 60 and lower) (Meigs, 1953).

A less precise, but useful, subdivision is into: 1. *semi-arid* – environments which allow the development of a more or less continuous vegetation cover, ranging from woodland to open grassland, but which are too dry or variable to permit secure, regular rain-fed cultivation of normal crops; 2. *arid* – vegetation is very sparse or absent, and is unlikely to include trees; there is no season in which crops could be raised using natural precipitation alone (Walker, 1979: 7); 3. *extremely arid* – most unlikely to have vegetation cover unless there is groundwater within a few metres of the surface.

Dryland vegetation cover can easily be damaged, and, once this happens, re-vegetation can be difficult. Soils are often deficient in humus or nutrients, particularly phosphates, or both, and what there is can be rapidly lost. There are likely to be seasonal and/or diurnal extremes of temperature, rain when it falls may be intense and erosive, and strong winds or bushfires are a risk. In short, drylands are vulnerable to land degradation.

Roughly 35% of the world's total land surface (40.0 million to 49.0 million km²) may be classed as drylands, roughly 14% of this is semi-arid (21.2 million km²), roughly 15% of this (21.8 million km²) is arid, and roughly 4% (5.8 million km²) is extremely arid (Furley & Newey, 1983: 309;

Independent Commission on International Humanitarian Issues, 1986a: 20; Matlock, 1981: 4). An estimated 37% of the world's drylands are in Africa, 34% in Asia, 13% in Australia, 8% in North America, 6% in South America and 2% is in Spain (Heathcote, 1983: 17). Somewhere between 500 million to 850 million people (roughly 17% to 20% of the world's population) inhabit drylands or depend upon them for a living. The bulk of these dwell in the semi-arid regions, where rates of demographic increase have often been considerable in recent decades (Ruddle & Manshard, 1981: 107; UNEP & Commonwealth of Australia, 1987: 4; Dixon *et al.*, 1989: *xv*).

It has been claimed that roughly 7% of the world's soils are more 'arid' than would be expected from the climate, and that some 9% of the vegetation cover is out of balance with climate (Eckholm, 1976: 60; Heathcote, 1983: 16–20). Caution needs to be exercised, because precipitation which seems adequate to maintain a vegetation cover may not be if, for example, the soil suffers from one or more of the following problems: fast drainage, crusts, is thin, has too high a salts or alkaline content, lacks nutrients or has poor infiltration characteristics. Other factors may well conspire to restrict plant growth, e.g. pests and diseases, extremes of temperature, bushfires, heavy grazing. In some situations, human activity is why soil or vegetation does not match with what the physical environment would seem capable of supporting, in others it may be that climate was more favourable in the past.

DESERTIFICATION

Terms used when discussing drylands degradation include: desertification, desertization, desert-encroachment, aridization, aridification and xerotization. Not only has there been a diversity of terms, but the same term has been differently defined by various authors (Eckholm & Brown, 1977: 7; Verstraete, 1983: 216; Wells & Haragan, 1983: 186; Grainger, 1990). The first two have been used to indicate change to more arid conditions, in some cases with no comment on cause; in one case (Glantz, 1977: 2) the two indicate difference in degree of degradation. There has been a tendency to use desertification to imply Man-induced degradation, and desertization – natural causes. In at least one case, desertification is used to mean irreversible degradation. Gorse & Steeds (1987: 2) distinguish between what they call 'desert spread' in semi-arid and arid environments and 'induced desertification' in more humid areas.

Desertification has become the most commonly used term . . . 'an unsightly word for an insidious problem' (Walls, 1982: 38). Probably first used by Aubréville (in 1949), there is still debate about definition of desertification; in spite of many major conferences, there are probably over 100 definitions, in some cases applied to a process of change, in others to the end state of a process of change. (Reining, 1978: 3; Dregne, 1985; Street, 1987; Adefolalu, 1983: 414; Gorse, 1985; Mabbutt, 1987; Mortimore, 1989). Definitions which mention 'spreading deserts' tend to obscure the fact that a large proportion of desertification occurs *in situ*, often well away from desert, itself a vague and unsatisfactory term, sometimes in quite humid environments (Goodland & Irwin, 1975).

Given the range of disciplines involved in study of desertification, it may not be that crucial to arrive at one overall definition, but, without it, synthesis of information is difficult. Given that desertification is one of the most serious problems facing the world, better terminology would make sense. For the purposes of this book, desertification may be taken to mean

Table 8.1. *Indicators of desertification.*

Physical indicators
decrease in soil depth
decrease in soil organic matter
decrease in soil fertility
soil crust formation/compaction
appearance/increase in frequency/severity of dust/sand storms/dune formation
    and movement
salinization/alkalinization
decline in quality/quantity of groundwater
decline in quality/quantity of surface water
increased seasonality of springs and small streams
alteration in relative reflectance of land (albedo change)

Biological indicators
vegetation
decrease in cover
decrease in above-ground biomass
decrease in yield
alteration of key species distribution and frequency
failure of species to successfully reproduce

animal
alteration in key species distribution and frequency
change in population of domestic animals
change in herd composition
decline in livestock production
decline in livestock yield

social/economic indicators
change in land use/water use
change in settlement pattern (e.g. abandonment of villages)
change in population (biological) parameters
demographic evidence, migration statistics, public health information.
change in social process indicators
increased conflict between groups/tribes, marginalization, migration, decrease in
    incomes, decrease in assets, change in relative dependence on cash
    crops/subsistence crops.

Sources: Reining, 1978: 5–8, 10; Kassas, 1987: 391.

the degeneration of ecosystems in semi-arid or arid regions, degeneration usually being measured in loss of primary productivity and/or species diversity.

Crucial questions

1. What are the indicators of desertification? What are the measurable aspects, how can these be measured, monitored, assessed? Can one region be compared with another? Indicators may be physical, social or economic (Reining, 1978; Olsson, 1983) (see Table 8.1 for a listing of the more obvious manifestations of desertification).
2. How is desertification perceived? What are the reactions of people, governments, non-government organizations (NGOs) etc?
3. Where is desertification occurring? The extent and degree of degradation. This is not always an easy question to answer as some governments have been/are reluctant to gather data on 'negative development', or do not have the facilities to do so.

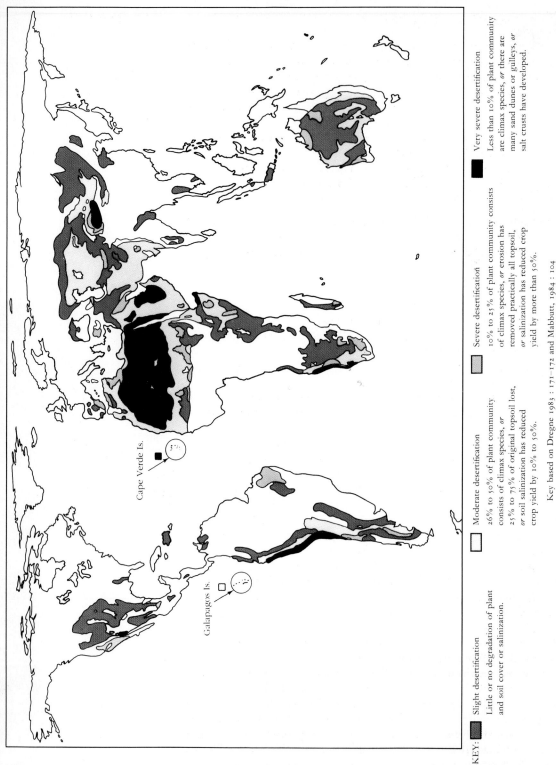

KEY:

Slight desertification

Little or no degradation of plant and soil cover or salinization.

Moderate desertification

26% to 50% of plant community consists of climax species, *or* 25% to 75% of original topsoil lost, *or* soil salinization has reduced crop yield by 10% to 50%.

Severe desertification

10% to 25% of plant community consists of climax species, *or* erosion has removed practically all topsoil, *or* salinization has reduced crop yield by more than 50%.

Very severe desertification

Less than 10% of plant community are climax species, *or* there are many sand dunes or gulleys, *or* salt crusts have developed.

Key based on Dregne 1983 : 171–172 and Mabbutt, 1984 : 104

Cape Verde Is.

Galapagos Is.

Fig. 8.1. World status of desertification. Source: author. Author sources: Barrow 1987a: 40.

4. What is the rate of desertification? How fast and how severe is the degradation?
5. What are the causes? There may be apparent 'direct' causes and/or 'covert', often indirect (in time and/or space), causes that are difficult to identify. Desertification may be the cumulative result of two or more, possibly unrelated, and, at first sight, non-threatening causes. If due to long-term, inexorable climatic change, mitigation efforts may be pointless.
6. What are the implications? What are the environmental social and economic costs?
7. Are there avoidance, mitigation and/or rehabilitation measures which can be applied? What is technically, environmentally, institutionally and economically feasible?

The awareness that desertification is a problem depends on the outlook of various groups of people; there may be abundant indications, but these may go unnoticed or unheeded (Heathcote, 1980; Spooner & Mann, 1982).

How great a problem is desertification?

Because the definition of desertification has not been precise, and monitoring has generally been poor, much of the statistics published are 'guesstimates' lacking accuracy. Air photographs and satellite remote sensing are often the best available means of establishing present extent, and, by comparing recent with past photographs, estimating the rate of change. Often, however, there is a need for better ground verification. As there is a continuum from slight to severe desertification, attempts to map categories of severity are inherently inaccurate. In 1977, the UNEP published a (provisional) *World Map of Desertification*. More detailed maps have been published since then, for example, that of Dregne (1983) but few give a reliable breakdown of degree of desertification. Figure 8.1 broadly indicates extent and severity.

Recent estimates suggest roughly one-third of the world's total land surface (around 48 million km²) is 'threatened' by desertification (Spooner, 1986; World Resources Institute & International Institute for Environment and Development, 1987: 71; Dixon *et al.*, 1989: 8). A 1983 estimate was that 47,063,000 km² were desertified, of which 8,773,000 km² was severely or very severely affected. More recent sources suggest 9,115,000 km² are desertified (Tolba, 1987a: 364). Roughly 52% of the world's drylands are probably affected to a slight degree, roughly 29% moderately, roughly 18% severely and about 0.2% very severely (Dregne, 1983: 174; IUCN, 1986: 11; UNEP, 1987: 20).

Table 8.2 gives a breakdown of desertification by region and land use (1985 situation). Whilst figures vary considerably, a number of sources agree that Africa has been badly affected. UNESCO (1977: Fig. 11.2) mapped areas of Africa considered to be at particular risk of desertification.

Rangelands seem worst affected, but, as more people depend upon rain-fed arable cultivation, so the threat to the latter could be said to be more crucial in that it affects food and commodity crop production. Dregne (1985: 19) estimated that 27.1 million ha of the world total of 126.3 million ha was significantly desertified. Ahmad & Kasses (1987: *viii*, 2) suggested that, of the world total food-producing area of around 13 million km², roughly 40 million ha were significantly damaged by desertification.

It is difficult to establish the extent and trends of desertification when agencies and individuals often use terms like 'significant' or 'serious' without

Table 8.2. *Percentage of dryland regions at least moderately desertified.*

Region	Rangelands	Rain-fed croplands	Irrigated lands	Total drylands
Sudano–Sahelian Africa	90	80	30	88
Africa south of				
Sudano–Sahelian Zone	80	80	30	80
Mediterranean Africa	85	75	40	83
W. Asia	85	85	40	82
S. Asia	85	70	35	70
Asiatic USSR	60	30	25	55
China and Mongolia	70	60	30	69
Australia	22	30	19	23
Mediterranean Europe	30	32	25	39
Latin America	72	77	33	71
North America	42	39	20	40

Note: includes subhumid regions with semi-arid and arid.
Source: based on Dregne, 1985: 28.

defining what they mean (see Fig. 8.2), estimating the rate of change is much more of a challenge. It is likely that the annual loss of land worldwide to 'significant' desertification is at least 50,000 km², an area larger than Belgium. Of that land, it seems likely that around 6,000,000 ha y^{-1} becomes 'irrevocably' unproductive and a further 21 million ha y^{-1} of 'potentially productive land' becomes 'economically useless' (UNEP, 1987: 120; Anon, 1987a).

What are the causes and processes?

Many statements in the literature are '... either weakly connected (shopping lists of "causes" unrelated to one another) or unduly hypothetical (plausible arguments not supported by case-specific data)' (Mortimore, 1989: 119). Table 8.3 lists categories of argument put forward to explain why desertification takes place. Whatever the cause(s), the process of degradation or desertification in all but the most arid regions generally involves damage to the vegetation cover. In the very arid areas, there is little or no vegetation to destroy so that in a sense there can be no desertification, although there can be erosion of soil/rock started or accelerated by the passage of man, animals or vehicles.

    Desertification can be the consequence of a complex mix of hidden and apparent causes (Warren & Maizels, 1977). Therefore, even though there may appear to be similar processes and causes at work in different regions, the reality may be very different, and interpretation needs caution (Spooner & Mann, 1982: 5; Dregne, 1983: 96). Another trap for the unwary trying to unravel the causes of desertification is that there are often 'feedback mechanisms', which means that there is a web of causation/feedback/causation, such that a physical cause might lead to a human feedback and that to further physical causes or vice versa.

    The way desertification proceeds may vary according to land use. Figure 8.3 illustrates, in a stylized manner, how yields might fall under different land uses.

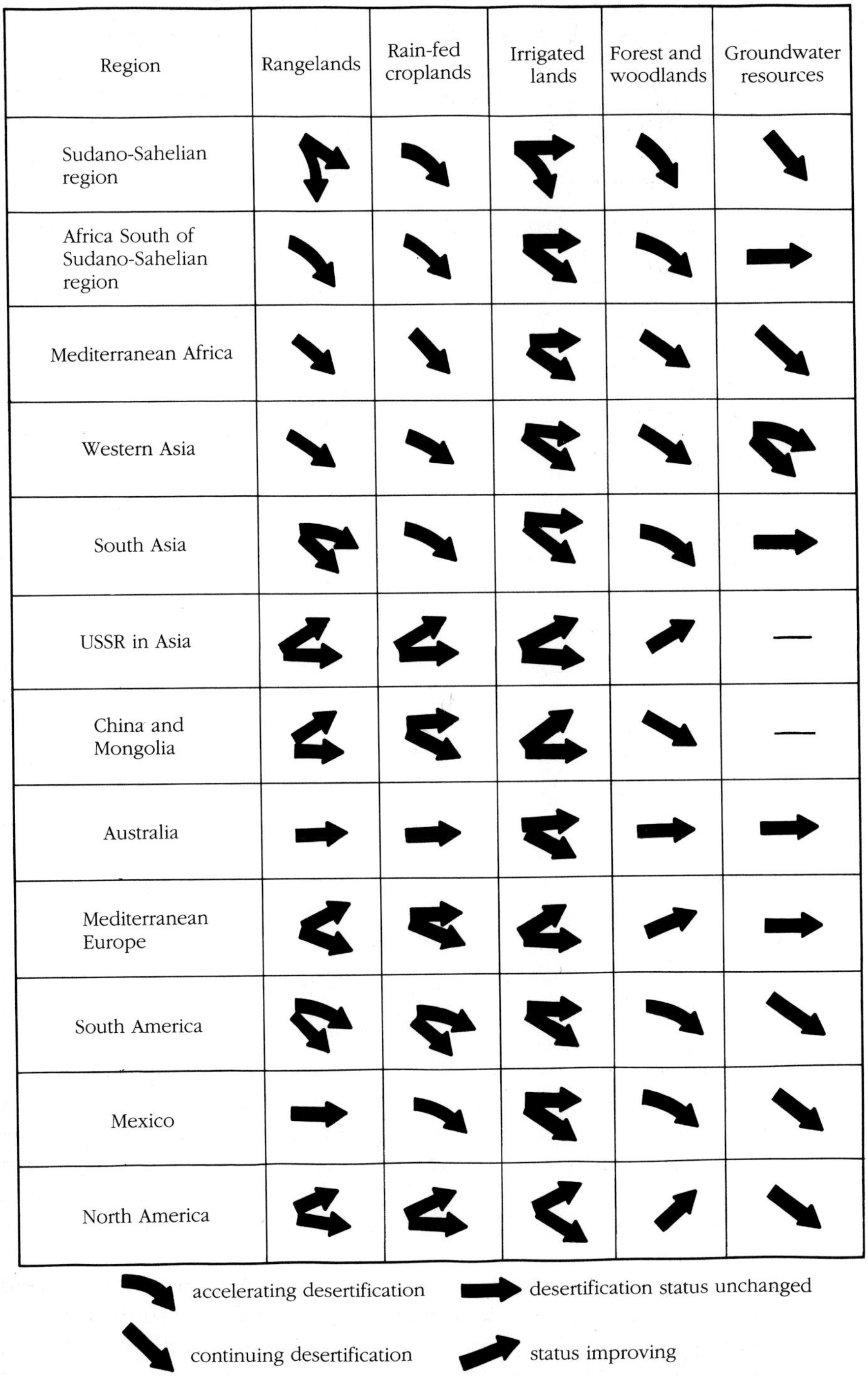

Fig. 8.2. Regional trends in desertification by land use category.

Region	Rangelands	Rain-fed croplands	Irrigated lands	Forest and woodlands	Groundwater resources
Sudano-Sahelian region	accelerating	continuing	accelerating	continuing	continuing
Africa South of Sudano-Sahelian region	continuing	continuing	accelerating	continuing	unchanged
Mediterranean Africa	continuing	continuing	accelerating	continuing	continuing
Western Asia	continuing	continuing	accelerating	continuing	accelerating
South Asia	accelerating	continuing	accelerating	continuing	unchanged
USSR in Asia	accelerating	accelerating	accelerating	improving	—
China and Mongolia	accelerating	accelerating	accelerating	continuing	—
Australia	unchanged	unchanged	accelerating	unchanged	unchanged
Mediterranean Europe	accelerating	accelerating	accelerating	improving	unchanged
South America	accelerating	accelerating	accelerating	continuing	continuing
Mexico	unchanged	continuing	accelerating	continuing	continuing
North America	accelerating	accelerating	accelerating	improving	continuing

Legend:

accelerating desertification   desertification status unchanged

continuing desertification   status improving

Fig. 8.2. Regional trends in desertification by land use category. Chart with arrows based on Environmental Conservation, 11(2) 1984, p. 100.

Table 8.3. *Categories of argument put forward to explain why desertification takes place.*

Natural causes:
Desertification is held to be primarily due to physical events: drought/climatic change, pest or disease outbreak. If so, possibly inevitable causes prevail and there are less opportunities to avoid/mitigate desertification although it might be possible to forecast trends and modify development to take account.

Human causes:
Population (Malthusian/Neo-Malthusian) arguments: desertification is blamed on growth of human population and/or livestock populations.
Structural arguments: social and economic structures and relations (patterns of ownership, rights of use and control of resources) are held to blame.
Political and economic causes arguments: political/economic factors which may be local or non-local (terms of trade, Third World debt, etc) are held to blame. The former might be countered by local people, the latter will require action outside the area suffering desertification.
Human fallibility arguments: desertification results from stupidity, greed, ignorance, short-sightedness of local and/or non-local protagonists (peasants/herdsmen, governments, developers), inappropriate technology or approaches (ill-informed 'do-gooders' may be a cause).
Resource exploitation: people are attracted into drylands to exploit the vegetation or soil for crops/livestock. However, there are situations where drylands are degraded for other reasons, e.g. nuclear weapon testing, mineral exploitation.

Natural causes of desertification

In drylands, plants often grow near their limits of tolerance. Vegetation patterns may form where topography concentrates run-off, collects precipitation or where plants are able to reach moisture, or the plants themselves have a growth form leading to circular or strip patterns with patches of bare ground. *Brousse tigree* ('tiger stripes') are formed by savanna grasses and herbs in, for example, Somalia, the Saharan fringes and in Central Australia (UN, 1977: 207; Heathcote, 1983: 83; Cole, 1986: 293, 344). With vegetation so close to the limits, even slight changes in environment can lead to more bare ground and/or species losses or change of species gradation, i.e. degradation (DeVos, 1975: 134).

Drought

A drought may be said to occur when a region has insufficient moisture to meet the demands of plants, people, livestock or wildlife. The shortage may be due to precipitation being significantly less than normal for the period in question (meteorological drought), or it may result from increased demand for moisture, if crops are altered to a more moisture-demanding type or because farmers alter their demands, i.e. it can be due to human attitude changes. An agricultural drought then occurs. Drought may be due to changes that prevent the absorption and storage of precipitation in the soil (hydrological drought) (Adefolalu, 1983: 412; Timberlake, 1985: 19; Glantz, 1987: 8; Mortimore, 1989: 11, 185).

Droughts are not restricted to any particular environment although they are especially common in certain regions especially tropical drylands. Droughts may be short-lived and localized, or widespread, or persistent and localized, or widespread; they may be recurrent with a clear pattern or random.

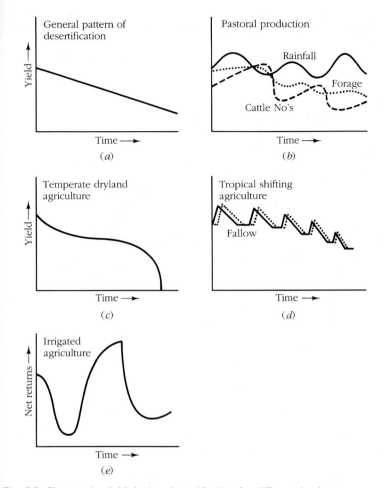

Fig. 8.3. Changes in yield during desertification for different land uses.
Key: (a) = General pattern.
   (b) = Approximation to situation under pastoral production.
   (c) = Approximation to pattern in drylands where persistent cropping
         overtakes the soil nutrients, reduces organic matter content and
         causes erosion.
   (d) = Pattern where drylands shifting cultivation has degenerated.
   (e) = A generalization of what happens in irrigation projects, a pattern of
         rising yields, breakdown, possible rehabilitation and so on. Source:
         based on UN (1977: 175– Fig. 2).

Drought can lead to desertification, but desertification can occur without there being drought. Drought often 'highlights' or triggers clear signs of desertification (Dregne, 1983: ix; 7).

Vegetation may suffer from drought, or drought may arise because vegetation has been damaged. Once the land surface changes, drought conditions may become more common or persist. There are a number of theories as to how drought might lead to further, more intense and more persistent drought, and desertification (for a review of degradation-induced drought, see Hulme, 1989). These 'feedback' processes may involve:

- reduced infiltration and/or water retention as vegetation thins, soil organic matter decomposes and soil parches. With reduced soil moisture, less cloud forms over the land, surface temperatures rise and airmass movements are affected (Charney, 1975; Charney et al., 1975; Mortimore, 1989: 148);

– degeneration of soil fertility as a result of decline in humus content
   soils then erode more easily and plant cover decreases;
– generation of enough airborne dust to affect air temperature and
   movements;
– clearing of woodland or overgrazing resulting in altered albedo and
   reduced evapotranspiration, downwind rainfall may decrease.

In West Africa vast areas of forest/woodland, which once transpired a lot
of moisture, have been removed from the path of winds that blow upon
drylands, and fears have been voiced that such winds now carry less rain.
The same might happen in Amazonia if forest clearance progresses. There is
evidence from southern USA/northern Mexico that differences in cattle
grazing practices can alter conditions of semi-arid rangeland. The USA had
better enforced limits on stocking; NASA remote sensing found the
difference to be clearly apparent with the summer daytime temperature rising
4°C higher just south of the border (Friedman, 1989). It is likely that such
grazing/albedo changes happen elsewhere and could initiate drought
(Otterman, 1974). Arnon (1981: 113) claimed to recognize such a desertification process for the Rajaputna Desert (India), where he claimed seventh-
century AD overgrazing altered vegetation leading to regional climatic
change that has meant more-or-less permanent desert conditions ever since.

When examining the role of drought in desertification, the following
questions should be addressed:

– Is there a pattern of droughts, can it be predicted?
– What are the causes (are all droughts in the region due to the same
   causes, is human action making droughts worse)?
– Are human activities making the land more vulnerable to drought
   and/or are cropping/livestock rearing strategies more or less vulner-
   able to drought?
– Can drought be avoided/mitigated?
– Are there feedback mechanisms operative?

There is abundant palaeoecological evidence of drought, for example:
mummified dinosaur remains are common in Jurassic deposits of around 140
million years ago (Bakker, 1988: 157) and in various regions Tertiary and
Pleistocene dunefields indicate past drier conditions. N. Indian, Africa and
the Americas have palaeodunes formed before 10,000 BP (Sing et al., 1974).
Raised shorelines around many of the world's lakes, and botanical evidence
in Amazonia and the Far East, indicate wetter and drier periods than present
within the last few million years (Allchin et al., 1978; Bryson & Murray,
1977: 48; Dalby et al., 1977: 65; Goudie, 1977: 88; Hare, 1977a, b; Lamb,
1982).

There has probably been a natural, progressive global desiccation during
the last 5000 or so years, but the change has not been uniform in time and
space (UN, 1977: 85; Bell, 1987: 84; Gregory, 1988). African drylands seem
to have been drier between 20,000 and 15,000 BP, wetter than now 12,000 to
7,000 BP; over the last 3000 years there may have been a gradual
reduction of rainfall, if any change (Beaumont, 1989: 197).

Separation of natural from anthropogenic causes of desiccation during the
last few thousand years is often dfficult. Authors refer to Roman cultivation
in now arid N. Africa as evidence of either, altered climate or desertification
due to misuse of the land. In reality there could be other causes, such as: the
loss of cheap slave labour; the incursion of nomadic pastoralists and/or
unwillingness or inability of farmers to maintain rain-fed farming systems
(Spooner & Mann, 1982: 53; Barrow, 1987a: 173).

There is a possibility that at least some droughts might be initiated by factors like: Milankovitch-type orbital variations; altered dust and ash levels in the atmosphere; fluctuations in global CO_2 level: changes in general atmospheric airmass circulation due to oceanic temperature variation; a large amount of snowcover over Eurasia and N. America (Gribbin, 1986). Some global-scale processes are affected by human activity, so some drought could thus be said to be indirectly due to human causes (Hare, 1979). If this is the case, past natural occurrence of drought might have limited value in forecasting future patterns.

A number of researchers have examined the recurrence of droughts (for example, for Africa: Schove, 1977; Glanz & Katz, 1985: 335). A table of drought occurrence for Africa, the Americas, Asia, Europe and Oceania, based on 1986 WMO data can be found in UNEP (1987: 321–3).

Much attention had focused on claims that the Sahelian–Sudanic Zone of Africa has suffered more drought in the last 30 years because the pattern of precipitation has changed, becoming higher over the Mediterranean, and lower and/or more erratic in distribution in time and space south of the Sahara. One assumption is that these changes are due to a southward shift of the Inter-Tropical Convergence Zone, possibly in response to oceanic temperature changes, caused by salinity variations that bring deeper cold water to the surface from time to time, or to variations in snowcover over Eurasia, where heavy spring snows delay the rise of air pressure over Eurasia which 'drives' rain-bearing monsoons to India and possibly other parts of the world (Gee, 1988a). The cause of these changes could be the 'greenhouse effect', volcanic dust pollution, or both (Charney et al., 1975; Glantz, 1976: 214; Bryson & Murray, 1977: 101, 111–14; Nicholson, 1983; Gribbin, 1985: 1986).

There is growing evidence that rainfall fluctuations in many regions are linked to large-scale ocean–atmosphere interaction (WMO, 1986; UNEP, 1987: 303). One such ocean–atmosphere interaction which has attracted attention of those concerned with drought in the Sahelian–Sudanic Zone, Australasia, S. Asia and Latin America is the El Niño–Southern Oscillation (ENSO), (Lockwood, 1984, 1986; Allan, 1988). El Niño events are manifest as episodes of warmer than normal sea surface temperatures particularly off Peru and Ecuador. In 1982, sea temperatures off Peru rose by 10 °C leading to wind system disruptions in the eastern equatorial Pacific (Boyle & Ardill, 1989: 62). There are indications that El Niño events caused flash floods in Peru in the past; in AD 600 and AD 1100 such flooding seems to have severely disrupted local cultures (New Scientist, 125 issue 1706: 30). There appears to be a strong link between El Niño and ocean–atmosphere events in the Pacific, particularly the air pressure variations and thus wind system changes known as the Southern Oscillation. There are other airmass circulations which possibly determine climatic conditions, for example, the Quasi-Biennial Oscillation, which some believe is a factor which might play a role in the depletion of Antarctic stratospheric ozone.

In 1982–83, severe drought in Australasia was associated with an intense ENSO event. In 1986 and 1987, it was possible to predict ENSO events as much as nine months in advance (Gribbin, 1988a), and Sahelian–Sudanic Zone rainfall 18 months in advance (Anon, 1987b). Once the ENSO is better understood, it may be possible to forecast drought in Africa, in areas of India dependent on the southwest monsoon, and in Indonesia, S. Africa, Papua New Guinea, Amazonia/Northeast Brazil, Peru and Ecuador (Land, 1987).

Grazing by wild animals, animal and plant invasions

Wild animals or feral livestock may degrade vegetation enough to initiate desertification. Some animal species respond to environmental opportunities with a population 'boom', and may overgraze. One suggestion is that termites, common in many semi-arid environments, may aggravate heavy grazing by wild herbivores or domesticated livestock, and 'tiger stripes' vegetation may result from such damage (DeVos, 1975: 148; UN, 1977: 207). There might be situations where locust or grasshoppers denude vegetation cover enough to trigger desertification. Animal species introduced into a region may multiply unchecked by natural predators or diseases and overgraze: in Australia, the rabbit has done sufficient damage in some areas to initiate desertification.

Locust invasions Locust invasions have been recorded in Africa and the Near East since *c.* 3300 BP (*Exodus*, 10: verse 12–verse 19). The desert locust and the red are the main problem, spreading if conditions in a region alter to favour their increase. This is likely to be caused by a reasonable rainfall, but conditions may be made more favourable by human activity, which leads to suitable 'nursery' areas. DeVos (1975: 152) suggested that irrigated land and greenery alongside canals could give locust an initial breeding site, better than would be provided by nature.

Five species of locust cause most problems in Africa (see key of Fig. 8.4) plus grasshoppers like *Kraussaria angulifera* and the rice locust, *Hieroglyptus daganensis*. The problem is not confined to Africa; grasshoppers and locust, the former are less migratory, can cause problems throughout the Tropics/subtropics, for example, in Australia the locust *Chortiocetes terminifera* can cause problems after rains (Goodall & Perry, 1981: 90). There are also species in Latin America and N. America that can cause problems (Heathcote, 1983: 1; Winstanley, 1983).

Locust problems generally follow good rains (at least 25 cm) in an area normally fairly dry. This provides suitable conditions for mass egg-hatching of locust eggs which can lay dormant in dry soil for some years. The second controlling condition appears to be air temperature. Locusts take from 10 to 71 days to hatch, depending on air temperature, and, when ready for flight, they require an air temperature above 20 °C. When conditions are ideal, three or four generations of locust can be produced in a year. The locust, particularly the desert locust, is highly mobile as 'hoppers' on the ground and as flying adults which are transported downwind (Wells & Haragan, 1983: 197). A swarm of locusts, which could be as much as 40 km × 6 km in size, can consume a vast amount of vegetation in a very short time, and, in semi-arid environments, this sort of damage can lead to wind and water erosion and vegetation may take a long time to recover; to the disadvantage of farmers and pastoralists.

Since about 1986, all five of Africa's problem species have increased, particularly in Eastern, Central and Southern Africa and in the SSZ, Mali, Senegal, Niger, and Ethiopia they have had severe problems since 1986 (Godwin, 1986; Jago, 1987). The increases are not just because of favourable environmental conditions. In 1986, one of the main anti-locust organizations closed (the Organisation International Contre le Criquet Migrateur African – OICMA). This left the task of control mainly to the FAO and the Organisation pour Lute Antiacridien et Lutte antiaviaire – OCLALAV, which has been underfunded. Underfunding, rising costs of pesticides, plus a ban on the effective compound dieldrin, and civil unrest which has hindered

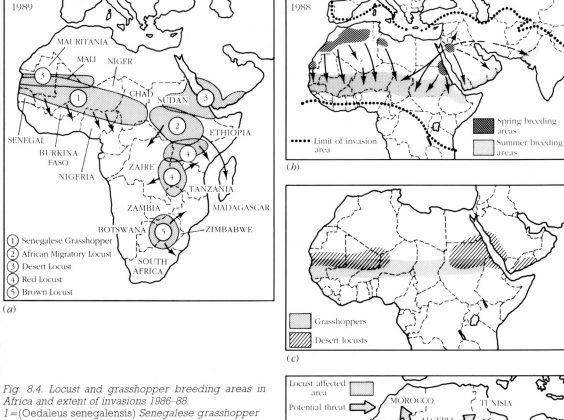

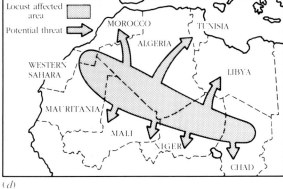

Fig. 8.4. Locust and grasshopper breeding areas in Africa and extent of invasions 1986–88.
1=(Oedaleus senegalensis) Senegalese grasshopper
2=(Locusta migratoria migratoriodes and L. migratoria capito) African migratory locust
3=(Schistocerca gregaria) Desert locust
4=(Nomadacris septemfasciata) Red locust
5=(Locusta pardalina Brown locust
(a) Main breeding areas (approx.) of five main locust species 1987–88 (various sources). Arrows indicate typical direction of invasion; (b) September 1988 situation, as bad as any year on record to that date MacKenzie, 1988c: 26); (c) Typical locust/grasshopper breeding pattern, 1987; (d) Potential threat to countries around the Sahara.

access for monitoring and control, and an apparent recession in the threat before 1986, meant that control has declined in the last ten years. Yet, with modern satellite remote-sensing, monitoring and control should have improved. The last big locust invasions were in 1963. In some regions, land development has helped to increase locust/grasshopper problems. For example, in Madagascar, the increase of grassland, as forest has been removed, has favoured breeding of L. Migratoria capito (Olson, 1987: 82).

There has been the suggestion that locust can cause drought, in that the insects denude enough vegetation to alter the albedo of an area which, in turn, causes weather conditions which prevent or hinder rainfall. This is unproven and Winstanley (1983: 200) suggests that locust invasions tend to follow droughts rather than precede them.

By 1987, the EEC, concerned that there might be a spread from Morocco, North Africa or even from the Sudan to S. Europe, spent over US$ 62,000 in

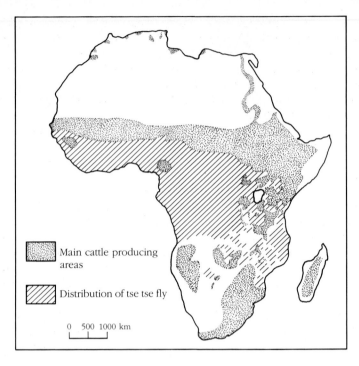

Fig. 8.5. The distribution of cattle and tse tse fly in Africa. Source: *Rapp* et al., *1976:*
33 (Fig. 2.2); IIED, WRI, World Resources Institute et al., *1987: 224 (Fig. 14.3).*

aid to African locust control (Johnson, 1987). A recent press article
suggested that, in 1988, control of locusts in Africa cost over £30 million. In
spite of this expense, a few locust managed to reach Wales and South West
UK in October, 1988 and, something previously unrecorded, specimens of
Shistocerca gregaria were recorded from Martinique, Surinam, St Vincent,
Trinidad, Tobago, Dominica and Antigua (*The Times*, 3/5/88: 8; 21/10/88:
24). Saudi Arabia suffered severe problems in October 1988, and there were
fears that swarms would reach Pakistan, India and Southern Europe (where
a cold spell killed off some invaders). The 'renaissance' of the locust since the
1960s stresses that control of land degradation is a delicate and on-going
process; a few years of success are no indication that a problem has ceased.

Tse tse fly The presence of the tse tse fly (*Glossinia mortisans* and *G.
tachinoides*) has effectively denied large areas of subSaharan Africa (at least 10
million km²) to livestock production (Fig. 8.5) (Ford, 1971).
    The control or eradication of tse tse, or an effective and cheap treatment
for the disease they carry, *nagana* in livestock and in Man, sleeping sickness
(African trypanosomiasis), would open up vast new areas to cattle. This
might well have more bad than good impacts.
    There are a number of proposed means for controlling the tse tse and the
disease it carries, ranging from spraying with pesticides, trapping the flies
with attractant pheromone compounds, mass release of sterile male flies and
drugs and vaccines to counter the trypanosome (Allsopp *et al.*, 1985). If the
wrong pesticides are widely used in an attempt to control tse tse, tremendous
damage could be caused to wildlife, soil flora and fauna and riverine animals
(*Unasylva*, 1978–30, 18–24; *The Ecologist*, 1985–15, 27–35; *IUCN Bulletin*,
17, 92; Linear, 1982; 1985: 233). The worst threat, however, is that, if
constraints on the use of this 10 million km² were removed through effective

tse tse control, bush clearing would accelerate, cattle numbers would rise fast, and there would be both considerable increase of individual pastoralists with their livestock and a risk of a 'hamburger-connection' – large-scale beef ranching to supply meat to the developed nations (DeVos, 1975: 149). The longer the delay before these lands can be used, the better, for improved more environmentally 'friendly' land-use management strategies might be developed and disseminated.

A similar situation exists with respect to the blackfly (*Simulium damnosum*), carrier of river blindness (onchocerciassis). People and livestock are kept out of areas of scrub and woodland near certain types of stream where this pest is abundant.

Quela birds Over large parts of subSaharan Africa, the quela bird: the red-headed dioch (*Quelea erthrops*) and the black-faced dioch (*Quelea quelea*) cause great damage to crops. In the Guinea savannas of the SSZ, these pests can strip farmers' rice, millet or sorghum crops, especially fields which mature early, as may be the case if someone adopts a new seed variety. Ruined farmers may then be forced into land misuse to try and obtain alternative food supplies, and desertification can ensue. Farmers, who might otherwise intensify production from a limited plot of land, may continue to practise extensive cultivation, for fear of crop loss to *Quela* from well-managed fields. Consequently, gradual decline of poorly managed non-intensively farmed land continues.

The resistance of a vegetation cover to overgrazing might be improved by introducing alien species, for example, African grasses to South American savannas or leguminous forage species like white clover of alfalfa to Australia. Such introductions require caution, for they could damage natural flora and fauna or trigger soil acidification. In parts of the USA/Mexico, introduced 'salt cedar' (*Tamarix* spp.) raise salt from below ground. And such deep-rooting, actively transpiring phreatophytic plant species may lower groundwater causing sufficient damage to the native vegetation to start desertification. A change in vegetation, as an invading species takes over, could, alternatively, mean less transpiration loss, raised groundwater and desertification through water logging and salinization.

Drought may debilitate a crop so that weeds become a problem; being more robust they better withstand drought. Even if rains return, the farmers' yields may be so depressed by the weed infestation that they neglect their land or try to reduce fallow periods and damage soils in an effort to grow more. Such a 'downward spiral' leading to desertification has been associated with 'witchweed' (*Striga* spp.) which, in subSaharan Africa and India, can reduce grain crops, especially sorghum or millet by 90% (Nour *et al.*, 1986).

Fire

Fire can be started by natural causes such as lightning. However, there is some doubt that natural 'wildfires' have sufficient effect on vegetation to actually cause desertification unless the vegetation is altered by Man. Vegetation is likely to be adapted to natural fires so that it has the ability to withstand burning and/or re-seed or re-sprout. Prevention of natural fires may lead to alteration of natural vegetation cover and possibly land degradation. In some regions, Man initiates so many 'wildfires'/bushfires that the recurrence interval between burns becomes so short that vegetation and soil deteriorate.

Human causes of desertification

There are situations where desertification results from natural causes, but these are triggered or aggravated by Man. There are situations where, if things remained undisturbed by Man, degradation may well have been much less and/or slower to develop (UN, 1977: 173; Goudie, 1981: 46; Lateef, 1980: 4). There are situations where purely human causes operate. And there are situations where causes are a complex mix.

Increasing human populations

It is often argued that desertification results from too many people for the environment to support (Hardin, 1968; DeVos, 1975: 168; Dalby *et al.*, 1977; Ruddle & Manshard, 1981: 116). However, there are regions with severe desertification, for example, Australia and large parts of subSaharan Africa, where there are fewer than 16 persons per km² – for comparison, at the time of writing, China's average population density was about 100 per km² and India's about 225 per km². Such figures are a little misleading, for most of the population in, say, China is concentrated in much less than the total land area, an average thus gives rather a distorted picture (Bell, 1987: 83). Why then is degradation occurring where human populations are so low? Franke & Chasin (1980: 117) suggested that, in West Africa, degradation takes place because there is insufficient labour, without which roads cannot be put in or maintained, agriculture cannot be sufficiently intensive and the economy cannot be developed. Bush-rotation – shifting cultivation – farming is disrupted when population growth happens suddenly, so that land use has not had a chance to intensify, or because there has been increase, but not enough increase, in numbers or, because labour is in short supply for some reason. These conspire to discourage intensive, sedentary cultivation (Timberlake, 1985: 39).

In rangelands of Australia and Western USA, desertification of low-population areas is primarily the result of a few ranchers carrying too many stock. Elsewhere, caution is needed. A low average population may obscure local overpopulation: population above the level which the land could sustainably support and, in particularly vulnerable environments, even a light population may be enough to do damage.

While it is often difficult to establish a definite population increase–land degradation relationship, there are many drylands where population has markedly increased. In Rajasthan (India), for example, population has risen from 36,000 to 96,000 in roughly 70 years (Ruddle & Manshard, 1981: 116); in Africa's Sahelian–Sudanic Zone there is reputed to have been a 2.5% per annum population increase, which means that by AD 2110 it will be double what it was when the 1968–73 drought began (Grainger, 1982: 53). The challenge is to establish what the 'critical population', human and livestock, is for each ecosystem.

Overgrazing by domestic livestock

Overgrazing and its impacts are not fully understood and terminology is confused. Overgrazing can have a range of effects (see Table 8.4) and can result from a complex of causes. At the general level, there does seem to have been an increase in stock in many drylands. Between 1955 and 1976, cattle numbers in developing countries are estimated to have risen by 34% and sheep and goats by 32% (Arnon, 1981: 111). Herd/flock increases are, in part, due to better veterinary care for animals and to better healthcare for

Table 8.4. *Possible effects of overgrazing.*

Reduction of vegetation cover and probably trampling. Depending on the type of livestock, may cause compaction and reduced infiltration or loosening of the soil surface which increases erosion. The effects may resemble a drought, even if precipitation has remained unchanged.

By reducing savanna grass cover, grassland fires become less frequent and bushes/trees increase. A false impression may be given that things are flourishing. However, the reduction of grasses and herbs under the growing scrub may allow greater soil erosion when it rains and reduction of infiltration. Also, dry matter accumulates under the bush and trees where livestock no longer graze; when fire finally starts it is more intense than previous grassland bushfires, and does far more damage to vegetation and soil (Bell, 1987: 84).

Unpalatable, spiny or difficult-to-graze plants tend to survive, other plants tend to decrease. The effect may be patchy. Where there are few ungrazed plants vegetation may be stripped; elsewhere, where grazing is unattractive, there is little degradation.

Alteration of tree/shrub regeneration. Scattered savanna trees/shrubs or forest may be prevented from regenerating, e.g. in Africa, *Acacia albida* is vulnerable to seedling damage through excessive grazing. Some savanna/woodland species will not successfully regenerate unless their seeds pass through the digestive tract of a grazing animal, either to kill damaging insect larvae or to break dormancy, this includes some *Acacia* spp. Some plant species' seeds germinate and survive better where existing vegetation is disturbed, for example, by overgrazing or livestock wallowing. Overgrazing may thus favour regeneration of some species and hinder others. Thus, the result of overgrazing can be replacement of grassland by bush or scrub, sometimes the opposite may happen.

Overgrazing may raise dust. This may be sufficient to cause more stable atmospheric conditions with subsiding airmasses the result of which could be a reduction of precipitation. It has been suggested that this process operates in Rajasthan (India) and the Sahelian–Sudanic Zone (Bryson, 1967).

humans, particularly immunization against diseases like smallpox. The blame for overgrazing has generally been levelled at peasants/herdsmen or on inclement weather/climate change. Ecologists have often blamed 'mismanagement' resulting from traditional patterns of land use, particularly where communal land ownership and individual herd ownership coincide. Social scientists are more likely to blame external factors, for example, expansion of large ranches or the breakdown of traditional grazing controls as a result of 'modernization', like the use of trucks to make new areas accessible to livestock. Beaumont (1989: 181) observed that it is possible for 'modernization' to cause the loss of youth from the rural areas; consequently those who are older or who have family commitments may tend herds/flocks nearer villages. Traditional range can thus be neglected, and, with trucking livestock, new areas may come under pressure.

Accurate identification of cause(s) of overgrazing may be difficult and the concept itself causes problems. Western concepts of 'correct' grazing level, 'resilience' and 'overgrazing' may not be appropriate, dryland herders may well have a strategy that allows for overgrazing. In drylands, annual variation in vegetation productivity is likely to be greater than short-term progressive decline of vegetation (Homewood & Rodgers, 1987: 113; Mortimore, 1989: 209, 213). To a pastoralist, the basic unit of land is not productivity per animal, and it makes sense to maximize production in good rainfall times and to lose production in bad. Migration, if possible with livestock, may help reduce bad-times' losses (Mortimore, 1988: 64).

There may be incentives for pastoralists to 'overgraze'. By doing so, they might reduce the risk of damaging bushfires and control taller grasses that harbour ticks which carry livestock diseases. Studies of pastoralism have tended to see stable production as desirable, implying stocking restrictions matched to the worst possible rainfall conditions, studies have also tended to assume one or a few years' data describes every year, whereas it is unlikely to do so.

Pastoralists may begin to overgraze their pastures because their traditional grazing-damage reduction or response and drought-avoidance strategies have broken down (Sandford, 1983: 475–8; Christiansson, 1988; Falloux & Murkundi, 1988). Overgrazing may also be the result of:

- Hindered migration.
- Government efforts to 'sedentarize' the people and their stock.
- The sinking of wells or the provision of watering places, food-aid distribution centres, healthcare posts, trading centres, which tend to attract and hold pastoralists too long in a given locality. A tear-drop-shaped piosphere of overgrazing/trampling, the head of which faces into the prevailing wind, is likely to form around the attraction.
- Commercialization of production which causes pastoralists to increase stock and/or attracts in large-scale ranching.
- Health and/or veterinary care which has led to increases in human and/or livestock populations.
- Loss of traditional administration of grazing rights.

Sedentarization has been a common cause of desertification, the motives for its promotion vary from a desire by authorities to make it easier to provide modern services to scattered peoples, to a wish to establish closer rule. For example, Rezah Shah of Iran attempted the latter in the 1920s, when he tried to sedentarize the pastoralists of the Zagros Mountains to curb their political power (Beaumont, 1989: 181).

Large-scale ranching has become a major cause of deforestation and of overgrazing. In Central and South America, and in parts of Africa, large-scale ranching has grown in response to increases in the world market prices of beef. In the USA, users of beef have for some time found it cheaper to import it from Brazil or Honduras rather than produce it in-country. This, so-called 'hamburger-connection', also promotes ranching elsewhere, for example, in E. Africa as a response to cheap beef demand in Europe. In North East and Amazonian Brazil, rising land values and tax incentives make inefficient and land-damaging large-scale ranching an attractive proposition to the rich investor. Even if the cattle fail to make a profit, the tax write-offs against ventures elsewhere in Brazil and land speculation give handsome returns (Branford & Glock, 1985; Joss et al., 1986: 107).

Tended goats, cattle and feral livestock are often blamed for deforestation and overgrazing. It is uncertain whether goats damage vegetation enough to cause serious land degradation as often as it is claimed they do. Goats can consume large amounts of woody material and may deliver the *coup de grâce* after cattle grazing, bushfire or fuelwood collection has already caused ruin (Spooner & Mann, 1982: 44). Dunbar (1984: 33) suggested that, because goats prefer bush and tree vegetation, they open up some savanna woodlands, increase the groundcover and so might actually reduce soil erosion. Usually, it is the herders who strip the trees, set fires to improve grass growth or who keep goats in a locality too long until damage is done.

'Undergrazing'

Decreased grazing, by wild animals or domestic stock, can result in vegetation change. Typically, herb and grass species diversity falls and

Table 8.5. *Actual and sustainable numbers of people in the SSZ.*

Zone	Crop/livestock sustainable population (1)	Actual rural polulation (2)	(1)−(2)	Fuelwood sustainable population (3)	Actual total population (4)	(3)−(4)
			(million)			
Saharan ⎫ Sahelo–Saharan ⎭	1.0	0.8 ⎫ 1.0 ⎭	−0.8 ⎫ ⎭	0.1	0.8 ⎫ 1.0 ⎭	−1.7
Sahelian	3.9	3.9	−	0.3	4.0	−3.7
Sahelo–Sudanian	8.7	11.1	−2.4	6.0	13.1	−7.1
Sudanian	8.9	6.6	2.3	7.4	8.1	−0.7
Sudano–Guinean	13.8	3.6	10.2	7.1	4.0	3.1
Total	36.3	27.0	9.3	20.9	31.0	−10.1

Notes: *The SSZ subzones used in this table are those shown in Fig. 8.6.
The World Bank (1985: 13, 26) concluded that:
1. Woodland/forest is vulnerable, given fuelwood demand and, in five of the six belts of the SSZ actual population exceeded sustainable population.
2. Fuelwood supplies were inadequate in the Sahelian, Sahelo–Sudanian and Sudanian belts.
3. The indications were that the Sahelo–Sudanian Belt was most at risk, i.e. the central belt of the SSZ, a conclusion echoed by Gorse (1985: 10), who suggested desertification control should focus on this belt and that people should be relocated to the Sudano–Guinean Belt.
Source: World Bank, 1985: Table 4, p. 26.

shrub/tree species become more common. As shrubs/trees increase, the groundcover below may thin and/or become more rank in growth; the result may be increased soil erosion and/or more intense bushfires.

In Africa, there is evidence in some regions that human and livestock populations have fallen, probably due to diseases, and scrub has become more widespread than previously. In North America, settlers killed off buffalo (*Bison bison*) herds in the late nineteenth century resulting in vegetation changes. Considerable shrub growth formed on the English downlands after myxomatosis reduced rabbit populations in the 1950s. Poaching or disease can reduce wildlife grazing, and game/livestock grazing may fall following drought, herd restriction legislation and falling market prices for meat or hides.

Fuelwood forage and dung collection

The earliest discussions of dryland degradation blamed tree clearance (Stebbing, 1935; Mortimore, 1989: 13). When wood is exhausted, desperate peasants and merchants collecting for urban consumers may resort to gathering animal dung and crop residues. Once that happens, soil degradation is pretty much assured. The World Bank (1985) suggested fuelwood is a crucial factor in the degradation of the Sahel (see Table 8.5).

Khartoum and Nairobi, to cite but two examples, have surrounding zones depleted of wood and dung for as much as 300 km from urban limits. Some have called these areas 'fuelsheds'.

It is possible that, in some situations, shortage of fuel, and thus demand for it, may not be the cause of de-vegetation, it may be the result of de-vegetation (Harrison, 1987a: 206). However, in many regions of the world, unless the poor are given economically viable alternatives, fuelwood, dung, forage and crop residue collection are unlikely to diminish (Prior & Tuohy, 1987; Whitney, 1987).

Social, political and economic structures and relationships that may trigger desertification

Land degradation has often been seen as the result of social and economic relationships (UN, 1977: 280; Gradus, 1985; Wijkman & Timberlake, 1985). Franke & Chasin (1980: 15) blamed the ecological deterioration in the Sahel on '. . . international capitalism'. Often at the root of the problem is conflict between public interest in the long-term and private, short-term resource exploitation. Where land is held in common, or where tenure is insecure, there is little incentive for the individual to minimize degradation.

Breakdown of established authority can cause desertification. For example, erosion of respect for heads of extended families due to cultural change; decline of traditional systems of tribute/tribal domination; inappropriate intervention by central government, such as the imposition of an outsider as a decision-maker. The new administrator is unlikely to achieve what the traditional leader(s) could because the local people do not respect and obey and they generally lose incentive to tackle problems (Timberlake, 1985: 133). Governments increasingly tend to enforce national or state boundaries, attempt to sedentarize nomadic/semi-nomadic peoples and develop dryland regions, all of which tends to hinder migration and drought/overgrazing avoidance. In various countries, scattered populations have been relocated by force or encouragement, into new villages because a state may wish to offer services like schools and healthcare more cost effectively or to subjugate and tax people more easily, or it may simply see the un-sedentarized as a 'stigma of backwardness'. New village formation may lead to concentration of demands on the land causing 'belts' of degradation near settlements, for example, in Tanzania around many *ujamaa* villages.

In Niger and Burkina Faso, the Tuareg once raided and 'taxed' savanna farmers, when this was controlled arable farming, e.g. that of the Iklan in Burkina Faso, increased, reducing fallows and putting land under stress. At the same time, the Tuareg were deprived of a vital link in their drought-avoidance strategy (Franke & Chasin, 1980: 68). Similar events have taken place in Kenya (Mabbut & Wilson, 1980: 6; Little & Horowitz, 1987: 195). The decline of trans-Saharan caravan routes led to impoverishment and land damage in some regions as people depended more on what they could win from the soil.

The spread of cash cropping is often seen as a cause of desertification but it is one thing to chronicle the process of ecological change and another to demonstrate its relationship with the impact of capitalism, although it does seem likely that cash cropping may prompt arable or livestock production in environmentally unsuitable locations. Urban-biassed economic policies seldom give much support to peasant agriculture, market prices are allowed to fluctuate and tend to be kept so low, to satisfy the city-dweller voters, that the producers get inadequate returns. Things are little better for many herders. Taxes and middle-men take a large portion of their profits in good years so little is available for improving land management. In remote areas, herders may have little incentive to sell livestock, cash is of little use if there are virtually no things on which to spend it, the herders' beasts are a more 'concrete' form of wealth and are unlikely to be reduced in numbers.

There is a risk that those engaged in cash cropping may be forced by falling market prices to step up production effort, greed or a failed crop may have a similar effect: a 'spiral' whereby the producer has to produce more to pay for inputs and/or compensate for falling produce prices. In parts of the Sahelian–Sudanic Zone, smallholder groundnut production has followed this pattern and has led to desertification. Where herders and farmers are not integrated, the expansion of arable cash-cropping may also force the herders to abandon traditional grazing lands and overgraze what is left to them by farmers or larger producers (Sinclair & Fryxell, 1985).

If high market prices for agricultural produce coincide with above average rainfall, if there is an innovation in seed or a fall in rural wages, in short, if there is anything which reduces production costs, boosts yields or makes cultivation/herding seem more attractive, people are likely to make greater use of marginal land. Any setback: for example, less than average rainfall or wage rises, can damage agricultural production and set off land degradation.

In some countries, the response to rising population has been to attempt to resettle people in 'vacant lands', often at great cost, and seldom with sustained success. There have been/are such programmes in Indonesia, Amazonian Brazil, Peru, Ecuador, Bolivia, Malaysia and in various African countries. These programmes have been a significant cause of deforestation and, in some cases, the settlers have failed to adapt to their new environments and their fall back – shifting cultivation degrades the land.

Where the active male population is lured away from the land by opportunities for wage labour in mines, city industry, tourism-related employment, or simply because the towns are attractive to youth, the old, the women and the children are left to cope with the farming for at least part of the year. Agriculture then becomes less intensive and land degradation may develop.

Two phenomena which may lead to land degradation are: social differentiation and marginalization. The former may be defined as the process of growth of inequality between sections of local, regional or national society. The result is marginalization: the retreat of farmers or herders to areas of poor productivity or some other disadvantage(s) – areas which are often vulnerable to land degradation. The two phenomena can be due to: appropriation of land by richer landowners; by the creation of state reserves, conservation areas, game parks; by the redistribution of land to groups favoured by the state; warfare/unrest; threat of disease, pests or natural disaster; simple lack of available land (Glantz, 1987: 6). Peasants may seek out marginal land to escape debt, to pursue new opportunities or to exercise some vague 'frontier spirit'.

Human fallibility as a cause of desertification

Unrest is a common cause of land degradation, either directly (see Chapter 11), or because human populations are uprooted or disorientated, suffer trauma and loss of livestock, seeds and tools, and may become refugees, in all probability malnourished, poor and in an unfamiliar, and possibly, hostile environment. Unrest also involves expenditure that might have been used for anti-degradation work such as control of pest insects, monitoring of erosion, etc. Unrest may take the form of tribal conflict, terrorism, full-blown warfare or inadequate rule of law over those who would exploit others or the land.

Greed, ignorance or fashion may result in excessive demands for resources. A change in taste can quickly lead to abandonment of traditional crops, possibly in favour of new less robust, less nutritious and more land-damaging ones (Mabbut & Wilson, 1980: 22). Veterinary care may well improve, but, with no complementary provisions for culling and marketing excess livestock, overgrazing problems are likely to follow.

Use of off-road vehicles: cross-country motor cycles, 'dune-buggies', jeeps, etc has increased. California and other arid areas of the USA, Australia and parts of game parks in Africa have suffered (Dregne, 1983: 123; Onyeanusi, 1986), and there are signs that Europe will have difficulties as sales of such vehicles rise. In some areas of the UK, country lanes are becoming deeply gullied as a result of recreational vehicles.

WHAT ARE THE IMPLICATIONS OF DESERTIFICATION?

Demographic analyses suggest that, by the early 1980s, between one-sixth and one-fifth of the total world population were significantly to seriously affected by desertification (UN, 1977: 7; Mabbutt, 1984: 105). Ahmad & Kassas (1987: *viii*) suggested 57 million were affected in 1977, by 1984 this had possibly risen to 135 million (El-Moghraby et al., 1987: 227); Kassas (1987: 391) put the figure at about 850 million significantly affected. In Africa, by the late 1980s, it seems likely that over 108 million were affected, 61 million seriously (Harrison, 1987a: 141).

It is difficult to accurately establish how much actually, or potentially, productive land has been lost to desertification, nor how much money has been diverted from other needs to combat the problem. Mabbutt (1987: 372) suggested that, worldwide, desertification caused an annual capital loss of about US$ 13 billion (at 1975 values); Kassas (1987: 391) gave what he considered a conservative estimate that worldwide dryland degradation cost US$ 26 billion a year in lost agricultural production–equivalent to enough to feed roughly 80 million people with wheat for a year. Sixteen of the 30 poorest, least-developed countries are severly affected by desertification (Ahmad & Kassas, 1987: 4).

Figures are not accurate, but give some indication of the scale of the problem. Between 1978 and 1983, according to Dregne (1984: 117), bilateral and multilateral aid donors spent US$ 10 billion on projects with an 'anti-desertification' component, of which he suspected less than one-tenth was used for actual field control of desertification. Between the mid 1970s and 1984, aid donors spent at least US$ 600 million on combating desertification of African rangelands (IUCN, 1986: 29). Official development assistance to the Sudano-Sahelian Zone (CILSS member states) was running at about US$ 40 per caput for the region in 1982, and total expenditure seems to have been at least US$ 7.45 billion between the late 1970s and 1982. However, less than 1.5% of that seems to have been spent on ecology/forestry projects. 'Anti-desertification' work can encompass many things that have little direct connection with land degradation (Grainger, 1982: 40). In 1986, UNSO was funding desertification control projects costing US$ 47.6 million (Tolba, 1987a: 367). Franke & Chasin (1980: 138) give details of EEC, IBRD, UN, OPEC and USA assistance to the Sudano-Sahelian Zone, in US$ between 1974 and 1979.

The sum needed to combat desertification in the future is going to be very large: in 1982, it was estimated that, between then and AD 2000, US$ 1.8 billion per year would be required, a sum equivalent to about 5% of what nations were then spending on armaments (Tolba, 1987: 19). Ahmad & Kasses (1987: *viii*) estimated that a 20-year worldwide programme to arrest desertification would cost (at 1987 prices) roughly US$ 4.5 billion a year, US$ 2.4 billion of that needed in developing countries. Such sums are well beyond 1987 levels of donor assistance to the Third World for everything. Rather than preach despair, Ahmad & Kassas (1987) suggested how funding might be found.

There are regions which may benefit from desertification: those which receive fertile wind-blown dust (in some cases this becomes loess) or river-borne silt (river floodplains mainly) that has eroded from the desertified badlands.

DESERTIFICATION PROBLEM REGIONS

Africa

Africa has been described as a continent on the brink of disaster. Roughly 12 million ha of subSaharan Africa is arid or semi-arid and, in those regions, are to be found 40 million people and 80 million livestock (Joss *et al.*, 1986: 503). As much as 742 million ha of Africa, *c.* 26% of the total land area and 85% of the total dryland area, has suffered, or is undergoing, moderate or severe desertification, most of this in the drylands (Timberlake, 1985: 61; Harrison 1987a: 141). Africa's physical environment is deteriorating, per caput production of food grains is falling; in some regions population growth rates are amongst the world's highest and national economies are in disarray. Africa is, and will probably remain for decades, one of the greatest challenges to world development (UNEP & Commonwealth of Australia, 1987: 3).

The Sahelian–Sudanic Zone (the Sudano–Sahelian Region or Sahel)

Stebbing (1935) was one of the first to draw attention to desertification south of the Sahara. Between 1968 and 1974 the Sahelian–Sudanic Zone (SSZ) suffered the latest of a series of known droughts (see Fig. 8.6). The situation became so bad that the UN convened the UN Conference on Desertification in Nairobi (Kenya) in 1977 to discuss the situation. In spite of that, and many subsequent conferences, and massive foreign aid, the situation has probably become worse. The IUCN (1986: 34) estimated roughly 90% of SSZ rangelands, 80% of SSZ rain-fed farmland and 30% of SSZ irrigated farmland were at least moderately desertified, and it seems that at least 49 million people were affected in the late 1980s (Mortimore, 1988: 61). A massive literature has been generated by the 1968–74 SSZ drought. For a list of bibliographies see: Franke & Chasin (1980: 142); also the OECD Development Centre have published a series of bibliographies (Beudot, 1987); a special issue of *Bulletin – Société Languedociènne de Géographie*, 18 (3–4) also provides extensive references.

The majority of the SSZ population live between the 350 and 800 mm y^{-1} isohyets (see Fig. 8.6), concentrated particularly in the south and east of the Zone IV. The distribution is uneven, possibly 80% live in 25% of the total area, and 40% in but 6% (Gorse, 1985: 7). The most populous regions are probably the Senegalese groundnut-growing basin, the Gambia and the Burkina Faso, Mossi Plateau. Together these are but 2% of the SSZ but have 24% of the total population. Mauritania had a population growth rate over the 20 years up to 1985 of 8.6%, some of which was due to immigration from

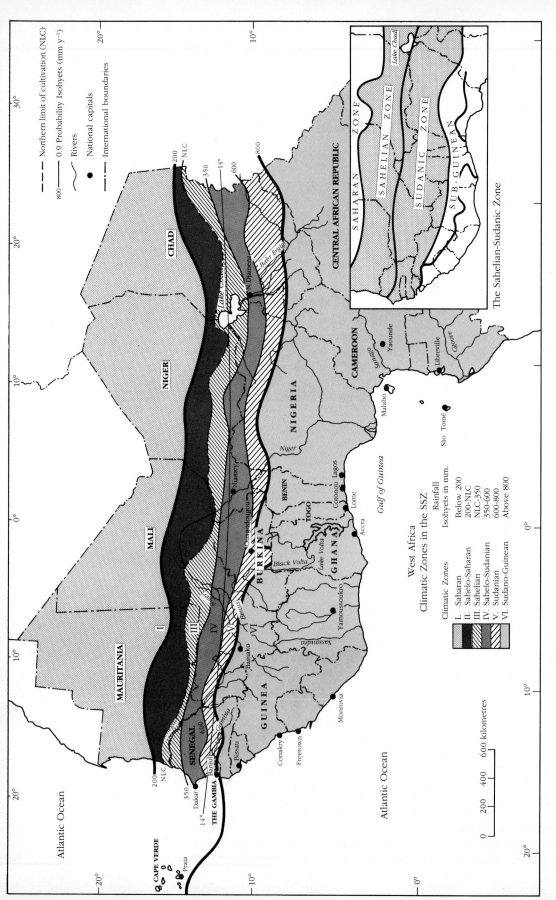

Fig. 8.6. *The Sahelian–Sudanic Zone climatic subdivision (rainfall). Sources: Main map. World Bank 1985 p. vi modified. Inset map. Barrow 1987a: 41 Fig. 1.6*

other regions (Gorse, 1985: 7). In 1985, in the Gambian SSZ, the population density was about 60 persons per km², in the Senegal SSZ about 28, in Burkina Faso about 22 in Mali, Niger and Chad it was around 6, 4 and 3 respectively (World Bank, 1985: 38). By AD 2000 the SSZ will probably have a population of around 54 million, compared with 19 million a few years before the drought of 1968–74 (World Bank, 1985: 7). It therefore seems likely that future drought will have at least equal effects to that during the 1960s and 1970s.

The impact of the 1968–74 drought is difficult to assess. In some regions virtually all livestock were lost or had to be slaughtered, the SSZ, as a whole, probably lost 25% of its livestock by 1973. There was great human suffering: in Burkina Faso, Chad, Mali, Mauritania, Niger and Senegal possibly 100,000 (perhaps 250,000) died between 1968 and 1973 and problems continue (Grainger, 1982: 39; IUCN, 1986: 20). An indication of the degree to which SSZ soils degraded during the drought is given by records of dust blown from the SSZ to the West Indies c. 4700 km to the west: in 1967/8 receipts were 8 microgrammes per m³, in 1972 it was 15 and in 1973 had grown to 42 (Mann, 1987: 85).

Given the variation of ecological conditions, ethnic groups, and land use strategies, it is difficult to trace causes and virtually impossible to recognize a single general process of SSZ desertification, though meteorological drought may often have been the 'trigger' or 'accelerator'. There is no guarantee that, with the return of 'normal' rains, desertified land will recover quickly or fully.

Precipitation over the SSZ is related to the position of the Inter-Tropical Convergence Zone, nowadays more commonly termed the Inter-Tropical Discontinuity. This precipitation is variable, both annually, due to changes in weather patterns, and locally, as much comes from storms which seldom follow the same track exactly. At the best of times the SSZ is drought-prone (Foster, 1986: 13; Glantz, 1987: 4). Droughts have been recorded for: AD 1446; the 1560s; 1910–14; 1940–42, the 1968–74 drought should thus have come as no surprise (Glantz, 1976: 4; UN, 1977: 4).

The IUCN (1986: 23) could find little compelling evidence for climatic change during the last 2000 years; the amount of precipitation in 1968 was sufficient, but it was ill-timed, finishing too early. Foster (1986: 19) suggested that SSZ rainfall has been considerably lower since 1968 than the average for 1900–1960; 1970, 1971 and 1972 were below-average rainfall years and Lake Chad shrank by one-third between 1968 and 1973 (Glantz, 1976: 77; Schove, 1977: 41). Grainger (1982: 40) suggested the 1968–74 drought was not as severe as the 1910–14 drought, but its effects have been greater.

Roughly three-quarters of SSZ people depend on rain-fed cultivation. Some regions depend heavily on livestock, for example, 80% of Somalia is rangeland and supports 60% of the population (Joss et al., 1986: 89). There are regional differences in adoption of cash cropping. The SSZ is thus by no means uniform in land use. As a whole, the SSZ has proved better over the last 20 years at increasing export crops, especially groundnuts and cotton, than improving food production for rural peoples (Kassas, 1987: 393). There have been more general changes in cultivation, in particular, the ox-drawn plough has spread. There has been breakdown in many regions of traditional land uses, for example, millet/sorghum and gum-arabic producing Acacia tree or shea-butter tree (*Butyrospermum paradoxum*) plus grazing agropastoral systems, and many pastoralists and cultivators have had their control over land reduced (Swift, 1977; IUCN, 1986: 30).

Better-than-average rains over the SSZ in the 1960s encouraged expansion of grazing into some marginal land and an increase in stock numbers. Winstanley (in Glantz, 1976: 199) estimated SSZ livestock rose by 46% between 1960 and 1970. During the years of less-than-adequate rainfall these herds destroyed rangeland.

An interesting theory is that, under normal rainfall conditions in the SSZ, the ratio of grassland to scrubland areas fluctuates, the periodicity of this depends on grazing intensity and the frequency/intensity of bushfires and/or cultivation. The 1968–74 drought might have upset such periodic successional change, grassland failed to fluctuate to scrub thickets and, instead, changed to grass patches/bare soil initiating desertification (IUCN, 1986: 21).

Many of the efforts to identify causes/processes of desertification in the SSZ have involved comparison of 'actual' with 'sustainable' human or livestock numbers. Not all researchers acknowledge, like the World Bank (1985), the inadequacy of the available database and the danger in using the concept of carrying capacity. Little & Horowitz (1987: 319) also warned of the risks of adopting a simplistic concept of carrying capacity in drylands. Comparisons of 'actual' and 'sustainable' populations made by the World Bank are given in Table 8.5. Similar efforts have been made by the FAO (IUCN, 1986: 26–28; Gorse & Steeds, 1987: 122), and differ somewhat.

To summarize, one may postulate three broad possibilities:

1. The SSZ drought was the result of a long-term, natural climatic trend. If so, degradation will probably get worse and will be difficult or impossible to resist.
2. It was due to short-term fluctuations, and thus it makes sense to try to weather-out future SSZ droughts.
3. It resulted from local causes which are complex and vary from place to place in the SSZ. Better management of land use should be effective in ameliorating future degradation.

The Republic of Cape Verde

The Cape Verde Islands have apparently suffered 27 years of declining precipitation (Heckmann, 1985). With 94% of the Islands' agriculture rainfed and the population relying mainly on wood for cooking and heating, desertification has become so bad on some islands that there has been speculation they may have to be abandoned (Timberlake, 1985: 134). In addition to supposedly decreasing rainfall and fuelwood collection, goat grazing and sugar production have been blamed for the degradation.

The Sudan

Between 1968 and 1974, rainfall was inadequate or fell at the wrong time, especially in the central and western Provinces of Kordofan and Dafur and in the east, along the Red Sea and border with Ethiopia (Timberlake, 1985: 26; Buckocke, 1988), and there was severe drought in 1984/85 (Little & Horowitz, 1987: 213). As in the SSZ, there has been recurring drought, e.g. in 1886 and 1910–1914. Perhaps 40% of the total population of the Sudan had lost their livelihood by the late 1980s because of drought/desertification, and in N. Sudan, Hindley (1987) reported dune movement.

Sudan produces roughly 85% of the world's gum-arabic, much of this by traditional agro-sylvopastoralists tapping *Acacia senegal* and *A. seyal* (see Fig.

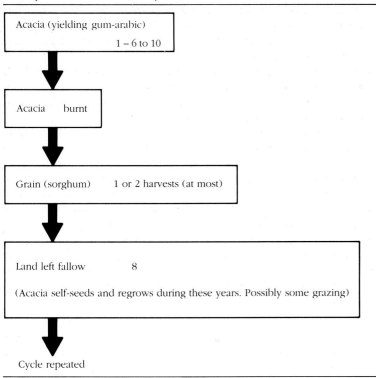

Crop	Number of years
Acacia (yielding gum-arabic)	1 – 6 to 10
Acacia burnt	
Grain (sorghum)	1 or 2 harvests (at most)
Land left fallow	8
(Acacia self-seeds and regrows during these years. Possibly some grazing)	
Cycle repeated	

Fig. 8.7. Gum-arabic/grain/fallow cropping cycle.

8.7). The production strategy has been in decline, making farmers in many regions, but notably Kordofan Province, and White Nile Province, more vulnerable to drought (DeVos, 1975: 49; Olsson, 1984).

The ecologically balanced gum-arabic/grain strategy apparently fails as population increases. Typically, efforts are made to increase grain production, the fallow period is reduced, grazing during the fallow is increased, and rising fuelwood demand leads to Acacia cutting. Acacia regeneration falters, either the worthless (in terms of gum production) *A. tortilis* takes over or, if grazing is very heavy and the *A. tortilis* seed-pods are eaten, tree cover disappears. The reduced tree cover and increased grazing leads to more wind erosion.

In some parts of the Sudan, fuelwood cutting is a major cause of desertification (Whitney, 1987) (see Chapter 4). There have been recent attempts to reforest with *mesquite* (*Prosopis* spp.) and Acacia to re-establish traditional gum arabic/grazing systems (Little & Horowitz, 1987: 95).

Borehole-sinking is frequently a cause of overgrazing, especially since the 1960s, to the extent that where the land is underlain by the aquifer-poor 'Basement Complex' desertification is less pronounced (El-Moghraby *et al.*, 1987: 228). Civil warfare has played a significant part in Sudan's desertification problem, especially in the south.

Ethiopia

It has been suggested that Ethiopia should be able to feed at least twice its present population, yet there has been widespread famine (MacKenzie,

1987a, b: 54; Kebbede & Jacob, 1988). In the worst-hit regions: Tigray, Wallo and Eritrea Provinces, the trigger appears to have been 3 years of drought followed by heavy rainfall (Wood, 1977 gives a chronology of Ethiopian droughts). Because much of the lowland has heavy clay soils and low rainfall, probably over 80% of the people farm the highlands, and keep about 70% of the cattle. It is common for farmers to till or graze slopes with a gradient greater than 25 degrees (Milas, 1984: 168; Kebbede & Jacob, 1988).

Much of Ethiopia's farmland was held as large estates before 1975, and, before the 1970s, the peasantry were heavily burdened with taxes and could spend little on land management. After 1976 there was redistribution to peasant associations which opened up fallow areas but lacked the skill or motivation to take adequate care of them. Population increase resulted in reduction of fallow, while fuelwood and dung collection removed tree cover and degraded the soil. At the turn of the century, roughly 40% of Ethiopia seems to have been forested. In 1984, various estimates put the extent of forest at between 2% and 4% (Timberlake, 1985: 129; MacKenzie, 1987a, 55).

In Eritrea Province from 1963–85, and in Tigray and Wallo Provinces from 1976 to 1985 there has been insurgency.

The Malagasy Republic (Madagascar)

Roughly 70% of Malagasy's forest has been cleared and replaced by savanna grasslands, 65% of which are at risk of desertification (Darkoh, 1987: 27). Overgrazing is a serious problem especially in the grasslands of the Central Plateaux and in the semi-arid south. Shifting cultivation (*tavy*) and recurrent bushfires in the disturbed areas are blamed for much of the forest loss. In recent years, an estimated 150,000 ha y^{-1} are believed to have been lost through these causes (Chown, 1986).

Angola, Botswana, Tanzania and Zimbabwe

Botswana is one of the most desertified African countries south of the SSZ. Overgrazing by cattle seems to be a significant cause, and, in part, stems from the commercialization of production. Darkoh (1987: 31) noted that European Economic Community subsidies had raised Botswanan market prices of beef 60% above the world market level after 1971. Opportunities to earn the large profits from cattle have led to a breakdown of traditional transhumance and increasing use of marginal land in the Kalahari sandveldt of western Botswana (Rapp et al., 1976: 171).

Hindered access to land, drought, warfare and influx of refugees has caused considerable dryland degradation in East Africa (Darkoh, 1987: 29). Kenya has had severe soil erosion related to overgrazing and fuelwood collection since the 1930s (Rapp et al., 1976: 165). In Tanzania, there is a general problem of overgrazing and reduction of arable fallows upon which are superimposed local complications caused by the concentration of people and livestock in localities that cannot support them.

Southern Africa

The grasslands of Southern Africa are mainly at quite high altitude and suffer frequent rainfall shortages. Pasture degradation, often due to overgrazing and soild erosion, are widespread, and in some areas duststorms are common (Furley & Newey, 1983: 261).

At the start of the twentieth century, N. Africa is believed to have had about 8 million ha of productive alpha grass (*Stipa tenacissima*) rangeland; by 1976 at least half of that had been lost or severely degraded (Rapp *et al.*, 1976: 8). Mauritania, Morocco, Tunisia, Algeria, Libya and Egypt are all suffering varying degrees of land degradation. In W. Egypt, Landsat information recently showed considerable dune movement (Eckholm & Brown, 1977: 11; Hindley, 1987). Mauritania has problems with sandstorms and moving dunes, with Central and Southern Mauritania worst affected. Between 1960 and 1970, Mauritania had 43 recorded sandstorms; between 1970 and 1980 there were over 430, 240 in 1982 alone (Middleton, 1988). There are indications that camel, sheep and goat grazing, plus fuelwood collection (between 1977 and 1987 Mauritania's 'forest' cover fell from about 3% to about 1%), has increased wind erosion (Gaye, 1987; Anon, 1987c: 49). Goodall & Perry (1981: 377) firmly blamed human causes for N. African land degradation, particularly population growth since the 1930s.

In Tunisia, unwise cereal cultivation on sandy soils using mechanical ploughing, plus overgrazing and fuelwood collection are blamed for desertification (Rapp *et al.*, 1976: 127). Clark & Munn (1986) reported a trebling in goat numbers in Morocco between 1931 and 1952.

South Asia

Land degradation in South Asia is widespread and has been going on for millenia; today possibly 70% of the subcontinent is desertified (World Resources Institute *et al.*, 1987: 278).

One of the worst-affected regions is the Rajasthan 'Desert' of northwest India and Pakistan. This is a semi-arid area surrounding the Thar Desert which has suffered a series of recent droughts, one of the worst being in 1986, which some suggest mark a trend toward drier conditions (UN 1977: 14; Mooley & Pant, 1981). Goodall & Perry (1981: 479) pointed out, that with 46 persons per km^2 in the early 1980s, the Thar Desert was one of the most densely populated drylands.

In the Indus Basin, irrigation-related salinization/desertification is a severe problem (see Chapter 9).

Sri Lanka has a Dry Zone where the rainfall can be less than 650 mm y^{-1}; large areas of these drylands are degraded (Heathcote, 1980: 4). Since the late 1960s foreign exchange problems have driven up food prices and many cultivators have reacted by expanding production in the Dry Zone in the form of damaging *chena* shifting cultivation.

China and Mongolia

Roughly 69% of the People's Republic of China and Mongolia are at least moderately desertified and much is under serious threat (World Resources Institute *et al.*, 1987: 278). In China, records indicate there were problems by 2000 BP. The worst-affected areas are the rangelands, especially in Western China bordering the Gobi Desert and parts of the loess soil regions of Northern China (see Chapter 10). Forrestier (1989) cited estimates that China's deserts were growing at around 1560 km^2 y^{-1}, so that, by AD 2000, there will be roughly twice the desert there was in 1949, unless control is achieved.

About 5% of Asian USSR is desertified (World Resources Institute *et al.*, 1986: 278). There is considerable overgrazing in the cool and temperate semi-arid lands of the Southern USSR Ukraine to Caspian Sea region and the Turkmen Republic (Turkmenistan). Fuelwood collection and the salinization of irrigation schemes has also led to degradation. The greatest difficulties are probably in North Kazakhstan, Western Siberia and Eastern Russia's 'Virgin Lands'. In the latter regions, roughly 40 million ha of dry grasslands were ploughed up between 1954 and 1969 to dry-farm cotton, winter cereals and fodder. Although the USSR's grain production climbed 50% in 6 years, there followed a slow decline in soil fertility of these steppelands. In 1963, there was drought, the strong, dry *sukhovei* winds stripped away the exposed soil and when rains returned, there was severe run-off erosion. Between 1962 and 1965, as much as 7 million ha were moderately damaged, and at least 3 million ha were lost to cultivation (Eckholm, 1976: 56).

There are severe difficulties associated with riverwater extraction to irrigate lands in Southern USSR to the north of the Caspian Sea (for a map and case-study see Beaumont, 1989: 386–99). These irrigated lands are suffering salinization and require heavy applications of fertilizers and pesticides to produce crops like cotton. The extractions have caused considerable fall in level of the Aral Sea, leading to marked increase in the Sea's salinity and the death of most of its once-rich fish stocks. Severe salinization and agrochemical pollution, plus falling water-tables are causing desertification around its shores. The shrinking of the Aral Sea will, if it has not already done so, lead to climatic changes in Central Asia, as there is now a reduced body of water to moisten westerlie winds in summer and warm them in winter. Recent reports suggest the Aral Sea has lost 69% of its water (*The Sunday Times*, 4/3/90).

Latin America

Soil erosion was occurring in Central Mexico, as a consequence of cultivation, by 3500 BP (*New Scientist* 125, issue 1705: 29).

According to Dregne (1984: 117, 211), roughly 56% of S. America is suffering moderate or severe desertification, other estimates put it higher – the World Resources Institute *et al.* (1986: 278) suggested that 71% of Latin America, including Mexico, was desertified. Argentina has problems, especially in the States of La Rioja, San Luis and La Pampa. The western and southern Argentine *pampas* (where rainfall is often less than 450 mm yr^{-1}) have suffered less than the wetter eastern and northern *pampas* which are more attractive to settlers. Overgrazing has been severe enough to markedly raise the silt-load of Argentine rivers such as the Rio Plata. In Western Argentina, irrigation-related salinization has become a real problem.

North East Brazil, especially the *sertão* and the *cerrado* lands, have a long history of drought; these are recorded for: AD 1587; 1825; 1877–9; 1930–32; 1936 and 1981–6. In 1986, drought affected at least 26 million people in the States of Ceara, Piaui, parts of Pernambuco, Paraiba, Riogrande Norte and northern Bahia: an area roughly the size of Western Europe (Anon, 1986). Studies suggest much of the desertification results from human causes, though drought is a 'catalyst' (Hall, 1978: 19; Ichikawa, 1983). There is a history, in Northeast Brazil, of cash crop monoculture on large estates, mainly sugar before the nineteenth century, and, since the nineteenth century, cotton. Smallholders concentrated on subsistence food production. Drought has tended to drive poor 'Nordestinos' off the marginal land, and then commercial agriculture takes over (Anon. 1984), there is also a land tenure/land access problem. Aid efforts have tended to help the large landowners and many of the poor, have, in desperation, resorted to woodcutting in order to produce, and sell, charcoal to townsfolk. Recent droughts have been forecast well beforehand, but counter-measures seem to have been poor.

The Mediterranean and Mediterranean-type drylands

The Mediterranean-type drylands are to be found along the subtropical western margins of the continents between *c.* 30 degrees and 40 degrees north and south of the Equator. Biogeographers recognize five Mediterranean-type regions: the Mediterranean-proper, and parts of: California, S. Africa, Peru, Chile and Australia, where plant growth occurs mainly in spring and is checked by summer drought. Local relief tends to have marked effect on rainfall and erosion; rainstorms cause spectacular damage. There has been considerable human disturbance of these regions and it is usual for natural forest to have been replaced by an overgrazed and frequently burnt scrub cover (Furley & Newey, 1983: 264–70). Plato over 2500 years ago commented (in *Critias*) on degradation in Attica (Greece) and, in the region of present-day Jordan, Israel and Syria deforestation and erosion was well under way by 6000 BC (*New Scientist*, 125 issue 1705: 22).

Europe

Possibly 50% of Spain, much of this Mediterranean Spain, is arid or semi-arid and, according to Dregne (1983: 183, 218), roughly 60% of those drylands are moderately desertified. In the Ebro Basin, the problem is growing, and seems to be due to the extension of cereal cultivation into marginal lands. Elsewhere, overgrazing and the practice of burning off brush to encourage pasture are responsible (Ruddle & Manshard, 1981: 206; Fantechi & Margaris, 1986: 3–8; Arianoutsou-Faraggitaki, 1985). Portugal, Sicily, Sardinia and the Italian Mezzorgiamo are affected by drought/desertification, in Sardinia, in recent years, the rains seem to have faltered, some suggest because of the 'greenhouse effect'. Turkey is badly affected, especially in its south and around the Black Sea.

Australia

Australia has vast areas of degraded land, yet rural population is low, and cultivation and livestock rearing are relatively recent developments. Aboriginal peoples, present in Australia by 60,000 BP, have probably increased the incidence of bushfires above natural levels for at least 30,000 years, and may have caused the extinction of some large marsupial grazing animals. However, dryland degradation has increased markedly since Europeans began to spread through the land in the mid eighteenth century.

Roughly 25% of Australia's drylands are virtually unoccupied because they are too remote and the grasses are unpalatable to livestock. But, of the remaining 75%, most is moderately desertified, particularly the drier *Atriplex maireana*-dominated woodlands of New South Wales, South Australia and Victoria, especially in the Murray River Basin. Before European disturbance, there were probably about 77,000 km² of *mallee* scrub, a collective name for dry woodland/scrub dominated by *Eucalyptus uncinata*, *E. dumosa* or *E. incrassata* with grasses like *Triodoka* spp.; since the 1840s this has been badly degraded. Both the *Atriplex*-woodlands and *mallee* scrub areas have tended to suffer from raised water-tables, leading to salinization and increased run-off erosion and gullying. This is often a result of reduced evapotranspiration losses following the clearance of the brush or trees (Douglas, 1981: 55; Heathcote, 1980: 60). The introduction of the rabbit has caused serious rangeland damage, although myxomatosis helped to control the problem from the 1950s until recently (Vines, 1987). Bushfires have become more of a problem in recent decades, especially in Southeast Australia and Victoria, probably as a result of rangeland and woodland disturbance.

In Western Australia alone, lost production due to desertification was recently estimated to be around A\$ 94 million/year (UNEP & Commonwealth of Australia, 1987: 15). In the Murray River Basin, salinization, much of it through faulty irrigation and poor drainage, is an increasingly costly problem and has already damaged considerable areas sufficiently to remove them from production.

In the 1980s, efficient, cheap scrub-clearing methods were developed; these plus 'stump-jump' ploughs, steam-shipping, the Suez Canal and the repeal of the Corn Laws in the UK (1846) made wheat farming in the *mallee*-type drylands areas with roughly 250 to 300 mm y^{-1} rainfall an attractive proposition (Clark & Munn, 1986: 61). From the 1840s to the present, grain production in these regions has shown a relationship with world market prices for wheat, and with agricultural innovation, such as the ability to correct trace mineral deficiencies in soils. This is illustrated in Figure 8.8. At

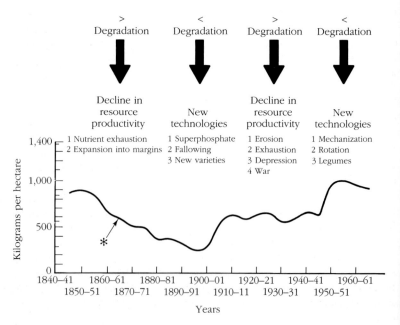

Resource productivity and technological adjustments
in commercial farming, South Australia

∗ Improvement in scrub clearing and plough

Fig. 8.8. *Resource productivity and technological adjustments in commercial farming in South Australia: 1840–1961. Source: Based on UN, 1977, p. 273, Fig. 3.*

various times, soil damage and wind erosion have become a problem, and in many respects the situation is reminiscent of the USA 'Dustbowl', especially in the Murray *mallee* region (Heathcote, 1980: 60; Beaumont, 1989: 176).

New Zealand

Drier regions of New Zealand are vulnerable to overgrazing and bushfires, for example: parts of Otago where the annual rainfall averages less than 760 mm and there are dry Föhn-type winds. Before the arrival of Europeans, between roughly AD 1000 and 200 BP. Maori peoples had set fires to grassland and woodlands. There has been greater disruption of vegetation, landslides and gulleying since European settlement, much caused by the introduction of grazing animals like the red deer and, above all, livestock, and by deforestation for fuel and timber. Before the arrival of Man, New Zealand had no native grazing mammals, so vegetation was ill adapted to survive the pressures placed on it.

North America

North American aboriginal peoples probably set fires to drive game at least 20,000 years before Europeans arrived. Damage, however, accelerated in the nineteenth century, especially after the opening of the railroads. In 1870, just as railroads were spreading into the Great Plains, there were probably over 15 million bison (Beaumont, 1989: 310). By 1885 only a few had escaped hunters and their place had been taken by cattle, which have different, more damaging, grazing habits. Railroads supported cattle ranching in the USA and Canada, and led to widespread overgrazing. In New Mexico and Arizona, Navajo Indians became sheep herders and caused rangeland damage.

In the USA, inadequate control over federal-owned rangeland meant that overgrazing was difficult to cure (Kassas, 1987: 393). By the early 1980s, there were an estimated 450 million ha of desertified land in the USA, Canada and Mexico one-third of which was severely affected (Dregne, 1983: 199). World Resources Institute *et al.* (1987: 278; 1987: 67) suggested that 40% of N. America was desertified, and, of *c.* 357 million ha of USA rangeland (including that in Alaska): 32% was in good condition, 28% in fair condition, 28% in poor condition and 12% in very poor condition. This is the situation in the world's richest nation, where funds should be available for control of land degradation, and where history should have made people aware of the need for such control.

The worst-affected regions are Southwest USA, especially around the Sonoran Desert (Arizona) and the Chihuahuan Desert (Mexico). There has also been considerable wind erosion during droughts in the mid-west. Within the last few decades, salinization has become a rangeland problem in the northern Great Plains, due apparently to rising groundwater in glacial soils overlaying impervious shales. These lands were once cultivated before becoming grazing land. Presumably the new rangeland has lower evapotranspiration losses than earlier vegetation and water-tables have risen (Heathcote, 1980: 37).

Broadly comparable to the steppes of Eurasia, tall-grass, mixed-grass and short-grass prairies once covered large areas of Manitoba, Alberta (Canada). Kansas, Oklahoma, Colorado, Texas and parts of New Mexico. Hot in summer, cold in winter, and often with less than 400 mm y^{-1} of, mainly summer, rainfall, these grasslands are largely 'marginal land'. Overgrazing

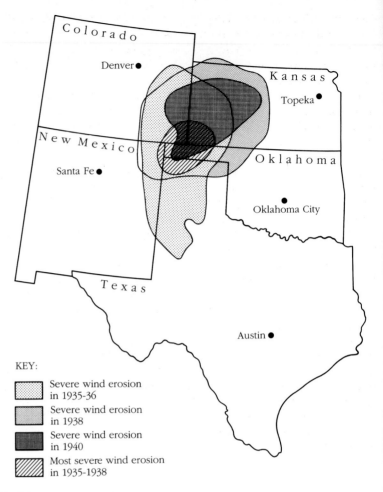

KEY:

Severe wind erosion
in 1935-36

Severe wind erosion
in 1938

Severe wind erosion
in 1940

Most severe wind erosion
in 1935-1938

Fig. 8.9. Extent of the USA 'Dust Bowl' region affected by severe wind erosion in the 1930s. Source: Worster, 1979: p. 30 (no Fig. number in that source).

has altered the tall- and mixed-grass prairie to short-grass prairie with scattered shrubby plants like *mesquite* (*Prosopis* spp.) that are unpalatable to livestock. Following the First World War, the short-grass prairies were increasingly ploughed up to grow wheat or maize. Drought and desertification dogged this exploitation, especially in the southern mid-west 'Great Plains which, by 1935, were so degraded as to be called the 'Dust Bowl' Bonnifield, 1979; Heathcote, 1980: 36; Svobida, 1986) (Fig. 8.9).

There is a long history of recurrent droughts going back at least several thousand years (records show severe droughts before the 1930s, in: 1854–60; 1864–65; 1873–80; 1890–95; 1910–14). Drought discouraged exploitation of the 'Dust Bowl' until after the end of the First World War, when wheat prices increased and the introduction of tractors and combine harvesters cut labour costs and made sparse-seeding with grain an economic proposition. In the 1920s, there were series of wetter-than-average years, sharecropper-farmed arble land and rangeland was converted to large-scale, mechanized grain production with little fallowing and little use of fertilizers. In 1931, drought re-appeared and persisted into 1932; by 1934 problems were widespread. Farmers were either slow to perceive the danger or, more likely, were trapped by debts acquired in bying farm machinery into continuing to try and produce. To compound the misery, grasshoppers added to drought damage (Saarinen, 1966), and the light sandy loess soils were predisposed to wind erosion. For several years duststorms were generated and were felt as far away as Chicago, New York and Washington DC. At least 80 million ha were badly damaged and 20 million were abandoned (Eckholm, 1976: 50; Kassas, 1987: 393).

The Canadian prairies seem to have suffered less than those of the USA, in spite of drought in 1934, 1961 and 1988. Nevertheless, desertification has been considerable and was costing C$ 600 million per year in 1987, and was expected to rise well beyond that (UNEP & Commonwealth of Australia, 1987: 20).

Drought in the USA mid-west did not cease in the 1930s; there were serious ones in the 1950s, mid 1970s and 1988. The recent droughts seem to be due to stationary high pressure air masses, as, in all probablility, were earlier ones.

Whatever the cause of droughts, mismanagement of land has made their impact worse. The mismanagement was not because of overpopulation, national poverty, ignorance or warfare; rather, it was the result of a decision by individuals to exploit a region for all it is worth (Russel, 1988).

The 'Dust Bowl' is important in that it has probably done more than any other Man–land mishap to promote soil conservation and environmental concern. In 1935, the Soil Conservation Service of the USA, part of the US Department of Agriculture, was founded largely as a response to 'Dust Bowl' problems. The Service has done much good work countering land degradation in the USA and elsewhere, yet, in the mid 1970s, rising grain prices triggered a new increase in exploitation of the prairie lands. Drought struck in 1974 and 1975, harvests fell c. 15%, and erosion and bushfires increased. Despite the lessons of history, despite institutions and policies intended to control degradation, the problems of the 1930s were being repeated (Matlock, 1981: 39; Heathcote, 1980: 120).

South East Asia

Rank, largely useless, dry lalang (Imperata cylindrica) grasslands have increased in Central Java, Eastern (Island) Java, Thailand, Malaysia and Vietnam following deforestation. If burnt over, the grassland can degrade further until there is full desertification.

DESERTIFICATION MONITORING AND CONTROL

Recognition of indicators of desertification is a step towards monitoring, the next is to establish standards and set up reliable measurement. One obvious, but often overlooked, need is to ensure that the time of measuring is noted, and is comparable between stations, although, with marked rainfall variation, even such measurement will be difficult to compare meaningfully. Even if widely accepted standards are adopted, desertification is often the product of a complex of causes, so comparison of site with site needs great caution (Rapp, 1976). Governments are generally reluctant to gather data on 'negative' development like desertification. That, coupled with the shortage of personnel and funding, has hindered national monitoring.

The FAO and UNEP have been mapping and monitoring desertification, especially since 1979. In 1983, the UNEP selected the Environmental Systems Research Institute to create a geographical information system to be used for monitoring and mapping world desertification hazard. In 1986, the Desertification Control Programme Activity Centre of UNEP was set up to establish a database on desertification.

Who is fighting desertification?

Between 1950 and 1962, UNESO ran an Arid Zone Research Programme which provided valuable information on the drylands; this was continued under the Man and Biosphere Programme from 1974. In 1973, the UN established the UN Sudano–Sahelian Office (UNSO) to co-ordinate efforts to aid the 19 SSZ countries. UNSO's brief was later expanded to include SSZ desertification avoidance/control. In 1973, eight SSZ governments: Mali, Mauritania, Niger, Senegal, Burkina Faso, Chad, the Gambia and Cape Verde established the Permanent Inter-State Committee for Drought Control (Comité Interétat pour la Lutte Contre la Sécheresse dans le Sahel – CILSS). This aimed to attack SSZ drought and desertification. In 1976, under the aegis of the OECD, various western aid agencies formed the Club du Sahel to organize and administer donor-to-country aid programmes, and to improve co-operation between SSZ countries and between donor countries and the SSZ, the main aim was to get regional food self-sufficiency rather than simply fight desertification. The OECD published a *Strategy and Programme for Drought Control and Development in the Sahel* in 1977 (OECD, 1977). In Southern Africa, the Southern African Co-ordination Conference (SADCC), and, in Latin America, the Andean Pact have made provisions for desertification control. In 1977, in response to the crisis situation in the SSZ, the UN General Assembly called for a Conference on Desertification, this Conference (UNCOD) was held in Nairobi (Kenya) and issued a Plan of Action to Combat Desertification (PACD). The UN Environment Programme (UNEP) was charged with administration of the PACD; UNCOD widened its concern to cover other regions of the world, and began this by circulating a questionnaire to check the desertification status of various countries; the results were patchy and unsatisfactory.

The PACD was a broad-based document, more concerned with rural development than with control of desertification. In effect virtually any development assistance in drylands tended to be called 'anti-desertification', hence many of the figures on costs or control measures are misleading. The UNEP set up three groups to assist in administering the PACD:

1. The Desertification Branch of UNEP – with the role of carrying out programmes (i.e. implementing the PACD) and acting as 'catalyst'/co-ordinating body. By 1984 it had caused *c.* 30 countries to assess their desertification status and prepare control proposals for submission to DESCON (see following).
2. The Consultative Group for Desertification Control (DESCON), was to secure funding for projects and to screen anti-desertification projects.
3. Inter-agency Working Group on Desertification Control (IAWGDC). This was charged with facilitating co-operation among UN agencies and to develop a plan of short- and long-term objectives for the PACD. IAWGDC was also to prepare an annual report on progress with PADC.

Apart from generating acronyms, what did these efforts achieve? The PADC stated what should be done, but not how it could be achieved. The general conclusion is that it failed to generate adequate political support, although its proposals were probably quite sound (Grainger, 1982: 41; Spooner & Mann, 1982: 4; Mabbutt, 1984; Tolba, 1987a). UNCOD was underfunded – by the end of 1983, it had received less than US$ 50,000 virtually all from developing countries (Tolba, 1987a: 366). In 1983/84, after 7 years activity, UNCOD called for a General Assessment of Progress on PADC. Questionnaries were sent out to over 100 countries – the returns were poor. At a UNEP special meeting in 1984 it was admitted that PACD had been an almost total failure (Timberlake, 1985: 60). In 1984, only two of the hundred nations recognized to be affected by desertification had proposed a National Plan of Action to Combat Desertification, in 1987 this had grown to six! These Plans were deemed essential by UNCOD (Tolba, 1987a: 367). Timberlake (1985: 60) regretted that desertification control had not been made the responsibility of the FAO and/or UNDP, rather than the UNEP which was comparatively underfunded, understaffed and had far less political clout. In 1986, the UNEP and the East–West Center, Hawaii and the Australian Government in an attempted to initiate renewed anti-desertification effort held a conference in Canberra which focused on the economic significance of the problem. A Strategy for Rehabilitating the Sahel and an Action Plan to facilitate this was published by the IUCN (1986), the intention was to work over 15 years and generate money at the local level.

In general, apart from local gains, successes have been restricted to parts of the USA, China and the USSR; elsewhere desertification had increased. Iran made some progress in the 1970s, and Libya and some other N. African countries are attempting dune stabilization/afforestation. In the last decade, Third World debt problems have, if anything, made desertification control less likely. There has also been a tendency for authorities to design control measures after focusing on physical symptoms, even when the causes are socio-economic.

Cost of desertification control

Dregne (1983: 172; 1985: 28) argued that most of the world's desertification could, in theory, probably be reversed with presently available technology. Provided enough soil remains, and plant cover can re-seed/be reseeded, desertification should not be total and irreversible. In practice, control/rehabilitation will be determined by economics and institutional factors (Dixon et al., 1990). The UNEP & Commonwealth of Australia (1987: 4) suggested that US$ 4.5 billion per year would, if effectively spent, prevent roughly US$ 26 billion lost productivity, i.e. the costs are huge but should be weighed against the costs and consequences of no action/expenditure. Forse (1989) noted that less than 10% of the aforement-ioned US$ 4.5 billion had been raised in 1988/89, and there is heated debate as to whether what had been raised was spent wisely. Ahmmad & Kassas (1987) suggested how funding might be generated. At present, hope for funding may well lie in 'debt-swap' approaches like those adopted to fight deforestation (see Chapters 5 and 6).

WHAT CAN BE DONE?

A major problem is to improve land use planning in drylands. There is also a need to train personnel and to overcome political and institutional constraints. Regional co-operation will have to be improved. Funding will be required on such a scale that efforts must have international backing (Tolba, 1987b: 111; Dixon et al., 1989).

There has been quite a lot of work on desertification control techniques (DeVos, 1975: 179; Kirmse & Norton, 1984), but establishing the necessary institutions, management, and funding has had less success. Over the last five years or so, there have been developments within community development, farmer/peasant education and 'grass-roots' planning that will help desertification control efforts.

Overgrazing and trampling by livestock can be countered by developing feedlot-rearing rather than free grazing. Beaumont (1989: 213) stresses the need to prevent overgrazing at critical times, in particular when seed is being set. Once seeds have been dispersed (or bulbs/tubers developed), then overgrazing poses much less threat. If grazing animals prevent seeding/bulb and tuber development, possibly through grazing in a few critical weeks of the year, then rangeland recovery will be, at best, slow and degraded. The possibilities for diverting investment in livestock to other alternatives should be investigated where there is a risk of overgrazing (Mortimore, 1989: 219). Where bushfire is a cause of desertification, improved control should be considered.

Measures which can be used to mitigate or avoid desertification, such as: appropriate forestry, fuelwood-supply plantations, dryland cropping strategies and range management have received more attention in the last decade. The challenge now is to:

1. Assemble appropriate 'packages' of crops, livestock, soil management, possibly alternative livelihoods, drought insurance/avoidance, etc, to suit each region.
2. To disseminate such 'packages', 'tune' them to local needs/constraints and sustain them by providing necessary inputs and, above all stable, appropriate institutions able to ensure efficient management.
3. To rehabilitate already degraded land where possible.

9 Non-erosive soil degradation

BECAUSE SOILS and other local conditions vary so much, it is difficult to generalize. Nevertheless, soil degradation might be defined as: a reduction of the current and/or future capability of soil to produce, in terms of quantity, quality, goods or services (Dregne, 1987; Higgins, 1988: 2). Soil degradation can be both quantitative: loss of soil due to erosion, mass movement and solution, or qualitative: decline in fertility; reduction of plant nutrients; structural changes; changes in aeration/moisture content; change in trace elements, salts, alkaline compounds; pollution with some chemical compound; change in soil flora or fauna. Soil degradation can be a natural phenomenon, for example: leaching of glacial soils, fragipan formation, laterite/plinthite formation, or anthropogenic. Soil is generally formed at a very slow rate, typically a few millimetres per century, soil removal can easily take place at a rate of several centimetres per year or more. Soil renewal/replacement depends on a complex of factors that can easily be disrupted. Although potentially a renewable resource, soil can become a non-renewable resource if mismanaged. Some soils require much more careful management than others.

The process of soil degradation may be difficult, and very costly, to halt or reverse once it gets under way. In some cases it may well be virtually impossible to reclaim or rehabilitate an area that has been degraded. This is particularly the case if vital seeds, fungi and soil organisms are lost, and, with such loss, there is also likely to be altered microclimate.

Soil degradation is one of the most crucial problems today, a problem that is accelerating, and one that tends to get too little attention from governments and people. Soil degradation is afflicting developing and developed countries from the Equator to the poles (Greenland & Lal, 1977: 5; Bridges, 1978). Oil has become a widely traded commodity in the second half of the twentieth century. The world was quick to recognize an 'oil crisis' in 1973/74, yet, in spite of the fact that soil degradation affects all people, millions of them directly, and in spite of soil degradation being a serious problem in many regions long before the 1970s, soil degradation has had much less attention. Possibly, worry about an oil crisis helped blinker people. Ironically, as oil reserves are depleted, soil resources will become more and more valuable because: 1. with less energy and artificial fertilizers, agricultural strategies will have to be revised; 2. it may well be necessary to grow crops to substitute for the energy and industrial raw materials presently obtained from petroleum as well as produce food crops.

Study and control of soil degradation is beset by many difficulties: data is often inadequate; the processes of erosion may vary over time, and monitoring has seldom been continuous or on-going. Occasional, frequently inaccurate, measurements give a distorted view. Much more research is required if satisfactory land management is ever to be achieved (Thornes, 1985; 1989).

For many years, soil degradation over wide areas of the globe has been masked by improving agricultural yields. These yield improvements have frequently been accomplished at the expense of accelerated soil damage. There must come the time where soil damage reaches a critical point, where gradual degradation shifts to catastrophe. There will be large areas, some of them vital for food/commodity production, where technology will not be able to boost yields to compensate for soil damage. Indeed, there are already signs in some regions that technology and crop improvement have reached a 'plateau' (Brown *et al.*, 1984: 54; Canter, 1986: 1). Soil degradation may result in feedback mechanisms, such that damage to soil sets in motion a chain of causation leading to further, greater decline (Nortcliff, 1986).

At present, soil degradation is mainly associated with farming, grazing, logging and mining. However, in the future, soil degradation may become more general, not just linked with land use, but affecting untouched, natural landscapes as well as those used by Man, if there is serious acid deposition, 'greenhouse effect' climatic change or radioactive fall-out contamination.

CAUSES OF NON-EROSIVE SOIL DEGRADATION

Considerable soil degradation can occur without there being any erosion; indeed, it is likely to predispose a soil to erosion, as a consequence of: compaction, salts/alkali accumulation, burning, chemical changes, oxidation of organic matter, etc.

Compaction and burning

If forest or savanna are cleared, there may be considerable variation in the subsequent degree of degradation depending on how the clearance was conducted. Much depends on how much compaction occurs, and how much of the plant nutrients are lost after vegetation is cleared. When vegetation is burnt, a lot of nutrients are carried away in ash, soot and smoke. Much of the remaining ash may be blown or washed away if there are heavy, rather than gentle, rains soon after the fire. If there has been a particularly fierce and hot burn, soil micro-organisms and soil organic matter may be destroyed and there may be chemical changes in the surface layers. The timing of the burning relative to seasonal rains is important, both in affecting the fierceness of the burn, and in determining how long may elapse before heavy rain strikes the burnt ground. Even on the same soil, the following clearance strategies could have different consequences:

1. Hand removal of vegetation – little soil compaction, some selected trees might be left to control erosion.
2. Use of bulldozer – much compaction of soil, little control over what vegetation is left. Generally more destructive than hand-cutting and burning. A single farm tractor pass may well cause a 70% reduction of soil porosity.
3. Bulldozer-clearing, plus burning of cut vegetation is particularly likely to result in land degradation (Little & Horowitz, 1987: 81).

In the UK, tractors, combine harvesters and items of towed farm machinery typically weigh between 10 and 15 tonnes and can cause serious long-term compaction, especially on heavy clay soils (Wolman & Fournier, 1987: 145). Trampling by livestock and animals used to till the land can cause compaction, but this is likely to be less than that resulting from mechanized cultivation. Clay–loam soils may become compacted when the clay content washes down the soil profile.

Decline of soil fertility

Soil fertility is a function of a wide range of factors, but, most crucial, are the availability of plant nutrients and adequate, but not excessive, moisture. There are many ways of assessing the fertility status of a soil, ranging from electronic probes and chemical soil tests to falling yields or the presence of 'indicator species' of weeds. In parts of Africa, the appearance of witchweed (*Striga* spp.) generally shows a fertility decline is taking place.

Loss of soil organic matter

The loss/exhaustion of soil organic matter, and the nutrients used by plants, can occur in virtually any environment, but is most dramatic in drylands. Organic matter is important in maintaining soil structure, supporting micro-organisms and in the retention of plant nutrients. As organic matter is concentrated near the surface, this valuable material is generally the first to be lost. Once the organic carbon content falls below about 2%, a soil is likely to be easily eroded (Kirkby & Morgan, 1980: 286). Loss of soil organic matter should therefore make a good indicator for those wishing to monitor land degradation. Surprisingly, it is seldom measured on an on-going basis.

Loss of organic matter may result from removal of crops, fodder, woodfuel and dung and bushfires, or stubble-burning, or overgrazing without the return of any material to compensate. It may also result from alteration of soil drainage, or tillage that accelerates oxidation of organic matter. Peaty soils tend to suffer oxidation of organic matter if drained, and can shrink alarmingly as a consequence. In drier climates, the loss of soil organic matter generally leads to a reduction in retention of soil moisture and, with this, a decline in vegetation cover, crops or natural plants, which, in turn, leads to increased erosion. A feedback can thus arise, as organic matter/moisture in soil falls, so plant cover declines and thus renewal of organic matters in soil is further reduced.

Tropical moist forests produce a lot of organic matter, both litter and root debris; soil micro-organisms rapidly break this down and it is re-absorbed by the vegetation. If the forest is cleared, the breakdown of organic matter generally remains high, but the supply of material ceases so that a decline of soil organic matter takes place. The soil exposed to sunlight is warmed more than it would have been under tree cover and may dry out more. It is common for a crust or plinthite deposits, duricrusts or cuirassic deposits, to develop after forest clearance (Nye & Greenland, 1960; Lewis & Berry, 1988: 133).

Problems with dung

Where fuelwood is scarce, people turn to dried animal dung for fuel and soil organic matter content can then decline (Wolman & Fournier, 1987: 203). Agarwal (1986: 26) pointed out that use of cattle dung has a high opportunity cost in terms of lost agricultural output had the dung been used to manure the soil. As well as leading to soil damage, it is likely to lead to increased area of cultivation to get the same crop. Agarwal estimated that, for every tonne of cattle dung burnt in India, roughly 50 kg of potential food grains are lost. Worldwide, it is likely that over 400 million tonnes of cattle dung are burnt every year in the Third World (World Resources Insitute *et al.*, 1985: 7; Agarwal, 1986: 26). India is a particularly heavy user of cattle dung, consuming at least 73 million tonne y^{-1} (*c.* one-third of total biomass used for energy). Dung is also much used as fuel in the Peruvian *altiplano* (Foley *et al.*, 1984).

Where fuelwood has to be purchased, dung may be more economical for a household. Reduction of dung usage for fuel may not necessarily follow planting of trees that provide wood for the market – it depends on relative prices of dung/fuelwood. Eckholm *et al.* (1984: 37) cite an Indian study which found that 1 tonne of dung applied to a field gave around US$ 8.0 worth of improved crop yield. The same tonne of dung, if used for fuel, could save the user purchase of fuelwood costing US$27 in the local market.

In Australia, low levels of soil organic matter has been a serious problem in some regions, in spite of there being no collection of dung and an adequate deposition by livestock. The problem was that there were virtually no indigenous insects capable of incorporating livestock dung into the soil. Livestock effectively removed organic matter which was not returned to the soil because it oxidized on the surface or was blown or washed away. The solution has been to import suitable dung-burying beetles (scarabs) (Jackson *et al.*, 1984).

Structural changes, 'laterization', crust and pan formation

Compaction and shrinkage through oxidation are not the only causes of structural change. Soil may suffer suffosion – the washing out, or the washing down profile of soluble salts like gypsum or common salt. Loess-type soils are vulnerable, and the problem may arise if land is irrigated. In the San Joaquin Valley, California, a considerable area subsided over 9 m through suffosion between 1925 and 1975. Some soils suffer a 'sealing' of soil fissures if they are cultivated, or mis-cultivated. Without pores and fissures to hold air and moisture, the soil becomes less fertile. Acid-sulphate problems afflict an estimated 12.6 million ha worldwide, 50% in Asia and the Far East. When this happens, the consequences are often bleak (Lal *et al.*, (1989: 66), (acid-sulphate soils are discussed later in this chapter).

A pan is a hard concretionary layer formed at, or beneath, the soil surface. Often pans form just below the cultivation depth; these are sometimes called plough soles. They can restrict roots, making crops or natural cover vulnerable to drought and trees vulnerable to wind-throw. They can also affect drainage leading to waterlogging and salinity/alkalinity problems. Once crusts (or duricrusts) develop, soil moisture recharge declines, vegetation finds it difficult to root, and sheetwash and gulley erosion increase as the land fails to absorb precipitation (Webster & Wilson, 1966: 32).

Laterite and laterization are not very precise terms, but, generally speaking, refer to the product and process of leaching leading to the concentration, consolidation and hardening of silicates (particularly Al_2O_3 and/or Fe_2O_3) to form layers, sometimes of great thickness. It is particularly common in the humid and subhumid Tropics. Depending on the nature of the materials involved, some authorities recognize: laterite, ferricrete' silcrete, calcrete (*caliche*): involving aluminium, iron, silica and calcium compounds respectively, (Goudie, 1973). The formation of laterites or plinthites and pans can be very rapid. Some tropical soils, often those beneath moist tropical forest or savanna harden as soon as they are drained or exposed to the air by tillage, road-cutting, etc. The effect of duricrust formation can be striking, the resulting scattered bush with bare patches of ground has been termed 'pedological leprosy'.

Acidification

Acid deposition has become a problem in nations with industrial development and/or widespread use of coal for fuel. The problem of air pollution-related acidification is spreading (see Chapter 4). Changes in crops and land use may also cause soil acidity changes, as may careless application of fertilizers. In Australia, for example, the creation of leguminous pastures, mainly with exotic white clover or alfalfa, has been known to cause soil acidification (Chisholm & Dumsday, 1987: 333).

The accumulation of toxic compounds and pest organisms

Salinization and alkalinization (alkalization) are among the main causes of land degradation (see next section). There are many toxic compounds other than salts or alkali compounds that may build up in soils naturally or as a consequence of development. Boron and selenium are naturally abundant in some soils and groundwaters; human activity may bring them to the surface or increase the level of contamination, if, say, poor-quality irrigation water is used on land. Boron, heavy metals, pesticides, herbicides, disease and pest organisms, radioactive compounds and many other contaminants may degrade soil following human activities ranging from warfare to sewage effluent disposal. These problems turn the use of organic wastes for soil improvement into anything but a simple, trouble-free process.

LAND DEGRADATION AS A CONSEQUENCE OF WATERLOGGING, SALINIZATION OR ALKALINIZATION

Rainfed agriculture tends to lose topsoil by water erosion and deflation. Irrigated agriculture tends to lose topsoil through waterlogging, salinization or alkalinization.

WATERLOGGING

Where drainage is impeded leading to saturation, i.e. soil interstitial spaces are water-filled, a soil may be said to be waterlogged. Some plant and animal species are adapted to waterlogged soils, some are not. If waterlogging of a soil occurs gradually, plants and animals may adapt or new species have time to colonize. If the waterlogging is relatively sudden, there may follow a period when existing organisms die or move away and new, adapted species have not colonized. As plant cover declines, soil erosion may occur unless there is standing water to protect the soil surface.

The post-waterlogging flora and fauna depend on many factors, including: the chemistry of the water and soil and upon how saturated vegetation and soil organic matter break down. In some environments, dispersal of flora and fauna that are adapted to wetlands is difficult; there may be no nearby sources of plants or animals and there may be little movement of birds or animals or floodwaters to carry organisms. It is likely that waterlogged areas will tend to acquire species found in the nearest ponds marshes and streams.

Waterlogging may be caused in many ways:

- altered land use may upset an existing precipitation: evapo transpiration relationship so that water-tables rise, even quite subtle changes of plant cover may have this effect;
- road and rail construction may obstruct drainage;
- poorly lined irrigation canals and/or reservoirs may leak and raise local or regional water-tables;
- irrigation schemes may 'leak' water raising local water-tables, there are large areas of the world where waterlogging/salinization due to this 'leakage' has reduced crop yields to levels below that obtained before irrigation development;
- rising sea levels or altered base levels, the latter often due to reservoir or barrage construction or inter-basin water transfer may cause waterlogging.

Altered land use might be the replacement of forest/woodland by shrubs annual crops or grassland and/or less obvious thinning or subtle species changes and/or compaction through land use. The reduction of evapotranspiration and/or the increase of infiltration due to altered groundcover changes in compaction, due, for example, to tillage of grazing land, and/or increased precipitation have attracted much attention (Ayoade, 1988: 254–7) In general, the replacement of tree cover with grass or shrubs is held to result in rising water-tables and possibly waterlogging, but it is not always the case. Much depends on what species are replaced and which replace, particularly their rooting depth. It is possible for very subtle vegetation changes, possibly only a change of one grass or herb association to another to alter regional water-tables. It need not be a gross change, from say grass to trees, although, in Western Australia, problems seem related mainly to the replacement of evergreen eucalyptus woodland, which transpires moisture year-round, with annual crops that transpire only during a relatively short growing season. By 1973, it seems at least 120,000 km² had been affected, the rising water-tables causing salinization and killing off of vegetation in lower-lying areas (Pereira, 1973: 76–81).

Where development impedes drainage, degradation can occur: up-slope where water is ponded causing waterlogging, which may kill trees and other cover until in time a wetland vegetation develops; down-slope where wetlands or better-drained areas may suffer through the loss of run-off or streamflows. Examples of such changes may be seen along the highways constructed in Amazonian Brazil where it is common to see woodland that has died off due to impeded local drainage.

Poorly lined irrigation canals and 'leaky' irrigation schemes cause widespread waterlogging and salinization, it is perhaps a little misleading to use the term 'leaky' with respect to irrigated land, for it is vital that enough water be applied to irrigated farmland to ensure a net downward movement of soil moisture to maintain a salt balance, i.e. the leaching away of salts. If a salt balance is not maintained, the land usually becomes salinized. The problem is that, where drainage is inadequate, waterlogging occurs, the leaching ceases, and salinization increases.

There are serious waterlogging difficulties associated with many large irrigation developments, for example: the Welton-Mohawk Irrigation Project (east of Yuma, Arizona, USA) (Beaumont, 1989: 274); also in the Grand Valley, California and over wide areas of the Indus Basin of

India/Pakistan, where in 1982 there were an esimated 8 million ha of waterlogged soils – 40% of which had become salinized (Barrow, 1987a: 298). Another estimate suggested that in the late 1970s up to 50% of Pakistan's huge canal irrigation area was waterlogged or close to becoming waterlogged (Little & Horowitz, 1987: 364). In the USSR, there has been similar 'leakage' problems associated with the Karz–Kum Irrigation Canal (Arnon, 1981: 123). In Egypt, as a whole, irrigation 'leakage' had led to the waterlogging and widespread salinization of about 80% of the total agricultural area (USDA, 1976 data cited in Beaumont, 1989: 256). In the 1960s, each year, as much land was being lost to waterlogging and salinization in the oases of Soviet Central Asia as were being brought into irrigated use. The situation had much improved by the mid 1970s, due to more attention to drainage and better water management (Mabbutt, 1987: 375; Beaumont, 1989: 392).

There has been waterlogging associated with many of the large reservoirs built since the 1950s for hydroelectric generation, irrigation supply or flood control purposes, e.g. around Lake Nasser, waterlogging has led to salinization and is endangering archaeological remains, and thus, indirectly, tourism.

Sea-level change has yet to become a significant cause of waterlogging but may well, especially in Bangladesh, the Nile Delta, the Netherlands and many other countries. Already Bangladesh has suffered increased salinization of farmland because seawater has pushed further into the delta system as withdrawals, and diversions of river water have reduced flows in the Ganges (Barrow, 1987a: 290).

Not all waterlogging is undesirable; at least a quarter of Mankind depend on rice, and much of that is cropped from flooded paddy-fields. Considerable areas of the Tropics and subtropics are deliberately waterlogged to form paddy-fields. Natural swampland also yields sago palm in parts of South East Asia and in parts of S. America and N. America wild rice. Paddy-fields may suffer much less soil erosion than alternative land uses, it is also likely that paddy production will be better sustained than rain-fed rice production. Provided agrochemical pollution does not occur, paddy-fields and associated ponds and channels yield fish and crustaceans, which can provide a valuable source of protein for people.

Waterlogged soils may yield methane, a 'greenhouse gas', which is increasingly important in global warming (see Chapter 3). Problems with acid sulphates may follow waterlogging, if it has been for long enough to cause the reduction of sulphate ions in the soil to sulphides under anaerobic conditions. If soils that have suffered such reduction are drained, they generally become very acid. If there is not enough calcium present to neutralize the reformed sulphate ions, an acid-sulphate soil may develop and be difficult to rehabilitate.

SALINITY AND ALKALINITY PROBLEMS

It is more likely that salinity problems will arise because of an excess of salt or alkaline materials. However, soils may suffer suffosion – the washing out of soluble salts which can result in subsidence and/or compaction. Loess or gypsum or silt rich soils are especially prone to this.

If a soil allows capillary rise of moisture, there is a very great danger that, if groundwater lies near enough to the surface, salts, and alkaline, sodic compounds, will be deposited in the root zone, the depth of soil between the water-table and the ground surface. Soils may contain residual salts that were already in the soil, or in underlying rocks, before Man used the land. These may have been concentrated by weathering, may have been carried to a natural depression by floods, or may have been in the soil if it was originally deposited under marine, or saline lake, conditions (this is known as primary salinization). Salts may also accumulate in a soil as a consequence of altered natural conditions or human activity. This is termed secondary salinization.

Lowlands, especially those which have endorheic drainage, are likely to suffer natural salinization. There are various reasons for secondary salinization (sodification, alkalinization or alkalization): there may be insufficient movement of water through the soil to carry away salt/alkali compounds; the water applied to the soil by irrigators may be of too high a salt/alkali content; groundwater may be too close to the ground. Each of these alone or in combination, can give rise to salinization/alkalinization. However groundwater at too shallow a depth is a particularly common cause.

A significant amount of salinization results from bad land management and/or bad irrigation supply systems and/or bad irrigation management that has led to excessive application of water and/or inadequate drainage. All of these can cause rising water-tables. In a loamy soil, the critical depth for the water-table has been calculated to be between 1.5 and 2.5 m below ground surface. Were the groundwater to rise higher, even if there was good quality groundwater or irrigation water, salinization/alkalinization would be likely (Kovda, 1980: 184; Holmes & Talsma, 1981). In some fine-textured soils there may be a risk even when the water-table is over 3.0 m below ground surface (Barrow, 1987a: 212–13). It should be noted that salts can migrate laterally as well as up and down a soil profile. Where land is poorly levelled or has a naturally uneven surface, there may be patches of salt build-up in the depressions.

Forms of salinization and alkalinization

A number of different salts or alkaline compounds may be present alone or in combinations in soil moisture in sufficient quantities to cause problems. Plants and organisms can be harmed by high concentrations of a single salt, toxic effect of a single ion, but more often, by high concentrations of more than one salt/alkali: the total dissolved solids effect. High levels of salt/alkali affect plants in a number of ways: they may prevent a plant from extracting adequate moisture from the soil by making the osmotic potential of the soil moisture greater than that within the plant tissue; in general, too much salt or alkali will hinder the extraction of nutrients from the soil and suppress plant growth; high salinity can reduce the conversion of ammonium salts to nitrate by soil micro-organisms which harms soil fertility.

Problems also arise if the balance in the soil between sodium and calcium plus magnesium is upset; when this happens, soil structure generally suffers (Barrow, 1987a: 97). Soils so affected lose permeability and become compacted. The actual concentration of salts/alkalis, which may be harmful in a given situation, depends very much upon the chemical characteristics of the soil, on the vegetation cover and on the management of drainage, irrigation or rain-fed agriculture.

Salinity/alkalinity in a soil is not constant; it varies from place to place even over short distances, depending on tillage, local soil quality, local topography, distance from surface to the water-table. Soil salinity may also vary in time, during the dry season, if there is one; when there is little rain to leach out salts, salinity may rise. Conversely it is likely to fall towards the end of a wet season. In drylands, salts can build up over a period of time if the land is cultivated and/or irrigated, but may be reduced if there is a suitable fallow period.

When high levels of soluble salts like sodium chloride or sodium sulphate accumulate in soil, provided there is less than 15% exchangeable sodium, i.e. that which is not chemically linked to clay particles, and which is therefore mobile), there may be formed a saline soil (solontchak or white alkali efflorescence soil), typically with a pH between 7 and 8.5. Often these soils have fluffy crystalline accumulations on, or near, the surface (Szabolcs, 1974: *iii*).

Abundant salts, and more than 15% exchangeable sodium, lead to the formation of alkali soils by alkaline hydrolysis. Thus this process is termed alkalinization (broadly synonymous terms are: sodification, sodication, solodization or soda alkalinization). Generally such soils have a pH of 8.5 or more.

If an alkali soil has little chloride content and abundant exchangeable sodium bicarbonate and/or sodium carbonate (over 15% exchangeable sodium), but little calcium, clay particles in the soil adsorb sodium and magnesium salts and swell, become impermeable and easily compacted; the process is known as hydrophilization. When this happens, rainfall or irrigation infiltration is hindered and plant roots/soil organisms may be starved of oxygen. Sodium hydroxides may also form and dissolve organic matter which can be deposited on the soil surface to form a dark efflorescence or crust, for which reason such soils are sometimes called black alkali soils, they are also known as solonetz or non-saline sodic soils. Typically, these solonetz soils have a pH between 8.5 and 10.0.

As a rough and easily remembered rule-of-thumb, sodium carbonates and bicarbonates lead to alkalinity, and sodium chloride and sodium sulphates lead to salinity.

Attempts to rehabilitate salinized soil can result in the formation of alkali soils if there is inadequate calcium in the soil to prevent sodium hydroxide build-up, which in turn leads to sodium carbonate formation (solodization).

Causes of salinization and alkalinization

Irrigation, or rather poorly designed and/or poorly managed irrigation, is a major cause of salinization/alkalinization in developed and developing countries. The problem occurs under free-enterprise economies and communism, in the Tropics, subtropics and, to a lesser extent, in temperate environments. The problem with irrigation is that, in most situations, if the management is allowed to falter, or if something goes wrong with the infrastructure, supplies or demand for water salinization/alkalinization may ensue and be difficult to counter. Few modern irrigation projects have functioned for more than 30 years, so how sustainable this form of agriculture is in the long term is unproven. What is clear is that, when things go wrong with irrigation, salinization/alkalinization can be very rapid.

There are four main reasons why irrigation causes salinization/alkalinization: leakage of water from supply canals; over-application of water; inadequate provision of drainage; inadequate application of water to leach away salts. When the latter is satisfactory, there is a real risk that salty return flows or groundwater will flow or seep into depressions and cause problems there.

In the Murray Basin (S. Australia) marine silts were laid down about two million years ago. Irrigation leaches salts from these soils, the river and groundwater become more saline and, when used for irrigation, cause salinity problems. In the Grand Valley, California, large areas of land are underlain by salty marine shales, irrigation raises the water-tables and mobilizes the salts.

In the wheat-belt of Western Australia, over 260,000 ha have been sufficiently affected by salinization to reduce or prevent cropping, largely because deep-rooting natural vegetation has been replaced with shallow-rooting cereals, and the reduced transpiration losses have led to raised water-tables. There are other areas of Australia, notably in Victoria, where around 100,000 ha are similarly affected (Chisholm & Dumsday, 1987: 15). Grove (1985: 61) reported similar changes in N. Nigeria. A rather different salinization process has been reported for southwestern USA, where, according to Farvar & Milton (1972), salt cedars (*Tamarix* spp.) tap saline groundwater that lies well below the ground surface and exude salt from their leaves, thus bringing salt to the surface.

Saline seeps may form where cereals are produced on dryland; soils underlain by slightly salty or salty subsoil, and where drainage is slow and the ground sloping. Depressions collect salts from the surrounding land to become 'seeps' (Dregne, 1983: 44). This is a serious problem in the northern Great Plains of S. Canada, and the USA, and in New South Wales and Western Australia. Fallowing may apparently have little effect and may even exacerbate the problem. Salt 'seeps' have been increasing since about 1945. They mainly appear on cultivated former rangeland, especially on the glacial soils of Alberta, Saskatchewan, N. Dakota, Montana, and S. Dakota). The cause appears to be an excess of soil moisture over evapotranspiration, apparently because the crop-fallow system increases water intake – mainly by trapping and holding winter snow which would blow away on natural rangeland. The blame for this form of salinization, therefore, seems to lie squarely with agriculturalists. The solution may well be to grow a deep-rooted summer crop like alfalfa to increase evapotranspiration (Wolman & Fournier, 1987: 381).

Altered precipitation, evaporation, evapotranspiration or run-off may trigger salinization/alkalinization. There may well be considerable change in areas affected by salinization as the 'greenhouse effect' develops. Szabolcs (1988) discussed the possible salinity changes in Europe resulting from the 'greenhouse effect'. His conclusion was that even a 1 °C rise in global mean temperature would cause considerable changes.

Where land is held on short-term tenure, cultivators will tend to neglect longer-term consequences and skimp on salinization management. Peasant farmers may prefer to use, or may be forced to use, shallow wells that yield saline water. Deeper wells, which cost more to sink and to pump, might give less salty irrigation supplies (Farvar & Milton, 1972: 285). In some regions of the Middle East, particularly Iran, relatively fresh supplies delivered by *quanat* have been supplemented in recent years by brackish water obtained cheaply from shallow boreholes. Inevitably there has been more salinization.

The extent, rate of increase and costs of salinization and alkalinization

It is difficult to get an accurate global estimate of the extent of salinization/alkalinization because the mode of occurrence and severity varies so much from locality to locality. Also, unless the problem is well advanced, the effects are insidious: there may be little perceived salinization, but crop yields or the range of land uses for an area may have been significantly affected. Some regions or countries have good maps, but all estimates of extent and

Table 9.1. *Global distribution of salt-affected soils.*

Area	Saline	Alkaline	Total	% irrigated area salinized
	(thousand ha)			
N. America	6,191	9,564	15,755	—
Mexico and Central America	1,965	—	—	—
S. America	69,410	59,573	129,163	—
Africa	53,492	26,946	80,438	—
S. Asia	83,312	1,798	85,110	—
N. and Central Asia	91,621	120,065	211,686	—
S.E. Asia	19,983	—	—	—
Australasia	17,359	339,971	901,430	—
Egypt	—	—	—	30–40
USA	—	—	—	20.25
China	—	—	—	15
Iraq	—	—	—	50
Pakistan	—	—	—	35
Australia	—	—	—	15–20

Source: Middleton, 1988: 17; Lal *et al.*, 1989: 65.

rate of change should be treated with caution. A real problem is one of standardization; one authority's 'significant salinization' may be orders of magnitude different from another's. The occurence of natural and man-made salinization/alkalinization have also made it difficult to measure the extent of degradation. It is, however, possible to equate much salinization with irrigation development.

There are few countries which do not have at least localized salinization/alkalinization problems. One suggestion is that there are around 25 million ha worldwide that are unusable for agriculture because of salinization (Kayasseh & Schenck, 1989). Worldwide, it has been estimated that, in the late 1980s, there are probably around 91 million ha of irrigated land; at least a third is in a poor state due to salinization, possibly over a half, i.e. roughly 30 to 46 million ha (Barrow, 1987a: 298).

Szabolcs (1971, 1974, 1988) gave a detailed country-by-country outline of distribution, extent and trends of salinization in Europe (Fig. 9.1 is based on his 1988 maps). In 1971, he estimated there were at least 20 million ha of salinized soils in Europe. Recent information on the extent of salinized land in Australia has been given by Williams (1987), and by Roberts (1987), who esimated that 2.0% of the continents' non-arid land was degraded by salinization. About 65% of Pakistan's agricultural land is irrigated, roughly one-third of that is affected by salinization (Table 9.1). Bokhari (1980: 174) surveyed 21 million acres (8.49 million ha) of the irrigated lands of the Indus Basin, and suggested that, by 1965: 18% was slightly saline; 11% moderately; 16% strongly. By 1978, the situation had apparently improved (on those lands) with falls of 6%, 3% and 6% respectively. Gupta (1979) and San Pietro (1982) have suggested that at least 7 million hectares of India were salinized or alkalized.

History has proved that salinization/alkalinization can overtake and ruin agriculture. The Tigris and Euphrates lowlands, in what is today part of Iran/Iraq, were once farmed by Mesopotamian civilizations – these areas are now mainly salty wastelands (Pearce, 1987a). Kovda (1983) suggested that salinization, natural plus Man-made, was possibly increasing at a rate of 1.0 to 1.5 million ha y^{-1} worldwide. More conservative estimates would put the figure nearer 160,000 ha y^{-1} (Barrow, 1987a: 298). While estimates are vague and inaccurate, the picture is clear that degradation is occurring in important areas of agricultural production and must inevitably impact upon Man's long-term well-being.

Accurate figures are hard to come by, but the scale of the costs is apparent by looking at regional or national expenditures that generally aim merely to contain the problem. The costs of land degradation due to salinization were calculated for the Murray–Murrambidgee River Basins in Victoria (Australia) to be rising at about A\$ 40 million/year by 1988 (Chisholm & Dumsday, 1987: 15). A 1985 estimate suggested Pakistan would spend US\$ 317 million over a few years to combat salinization (Barrow, 1987a: 293).

COUNTERING WATERLOGGING, SALINIZATION AND ALKALINIZATION

To control salinization/alkalinization, it is first necessary to recognize the type of problem and causes. In some circumstances, control and possibly rehabilitation may be practicable, in others it may not.

Waterlogging can be cured by drainage. Ditches, tile or mole-plough drains can be used to lower water-tables where there is sufficient fall available to ensure a flow of water out from the waterlogged soil. In some cases, a change of cropping strategy/fallowing/crop mix may be sufficient to lower water-tables. Where there is level terrain, pumping and water disposal system may be required.

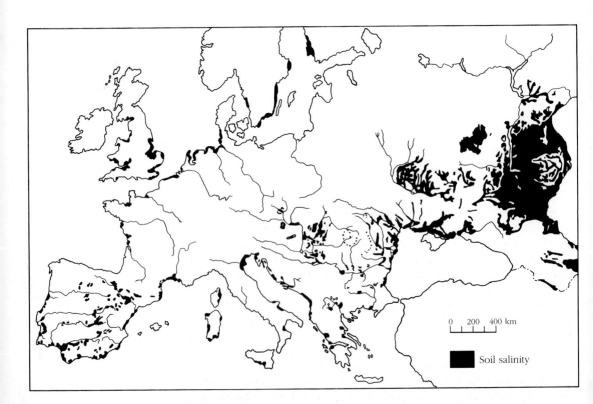

Fig. 9.1. Salinization in Europe 1988. Source: *Szabolcs, 1988: 8 (Map 1).*

In the Indus Basin, Pakistan's Salinity Control and Reclamation Programme (SCARP) have used drains and deep tubewells that are pumped to lower water-tables. This deeper water tends to be less salty than shallow groundwater and can be used to leach out salt. SCARP projects have been initiated at 5-year intervals since the 1950s, SCARP Project V began in 1987. A problem with drainage is that the contaminated water return flows have to be disposed of and may cause problems. If there is no suitable 'sump' area, then discharge into streams may hinder downstream irrigation, water use and aquatic or floodplain wildlife. On the Murray Floodplain, Australia, a common tree: *Eucalyptus camaldulensis* is increasingly showing reduced vigour because of soil salinization, much due to increased salt deposition by floods as a consequence of upstream return flow discharges.

The Colorado River (USA) is an example of a watercourse heavily loaded with salts leached from irrigation areas. Much of the Colorado's water is extracted above the Imperial Dam to supply California and the Welton–Mohawk Irrigation District. Before the Dam, Mexico got water across the border with an average *c.* 700 ppm salts. After the Imperial Dam, the Colorado's water averaged *c.* 1500 ppm as it crossed the border (Pearce, 1987a).

If the main cause of salinization is soluble salt(s) concentrating in the upper layers of the soil, reclamation is relatively easy. With many soils it is possibly to leach out salts, provided that sufficient water of reasonable quality, as precipitation or irrigation, is available, and that the water-table can be lowered by drainage or by pumping below the critical depth. It should be noted that leaching salts away will also remove nutrients; therefore it may be necessary to add fertilizers or composts to the soil to compensate, and the costs should be budgeted for.

In some situations, the water-table may be within critical depth of the soil surface because there is a perched water-table, i.e. there is an impediment to drainage in the soil. If the impediment is a lateritic layer, deep-ploughing may be sufficient to break it up, improve drainage and control salinization/alkalinization.

While it is theoretically easy to calculate the amount of water required to leach away salts and maintain a salt balance in the soil, i.e. a satisfactory steady-state whereby incoming salts deposited from irrigation water, etc, are compensated for by outgoing leaching water, it is, in practice, not so straightforward. Water may rise through the soil, carrying salts/alkaline compounds, relatively easily by capillary action via small pores and fissures. Getting water to drain down through these smaller fissures may be difficult, or virtually impossible if soil has become impermeable because of salinization/alkalinization, or because clay minerals have swollen. Clay soils have generally been more difficult to remove salts from. A promising treatment for such soils is to till them to about 50 cm depth, build bunds across the field to restrict surface flow and then irrigate (Wiseman, 1989). If soils have accumulated an excess of the element boron, this can be more difficult to leach out than more common salts.

If salts/alkaline compounds have become chemically linked to clay particles, chemical treatment may be required to dislodge them, i.e., it is necessary to replace exchangeable sodium – this is known as chemical amendment/amelioration. To rehabilitate saline–alkaline soils, the problem is to replace the exchangeable sodium ions which are linked to clay particles with calcium or other suitable ions, in order to reduce the sodium to calcium ratio, and then to leach out the replaced sodium and other soluble salts that are no longer bound to the clay.

Efforts to rehabilitate saline or saline–sodic soils must be cautious, for a mistake resulting in the leaching away of soluble salts leaving exchangeable salts bonded to the clay particles could convert them to alkali soils; their structure deteriorates and they are then very difficult to amend.

A common means of replacing exchangeable sodium with calcium is to spread a soluble calcium salt on the soil, usually gypsum, $CaSO_4$. Gypsum (sulphate of lime) is often available as an industrial by-product, and may become more readily available if thermal power stations adopt certain flue-gas treatments to combat pollution (Seneviratne, 1979; Kayasseh & Schenck, 1989). Even quite low application rates of gypsum (say 7.5 tonne per hectare) may be sufficient to allow crops to be grown. Powdered sulphur, aluminium and ferrous sulphate have also been successfully used for soil amendment; these hydrolyse, liberating sulphuric acid which acts to counter the salinity. The control of alkalinity in dryland soils often involves the use of acidifying agents like those just listed, but efforts can be expensive, largely because the soils are so impermeable that it is difficult to leach out contaminants. Some salinized/alkalinized soils lie above a subsoil with sufficient $CaCO_3$ or $CaCO_4$ for amelioration to be performed by simply ploughing so as to mix topsoil and subsoil (Kovda, 1982: 325). In some situations, soils can be improved by simply leaving them fallow so that rain washes out the salts.

A slower, less-effective alternative to chemical amendment is to grow, harvest and remove plants which are able to draw salts from the soil. Such plants might be rotated with crops, or might themselves provide some useful product such as thatch, fuel, food, paper pulp or straw for strawboard manufacture. This has been tried on the Gezeira Irrigation Scheme (Sudan), where a fodder crop: saltbush (*Atriplex* spp.) has been grown in rotation (one year in twelve) with the cotton cash crop. Other promising species include: *Prosopis spicifera*, *Suaeda fructicosa*, *Leptochloea fusca* and some of the rush family (*Juncus* spp.) (Barrow, 1987a: 220).

It may be possible, in some situations, to lower the water-table to below the critical depth by planting blocks or belts of deep-rooted plants which transpire a lot of moisture. Such plants would (hopefully) not compete for water with shallow-rooted crops. In parts of India and Pakistan, oilseed rape, pulses or wheat, all relatively deep rooting, are often planted after rice crops so that they use up the remaining moisture before the rains return, keeping the water-table lower than would be the case if just rice were grown – they also give valuable second or even third crops. Where salt/alkali reduction runs into difficulties, it may be possible to plant salt/alkali-tolerant crops.

LAND DEGRADATION AS A CONSEQUENCE OF AGRICULTURAL POLLUTION

Agrochemicals: pesticides, herbicides, fungicides, etc.

Before 1940, there was little land degradation through agrochemicals, modern pesticides were only just coming onto the market, herbicides were limited to sodium chlorate and a few other weedkillers which were little used for farm agriculture, fungicides were seldom used outside orchards, vinyards and market gardening, and hormones, antibiotics, and so on, had not been developed. Artificial fertilizers were being used in some areas, but had caused few problems. In some temperate countries there were local stream pollution problems with sheep-dip.

Table 9.2. *Some commonly used pesticides and their characteristics.*

Non-persistent	Persistent	Permanent
	Type	
Organophosphorus compounds	Chlorinated hydrocarbons DDT Cyclodiene organochlorines Aldrin Dieldrin Endrin Heptachlor	Compounds of mercury, arsenic, lead
	Characteristics	
Lose toxicity over growing season. While effective, can be more toxic to mammals than persistent pesticides. In combination, can exhibit strong synergistic effects in toxicity.	Slowly lose toxicity, with a half-life of two to five years, or longer under certain conditions; slower to degrade in colder climates and in soils that are clay-rich, dry, or contain large quantities of organic material. Moderately toxic to mammals, very toxic to fish and crustaceans. Tend to concentrate and persist in body fat; do not build up indefinitely – maximum concentrations reached only with repeated applications.	Remain permanently in the environment unless physically removed. Can be lethal to humans in sufficient concentrations; relatively easy to avoid, however, since they tend to be 'immobile'. Industrial activities are the principal means of mercury and lead introduction into the environment. Agricultural arsenic compounds are little used today.

Source: Compiled by author.

It was first really brought home to the general public that there was a pesticide problem by the book *Silent Spring* (Carson, 1962), yet there has been disappointing headway in reducing the pollution, rather it has grown exponentially (Pratt, 1965; Bull, 1982; Anon, 1985b). Modern agriculture in the western nations and, at least among large-scale producers, in the Third World, has become more and more dependent on pesticides. Until recently, efforts to improve agriculture concentrated on increasing crop yields, mainly through the use of 'improved' seeds of 'high-yielding' varieties, which respond favourably to fertilizer and irrigation, but which demand pesticides, fungicides and selective herbicides to protect them. If the economics are right, if there is no problem associated with the agrochemicals, all may be fine, for example: cotton yields could increase by 50% and apples by 100% (see Table 9.2). Such yield increases could help reduce demand for opening more land for agriculture. Unfortunately, there are usually side effects when agrochemicals are used, and a crop which lacks resilience to pests, disease and environmental fluctuations may not be a desirable thing in the long term.

The long-term effects of pesticide, herbicide, and other agrochemical use on the environment, particularly within the soil, is not clear. There may be an insidious loss of vital soil organisms which play important roles in decay, nitrogen fixation, the sulphur cycle and/or are of significance in symbiotic relations with crops (e.g. mycorrhizal fungi or soil arthropods). Predatory organisms, like insect-eating birds, which destroy pest organisms, are likely to be affected by pesticides, and may well be because they are carnivores at the top of the food web. The long-term effect may be a temporary kill of pests, which may then develop a resistance to the pesticide, a more permanent kill of predators and a resulting 'boom' in pest numbers. Agrochemicals may have catastrophic effects if they destroy earthworms, termites or pollinating insects; the latter can be especially vulnerable if a feeding area is contaminated.

Monitoring agrochemical use is not easy. Problems can arise even when very small amounts of pesticides, herbicides, etc, are present. There is such a wide variety of agrochemicals that detecting and monitoring is difficult. Compounds may degrade before, or after, application into different harmful substances, some of which can be long-lived in the soil. However, it is not an option to suddenly reduce the use of agrochemicals to control pests, because the loss of produce to them is so great (Wolman & Fournier, 1987: 230). There is no guarantee that users will apply agrochemicals correctly; it is not unusual for market gardeners to mix pesticides together and to apply these and chemical fertilizers at excessive rates (Ghatak & Turner, 1978).

There is a trend toward integrated pest management, which means simply the application of common-sense to pest control so as to target poisons more precisely at pests, to try and conserve predator species and to use other strategies as well as poisons: pest deterrents, breed crops with pest resistance, attract and trap pests, etc. There is nowadays more interest in so-called 'biotic' pesticides such as derris or pyrethrum – which are natural or synthesized copies of natural compounds that pose fewer pollution problems.

Use of biological controls can go wrong, a control organism may become a pest, a bacteria designed to kill one thing might mutate and damage something else. It has been suggested that, if new pesticides similar to the toxins of many spiders were to be used, insects might develop resistance, then spider predation would be hindered leading to increased numbers of insects.

In countries where schistosomiasis debilitates the human population, in addition to causing great suffering and probably reducing farming efficiency, there are possibilities for using natural plant compounds to control the snail vector with little risk of contaminating streams, soil or groundwater with chemical molluscicides which often contain potentially toxic compounds like copper (Barrow, 1987a: 283).

The UNEP runs an International Register of Potentially Toxic Chemicals which provides a database on the vast range of agrochemicals (the Register is not restricted to agrochemicals).

Agrochemicals: fertilizers, lime, etc

In many countries, nitrate fertilizers have become a vital part of agricultural production. Without them, yields would fall to uneconomical levels (Johnson & Cowrie, 1969). Recently, pollution has become a serious problem. A less obvious problem is that use of such compounds may mask what would otherwise be a plateau or a decline in production due to soil damage and soil erosion (Wolman & Furnier, 1987: 203). It is not artificial fertilizer use *per se* that leads to land degradation, but incorrect, clumsy use. Nitrogenous fertilizers, phosphate fertilizers and ammonium-rich fertilizers can be converted in the soil by *Nitrosomonas*, bacteria to nitrate compounds. Some of this nitrite is converted to nitrate by *Nitrobacter* bacteria. Some of the nitrates leach out to contaminate waterbodies and may also be converted by soil micro-organisms into nitrogenous gases which escape to add to the 'greenhouse effect'. In the last few years, the UK and parts of W. Europe have realized that nitrate pollution of groundwater and surface water is a serious problem.

It is not just overuse of fertilizer that has led to nitrate pollution, and simply cutting future application will probably not reduce nitrate release that much for a long time, unless land is managed to 'lock up' nitrates. Some of the problem arises because soil organic matter has been decomposing more rapidly in recent years in areas that are ploughed, so the problem is, in part, because of a shift from pasture to arable cultivation. In temperate environments, growing grass or broad-leaved trees rather than arable crops on soils especially prone to nitrate formation and leaching may help reduce the problem (Addiscott, 1988).

In Western Europe the practice of growing winter wheat is apparently one cause of increase in nitrogenous fertilizer use and releases. In the UK, the Government has begun to encourage farmers to restrict the use of nitrate fertilizers in areas where the use is likely to cause problems, and it seems likely that EEC regulations coming into force in the 1990s will encourage Europe to further restrict practices that lead to nitrate pollution.

There has not been enough time for all the effects of using agrochemicals: chemical fertilizers, pesticides, herbicides, fungicides, etc to become apparent. There may be slow, cumulative changes in soil chemistry, structure and populations of soil micro-organisms. There has been a vast increase in agrochemical use, many in developed countries. For example, in the last 100 years, the UK has increased chemical fertilizer use about 25-fold (Briggs & Courtney, 1985: 101).

Superphosphate fertilizer may make soils more acid if applications are not carefully monitored.

Farm slurry, silage effluent and waste from processing agricultural products

Silage effluent and livestock waste are a problem in Western Europe, and in parts of the USA. Deliberate and accidental disposal into streams and rivers has caused great damage to aquatic and wetland ecosystems. After rudimentary 'treatment', by allowing the waste slurry to stand in a lagoon, or tank, some of the material can be returned to the land. Unfortunately, there is often far too much waste to spread on the land, transporting the surplus elsewhere is costly, and storage is a risky, temporary solution. An 800-head herd of dairy cattle in Europe have roughly the equivalent potential to damage to the environment as the sewage from two medium-sized UK cites (Cardiff and Swansea) combined (*The Sunday Times* 5/3/89: A15). Dutch farms produced *c.* 96 million tonnes of livestock manure in 1988, but the land could safely absorb only about 50 million tonnes. The EEC is accumulating more than a butter 'mountain' while parts of the Third World desperately need organic matter for their soil. In parts of Europe, it has been recorded that ammonia, generated by decomposition of manure-slurry in the soil, or that vented from sheds holding large numbers of livestock, kills trees and certain types of moorland vegetation over quite wide areas (Armstrong, 1988).

Livestock slurry is likely to contain residues of growth-promoting hormones, heavy metals (some livestock feed has high levels of copper), and antibiotics. The long-term effect these may have on soil micro-organisms is unknown.

Land drainage

If land is drained, there may be subsidence, acid-sulphate soil formation, oxidation of soil organic matter, even spontaneous combustion of peat deposits, and a risk that contaminated drainage water might damage floodlands and wetlands (Boels *et al.*, 1982).

AVOIDING AGROCHEMICALS: ORGANIC FARMING

There is an increasing interest in Europe and the USA in 'organic' farming, i.e. the abandonment of pesticides, herbicides, fertilizers, etc, but not the abandonment of modern seeds, livestock, mechanization, sound, proven husbandry techniques and soil conservation. The market for organically produced crops is expanding. The process of conversion is, however, rather slow, taking several years before land can be certified 'free' of agrochemicals. Organic farming is not new, most farming was organic farming before about 40 years ago.

An interesting comparison of land degradation effects of organic and conventional agriculture has been made by Reganold (1989). The study examined two neighbouring farms in Washington State (USA) which were virtually identical in all respects, except that one became 'conventional', non-organic, in 1948 and the other did not. The indications in the late 1980s were that the organic farm's soil held more moisture and had a better soil condition. A comparison of soil loss indicated that the conventional farm lost 20.4 t ha y^{-1}, whereas the organic farm lost only 7.8 t ha y^{-1}. The average yields (for winter wheat in 1986) on the organic farm were 8% lower than those of the neighbouring conventional farm, but were 13% higher than the average for the region's conventional farms.

AREAS THAT ARE ESPECIALLY VULNERABLE TO SOIL DEGRADATION

Tropical soils

According to Moran (1987: 69–73): tropical soils vary in 'fragility', and tropical soils are far from uniformly distributed. Moran claims that, in many parts of the world, the problem of soil degradation was not one of erosion or loss of organic matter, rather it is of increase in acidity and decline in what is often already poor fertility. Moran suggested that:

> 81% of Latin American soils are acidic and nutrient poor;
> 56% of Africa's soils are acidic and nutrient poor;
> 38% of Asia's soils are acidic and nutrient poor;
> 33% of humid, tropical Asia has soils with moderately high base status;
> 12% of tropical Africa has soils with moderately high base status;
> 7% of humid tropical America has soils with moderately high base status;
> 61% of tropical America's soils have aluminium toxicity problems;
> 53% of tropical Africa's soils have aluminium toxicity problems;
> 41% of tropical Asia's soils have aluminium toxicity problems.

In Amazonia, according to Moran, 90% of the soils are phosphorus deficient and will probably require applications of the element if cultivation is to be sustained.

Acid-sulphate soil problem areas

In some soils, sulphate ions are reduced to sulphides due to anaerobic conditions; problems may arise if such soils are drained, thereby creating aerobic conditions. If there are not enough calcium ions present to neutralize the reformed sulphate ions, the result is a very acidic acid-sulphate soil. These are quite commonly formed where tropical wetlands, especially coastal lowlands, are drained. Acid-sulphate soils are difficult to rehabilitate and are one of the few soils that are unsuitable for rice cultivation.

Peaty soils and permafrost soils

Peat and peaty soils can suffer severe shrinkage if drained. They are also prone to underground fire, a recent problem in parts of Indonesia, wind erosion and biological decay. In the northern high latitudes, and in some uplands, soil may be frozen, with only the upper metre, or less, thawing during part of the year. These soils, which may cover 25% of the Earth's land surface – 20 million km², tend to be vulnerable to damage, mainly because they become saturated, and because vegetation cover is shallow-rooted.

10 *Erosive soil degradation*

SOIL EROSION, MASS MOVEMENT AND SOLUTION

IT IS DIFFICULT TO GIVE a precise definition of soil erosion, but a reasonable working definition is: the removal ('eating away') of soil material by water or wind at rates in excess of soil formation. Soil erosion is generally the culmination of a degradation process. Added to erosion are the effects of mass movement and solution, material dissolved away by moving moisture. Mass movement is the downhill movement of surface materials, including solid rock, under the influence of gravity, frequently assisted by buoyancy of particles due to rainwater. Mass movement can occur rapidly as landslides, rockfalls, etc, or much more slowly as 'creep'. As a result of mass movement, surface materials come to rest in a steady-state that depends on the material's character, the slope of underlying terrain, rainfall, and gravity (see Table 10.1). (For a review of soil erosion terminology see: Zacher, 1982: 27–45.)

Erosion, mass movement and solution act to remove material from a site, i.e. are responsible for quantitative soil degradation (Kirkby & Morgan, 1980: 2). These three processes are natural, worldwide components of soil erosion, and, in this chapter, soil erosion is used as an inclusive term. It is also worth stressing that, as Zachar (1982) put it: soil erosion is a 'disease' of landscape not just a 'disease' of soil, it relates to vegetation, climate, etc.

It is possible to divide soil erosion causes into: abiotic causes, due to inanimate processes, and biotic causes which relate to activity of living things. In any given situation, one or both groups of causes may operate, but not necessarily at the same time. Of the abiotic causes, water and wind are the main agents, human activity has come to dominate the biotic causes, indeed, may well, at least regionally, dominate all causes of soil erosion. Some refer to human activity-related erosion as anthropogenic erosion, others use secondary erosion, as opposed to natural or primary erosion. Potentially confusing is the use of accelerated erosion to imply 'resulting from human activity'. While Man has often accelerated soil loss well beyond natural rates, there are natural processes/events that can suddenly alter long-established 'natural' rates of erosion, for example, earthquakes, tsunamis, major storms and severe drought.

Once topsoil is removed, the subsoil may be more or less vulnerable to erosion. Often the former is the case, because the lack of organic matter in subsoil makes a protective vegetation cover more difficult to establish and unless the subsoil is clay-rich there is less to bind particles together. Erosion-resistant soil layers: pans, stony-layers, clay-bands, etc, will slow and possibly stabilize soil erosion. Thus erosion seldom proceeds in a steady

Table 10.1. *Types of soil erosion.*

Agent[a]

Water

SHEET (SHEETWASH) EROSION
Rain and overland flow of water removes soil particles, there may be slow and insidious
or rapid and spectacular loss of layers of soil. The former is especially dangerous because
it may not be observed and so no action is taken to counter it (El-Swaify et al., 1985: 3).

RILL EROSION
Flowing water concentrates into rivulets and carves small channels.

GULLY EROSION
Where rainfall cannot infiltrate the soil and, where slopes are sufficient, water will flow
and become concentrated (Hudson, 1981). May well be triggered or aggravated by
trampling or vegetation damage. If flow in an already established channel increases, a gully
may form. In Madagascar, there are spectacular gully erosion features of lateritic clay soils:
lavakas (Battistini & Richard-Vindard, 1972; Randrianarijaona, 1983), gully erosion is
common in India and on the lower slopes of the Andes (Brown, 1978: 18). Log-dragging
is a common initiator of gully erosion, especially in the humid tropics.

STREAMBANK COLLAPSE AND REMOVAL
Stream/river undercuts bank, material slides into river and is transported away. Important
in river basins with soft soils, like many rivers in the Amazon Basin.

subsurface erosion

PIPING
Large subsurface channels formed, may lead to open gullies, causes
debated (Kirkby & Morgan, 1980: 153).

INTRASOIL EROSION
Gravel and stony soils are especially prone. Finer topsoil gets washed down the soil profile
by rain, typically after vegetation is disturbed, it may stay in the depths of the subsoil or
may be transported away if there is sufficient underground flow of water.

TUNNEL EROSION(*SUFFOSIS*)
Especially common in loess soils, subsurface 'corridors' are washed out usually just above
a less permeable layer, which is often at the bedrock/loess contact. In final stages, this
resembles or becomes gully erosion (Zachar, 1982: 64–70).

STRUCTURAL CHANGE
Water causes structural change. Other factors may cause structural change that favours
erosion, e.g. salt accumulation, trampling, tillage. The formation of crusts may increase
erosion, at least locally if it leads to concentrated run-off. Where there are gentler slopes, it
may reduce dislodgement of material by raindrop action and so cut erosion. Crusts tend to
hinder infiltration and growth of a protective plant layer.

MASS-MOVEMENT (SOLIFLUCTION)
Movement, typical, but not always, of loose material due to force of gravity. Movement of
slushy mass can be very damaging, slopes and channels may be eroded and vegetation
overwhelmed. Avalanches of fast-moving snow and rock debris can remove large swathes
of forest and open up areas to other forms of erosion.

Wind (Aeolian erosion)

DEFLATION
Removal and transport away of loose soil, especially sands, sandy soil, light peaty soils or
loess. Typically, leaves localized hollows. Deflation can remove much valuable agricultural
land in times of drought. Problem, for example, in: USA – 'Dust Bowl'; UK –
Norfolk/Suffolk Brecklands; UK Vale of York; UK – W. Midlands, Lincolnshire, E.
Nottinghamshire; USSR – Ukraine; Argentina (Arnon, 1981: 110).

ABRASION
Wind, charged with fine rock or ice debris damages plants, erodes rock, equipment,
buildings and blows away the loosened material.

Note: [a] On the whole, wind erosion is less researched than water erosion.

manner through time unless there is a very thick and homogeneous soil and/or a relatively slow rate of erosion,

Not all places have erosion in excess of soil formation; there are localities which accumulate material, sometimes as a result of Man-induced degradation elsewhere, sometimes due to natural causes. Wind or floodwater may deposit sediment, volcanic ash or loess; an area with such accumulation may sustain agricultural production even though the standard of management is low. There are also situations where rock or subsoil readily form soil or allow plant growth, so that there may be fast recovery from erosion. Clays, shales and limestones may support herb and tree cover with virtually no topsoil present. Some of the world's most important food and commodity crop production regions are areas where accumulation of material matches, or exceeds, erosion, for example, the Nile Valley, lowlands adjoining the Ethiopian and Sudanese uplands, or the Amazonian *várzeas*. In the case of the Nile Valley and many of the major Indian floodplains, one might argue that upland farming/grazing has dislodged much of the sediment that helps sustain lowland cultivation.

The amount of erosion that will occur in a given circumstance is determined by:

1. Erosivity – the capacity (potential) of precipitation to cause erosion in given circumstances, i.e. 'aggressiveness' of climate. Erosivity is a function of intensity, duration, timing, and amount of precipitation.
2. Erodibility – the vulnerability of soil to erosion i.e. a soil property: its liability to have particles detached and then transported away. Erodibility is dynamic; it changes during say a storm, during the year or from year to year. Soils can vary in moisture content and with this resistance to erosion. For example, infiltration can alter if soil structure changes, this may be due to: seasonal activity of burrowing animals, swelling/shrinking or saturation of a soil during a rainfall episode trampling of compaction. Infiltration can alter if vegetation cover alters. Surface water flow causes much soil erosion, subsurface flow can affect surface flows.
3. Cover – natural vegetation, crop or covercrop that protects the soil.
4. Management – land use: crop, cropping method, cropping pattern, tillage method, use of mulch.

At various times of year, or over a period of time 1., 3. and 4. are likely to alter. Unless there is disruption, 2. is more likely to remain stable. If cover is removed, even briefly, erosion can markedly increase (Greenland & Lal, 1977: 6).

The amount of solution depends upon: 1. the character of the soil/rock. 2. the movement of moisture: amount and timing of flows. 3. the quality of the moisture; acid precipitation may act directly on rocks or may lead to acid soil moisture. Soil moisture may become contaminated with salts or other contaminants that accelerate or slow solution, either by altering chemical reactions or because they affect the permeability of the soil/rock and thus movement of moisture.

The relationship between erosion and vegetation cover is complex. If cultivation of an eroding/potentially erodible area of land ceases, or if there is some other land use change, the system might move toward plant cover becoming established or, it might move toward erosion until the land is badly damaged. It is important to be able to determine in advance which route will be taken; there may be situations where rehabilitation efforts are a waste of time. Thornes (1989: 48) presented a model based on differential

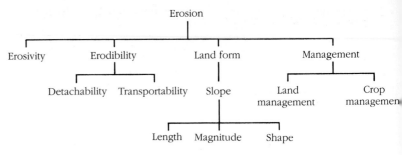

Fig. 10.1. Factors contributing to erosion.

equations describing change in rate of erosion and growth of vegetation. In practice, other factors would need to be added, such as grazing pressure, plant water demand, etc, which could give some idea of the likely vegetation cover–erosion relationship. It is apparent that, beyond certain limits, the vegetation cover–erosion relationship can suddenly 'flip' from a non-problem to a problem state.

Where airflows are not sufficiently slowed by vegetation, topography, etc, there is likely to be wind erosion, especially if the soils dry out. Wind erosion is episodic, arable cropping is likely to lead to seasonal peaks of wind erosion that coincide with periods when vegetation cover is reduced, soil is driest and most disturbed, and wind most erosive. Typically, such periods (for higher latitudes) are after spring tillage, or follow harvest before the arrival of winter snows or rain. Nearer the Equator, wind erosion rises during dry seasons or if there is drought. Erosive episodes may well be associated with winds that occasionally blow from some direction other than the usual prevailing wind. Certain winds like the *harmattan* (W. Africa), the *sukovey* (USSR) or the *pampero* (Argentina): may cause considerable vegetation damage, by uprooting plants and/or by desiccation of plants and soil, the land is then more prone to wind erosion (Gerasimov *et al.*, 1971: 72). Loose soil or sand may be removed by wind to erode deflation hollows or there may be a more general loss of upper layers of the topsoil.

MEASUREMENT OF SOIL EROSION

Soil erosion has been defined as: the gross amount of soil moved by raindrop detachment or run-off (wind effects should not be forgotten). Soil loss has been defined as: soil moved off a slope or field. Sediment yield has been defined as: soil delivered to a point under evaluation.

There are a number of ways in which soil erosion may be measured:

1. *direct measurement at site*
   - The time to remove a given depth of soil,
   - Depression of surface in a given time.
2. *modelling (analogue models)*
   - Simulate rainfall by spraying water onto a test bed and measure effect.
   - Shield a plot with, say, mosquito-gauze and compare effect after a given time with an unshielded plot to judge effect of precipitation impact (Greenland & Lal, 1977: 168). A plot may be protected from trampling/grazing by an exclosure. Levels within this plot can be compared with those outside; alternatively, metal pins or precise levelling can be used to check losses from a site.
3. *monitor stream sediment loads*
   - Accuracy is questionable – not all sediment will reach a stream, there may be sudden above-average releases, monitoring may miss these if not

Table 10.2. *Typical form of the Universal Soil Loss Equation.*

$$A = (0.224)\ R\ K\ L\ S\ C\ P \qquad (5)$$

where:

A = the soil loss kg m^2 s^{-1}
R = the rainfall erosivity factor
K = the soil erodibility factor
L = the slope length factor
S = the slope gradient factor
C = the cropping management factor
P = the erosion control practice factor

Source: For a detailed explanation see Hudson, 1981: 179–96.

constant or if severe flood damages equipment. Not all sediment reaching a stream will reach the monitoring point. There may be opportunities to use Man-made radionuclides, such as ^{137}Cs or ^{210}Pb from global fall-out, atomic accident or deliberate application to the land, to trace where eroded sediment goes and whether any location escapes erosion.

4. *empirical estimates*
   – Tolerance level (T-factor). This may be defined as the loss equal to the rate of new soil formation. Obviously, if this is exceeded, there will be a net loss of soil. Kirkby & Morgan (1980: 45) defined it as: the maximum rate of soil erosion that permits a high level of productivity to be sustained. It is not unusual, in, say, the USA to have soil losses at twice the tolerance level.
   – Universal Soil Loss Equation.

There is still debate about central aspects of soil erosion, for example, what proportion of the material moved by rain is initiated (loosened and dislodged) by rain? Some presumably is made ready for movement by soil organisms, wind action, etc, between rainstorms. One source of soil loss which can be high in areas of cropping, and which tends to be overlooked is loss on crops, that is material adhering to harvested roots, which is especially significant with potatoes, beet, yams and other root crops.

The Universal Soil Loss Equation

The Universal Soil Loss Equation (USLE) is a predictive 'tool' intended to estimate average annual field soil losses. It was developed in the 1930s by the US Soil Conservation Service, was improved in 1954 by the US Agriculture Research Service, and was further improved in 1978 by the US Dept of Agriculture. It is much used by consultants and planners worldwide to predict soil loss and to select appropriate agricultural practices and crops, in spite of being developed in the USA and, at least in part, being suited to the mid-western USA environment (Hudson, 1981: 179–96). It has now been better adapted for use elsewhere – particularly as a result of efforts by the International Institute of Tropical Agriculture (Ibadan, Nigeria), which has tried to 'tropicalize' it. Nevertheless, Chisholm & Dumsday (1987: 85), warned of its limitations in Australia.

The USLE considers a range of parameters (see Equation 5, Table 10.2) to derive a value for average annual soil loss (loss may nowadays be expressed in kg m^2 s). Problems arise when it is applied in areas where such data are imprecise or unavailable. Unfortunately expediency often forces developing countries to take such risks (Wischmeier, 1976; Wischmeier & Smith, 1960).

Table 10.3. *Typical form of an empirical attempt to assess wind erosion of soil – a Wind Erosion Equation.*

$$E = f\ (I,\ C,\ K,\ L,\ V) \tag{6}$$

where: E = soil loss by wind (erosion)
I = erodability factor – vulnerability to wind erosion
C = factor representing local wind conditions
K = soil surface roughness
L = width of the field in direction of prevailing wind
V = measure of vegetation cover

Source: modification of Hudson, 1981: 258–9.

Measuring wind erosion

For any given soil conditions, the amount of soil which will be blown away depends upon: 1. wind velocity and 2. roughness of the soil surface. Estimating the losses due to wind is more complicated than applying the USLE to water-related erosion, Equation 6, Table 10.3 gives a typical empirical method.

MONITORING EROSION

The ability to measure soil erosion is not enough. There is a need to be able to obtain a long-term picture of degradation in a given region, to be able to assess the current position, predict possible future trends and to try and compare one locality with another. Soil erosion is not often constant, it is more likely to take place as 'episodes' with periods of relative quiescence. For example, the UK winter of 1985–6 was very wet and saw more severe water erosion than usual. The present position may not be a true reflection of what an environment could once support, and present rates of erosion may not be maintained. Soil is seldom homogeneous, so soil degradation varies from place to place even over short distances and in the same place over time. Vegetation strongly influences erosion. Usually it protects soil, but there are situations where trees shed large, erosive droplets and have little ground-cover beneath – in such circumstances, erosion might actually be enhanced; this is a problem in some teak plantations. Land use can change, for example, growing autumn-sown cereals has become more common in the UK since the 1960s and this favours erosion.

Evidence of past erosion is provided by palaeo-erosion studies, for example, evidence from lake or marine cores (Holdgate & Woodman, 1976: 160). One common problem is the need to find common reference points at different sites; this may be possible if there are volcanic ash layers or by radio-isotope studies.

Some developed, and some developing, countries have set up soil erosion monitoring organizations but practices vary. Nor are many of the monitoring services long established, except in the USA where they date from the 1930s.

The UNEP has a World Soils Policy; this is intended to develop methodologies to monitor global soil/land resources. The problem is to collate and correlate national and regional data. The UNEP prompted the International Society of Soil Sciences (ISSS) to start production of a global soil degradation map (1 : 10,000,000 scale, scheduled for publication in 1990)

Table 10.4. *Some selected erosion rates.*

Region	Rate (t ha y^{-1})	Source
Ethiopia	296	1
Thailand	Lists rates	2
South East Asian rivers	Suspended sediment Loads	3
USSR steppes	Lists rates	4
USA Iowa	35 (average for State)	5
Czechoslovakia	62	6
USA average for all crop land	2 approx.	7

Note: Information on soil losses from croplands in various countries may be found in Lal *et al.*, 1989: 61.
Sources:
1. World Resources Institute *et al.*, 1987: 222.
2. El-Swaify *et al.*, 1985: 11–12.
3. Douglas, 1981.
4. Gerasimov, *et al.*, 1971: 172.
5. Canter, 1986: 17.
6. Parikh, 1988: 137.
7. Council on Environmental Quality 1977 estimate of average for all USA, from: Canter, 1986: 17.

and to establish a database. In late 1987, the UNEP, the ISSS and the International Soil Reference and Information Centre (ISRIC, the Netherland) agreed to a project: Global Assessment of Soil Degradation (GLASOD). This was seen as a first step towards global soil degradation assessment. Progress was outlined in the *SOTER Report, No. 3* (International Society of Soil Science *et al.*, 1988).

To establish seriousness of erosion, depth of soil has really to be compared with soil loss rate and rate of soil formation at a given site, e.g. a 1 mm y^{-1} loss and a soil 1 metre deep with no measurable soil renewal and, assuming plants need a minimum of 40 cm to root, would give roughly 600 years of production before the critical point is reached. If soil depth has been 45 cm, then there would have be a mere 50 years grace. According to Brown (1978: 22) over much of the Earth's surface, topsoil is seldom more than 30 cm thick.

Soil erosion may be continuous, seasonal or momentary, it may be slow, moderate or rapid. The crucial question is: what is the critical amount/rate of soil loss? Crude rates of soil loss have been calculated (in 10^9 t y^{-1}) for the world by Clark & Munn (1986: 56):

$$\text{pre-agricultural} = 16.4$$
$$\text{AD } 1860 \quad = 46.3$$
$$\text{AD } 1978 \quad = 91.1$$

On the world-scale, erosion seems to be out of control, often being well in excess of natural rates.

Possibly one of the best-studied regions, with respect to soil erosion, is the USA Great Plains, reflecting the lessons learnt from the 'Dust Bowl' in the 1930s, when there were as many as 13,354,376 ha devoid of vegetation and dust 'blizzards' sufficient to blot out the sun at midday. Figure 10.2 gives wind and water erosion rates for this part of the USA.

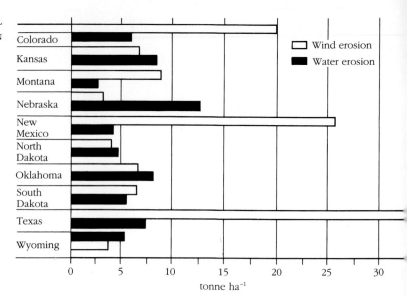

Fig. 10.2. Average annual wind and water erosion for the Great Plains USA (1981 USDA data). Source: Harlin & Berardi, 1987: 22 (Fig. 2.6).

THE COSTS AND EFFECTS OF SOIL EROSION

One may divide the costs of soil erosion into: direct (on-site) and indirect (off-site). The main direct cost is decline in crop productivity. Indirect costs include: siltation of reservoirs, canals, streams, with associated loss of water supplies, power generation capacity, flooding, increased dredging costs, etc; and landslide damage to roads, infrastructure, housing and landholdings. The direct costs are vast, the indirect costs are considerable and may sometimes be greater than on-site impacts. Many large and smaller hydropower and irrigation projects have been ruined by soil erosion (Repetto, 1986; Barrow, 1987a: 277).

Soil contributes considerably to the value of land. Once soil degradation begins, land values generally fall, the result may be virtually worthless, unsaleable wasteland (Chisholm & Dumsday, 1987: 83). Soil loss or deterioration does not have to progress to the point where cropping or grazing is impossible before it has effect. Slight or moderate degradation may be sufficient to restrict what can be grown due to insufficient depth of soil or poor-quality soil. It may also, by reducing available soil moisture, reduce the land's resistance to drought.

The costs of halting/repairing soil erosion are considerable and are not easy to calculate. Possibilities of halting/repairing soil loss depend upon the level of degradation, costs of control/repair and the potential returns after control/repair, and/or savings by reducing indirect impacts – like silting of reservoirs. Chisholm & Dumsday (1987: 91–5), examine the problems of estimating costs of soil erosion and costs of control. In crude terms, soil erosion in Australia probably caused a decline in wheat yields of between 6% and 52% in the period 1973–4 to 1983–4. In cash terms, that would be between A\$ 13 and A\$ 155 per ha over ten years (Chisholm & Dumsday, 1987: 90. A recent source (*The Times*, 30/8/88: 5) suggested soil erosion was costing Australia A\$ 2000 million a year. Doubtless, were figures calculated for the USA, UK, or parts of Africa, losses would be huge. India in the late 1970s, for example, probably spent about US\$ 6 million a year on fertilizers much just to match losses of soil.

Table 10.5. *Perceived causes of depressed agricultural production in subSaharan Africa 1975–83*.*

Country	Adverse weather	Political unrest	Inappropriate agricultural policies
Burkina Faso	–	2	1
Cape Verde	1	–	1
Cent. African Rep.	–	–	2
Chad	2	2	1
Ethiopia	2	2	–
Gambia	1	–	2
Ghana	1	1	2
Guinea	2	–	–
Kenya	1	–	1
Lesotho	2	–	–
Liberia	–	1	2
Malagasy Rep.	1	–	1
Mali	2	–	2
Mauritania	2	–	–
Mozambique	2	2	–
Senegal	2	–	2
Sierra Leone	1	–	–
Somalia	2	2	1
Tanzania	1	–	1
Uganda	–	1	1
Zaïre	–	–	2
Zambia	2	1	2

Key: 1 = moderate influence   2 = strong influence

Notes: * There can be little doubt that, in some of these nations, other factors have also been at work. For example; the 'debt problem' has starved agriculture and environmental management of funds; the demand for cheap food to feed urban masses has tended to keep rural market prices too low and thus offer farmers little incentive for more intensive farming, rather than damaging, inefficient, extensive farming.

Sources: based on Independent Commission on International Humanitarian Issues, 1986a: 58, Table 3.

CAUSES OF SOIL EROSION

The causes of soil erosion are often complex. Cultural, institutional, social, economic and environmental factors play varying parts. It is only quite recently that there has been more interest in the political, institutional and economic causes of soil degradation; the picture is still far from complete (Blaikie, 1985; Blaikie & Brookfield, 1987).

It seems likely that there are vulnerable environments, where soils are easily degraded and/or conditions hinder maintenance of a good cover of vegetation, and/or drought is a problem, and/or the rainfall is especially intense. A number of authors suggest that subSaharan Africa is more vulnerable than other world regions because its soils are erosion-prone, and that soil conservation measures are needed at much lower population densities than is usual elsewhere (Harrison, 1987a: 41). Table 10.5 lists some of the 'causes' of depressed agricultural production in subSaharan Africa.

Shifting cultivation

Shifting cultivation (land rotation agriculture) is widely blamed for removal of vegetation, burning and soil exhaustion. There is a massive literature, but not a lot of research into actual soil erosion effects. Given the huge range of diversity of strategy and variation in degree to which each strategy has been disrupted by various development pressures, assessing the effects of shifting cultivation is difficult. If traditional shifting cultivation has not broken down, it is probable that most eroded material would be held within the cleared plot boundaries by surrounding weeds, etc. There would be damage and losses from the use of fire, but not all shifting cultivators use fire to clear their plots. People often revert to shifting cultivation when in some way disadvantaged or disrupted, their practices then become clumsy and lead to degradation of the soil.

Livestock herding activity

Livestock have two main effects on soil: they remove vegetation exposing soil to wind and rain, and either trample the surface dislodging soil particles or compact the surface reducing infiltration. The result of these actions is to increase soil removal. The rates of damage and pattern of damage varies according to type of livestock and according to factors such as water availability and whether particular trails are regularly followed. Erosion is likely to be worst around boreholes and stockades where livestock are kept for the night.

Arable cultivation

There can be little doubt that ploughing is often the main or a major cause of land degradation. The degree of damage depends on the ploughing technique and upon the timing and vulnerability of the soil. Studies have shown that chisel ploughing causes less damage than mouldboard ploughing or disc ploughing (Reganold, 1989).

Fire

The effects of fire are two-fold: above-ground vegetation and litter is removed and, if the fire is sufficiently hot-burning, root and soil damage may occur. For this to happen temperatures of 900 °C or more have to be reached. Most fires subject the soil surface to less than 300 °C. When above-ground vegetation and litter burn, there are losses of nutrients, directly in the smoke and particles carried aloft, nitrogen in particular is lost, and, because the ash left on the surface is rich in potassium and is very easily blown away or dissolved by rainwater, potassium losses tend to be quite high (Briggs & Courtney, 1985: 150–6). Burning is not restricted to forest clearance. Agricultural production may produce low-value crop residue; for example, wheat or barley stubble may be burnt each year, and sugar cane fields may be regularly burnt to aid harvesting.

Human access and tourism

Walkers and vehicles may cause considerable damage. This tends to be mainly along specific tracks, particularly where routes converge. Tracks may collect rainwater and feed it to where it causes gully erosion problems. Off-road vehicles are becoming a problem in some countries, and tend to cause more widespread damage than pedestrians. Trail-motorcycles, 'dune-buggies' and jeep-type vehicles can start severe deflation in drylands or dunefields. In game parks, off-road vehicles may also cause problems especially in localities where animals congregate, such as around waterholes or salt-licks. In colder environments, skidoos and skiers can damage the vegetation cover protecting delicate tundra or alpine soils, which then easily erode during spring and summer. (Ski damage is discussed in Chapter 7). In very arid and very cold environments, tracks left by people, animals or vehicles decades ago may still show little sign of recovery. Trampling by walkers is a particular problem in peatlands, upland areas and in peri-urban areas where there is heavy usage (Chi Yung Jim, 1987). Tourist authorities may have to fence off vulnerable areas like sand dunes and provide erosion resistant pathways.

EXTENT AND RATE OF SOIL EROSION

Commercial causes

In many tropical lowlands, logging activities have been a major cause of soil erosion, especially along logging trails. Large areas of the world suffer soil erosion as a consequence of commercial agricultural demands. Cotton has proved to be a crop that is grown for commercial gain and which is often followed by soil erosion. Once 'locked into' a commercial production strategy, world market forces or individual greed may drive land use to the point of degradation.

Land drainage

If land is drained, there may be subsidence, acid-sulphate soil formation, oxidation of soil organic matter, even spontaneous combustion of peat deposits, and a risk that contaminated drainage water might damage floodlands and wetlands (Boels et al., 1982).

EXTENT AND RATE OF SOIL EROSION

As remote sensing, international co-operation and databasing improve, there are better chances for precise assessment of extent and rate of erosion. Problems will still remain: acute or chronic erosion may be readily visible, but much erosion is insidious, for example, a loss of 50 t ha y^{-1} amounts to only about 3 mm y^{-1} off a soil profile, difficult to recognize by remote sensing, but enough to affect agriculture in quite a short time if the soil is shallow. One monitoring problem is that there may be a natural rate of soil loss that has to be assessed and then checked against actual. If there is a mismatch then there might be a chance of erosion control by altering land use. It should be emphasized that, even without change in land use, soil erosion may vary if, for example, a region starts to get higher rainfall. Where there is a long history of land use, the worst phase of erosion may have passed, there may not have been much change in environmental conditions (e.g. climate) or land use, merely a burst of erosion which took place when the land use began and a new 'steady-state' or rate of deterioration was reached.

Zachar (1982: 462–81) attempted a global assessment of soil erosion, Figure 10.3 gives a broad indication of intensity of water erosion, and Table 10.6 gives approximate rates for various countries. However, it is probably wise to wait until the publication of the GLASOD maps, sometime after

209

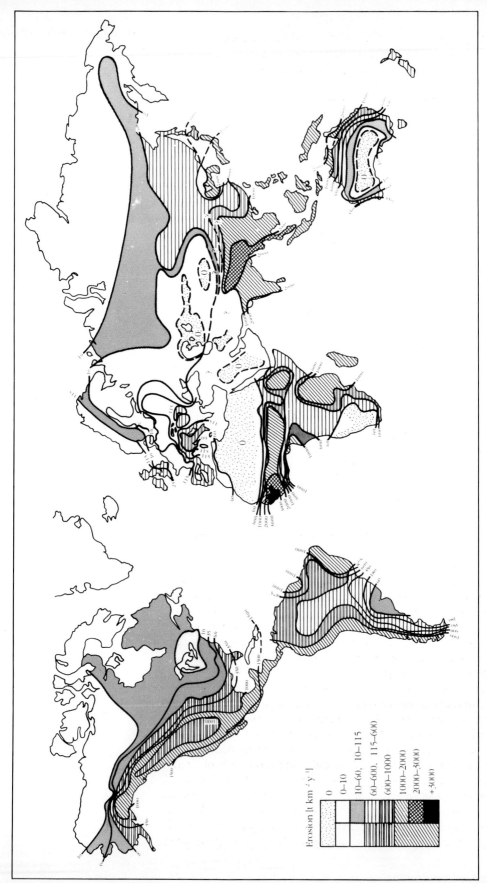

Fig. 10.3. World map of the intensity of water erosion. Source: Zachar, 1982: p. 468 (Fig. 193).

Erosion [t km⁻² y⁻¹]

	0
	0–10
	10–60, 10–115
	60–600, 115–600
	600–1000
	1000–2000
	2000–3000
	+3000

Table 10.6. *Magnitude of erosion from cropland in various countries.*

Country	Rate of erosion (t ha y^{-1})
Argentina/Paraguay/Brazil	18.8
Belgium	10.0– 25.0
Benin	17.0– 28.0
Burkina Faso	10.0– 20.0
China	11.0–251.0
Ecuador	210.0–564.0
Ethiopia	34.0
Guatemala	5.0– 35.0
Guinea	17.9 24.5
India	75.0
Ivory Coast	60.0–570.0
Jamaica	90.0
Kenya	5.4– 47.1
Lesotho	40.0
Malagasy Rep.	25.0–250.0
Nepal	40.0
Niger	35.0– 70.0
Nigeria	14.4
Papua New Guinea	6.0–320.0
Peru	15.0
Senegal	14.9– 55.0
USA	9.6
Tanzania	10.1– 92.8
Zimbabwe	50.0

Note: The data used in this table comes from a wide range of sources and is derived through a wide range of sampling methodologies; it is therefore not standardized and serves as only a general indication.
Source: based on Lal *et al.*, 1989: 61, Table III.

1990, before trying to get an accurate overview of soil erosion (International Society of Soil Science *et al.*, 1988).

Some generalizations follow which serve to emphasize the scale and widespread nature of soil erosion. Africa suffers a lot of erosion in seasonally dry regions as a consequence of arable farming and/or grazing livestock. Soils with less than 2% organic matter content, and soils with less than 5% clay content are vulnerable to erosion. Latin America seems to have more of a problem of decline of fertility and increasing soil acidity, phosphorus deficiency, and levels of aluminium high enough to kill crops are common in Amazonia (Moran, 1987: 70–4).

A large part of South Asia has been badly affected by soil erosion; El-Swaify *et al.* (1985: 3) estimated around 175 million ha of India's total area of 328 million ha were 'degraded'. China is increasingly afflicted by soil erosion, Forestier (1989) estimated roughly one-sixth of the total land was affected and, in valleys and lowlands, silt-laden rivers appear to be flooding more severely and frequently. Australia, has probably got about 38% of its non-arid (i.e. usable) land significantly eroded (Chisholm & Dumsday, 1987); possibly as much as half of Australia's farmland needs remedial treatment (*The Times*, 30/8/88: 5). It was estimated, in 1987, that 44% of the UK's arable land soil was at risk from soil erosion. In the last 200 years, the USA has probably lost at least one-third of its topsoil. By the late 1970s, about one-fifth of the world's cropland had been lost to soil erosion and about one-half of the world's cropland was losing soil at a debilitating rate (Brown, 1977: 18; Brown et al., 1984: 5; World Commission on Environment and Development, 1987b: 25).

Natural rates of soil erosion vary greatly and are, in large part, a function of vegetation cover. Undisturbed, semi-arid regions possibly lose around 1.0 mm y^{-1}. In temperate UK, in sites where vegetation is undisturbed (i.e. is 'natural'), erosion seems to seldom exceed 1.0 mm y^{-1} (Kirkby & Morgan, 1980: 3).

What are permissible rates of soil erosion?

There is little agreement in the literature, levels of 0.1 to 0.2 mm y^{-1} (4 to 20 t ha y^{-1}) loss are often described as 'acceptable' (Kirkby & Morgan, 1980: 5). As a rough guide, in the following section 25 mm y^{-1} loss is roughly equivalent to 400 t ha y^{-1}. In the USA, 11 t ha y^{-1} has been seen as 'acceptable', 180 t km^2 y^{-1} is seen by some as a cause for concern. Harlin & Berardi (1987: 219), however, warn that, with soil seldom replaced at more than 2.5 cm per 200 to 1000 years, the 'acceptable' level should be nearer 1 t ha y^{-1}. The ideal 'acceptable' rate would be one that matches, or is less than, rate of soil formation. In the UK, the natural replacement rate is 0.1 t ha y^{-1}. Compare this with losses of 20 to 50 t ha y^{-1} which are not uncommon in the UK. Zacher (1982: 86) felt that loss of over 0.5 mm y^{-1} (5 m^3 ha $^{-1}$) was a cause for deep concern, and classified soil erosion rates into:

> serious   – 40 to 130 years to lose the topsoil;
> severe   – 10 to 40 years to lose the topsoil;
> catastrophic – loss of topsoil in one or a few storms.

The serious/severe/catastrophic classification may be the most useful type of approach for it gives planners and people a clear idea of time to disaster unless action is taken, rather than what might be to them a meaningless numerical value.

Recognition of practical tolerance levels or T-factors is not easy. Natural and human activity-related soil losses must be monitored before anything else can be usefully done. What planners call 'acceptable' now may not be if sustainable development becomes a goal. One millimetre/year loss may have little effect in a human lifetime but, over several generations, it might, especially if the soil is thin. Depth of soil has really to be compared with loss rate and with rate of formation at a given site.

Bearing in mind the warnings just given, there are apparently typical values for virtually all parts of the world that are way in excess of 'acceptable'. For example, in the USA, Iowa, presently the first-ranking maize producer, second-ranking soya producer in the USA, and an important fodder-growing State, commonly has 35 t ha y^{-1} losses and in some areas 450 t ha y^{-1} (Canter, 1986: 17). Some parts of the People's Republic of China with loess soils apparently lose 4000 to 10,000 t ha y^{-1}. In the 'Dust Bowl' areas of the USA, mid-west records show wind erosion rates of around 10 mm y^{-1} at the height of the problem in the 1930s (Kirkby & Morgan, 1980: 3). In Haiti, things are so bad that one-sixth of the total population have reportedly left the island that once had good soils and a rich forest cover (Boyle & Ardill, 1989: iii).

AREAS THAT ARE ESPECIALLY VULNERABLE TO SOIL EROSION

Loess soil areas

Loessial soils are prone to compaction and waterlogging when cultivated. If the terrain slopes, then gullying or tunnel erosion is a risk. Severe erosion is common and, it would appear that the worst damage is done by occasional heavy downpours rather than by more frequent gentler showers. When dry, loessial soils can be easily blown away by the wind. There are such soils in: the USSR's 'loess belt', mainly in the Ukraine, S. Russian Plain, Soviet Central Asia around L. Baikal and in the Ob and Yenesei Valleys; in Nebraska, Iowa and Idaho, USA; the 'cover-sands' areas of Belgium, northern Germany, Bavaria, the Netherlands/German border region, Poland, China and Mongolia, Uruguay and S. Brazil. (Zachar, 1982: 469; Smil, 1984; Pecsi, 1987). The Peoples' Republic of China and Mongolia have between 275,000 and 530,000 km² of loess. Published estimates of depth vary, ranging from 10 to 200 m or more in thickness; a high proportion of this area has soil erosion problems (Pye, 1984). It is also very valuable fertile agricultural land.

The US Department of Agriculture recognizes a 'threshold for concern' of 180 t ha y^{-1} soil loss; parts of the China/Mongolia loess belt have erosion rates of between 4000 and 10,000 t km² y^{-1} (Grout-Smith, 1989). The loss is by both wind and water erosion, the later being mainly between July and September during heavy seasonal rains. So bad is the situation that it is possible to register seasonal variations of airborne dust in Hawaii which reflect springtime ploughing activity in nothern China.

Steep slopes

A significant part of the world's land slopes steeply. In the steepest slope areas, over 15 degrees gradient, mass movement, including landslides, mudflows and avalanche may be a problem. Avalanches damage vegetation and erode soil; rocks, soil or snow may be involved. Soils tend to be thin and prone to downslope movement, and tree cover will tend to be shallow-rooting and may be prone to wind-throw. In New Zealand and the Pacific islands, steep slopes seem to have been particularly vulnerable to erosion (Eyles, 1987). In some regions with rich soil and steep slopes, cultivation strategies have evolved to cope with the conditions, e.g. the rice-paddy terraces of Java and the irrigated terraces once farmed in many parts of Latin America, notably in highland Peru.

Dryland soils

Dryland soils and soils which dry out for long periods are prone to degradation, because they tend to lose their organic matter and become friable or impermeable (which results in strong surface flow when it rains), and because they tend to have a poor cover of vegetation.

CONTROLLING SOIL DEGRADATION

The first step in controlling soil degradation is to assess the problem, the second step is to identify an appropriate land use for the afflicted area; there may be a need for rehabilitation measures. The third is to implement such a land use, the fourth is to manage and maintain such a land use. Land capability assessment is increasingly used to identify appropriate land uses. The foregoing sequence may seem sensible but, in practice, there are a plethora of, often difficult to resolve, problems. Problems such as: how to fund corrective efforts; how to overcome lack of interest or resistance by local people; how to establish suitable institutional arrangements to initiate and manage soil degradation control; there may be a need to alter legislation to support certain groups of society – without such change, they may have no incentive or chance to improve land use.

There are situations where soil degradation can be easily controlled, possibly by selecting appropriate crops, but there are also situations where things are complex (Fig. 10.4 illustrates the sheer range of possible scenarios). Because of the complexity of the problems, and, because the relationship between agricultural productivity and soil degradation is non-linear, indeed, as soil degenerates productivity is likely to fall in an exponential manner, it is likely that computer mathematical modelling will be needed to predict the likely course of erosion and the best control strategy for a given locality (Thornes, 1989).

A problem with control of soil degradation is that the costs may begin immediately and be quite considerable, but the benefits may not appear for some time and may, at least in cash terms, and at least at first, be slow to

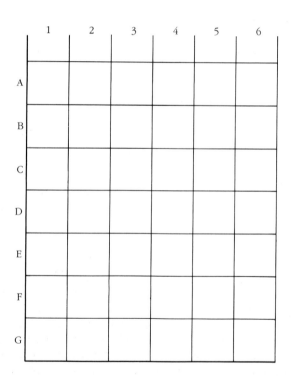

Fig. 10.4. Matrix of possible combinations of factors which might lead to varying degrees of soil degradation.
Key: 1=crop degrades soil; 2=crop neutral effect on soil; 3=crop improves soil; 4=good soil conservation practice; 5=neutral soil conservation practice; 6=bad soil conservation practice.
A=vulnerable soil; B=neutral degree of vulnerability; C=robust soil; E=damaging precipitation conditions; F=less problematic precipitation; G=additional factors leading to damage (e.g. locust attack, bushfire, etc). Note: The combination: 1,6,A,E,G is particularly bad; the combination: 3,4,C,F is particularly favourable.

accrue. Erosion losses and problems are likely to affect groups of people, especially poor people, the benefits from exploiting the soil are likely to benefit individuals, especially richer, more-influential individuals.

Measures for countering water erosion

There are four groups of practices which help counter water erosion: 1. those practices which help maintain or improve soil infiltration rates; 2. those practices which help safe disposal of excess surface run-off should precipitation exceed the infiltration capacity of the land; 3. those practices that help bind the soil together; 4. practices that reduce the impact of precipitation on the soil.

Measures for countering water erosion may be grouped into those which:

– *Slow overland flow and reduce raindrop splash effect.* This may be achieved by maintaining one or more of the following: vegetation ground-cover, a mulch layer, contour cultivation, bund construction, grass strips.
– *Reduce soil surface temperature.* This may be achieved through shading and/or mulching.
– *Improve infiltration.* This may be achieved through tillage, to open up the soil and by construction of structures to retain run-off moisture so that it can infiltrate.
– *Improve the organic matter content of the soil,* and possibly add plant nutrients (artificial fertlizer can be used to boost available plant nutrients but adds no organic matter). Add organic matter: manure, green manure, peat, etc.

There is much overlap between measures to control water erosion and those to control wind erosion. For example, techniques designed to maintain plant cover, bind the soil and minimize disturbance, such as: 'zero'-tillage; direct drilling of seeds; rod-weeding, a technique whereby a subsurface bar is dragged through the soil to break weed roots with relatively little damage to soil surface; mulching; soil conditioners. Measures that reduce run-off often reduce the effects of wind. Measures which reduce water erosion by improving or maintaining soil organic matter also help reduce wind erosion and generally improve soil moisture availability (Lal & Russel, 1981).

Excavations, stone-lines and bunds

To control erosion by water, a major goal must be the slowing of run-off flows over the soil surface. There is a huge diversity of widely used measures: terraces, along-contour stone-lines, grass strips, trash-lines, drains, banks, ditches, etc (see Canter, 1986: 134–9). Few methods are as easy to apply successfully as some would believe. There is a need to estimate likely run-off before measures can be safely selected and designed, but often this is not done. The result is that water is channelled to a point where it causes damage, or a system breaks down and causes damage where concentrated flows escape. There may be problems if the erosion control measures hinder tillage: terraced land may require as much as 6% more time to plough, terracing can restrict cropping patterns and take a significant amount of farm or grazing and land out of production. Somehow the measures have to be financed, labour has to be found to install and maintain them, and farmers have to be convinced the effort and loss of land is worthwile (Little & Horowitz, 1987: 32).

Funding and constructing soil erosion control/water conservation mea
sures, the two are often inseparable, tends to be a problem. Construction o
erosion control measures is not so much a problem of lack of tried and tested
methods as one of difficulty in getting labour in remote areas and motivating
people to maintain or renew structures (for information on construction o
erosion control/moisture conservation measures see: Leblond & Guérin
1988). In Ethiopia, one estimate suggested that it takes 150 man/days work
to dig 1 km of typical field terraces, to build 1 km of main terrace could take
350 man/days and 1 km of road may take 2000 man/days (Cross, 1983)
Moisture conservation terraces can last 20 years without much maintenance
once built, but their construction may take 742 man/days per hectare
protected. Terracing involves effort, this is no disadvantage if yields increase
enough, erosion declines and security of harvest increases – which may be
the case. But, some terracing and other soil conservation/moisture conservation measures may not be so attractive. It may, for example, make more
sense to farmers to allow their land to degrade and become migrant labour
than to try and boost yields and try to market more or better produce. The
roads and the market prices and demand for produce may make intensifica-
tion unattractive. Indeed, where there is a possibility of migrant labour,
rural workers may be, at least seasonally, scarce. In such circumstances,
getting people to construct and maintain soil conservation/moisture
conservation structures will probably be difficult. There is a chance in some
situations that, by providing terraces and so on, the farm profits and security
are boosted, the need for migrant labour earnings may be reduced, and
labour may return. Each situation will require careful assessment to establish
if this is the case.

In Peru, one USAID study showed that farmers accepted financial aid to
construct terraces. They then 'sub-contracted', paying labourers less than
the aid they had received, made a profit and thereafter neglected the terraces.
It seems that, in the region, there were sufficient opportunities for off-farm
wage earning to make terrace maintenance and better farming, with more
effort involved, unattractive. What is clear, is that to generalize can be
dangerous; each situation must be carefully assessed before too large and
costly a programme of 'improvement' is embarked upon. The value of soil
conservation, in the eyes of locals, may depend on transport, labour, market
and other factors.

There are situations where peasant farmers have willingly adopted erosion
control measures. For example, in Wollo Province (Ethiopia), farmers use
brushwood and stone check-dams to counter gulley erosion. Soil accumulates behind the check-dams and remains damp for some time after rains,
providing excellent farm plots (Conway, 1988).

Soil conditioners

There are a range of compounds that can be used to improve the fertility
and/or resistance of soil to water and wind erosion. Some simply seal the soil
surface, binding particles together so as to reduce dislodgement and
removal, for example, with oil- or rubber-based emulsions. Some treatments
simply cover the surface with a protective layer (mulch) which holds
moisture and delays run-off, improves infiltration and reduces the effect of
raindrop impact: there are many materials used as mulches with this in mind.
Both surface treatment with emulsion sprays and mulching help conserve
moisture and are useful as means of establishing vegetation where conditions
are difficult. It is possible to include seeds with some of these treatments so

hat seeding and mulching are done in a single pass. Some treatments and mulches are inert, others such as diluted sewage sludge, sugar cane bagasse, or other nutrient-rich waste, improve soil fertility as well as giving protection. There are risks with some treatments: sewage sludge is probably best used where trees are to be grown or landscaping is the goal, rather than on cropland, unless it is clear that the treatment has no risks of disease transmission or pollution of streams and groundwater by excess nutrients, heavy metals, etc.

There has been considerable interest in a 'new generation' of soil conditioners which can be very efficient at conserving moisture (some can hold 1000 times their own weight of water) and stabilizing soil. These may be added to soil as a surface film or incorporated as an additive in the topsoil. Greenland & Lal (1977: 101, 107) and Zachar (1982: 385–6) listed a number of such conditioners, including:

Polyacrylamides (PA)
Polyvinylalcohols (PVA)
'Curasol AE' (Hoechst)
'Humofina PAM' (Labofina)
'Petroset SB' (Phillips Petroleum)

Conditioners like PA can be useful, but probably cost too much for general use by peasant farmers, although *The Times* (25/10/88: 38) reported one project where PA used to establish Acacia plantations cost *c*. £1.60 per 100 trees established.

Green manures, organic fertilizers and chemical fertilizers

There has been much interest recently in developing strategies like alley-cropping, where shelter-belt shrubs or trees provide mulch or compost. There are plants which are particularly efficient at fixing nitrogen that might be grown alongside crops/pasture, or mixed with crops/pasture, or grown in rotation with crops/pasture, or which could be grown as hedges or farm woodland plots to provide leaves and twigs for mulch. As these nitrogen-fixers die naturally, are ploughed in, or are added as mulch/compost, the soil should improve in structure and organic carbon content. In overgrazed areas of tropical South America, legume/grass mixes are attracting some attention, for example, *Centrosema acutifolium* and *Andropogon gayanus* may prove valuable in Brazilian *cerrados* grasslands for maintaining soil fertility, protecting against erosion and improving grazing.

In coastal areas, seaweed can be a valuable soil additive, and it is one that could be more widely adopted. Away from coastal areas, aquatic weeds are often a nuisance but might prove to be a resource if collected and applied to cropland as a compost.

The advantage of these organic treatments over chemical (artificial) fertilizers is that they are: less demanding of the user in terms of rate application; there is less need for precision; there is much less handling risk; the release of nutrients is likely to be more gradual, so cutting pollution risks; timing of application is less critical and perhaps most important, the treatment adds organic carbon to the soil. There is debate, but it seems likely that, in the long run, maintenance of soil structure and fertility will require additions of organic material not just artificial fertilizers. This conviction, added to worries about the damaging effects of agrochemical use on the land and the consumer, has led to increasing adoption of organic farming approaches, so far mainly in richer nations (Arden-Clarke & Hodges, 1987).

Table 10.7. *Formula to determine shelter-belt spacing.*

$$L = 17H \, (Vt/V) \cos \alpha \qquad (7$$

where: L = distance apart of shelter-belts
   H = height of shelter-belt
   V = actual wind velocity measured at 15 m above ground
   Vt = threshold wind velocity (taken to be 34 km h^{-1})
   α = angle of deviation of prevailing wind from a line perpendicular to the shelter-belt

Source: Kirkby & Morgan, 1980: 273–6; Zachar, 1982: 380.

Groundcover plants

Groundcover plants provide protection from direct impact of raindrops shed intercepted moisture in drops that are less damaging than raindrops and have a dense mat of shallow roots which bind the soil. Things are more complicated if the groundcover is to be used beneath a tree or shrub crop where light levels may be low, and, if there are to be annual crops grown nearby, ideally the groundcover would fix nitrogen and improve the soil rather than compete with crops for moisture/nutrients. The choice of appropriate groundcover plants thus depends on a range of factors including: character of precipitation, the land use, the slope, etc.

Measures for countering wind erosion

Soils with a particle size range of 0.002 to 0.100 mm are more prone to wind erosion and transport. The following passage gives only a brief overview of the many technical measures available for erosion control (for further information see Weber & Stoney, 1989).

Shelter-belts and windbreaks

Windbreak is generally applied to non-living structures: fences of brush wood, wicker-worker, etc, and occasionally to small-scale plantings of, say aloe. Shelter-belts are larger-scale plantings which, when mature enough give protection for at least 20 times their height downwind. Care is needed in siting windbreaks or shelter-belts to ensure that they are at 90° to the most damaging winds, not necessarily the prevailing wind. Cross-sectional shape and the permeability of the barrier to airflow are also important; a shelter belt or windbreak should not be too wind-proof, it should 'leak' a little or there will be damaging eddies in its lee; about 40% porosity is generally considered desirable. Spacing and height also require attention (see Equation 7 in Table 10.7).

Shelter-belts are not instant solutions, they take time to establish. Care must be taken to ensure that local people understand the need for, and support the establishment of, shelter-belts or the erection of windbreaks. If they do not, damage is likely to occur. It is also important that the shrubs or trees used do not compete with nearby, generally shallower-rooted, crops or pasture for moisture.

Some trees or shrubs are particularly suitable for shelter-belts, for not only do they slow the wind, they also supply firewood, fodder, compost or mulch that can be used for soil improvement. There have also been impressive

results from using shelter-belts to conserve soil moisture in dryland regions
and thereby boost crop, possibly by as much as 30%, or for forage and
fuelwood (Barrow, 1987a: 157; Weber & Stoney, 1989: 137).

Stabilizing moving sand and soil

There are a great many ways, other than with shelter-belts, of holding soil in
place or catching that which has begun to move. Crops may be planted in a
suitable pattern, usually a grid-pattern (*coulisses*). Sturdy, soil/sand-trapping
grasses or herbs may be planted in a pattern that serves to stabilize areas of
soil erosion, for example, *Ammophila arenaria* has been found effective in
Europe for sand dune protection (Lenihan & Fletcher, 1976). Simply laying
a 'thatch' of tree branches may be helpful. It may also be worth spraying soil
or sand with compounds to stabilize it: latex emulsion; oil; waste paper or
fibres and water; shredded bark, to name but a few with or without seeds
incorporated in the mulch.

Reducing damage caused by agricultural activity

Mechanized cultivation can cause serious damage to soil. There is also a
possibility that inappropriate tillage can waste soil moisture (Barrow, 1987a:
156). Zero-tillage has been advocated as a measure to reduce degradation
during arable cultivation. Zero-tillage may demand the use of herbicide or
burning to control weed growth, although this may be avoided if special
ploughs are used. A wide horizontal blade is drawn through the soil, cutting
weed roots and disturbing the soil only around the supporting vertical blade.
A recent, promising development, is the 'gantry'. This consists of two sets of
powered wheels *c.* 12 m apart on a gantry from which tillage, spraying,
seeding and harvesting, etc, can be carried out. The wheels follow narrow,
fixed paths across the field so that there is little of the crop damage or soil
compaction associated with conventional tractors and farm machinery.
More efficient application of seed and agrochemicals should help to cut the
cost of farming inputs, and, more importantly, reduce the amounts of
potentially polluting fertilizers, etc, that are used. The system is being
developed by the Silsoe Agricultural Institute (UK), and seems to have great
potential, at least for farmers in richer nations and commercial farming in
developing countries (*The Times*, 11/9/89: 4).

Encouraging, supporting and enforcing soil degradation control

Separation of administrative/extension/education efforts from consideration
of soil protection techniques is not really practicable. Baker (1984)
highlighted what he saw as a 'conventional' perception of land degradation
which led to 'conventional' responses. Erosion is not just due to misuse of
vulnerable physical environments. Erosion is often because vulnerable
environments coincide with marginalized, powerless people who are forced
to degrade land. Effective soil degradation control requires certain things
(see Fig. 10.5).

It is possible for those seeking erosion control/reduction of soil
degradation to:

1. educate people in value of soil conservation;
2. offer grants and loans to tempt people to practise soil conservation;

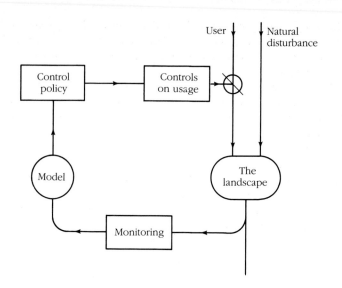

Fig. 10.5. Soil degradation control. Source: Based on Chisholm & Dumsday, 1987: 48
(no Fig. number used in source).

3. tax and/or fine those who cause erosion/soil degradation, if, say, it reaches
   a certain threshold;
4. manipulate the market: hold down or drive up prices, aid or hinder sales
   to encourage/discourage crops which are seen to lead to excessive
   erosion/soil damage;
5. discourage or prohibit practices or timing of practices that cause soil
   erosion/soil damage, e.g. discourage tillage of soil that is too wet or too
   dry, discourage stubble/crop residue burning, try to find alternatives to
   dung collection for fuel;
6. reward those who manage to cut soil erosion/improve soil quality.

Some of these options (3. and 6.) are potentially inequitable. A farmer may
take over a farm with a poor soil degradation record, or a farm with
especially difficult and vulnerable conditions, and would thereby risk being
penalized.

Historically, governments attend to land degradation only when public
opinion forces them to, usually as a result of perceived 'catastrophe'. In
effect, the management of land degradation, particularly soil degradation has
been response-to-crisis management (Chisholm & Dumsday, 1987: 47).

Yield decline is not linear – thus the earlier soil conservation is initiated,
the greater the potential benefits. Also, once a certain stage is reached,
rehabilitation efforts may be pointless as far as production from the land is
concerned, i.e. it is not cost effective.

There is a trend nowadays toward prevention of soil degradation, but it is
new and not very well established, especially in the developing countries
where resources are scarce. Another problem is that management often has
to be according to the best available understanding, often only partially
complete, of how the ecosystem and probably the society, functions. Errors
are inevitable and will continue to occur, even with the best efforts.

There are, of course, governments that offer tax incentives and grants to
encourage soil conservation. Australian Income Tax offers 100% write-off of
expenditure on structural works for soil conservation (Chisholm &
Dumsday, 1987: 239). Many irrigation management authorities regulate

water supplies to growers to help avoid over-irrigation and the likely consequences of waterlogging and salinization. Such an approach is likely to be much cheaper and more effective than remedial soil drainage or chemical treatment measures.

What is worrying is that, even in developed countries, soil conservation appears to have a low priority. In spite of decades of work by bodies like the US Soil Conservation Service, USA farmers were not managing soil as well in 1978 as they did 50 years earlier according to Brown (1978: 24). In 1988, damage to USA food and cotton production through soil erosion was estimated to be around US$ 43 billion per annum (Anon. 1988b: 29). Hudson (1987a, b) has discussed soil conservation strategies, and suggested that soil conservation might be more easily achieved if it were more closely integrated with agricultural extension. Indeed, he advocated that soil conservation be re-named 'land husbandry' and that the emphasis be placed on:

- prevention of erosion rather than cure;
- stressing the loss of production (to keep farmers' attention);
- stressing the potential of soil conservation for improving and sustaining production;
- promoting the use of local materials/practices;
- involving local community at all stages;
- making programmes more attractive, so that external incentives and subsidies are not necessary.

11 Land degradation through warfare, mineral extraction, industrial and urban development and increased movement of organisms

LAND DEGRADATION AS A CONSEQUENCE OF WARFARE

Conventional warfare

WARFARE, civil and international, can be a direct, or an indirect, cause of land degradation. Acts of war may cause considerable damage: cratering, fire, killing of livestock and people. The debris of war may remain long after hostilities cease, making land use difficult or dangerous. Warfare also disrupts economic and social activities and diverts manpower, money and equipment from other tasks, including environmental management. People affected by warfare or unrest are unlikely to practise careful, productive agriculture; they may, in any case, have lost livestock, seeds and tools. Those forced to become refugees are unlikely to get satisfactory new lands and may suffer trauma and problems of adapting to new environmens which hinders return to normal livelihoods, often for many years. The drive to obtain minerals, food and other supplies for war efforts is likely to mean a reduction of concern for environmental consequences, although it may lead to technological advances that might eventually be useful for countering land degradation (for example, satellites for strategic reconnaissance have led to earth resource monitoring and weather satellite technology).

In the past, the expansion and contraction of food and commodity crop production has often reflected periods of war. The demand for rubber increased after 1914, partly due to the demands for war equipment, partly because of the technological development: vulcanization, more effort went into its gathering, and plantation cultivation increased. Grain prices and expansion of grain production into marginal lands has often reflected warfare, for example, in the UK during the Napoleonic Wars and during the First and Second World Wars.

The second half of the twentieth century, 1945 – 1981, has seen about 133 wars or armed conflicts, mostly in developing countries and of relatively small scale (El-Hinnawi & Hashmi, 1982: 15). Conflicts like the Vietnam War or those between Egypt and Israel (1967 and 1973) have been quite large scale. Africa, in particular, has suffered from frequent conflicts, many of these, civil wars. With less than 10% of the world's total land area, the African continent had over half the world's total refugees in 1987.

Nations of the Far East, South Asia, parts of Latin America and Africa, spend quite large proportions of their gross national product (GNP) on their military forces. African countries, on average, spent 3.2% of their GNP on military forces in the late 1980s (Harrison, 1987a: 52). Money spent on troops and munitions or military hardware could have been spent on environmental management, improvements to agriculture, healthcare, education, etc, although troops may be used for land management work. El-Hinawi & Hashmi (1982) suggested that, since 1900, military expenditure globally has increased about 30-fold, absorbing huge amounts of natural resources.

Military considerations are often behind decisions to develop forest, remote deserts or islands. For example, in Amazonia, the 1960s and 1970s road-building was largely promoted by, and carried out by, the armed forces. Only Antarctica has been spared such development efforts, thanks so far to the Antarctic Treaty.

There are problems with unexploded munitions in many parts of the world. In parts of North Africa, between 5 and 19 million Second World War mines are still a threat, especially in Libya. In the Egypt–Israel–Palestine region, there are still mines and unexploded shells, etc from 1967 and 1973. In the Falkland Islands, there are extensive minefields left from the 1982 conflict. In Afghanistan, Iran–Iraq, Mozambique and Angola there are mines and other munitions to maim any peasant who tries to cultivate the land or graze livestock (Holdgate et al., 1982: 592). In Indochina, estimates suggest that there are over 2 million unexploded bombs and around 23 million unexploded artillery shells scattered over the countryside (Westing, 1984a,b).

Many of the world's farmers and pastoralists are going to face a threat for decades to come. European nations still maintain munitions disposal teams to deal with material left from 1914–18 and 1939–45. Modern mines are likely to be more of a problem to find than those of the 1930s and 1940s due to their construction with plastics to make them difficult to detect.

Warfare often causes bushfires. How much land has been lost to this is difficult to assess but it must be considerable. Bomb and shell craters are easier to recognize and map, in Vietnam there are an estimated 25 million, representing a displacement of roughly 3 billion m³ of soil (Gradwohl & Greenberg, 1988: 45). The Stanford Biology Study Group (1971) noted a single 500 lb (227 kg) high-explosive bomb could form a crater 14 m wide and 9 m deep. Between 1968 and 1969 alone, 3,500,000 such bombs were dropped in Vietnam, the Group also noted that 25 year-old bomb craters were still clearly visible in New Guinea; the damage can be slow to heal. Some areas of Vietnam, bombed in the 1960s, still had areas bare of vegetation in 1988 and considerable damage had been done to paddy-field systems (Kemf, 1988: 56). In Europe, areas of land degraded during the 1914–18 conflict were colonized by ruderal species, one of which, the red field poppy (Papaver rhoeas) has become symbolic of rememberance of the tragedy and sacrifice of war.

The indirect damage caused by war can be enormous. In Medieval Europe, the 'Hundred Years' War led to depopulation of whole regions, loss of farm labour and abandonment of land. The consequences were extensive neglect of farmland and pastures, widespread growth of brush and woodland and long-term changes in agricultural practices forced by labour shortage. During the Second World War, large areas of reclaimed land in the Benelux countries were deliberately flooded just prior to the German invasion, causing considerable damage. Timber resources have been damaged in Vietnam and elsewhere in Indochina, by bushfires during hostilities and, because the use of weapons left many metal shards in trees, these wreak havock in sawmills many years later if the wood is processed.

Chemical and biological warfare

Poison gases; e.g. chlorine and 'mustard gas' (phosgene), were used in
Europe during the First World War, and, in spite of being forbidden under
the Geneva Protocol of 1925, in some of the recent conflicts in the Middle
East, and in Africa. The use, during the 1970s and 1980s, of modern 'nerve
agents' has been suspected but there has been little conclusive evidence.
Although intended primarily as 'incapacitating agents' CS and 'teargas' -type
gases might affect wildlife. The USA used about 9 million kg of CS in
Indochina, mainly in S. Vietnam during the Vietnam War, Freedman (1989:
304) suggests it may have had serious effects on fauna.

Apart from the humanitarian issues, the effects of war gases on wildlife
and the soil is uncertain. Some chemical weapons can have long-lasting
effects, but most break down fairly fast. More problems have been caused by
leakage from manufacturing or storage sites. In the UK, there are sites where
soil contamination is high following storage or attempted disposal of gases
like phosgene in the late 1940s. In the USA, there was controversy about
contamination associated with poison-gas manufacture/testing at Dugway
(Utah) in the 1960s.

Great damage has been caused by chemicals designed to 'defoliate'
vegetation so as to deprive an enemy of cover or food crops. These defoliant
chemical compounds were briefly tried in Malaya (by the UK) in the 1950s
(Pereira & Thomas, 1985), but were most heavily used during the Vietnam
War. The main forms used were: 'Agent Orange': 2, 4-D + 2, 4, 5-T and
'Agent White': 2, 4-D + picloram and occasionally 'Agent Blue' (based on
picloram). Picloram is a very persistent and unpleasant compound. It seems
likely that these 'agents' were not very pure and contained a lot of the highly
toxic and very persistent compound: dioxin (or TCDD – a dioxin isomer). If
that was the case, the land degradation threat will still be active (Richards,
1984: Kemf, 1988). Agent blue was used against cropland and contained
cacodylic acid which is $c.$ 54% arsenic. The arsenic tends to accumulate in the
food chain, making agricultural use of the contaminated land risky, even
now (Stanford Biology Study Group, 1971). It has been claimed that, in S.
Vietnam alone, over 72 million litres of these defoliants were used (Wilkie,
1988).

It has been estimated that, during the Vietnam War, 40% of Vietnam was
treated and 44% of all rainforest/forest was defoliated particularly between
1960 and 1972 (Gradwohl & Greenberg, 1988: 45). Myers (1980: 116)
estimated that 20,000 to 50,000 km² of Vietnam's forests were damaged to
varying degree by warfare, most in what was S. Vietnam. The effect of these
chemicals on fauna and lightly contaminated plant life is unknown.
However, the impacts have probably been considerable as they persist, can
be toxic to animal life, and may cause mutation. Mangrove forests were
especially badly affected. Myers (1980: 116) estimated that 2600 out of
7200 km² that had been sprayed were killed. In 1968, the US Department of
State studied the ecological effects of defoliant use, apparently until about
1966 mangrove forests had been particularly heavily treated.

Defoliation in Indochina has, in many cases, caused permanent destruction of cover, or marked, possibly permanent, change in the character of
vegetation rather than temporary leaf loss. In Vietnam and Laos, large areas
of deciduous forest were killed and recovery has been very slow and
sporadic (Freedman, 1989: 304). Where vegetation on steeper slopes was
sprayed, there has been considerable soil erosion. Large areas of Vietnam's
woody vegetation, especially *Melaleuca* spp. woodlands, has been replaced by

grassland, the water-tables have risen and woody cover is unlikely to ever recover. Of little value for grazing or cultivation, these grasslands have been dubbed 'American grass' by the Vietnamese. (Detwyler, 1971: 532-46; *Environmental Conservation*, 11: 147; Kemf, 1988). In some mangrove forest areas, defoliation exposed soils to sunlight and laterization took place, or soils drained and acid-sulphate soils developed making reforestation unlikely.

Since the Vietnam War, there have been efforts to replant mangroves, at a rate of about 300,000 ha a year, especially in the Mekong Delta and in the Gulf of Camu, but about 20% of the defoliated areas remained bare in 1988 (Kemf, 1988). In N. and S. Vietnam, defoliation, plus the effects of explosive bombs, napalm and deliberate bulldozing of forest, probably destroyed about 22 million ha. In S. Vietnam, at least 5.6 million ha of upland forest were damaged (Kemf, 1988: 55). The USA apparently recently came close to using herbicide ('spike') sprays from aircraft against illicit coca (source of cocaine) fields in Peruvian jungle areas (Wilkie, 1988).

There has been no recorded use of biological weapons so far, although there might have been tests in Mongolia during the 1930s. There have been situations where European settlers have promoted the spread of serious diseases like smallpox or measles amongst aboriginal peoples in parts of Amazonia and probably elsewhere. Diseases spread accidentally by the Spanish during the Conquest of Latin America probably did as much as anything else to alter Andean land use. Before the Spanish Conquest, there were extensive and sophisticated hillside, irrigated terraced fields in Peru, Colombia, Ecuador and other parts of Latin America and in the *altiplano*, and in other wetlands there was drain and raised-bed (*chinampas*) agriculture. After the Conquest, few of these systems remained in operation and productive cropland became less-productive grazing land or rain-fed cropland, probably through disease-related depopulation.

During the First and Second World War there were fears that anthrax (*Bacillus anthracis*) would be used as a weapon. It was not, but experiments to develop offensive, defensive or retaliatory capabilities by the UK left Gruinard Island in Scotland heavily contaminated. The Island was 'decontaminated' and sold by the Ministry of Defence only in the late 1980s, and caution is still exercised over access to it. The use of persistent organisms like anthrax (and other diseases such as foot-and-mouth diseases of livestock or tick-borne infections) by nations at war or terrorists would have a serious effect on the possible land use of areas for a long time. The introduction of livestock diseases, insect, pests of crops, Man and animals would present few problems to anyone determined enough, and with access to resources; even simple failure to control locust breeding in remote areas may affect surrounding territories.

Developing bacteria, viruses, fungi, etc. for infecting crops or livestock is not very difficult, the main constraint so far, which, thankfully, has prevented use of biological weapons, is the difficulty in restricting the spread of infection to an enemy nation. With modern genetic 'engineering', the latter difficulty might be overcome. There is also a risk that some organism 'engineered' for peaceful use, for example, a bacteria used to enhance frost resistance of vegetables or a virus spray to kill cabbage-eating caterpillars, might mutate or, in some indirect way, become a problem, say, by passing on genetic material to some other organism that then becomes a threat.

Environmental warfare

The deliberate manipulation of the environment for military purposes has occurred on a small scale, as 'scorched-earth' actions for centuries. Armies have commonly set fire to crops and forests or have diverted streams from townships under siege. (The Amu-darya which flows into the Aral Sea was diverted during the campaigns of Ghengis Khan to subdue people in the region). The diversion of large streams is now relatively easy and could deprive a whole nation of irrigation and domestic water supplies, without war having been formally declared. During the Iran–Iraq conflict, large areas were flooded to hinder troop movements (Westing, 1984b).

Alteration of regional weather patterns, snowcover, triggering of earthquakes, tsunamis, etc are, thankfully, still in the realms of science fantasy, but are not impossible. There have been suggestions that extra low-frequency radio transmissions or strong microwave transmissions might be used to degrade environments some distance from the source (Smith & Best, 1989).

Nuclear warfare

Nuclear munitions have already degraded large areas; there has been pollution resulting from weapons manufacture, use (at Hiroshima and Nagasaki in 1945) and testing. Before the 1967 Test Ban Treaty, there were worrying levels of atmospheric fall-out, and testing has contaminated or blast-damaged parts of the USA, USSR, China, Australia, the Pacific islands (notably, Eniwetok Atoll, the Marshall Is., Christmas Island and Bikini Atoll), Pakistan and India. The Marilanga Test Area of Australia is still contaminated in places although the last test was over 35 years ago. Between 1945 and 1978 there were at least 1165 nuclear test explosions worldwide, around 130 of these were wholly above-ground (El-Hinnawi & Hashmi, 1982: 15). Since the 1950s, there have been over 250 nuclear tests in the Pacific and testing still continues on Muraroa Atoll.

A large literature has grown up on the established, and what are believed to be the likely, effects of nuclear warfare. There are many variables involved should an exchange of nuclear weapons take place which may determine degree of land degradation:

- *Scale:* this could vary from one terrorist device of low yield, or even no nuclear fission as such, but rather the explosion of a device intended to scatter toxic, radioactive material, to a full-scale exchange between 'superpowers' of possibly several thousands of warheads, some of high yield. The detonation of a nuclear weapon at very high altitude (just outside the atmosphere) could generate a widespread nuclear pulse, wrecking electronic and electrical equipment so as to put out of action: phones, computers, TV, radio, most motor vehicles and aircraft, etc. The economic chaos would probably lead to considerable land use change.
- *Timing:* the exchange might cause more damage at certain times of year, at least if the exchange is not a very extensive one. A long, drawn-out exchange over weeks or months (perhaps a little unlikely) may cause more damage than a short, intense exchange.
- *Targetting:* if 'dirty' targets: fuel refineries, chemical factories, nuclear power stations, etc, are hit, then pollution will be much increased.
- *Type of warheads:* the yield (destructive force) of nuclear weapons varies between less than 1 kiloton and over 50 megaton, a considerable

range. Some nuclear weapons are relatively 'clean', particularly the so-called neutron bomb, and yield less fall-out than other types. Contamination also depends on where the warhead detonates; an air-burst well above ground or the ocean will probably draw up less debris and so yield less fall-out, though it may cause more widespread urban and forest fires.

At least seven nations have nuclear capability, i.e. have exploded nuclear bombs, even if they have not stock-piled weapons. Other countries, soon will have, or could easily have, such capabilities by AD 2000. In the early 1980s, there were an estimated 50,000 nuclear warheads (Barnaby, 1982: 77). The potential for nuclear war is significant; the scale of damage to the environment if such an event were to happen seems likely to be very considerable. There is little doubt that non-combatants as well as combatants would be very severely affected, directly and indirectly.

Some nations still test, although this is mainly underground; France has reputedly exploded around 300 devices since the 1950s on Pacific islands (El-Hinnawi & Hashmi, 1982). There have been sinkings of vessels with nuclear reactors for propulsion and/or carrying nuclear weapons at sea; on land, there have also been incidents: one was the re-entry and disintegration over Canada of a radioactive satellite power source whch caused localized contamination of a little-populated region. There have also been aircrashes involving nuclear weapons, one such incident occurred near Palomares in Spain in the 1960s and appears to have involved the removal and disposal of large amounts of contaminated soil from several km².

The effects of nuclear weapons are likely to include: blast and direct radiation damage to organisms and the Earth's surface: heat-flash damage; radioactive fall-out: release of toxic chemicals and generation of CO_2 and NO_x by fires, the latter possibly upsetting ozone layer and altering UV-B receipts at the Earth's surface (Harwell & Hutchinson, 1985). Upset to world trade and telecommunications would mean a severe disruption of supplies of petroleum products, fertilizer, seeds, pesticides, etc, plus a loss of market for food and commodity crops. Even if the impacts of the war were restricted to the Northern Hemisphere, farmers in the Southern Hemisphere would be badly hit and many would probably degrade or abandon their land when deprived of returns and inputs.

There has been considerable controversy over the 'nuclear winter' effect hypothesis, which suggests that the weapons, plus the fires they start, would generate so much dust, gases and soot that the whole globe would probably have abnormal climatic conditions for some indeterminate time, after the exchange (Bondietti, 1982; Westing, 1987; Ginzburg, 1989; *Ambio*, XVIII issue 7 considers the possible impacts of nuclear war; Botkin *et al.*, 1989: 157–64).

There is some indication from the effects of large, natural forest fires that a 'nuclear winter' is a risk (Bach, 1986: Turco *et al.*, 1983; Greene *et al.*, 1985; *Journal of Bioscience*, 1985). If a war led to temperatures in the Tropics being depressed by as much as 6 or 7°C for more than a few days, which has been suggested as a possibility, the effect on plant life would be catastrophic (Freedman, 1989: 315). In some latitudes, plants and some wildlife may get a little protection if the 'nuclear winter' takes place after the first frosts, by which time organisms are 'hardened' and are dormant or covered with a protective layer of snow (Harwell & Hutchinson, 1985). Conifers seem to be particularly sensitive to radiation damage (Westing, 1987); pollinating insects would probably suffer, and areas of burnt forest or grasslands would probably lose nutrients and soil through leaching and erosion.

LAND DEGRADATION AS A CONSEQUENCE OF MINING AND QUARRYING

Mining and quarrying does not always result in permanent land degradation; some of the most aesthetically pleasing landscapes and valuable conservation sites owe their origin to it. Unfortunately, while mining/quarrying is active, considerable environmental damage can occur (Detwyler, 1971: 325; Goodman & Bray, 1975).

One may divide mining/quarrying into: surface mining and quarrying and subsurface (or deep mining). The latter may be done by drilling quite small diameter boreholes.

Surface mining

There are various types of surface mine:

- open-pit quarries – little overburden is removed;
- strip-mining – typically, more overburden than mineral is removed;
- hydraulic mining – river sediment is washed to separate out minerals/gemstones. Some forms of hydraulic mining are used in open-pit quarries, e.g. gravel-pump tin mining in Malaysia.

There has been widespread quarrying in Europe for metals, building and roadstone from Roman times. Cathedral construction in Medieval times led to demand for certain types of stone. Specialist needs were also met by quarrying: roofing slate; decorative stonework, particularly marble and alabaster; limestone, for mortar, agricultural lime and for smelting; rocksalt, for human and livestock use; millstones, for milling flour and later industrial processing. In the UK, Poland, Holland and Germany, there has long been a demand for kiln-fired clay-bricks. Brick-pits have been dug in many parts of the UK and Europe, for example, around London. Once abandoned, these excavations have proved valuable for domestic refuse disposal and recreational use.

Since the Second World War, cement and concrete has come to be used more often as a construction material and has resulted in extensive quarrying of chalk or limestones. The manufacture of cement has generally led to serious localized dust pollution. Limestone is also in great demand for the chemical industry, for aggregate and building stone (Stanton, 1989). Demand for sand and gravel has increased roughly in line with the increase in demand for concrete/cement.

Some of the earliest large-scale surface mines were for peat, and the flooded workings have given the Claires region of France, parts of Belgium and the Norfolk Broads of eastern UK a distinctive pattern of shallow lakes and ponds.

The extraction of coal increased considerably after AD 1752. Until the nineteenth-century most came from small subsurface deep mines or open bell-pits; deep mining increased in the UK and other countries in the nineteenth century and in the first half of the twentieth and, after the 1940s, surface coal mining production overtook deep mines production. This largely reflects the development of heavy mining equipment capable of stripping and transporting overburden, but also follows the exhaustion of high-value coal reasonably accessible to deep mining, and to rising labour costs and reluctance of mines to work below ground. By 1971, four-fifths of the USA's solid fuel and ores came from surface mines (Bradshaw & Chadwick, 1980: 163).

Open-cast surface mining causes the following disruptions:

1. Removal of overburden and mineral(s) creates a large hole in the ground. If care is not taken, there may be species loss, dust pollution, noise and disruption related to transport and processing of mineral(s).
2. If a lot of the mineral(s) is/are removed, and the overburden is returned, once it settles there may be a depression. Subsidence may also be associated with deep mining.
3. Re-establishing vegetation on the restored mine site or the abandoned, unrestored mine site may be a problem (James, 1966). There may no longer be plants to re-seed the site, soil may have been damaged, vital fungi, bacteria, etc, may have been lost. Or, there might be toxic levels of various elements, plus a mineral-rich, humus-poor soil.
4. The overburden may be stored, at least temporarily, as spoil heaps, these can be unsightly and dangerous, they are prone to landslides and/or may have toxic compounds leached from them or may even catch fire spontaneously due to the oxidation of bituminous matter (Lenihan & Fletcher, 1976: 70). Spoil tips may also be re-worked at a later point in time if extraction processes have been improved, and, with this, renewed pollution, noise, etc. Deep mines also generate spoil heaps.
5. There is a risk that workings will flood. This may have beneficial (recreational and wildlife potential) as well as negative impacts.
6. Noise, dust and vibration from machinery and explosives causes disturbance.

A problem with surface mining is the overburden. If the mined area is to be rehabilitated, then storage practice is crucial (Doubleday, 1974; Down & Stocks, 1977). It may be necessary to separate topsoil and subsoil/rocks to ensure the former is not compacted, buried or in any other way damaged. Even with the best storage, organisms like earthworms suffer. A common strategy is to remove overburden, and, if need be, conserve it, extract the mineral(s), partially fill the excavation with refuse or other waste and then return the overburden and re-vegetate the site. Problems arise if the overburden contains toxic materials, lacks humus or has had nutrients leached from it. If any of these have occurred, re-vegetation can be difficult. Restoration is seldom perfect: even if contours are reformed with the spoil and the area is re-vegetated, it is unlikely that subsurface drainage will not have been drastically altered (Jordan et al., 1988; Laidler, 1989).

Hydraulic mining, the extraction of sediments from river bed or banks and then the washing of the material, causes relatively limited excavation damage, unless large floating, bucket-chain tin or gold dredgers are used, but usually there is a lot of waste silt (tailings). In Malaysia, Thailand, California, Australia and parts of Brazil, tailings are a problem. The material is seldom toxic, but it is usually rather infertile sandy material and it gets spread by floods to choke streams and coat farmland near rivers. In California, nineteenth-century gold miners released huge amounts of tailings. This material is still mobile and causes flooding and siltation problems (Beaumont, 1989: 155). Near Kuala Lumpur, Malaysia, large areas of tin tailings have proved difficult to re-vegetate.

Lead, copper, gold and other non-ferrous mining tailings may be difficult to re-vegetate, either because they have a lot of these metals in them or because they are contaminated with chemicals like cyanide which are used in extraction. Some tailings can be very acidic with a pH of 4.0 or less, some are fine-grained enough to be unstable if built up as a waste tip. The UK Cornish china clay (kaolin) mines produce over 5 million tonnes a year of silica sand which are difficult to stabilize and re-vegetate. Fluorspar mine tailings are toxic and difficult to re-vegetate (Chadwick & Goodman, 1975: 350–84). The escape of ore processing chemicals, liquid slurry or material leached from spoil heaps or tailings can cause problems, mainly to river systems and coastal environments, but sometimes to floodlands and low-lying areas, or to land affected by drainage water carrying contaminants.

Cyanide and mercury contamination is becoming a serious problem in Amazonia, where many small gold mines use this form of processing, and simply discharge the residues into rivers. The Ok Tedi Copper Mine in Papua New Guinea has caused considerable damage with its tailings and pollutants and much social unrest (Hyndman, 1988). 'Red mud' left after processing bauxite to aluminia for making aluminium is very alkaline and has a high content of sodium hydroxide or sodium chloride. If this 'red mud' escapes into streams and gets deposited on floodlands, it can cause considerable damage.

There are regions that are naturally rich in heavy metals and may consequently have a sparse vegetation cover. Soils derived from serpentine are often rich in nickel, cobalt or iron and form badlands in parts of California and Zimbabwe. It is not uncommon for savanna soils to have high levels of selenium. Cattle grazed over such land may develop 'blind staggers' due to the poison accumulated from the forage.

Some regions have been heavily degraded by deep mining, for example: the gold mining region of the Witwatersrand (S. Africa) or the Copper Belt of Zambia. In the latter region, not only has mining had a direct impact, the demand for timber for fuel and pit-props to smelt the ore has caused tremendous devastation to forest and woodlands (Lewis & Berry, 1988: 369). Over 3000 years of copper mining and smelting have left their mark on Cyprus, much of the Island's forest must have been burnt for charcoal. In the Harz Mountains of Germany, there is also a long history of mining and related deforestation. A gold-rush at Coolgardie in Australia between 1892 and 1910 (and, to a lesser extent, in the 1930s) established townships forced to depend on salt water ponds. Wood was used to run desalination stills and this caused deforestation of vast areas (Beaumont, 1989: 159). In many countries, for example, Amazonia, mineral extraction and hydroelectric development tend to be associated. The availability of hydroelectricity powers mining and processing and helps make the mineral extraction profitable. The dams to provide the power may flood large areas of lowlands and affect downstream flood regimes which, in turn, may degrade large areas of floodlands and estuaries.

Blasting and mechanical operations associated with surface mining has some impact; the noise travels, debris may be scattered damaging nearby land and infrastructure, and dust is generated. Surface mines often flood, for example, in the UK over 1000 ha of ponds were created every year by gravel and sand extraction in the 1980s (Chadwick & Goodman, 1975: 216). In the USA, in the mid 1960s, over 10,000 km^2 had been disrupted by surface mining (Detwyler, 1971: 348–369). Some surface mines in Malaysia are over half a mile deep, e.g. the Sungai Besi Tin Mine, Serdang, Malaysia. When economic conditions generate the impetus, it is likely that there will be very large-scale development of oil-shale in Alberta (Canada), and possibly elsewhere (Bradshaw & Chadwick, 1980: 171).

Deep mining

Deep mines may be shafts sunk vertically until minerals are reached, or they may follow a mineral vein or lode. Where a mine has a sloping shaft, or follows a mineral horizontally into a hillside, it is generally termed an adit. Three problems are associated with these deep mines: subsidence; spoil heaps; and mineral-rich water pumped from, or seeping from, the mine. The water draining from mine workings or leaching from spoil heaps is often acidic and ferruginous due to the breakdown of iron pyrites (FeS_2). Water from uranium mines such as those in Colorado can have a low pH and some radioactivity. Some mines have waste that is high in molybdenum which makes it difficult to establish vegetation on the waste (Chadwick & Goodman, 1975). There are Roman lead mines in various parts of Europe that are still poorly re-vegetated.

Subsidence depends on the rock structure and character, upon the mining technique used; if some 'pillars' are left, collapse may be reduced or prevented, and upon the depth at which mineral extraction takes place. Subsidence may damage roads, housing, etc, and may give rise to water-filled hollows.

Extraction of minerals by borehole

Water, petroleum, natural gas and salts, are obtained by borehole, and sometimes come to the surface under pressure, obviating the need for pumping; sometimes the material has to be pumped up and may require injection of solvents, detergent or steam down a second borehole or down an inner pipe within the etraction borehole to be 'purged' from the source rocks or trap structure. There are possibilities that, in the future, coal may be gassified below ground by starting partial combustion and sustaining it by pumping oxygen and other gases down one borehole, the gas produced being extracted at another.

On-land oil pollution sometimes happens if a borehole suffers a well blowout. However, the effects tend to be quite localized. Pipeline leakage is surprisingly rare considering that worldwide there are over 64,500 km. Test spills suggest that tundra and temperate environments will, in the long term, suffer only slight to moderate damage from petroleum spillage. Salt marshes and mangrove swamps are frequently affected by marine oil spills; moderate spillage may cause serious damage, light spills may actually be slightly beneficial (Freedman, 1989: 151).

Extraction of minerals from boreholes can cause subsidence. If a reservoir rock (the rock holding the mineral) collapses when a mineral is extracted, due to the pressure from the overburden, it is unlikely that mineral fluids or water will ever collect in those layers again. Extraction of petroleum from the Wilmington Oil Field under Longbeach, California has led to over 27 feet (c. 9 m) of subsidence in some areas between 1933 and 1936 and several shallow earthquakes (Detwyler, 1971: 370). Mexico City and Jakarta have a similar degree of difficulty due to extraction of water from aquifers.

Indirect impacts of mining

Mining can attract migrant workers. The Copper Belt of Zambia or the Serra Pelada Goldmine of Brazil drew manpower from the surrounding regions, with the result that labour shortage caused neglect of farmland (Lewis & Berry, 1988: 370).

Rehabilitation and restoration of land degraded by mining and quarrying

Not all sites of mining require rehabilitation, provided they are not a safety hazard. Given time, old quarries, pits and spoil heaps can become valuable conservation and recreational sites. Larger, unflooded pits provide refuse disposal sites and, in warmer climates, flooded pits may have use as reservoirs and fishponds. Rehabilitation of large-scale open-cast mining can be costly: Chisholm & Dumsday (1987: 360) cite costs from A$ 500 to A$ 10,000 per ha.

LAND DEGRADATION AS A CONSEQUENCE OF INDUSTRIAL ACTIVITY AND DISPOSAL OF DOMESTIC AND INDUSTRIAL WASTES

Pollution may be defined as the release into a shared environment and against common interest, of an offensive by-product or waste. Alternatively, one might define a pollutant as something in the wrong place or in the right place at the wrong time. Noise, microwave, and radio-interference, radiation of various forms, smells, aesthetic problems, etc, which are hardly material (in the sense that dust, gas or soot are), are forms of pollution. Pollution can be primary, that is, it has a direct effect on the environment, or secondary, the product of photochemical processes or interaction with moisture and other pollutants after release. Pollution may take place on a local scale, a regional scale or a global scale, and there may be cumulative and insidious or immediately apparent, short lived or long lived.

Pollution problems may only occur, or become apparent, when a 'threshold' is reached. Below that point there may be little clear indication that a problem has arisen. Many pollutants are concentrated by organisms as they metabolize, and so become 'magnified'. A 'safe' background level of a pollutant may reach dangerous levels particularly in organisms, at the top of the food-web, which prey on others.

Pollution may take place in water or the atmosphere, there may be exchanges between these separate systems: airborne dust may settle into water and, at a later stage, spray may dry and become dust again. Pollution may originate as a point source: for example, a single waste-discharge pipe or an explosion at a chemical factory. Pollution may be released from a line source: a road treated with salt or upon which vehicles travel using leaded petrol. Pollution may come from an extensive area, for example, a large open-cast mine, a burning forest, an urban area – this is an area source. Release from any of these sources may be instantaneous and isolated, instantaneous and repeated or periodic, single or multiple 'puffs' of pollution. Releases from any of these sources may be a, more or less, continuous 'stream' of pollution.

The point of release might be at roughly ground level, or at some height above the ground. If above ground, released material will disperse according to its particle size and weight, windspeed, precipitation conditions and the height of release. Some pollutants may be carried by insects or other organisms; indeed, the organisms themselves may be seen as pollution by a householder, these vectors can follow a wide range of routes and may travel against the wind, certain ant species may travel along piping ducts, 'hitch rides' on motor vehicles, ships or in aircraft. Some pollutants are stable and change little after release, some break down into harmless compounds, and

some into harmful compounds. A persistent compound could become
global threat even if released intermittently at a few point sources.

Land degradation caused by domestic wastes

There are basically two types of domestic waste: sewage/nightsoil and refuse
(garbage or trash). Domestic refuse is a problem around households where
there is inadequate collection and disposal, the tendency being for
householders to fly-tip the waste. The result is unhealthy and aesthetically
unpleasant, but there is unlikely to be much real contamination of soil.
Where a collection and disposal system is operated, the areas around the
disposal site will probably face difficulties in all but the most advanced
countries. There are several options for disposal: landfill; recycling or
recoverable material and/or incineration; dumping of waste at sea; com
pression of waste and use for landscaping or coastal defences. Incineration is
expensive, unless the heat is recovered for domestic, district heating or
power and, without costly anti-pollution equipment, the smoke will
contaminate the atmosphere, adding to acid deposition problems.

Landfill disposal presents a number of problems. Noise, smell, rats,
carrion-eating birds and flies are common difficulties. The main effect of
these is on land use and land prices close to the tip, particularly downwind in
the direction of the prevailing wind. Landfill sites take up space, and
continue to be unusable for certain purposes long after disposal has finished.
A landfill site, that has been sealed and landscaped, is likely to suffer
subsidence, may leak water contaminated with a wide range of toxic
materials and may generate enough methane to be a hazard or a useful source
of power for electricity generation or district heating for decades. In the UK
this refuse-generated methane could provide the equivalent of around
million tonnes or coal a year (Richards, 1989). If unused, this methane joins
the globe's 'greenhouse gases'. The escaping leachate is most likely to
contaminate nearby low-lying land, streams and possibly groundwater.
Methane leakage and 'hot-spots', where oxidation generates heat, prevent
the use of the land for housing, industrial development or car parking.
Unless the landfill site is underlain by impermeable rocks, the area should
be 'sealed' before tipping with a layer of clay or silt (which may be less
prone to cracking). A cap-layer over the top and sides of the site of the tip
help to prevent leakage of gases and contaminated water. Unfortunately
sealing has often been unsatisfactory, or the solution is temporary, given the
tendency of sealing layers to crack. The risk of the seal being breached by
burrowing animals and plant roots seems to be minimal because these are
discouraged by the gas and heat before they penetrate very far.

In the Third World, some refuse recycling is likely to take place
spontaneously, as the poor of urban areas collect paper, tin, glass, etc, and
make use of it in various ways. However, there is little money to spend on
adequate incineration, compaction or proper landfill disposal of what
remains. Cities like Lima (Peru) have vast, unsightly and unhealthy refuse
tips occupying large areas of urban land.

In Western countries, since the invention of the water-closet in the second
half of the nineteenth-century, sewage disposal has involved the operation of
costly and complex water and waste-conveying drains. There are few
impacts in the areas where these sewage systems are charged, except where
maintenance or design has been inadequate or if flooding or subsidence
occur.

Unfortunately, few nations have installed sewage systems which separate storm water, sewage, and industrial effluent. In the future, in order to reduce eutrophication of inland waters and coastal seas, it is likely that more advanced sewage processing will be needed and on-land disposal will increase, using techniques like wet oxidation (Beard, 1989). There are problems associated with disposing of sewage on land; it is costly and there may be high levels of heavy metals, detergents, antibiotic and drug residues and harmful organisms. Much of the heavy metal contamination comes from industrial activity like plating and galvanizing, tanning, electrical and chemical manufacturing. Zinc and cadmium are a particular problem and their effect on soil organisms is not fully understood (Gillen & McGrath, 1989).

In countries where there is not a water-based sewage system, there may be fewer problems in disposing of waste, for nightsoil is less likely to have detergents or industrial wastes mixed with it. In countries such as the People's Republic of China, nightsoil can be treated as a valuable resource to be returned to the land or fed into fishponds. Such use, by intensifying production, may help take the pressure off the land for expansion of agriculture.

Land degradation caused by industrial wastes

There is such diversity of industrial waste that generalization is difficult. Where industry produces particularly toxic airborne pollutants such as copper, mercury or nickel smelting, extensive areas may suffer vegetation and soil damage and this can be difficult to rehabilitate. Heavy metals, radioactivity in some toxic compounds like dieldrin may be very slow to break down. The soil therefore has either to be removed, and carefully buried below an uncontaminated layer, with measures to prevent accidental exposure or leaching out of the hazardous compound, or treated chemically to neutralize or leach out the pollution for safe disposal (Hutnik & Davis 1973). This requires expertise and can take a lot of funding and time to do effectively, as was the case in the Lower Swansea Valley, UK (Oxenham, 1966; Hilton, 1967). Milne (1989) reviewed the UK contaminated land situation and noted rehabilitation costs could easily reach £200,000 per ha. If treatment is inadequate, for example, if burial is too shallow, plants may simply root into the toxic material and die when they reach a certain stage of maturity.

A worldwide problem is that records on industrial waste disposal are unsatisfactory; there may be a dangerous pollutant or a 'cocktail' of dangerous compounds buried at a site and no one is really aware, or, if they do recognize a problem, assessing its precise character is difficult. As with landfill disposal of domestic refuse, there is a risk of toxic or inflammable or radioactive gases or leachate from industrial waste.

A number of mineral processing and industrial activities cause sufficient pollution to drive down the value of nearby land, e.g. cement manufacture or tanning. Brick or tile manufacture and the steel industry can generate dust, hydrogen fluoride and silicon fluoride in sufficient quantity to pose a health hazard.

Heavy metals pollution, e.g. copper, mercury, lead, nickel, vanadium, cadmium and cobalt are a widespread problem. The sources range from use of leaded petrol to smelting non-ferrous ores or the combustion of fossil fuels. Some lichens and bryophytes are sensitive to airborne heavy metals, earthworms are sensitive to copper and zinc. Most vascular plants are sensitive to heavy metal pollution, although there are some species that are very resistant, for example, those metalophytes adapted to copper or nickel-rich soils (Baker *et al.*, 1988; Freedman, 1989: 71). It may be possible to use these species to landscape toxic spoil tips or even to plant, harvest and dispose of them and thereby gradually remove heavy metals from a soil, suitable species include *Alyssum corsicum* and *Sebertia acuminata* (Tyler, 1984).

Land degradation caused by burial of the dead

It is a little insensitive to discuss the issue of human burial along with waste and refuse disposal. However, many cultures require non-cremation disposal of bodies, and this may require quite large areas of land if environment and beliefs preclude catacombs or ossuaries. Land used for burial is seldom used for anything else, and so, like urban sprawl, it must be counted as a cause of land degradation in that crop production, etc, largely ceases.

Land degradation caused by power generation

Electrical power is presently generated by: hydroelectric turbines; coal, oil, natural gas, methane, peat or wood burning thermal power stations; nuclear fission power stations; wave power; wind turbines; estuarine barrages; geothermal power stations; solar generation. Hydropower generation, at present, generally means dams and flooding of land and often dislocation and resettlement of people.

Hydroelectric dams often flood acres of richest soil, of greatest bio-diversity and often, of heaviest population. The direct impact and indirect land degradation can therefore be considerable. By regulating river flows, dams can damage downstream flood plains, wetlands, mangrove swamps, etc, by raising local water-tables, reservoirs formed behind large dams can cause waterlogging and salinization (Barrow, 1987a: 268–86).

Most of today's thermal power stations liberate pollutants which cause land degradation directly, and indirectly through the 'greenhouse effect'.

Nuclear fission generation at its present level of development has the disadvantage of cost and risk of land degradation through accidental release of radioactivity. Solar heating/power generation can take space, is costly, and has specific site requirements. Geothermal power generation is presently restricted to a few places where natural steam or hot water are easily tapped as in Iceland or New Zealand. However, there are possibilities that, in future, boreholes may be sunk in areas where there is no at-surface geothermal source, so that injected water can be raised in temperature enough for district heating and/or power generation. There is little land degradation associated with the use of geothermal energy, but there may be a problem where 'wet geothermal generation is developed, of disposing of hot and mineral-rich water, which could affect streams and low-lying land.

Estuary barrages, while non-polluting and a means of cutting 'greenhouse gas' emissions that may cause sea level rise, could cause considerable damage to coastal salt marshes and estuarine floodlands, there may also be a problem in draining low-lying lands once an area behind a barrage ceases to have tidal movements. So far, there have been few such barrages. Wind turbines will probably become more widespread; at present, there are extensive facilities in parts of the USA, and there will soon be in the Netherlands and Denmark. The main impacts are aesthetic, noise, and possibly radio/TV interference and wildlife disturbance, but, compared with other generators, they are non-polluting, fairly cheap and relatively little and will be lost after they are installed. Wave power is at present little used and takes up little land; the main impact would be if wave power helped reduce thermal power generation.

Many thermal power stations produce fly ash which settles downwind, a big power station can yield 2 tonnes a minute for 24 hours a day. Not all ash escapes, indeed, in newer stations, most is removed from the flue gases (it still has to be dumped somewhere or used for building materials). Fly ash is generally inert, although it can have a high boron and soluble salts content, so rehabilitation of ash dumps is not too difficult (Chadwick & Goodman, 1975: 287).

In 1985, nuclear power stations provided about 18% of the world's total electricity. Some countries rely more upon this power source than others; France generated about 65% of its electricity by this means in 1985, the nations with the most nuclear stations at that time were: the USA, France, USSR, UK, Japan, Canada, W. Germany, Sweden and Spain. Sweden has now begun to decommission all her nuclear stations (Middleton, 1988: 41).

Nuclear power station accidents have been rare. Chernobyl (1986) being the worst such incident. A reactor fire occurred at Windscale, Cumbria, UK in the 1950s (not a power station) and contaminated large areas of grazing land, and there was a near melt-down at Three-Mile-Island, USA in the early 1980s which, by 1988, had cost over US$ 1 billion to clean up. As a consequence of the Chernobyl accident, there have so far been 33 fatalities recorded (plus 2000 people contaminated enough to make serious cancer a real risk to them in the long term). Around the Chernobyl power station, an area at least 30 km wide has been so contaminated that humans and livestock have had to be evacuated for the foreseeable future. Mould (1988) reported that 135,000 people were evacuated, and that the area of 'significant' contamination is over 1000 km². This contaminated land was an imporant souce of vegetables and other foodstuffs for the USSR. There was also significant deposition of radioisotopes in parts of Scandinavia, Western Europe and the UK, mainly where radioactivity was washed to the ground by rainstorms over uplands. The fall-out has been much slower than expected to disperse and has disrupted livestock production in upland Wales, Lapland and parts of Germany, Norway and Sweden, where reindeer have been contaminated enough to make necessary a ban on their consumption for meat.

There was some luck involved in the Chernobyl accident, for if radioactivity had reached the River Dneiper system, in any quantity, a vast area of agricultural land could have been contaminated. It was also luck that the city of Kiev, with c. 2.5 million population, the USSR's third city, was not significantly affected. Chernobyl serves as an expensive, but mercifully relatively gentle, warning to other nations contemplating nuclear power generation. It is estimated that entombment of the reactor alone cost over £2000 million by 1988. Another source suggests cost of roughly US$10 billion by 1989 (Boyle & Ardill, 1989: 175; O'Neill, 1989: 59). Mould (1988) noted that there were 14 reactors like the one at Chernobyl in service and a further eight under construction in the USSR, plus several similar versions in India. The risks of nuclear power generation have to be weighed carefully against the risks from fuel-burning thermal stations. Both pose the risk of land degradation if, misdesigned or mismanaged. In addition, nuclear stations can be affected by natural or terrorist disasters.

One benefit from the Chernobyl accident has been that it has given researchers a marker 'horizon' useful in studies of soil loss from land and the pattern of re-deposition (Bonnett et al., 1989).

Land degradation caused by nuclear waste disposal

Nuclear waste is produced by power generation, industrial use and weapon manufacture. Some waste is highly radioactive for many thousands of years. Keeping such material isolated from the environment, disposing of the waste heat it generates, and ensuring that the material cannot become concentrated in such a way as to risk a 'critical mass' or near 'critical mass' developing and causing a violent reaction, for thousands of years is a challenge.

The disposal of nuclear waste is expensive, both in the infrastructure involved and because a disposal site is likely to have an effect on land value and land use nearby, for real or imagined reasons. In the past, the solution was to pump radioactive material out to sea, down deep boreholes, store it in tanks or sink it in drums well offshore. The USA Department of Energy recently estimated it will have to spend US$ 100 to 150 billion to deal with problems caused by such disposal down deep boreholes or in tanks (Charles, 1989). Nuclear or hazardous chemicals effluent pumped down deep boreholes can contaminate groundwater, in many cases virtually permanently, and by lubricating joints between rock layers may cause earthquakes – as at Perry, Ohio or Rocky Mountain Arsenal, Colorado.

In 1957, in the Kyshtm area of the Urals (USSR), a radioactive waste dump is believed to have exploded, contaminating many hundreds of km². Several villages were permanently evacuated and wetlands and streams were affected (Boyle & Ardill, 1989: 177). The numbers of people and livestock involved were not reported.

Land degradation caused by transportation

In the USA, by 1984, about 129,000 km² were under roads and c. 3000 km² were covered by parking lots; other nations have lost significant areas to these land uses (Ramade, 1984: 149). In addition to the loss of agricultural land beneath tarmac and concrete, road and rail transport cause degradation by acting as line sources of: lead compounds from cars burning leaded petrol, exhaust gases from road vehicles, salt from winter salting in cooler environments, asbestos from wear of vehicle brake-pads, clutches, tyres, etc where these are still permitted to contain asbestos. There are indications that, along some busy flight routes, aircraft cause sufficient pollution from the fuel they burn to increase the acid deposition damage to alpine vegetation. In drier environments, unsurfaced roads usually generate a lot of dust (Canter, 1986: 182). Noise pollution is frequently associated with transport and may disturb wildlife and humans. Where noise is excessive, land values may be depressed.

In the early 1970s, there was widespread concern that supersonic airliners would cause damage to stratospheric ozone. So far this has proved to be minimal probably because there are so few.

Land degradation caused by urban expansion

There has been considerable 'urban-sprawl' since the 1920s. In developed countries cities grew by roughly 2.5-times between 1920 and 1960. In developing countries the increase was roughly eight-fold (Arnon, 1981: 134). It is not unusual for urban expansion to take some of the best agricultural land for the simple reason that towns have tended to grow up in lowlands or on plateaux, especially near rivers where the soil is good. The impact of urbanization is not only felt through the physical presence of buildings; demand for fuelwood may lead to damage to forests for hundreds of kilometres, and the lure of the city may draw farm labour from the land for thousands of km² and thereby upset efficient landuse causing degradation.

INDUSTRIAL AND ENERGY CROPS AND LAND DEGRADATION

The use of livestock slurry for biogas generation might solve the land-disposal problem and cut the releases of methane to the atmosphere. Some countries produce, or plan to produce, bio-fuels, particularly alcohols and vegetable oils like sunflower. Brazil already has a large alcohol production programme based on cane sugar, cassava or sorghum as feedstocks. In the USA, and in some African nations, maize is the favoured feedstock, elsewhere wood has been used and there have been proposals to use aquatic weeds like water hyacinth.

Brazil produces alcohol mainly in medium-sized regional distilleries. This has resulted in widespread river and wetland eutrophication because every litre of alcohol produced results in $c.$ 13 litres of effluent. By 1985, the impact of effluent from alcohol production exceeded the impact of all Brazil's human sewage effluent. There is a second impact of such energy crop production, either farmers have to find new land to subsist, or unused land is cleared to produce the feedstock. Alcohol production thus adds to the pressures on the land, this has to be set against the benefits from reducing vehicle emissions of part-combusted hydrocarbons and other petrochemical pollutants when methane or alcohol is burnt. Plastics, cellulose, and a wide range of products might, in the future, be produced from crops rather than from petrochemical sources. Rayon and other Man-made textiles are already heavily dependent on cellulose from mangrove forests or conifer plant-ations. In the long run the demand for land to produce industrial crops will probably increase.

LAND DEGRADATION THROUGH ELECTROMAGNETIC POLLUTION (EXCLUDING RADIOACTIVITY)

Recently, there has been debate over the effects of electromagnetic radiation on the environment and living organisms. There is no doubt that telecommunications, computers and other electrical equipment can be affected, and this may make some areas unsuitable for certain types of activity, there is also a chance that land and organisms near high-powered radio transmitters, radar stations and microwave sources, and along the route of high-voltage power transmission lines may suffer. There is presently little reliable published information on such effects, particularly that which might be generated by power cables. Smith & Best (1989) did, however, attempt a review of the field effect of power lines.

LAND DEGRADATION AS A CONSEQUENCE OF PLANT AND ANIMAL 'INVASIONS', INTRODUCTIONS AND 'ECOLOGICAL EXPLOSIONS'

A plant or animal species may spread by natural dispersal and by deliberate' or inadvertent, human introduction to areas where it was previously absent. The newly dispersed alien species may cause no problems and become an additional exotic component of the flora or fauna, or it may cause problems immediately, or after a delay, possibly of many years. Whatever the manner of its arrival, to survive, the 'invading' species must find a suitable vacant niche; to become a problem it will have to compete with indigenous species and come off best (Holland & Olson, 1989; Mooney & Drake, 1987).

If the competition among species allows an 'invading' or native species to overcome natural controls: predation, environmental factors, disease, etc, and increase in numbers at a rapid pace, this is what Elton (1958) termed an 'ecological explosion'. This may possibly be as a consequence of human activity which disrupts ecosystems, a natural disaster or some advantage gained by the organism, possibly as a result of mutation. Sometimes a species arrives in numbers sufficiently large to damage the environment, as may be the case with swarms of locust blown on the wind to new localities.

Problems caused by dispersal of organisms to new areas are not new, it is a part of life. A plausible explanation for the extinction of the dinosaurs at the end of the Cretaceous (*c.* 65 million years BP), is simply that there was sufficient change in sea level to allow movements of species to new regions with resultant changes in inter-species competition and outbreaks of disease (Bakker, 1988: 442). However, in recent decades, humans have increased the movement of organisms to levels well beyond normal natural levels. The consequences of such dispersal can be very serious in environmental, economic and social terms.

The barriers to dispersal of organisms: mountains, sea, rivers, deserts, forest areas, etc, are increasingly overcome as Man travels more and more, and at a faster pace, and organisms 'hitch rides'. With the use of freight containers, animals and plants which would never have withstood a long sea voyage or air travel in the past now have more chance of establishing themselves in new areas. Man carries organisms by mistake and he has deliberately introduced a vast range of plants and animals to various parts of the world. For example, at least one-third of the UK flora are introductions, and 20 of the UK's 67 wild mammals are introductions (Martin & Klein, 1984).

Introduced or invading plants that have caused land degradation

Bracken (*Pteridium aquilinum*) is increasingly a problem in the UK, particularly in uplands. Once established, bracken can poison livestock and exclude many herbs and grasses, the spores are carcinogenic and may pose a threat to Man and livestock if they contaminate water supplies in quantity (Sykes, 1987). The cause of the increase is probably a combination of excessive grazing damage or too-frequent burning of woodland and moorland (Lenihan & Fletcher, 1976: 116–28). In 1985, bracken covered an area of the UK equivalent to the whole of the county of Devon (Anon., 1988h). In the northern Great Plains (USA) the pricklypear cactus (*Opuntia polyacantha*) is a pest that is displacing other more useful plants.

A plant which owes its origin to humans, the dune cordgrass (*Spartina townsendii* – a natural cross between the European *S. Maritima* and a related species introduced in the nineteenth-century from the USA: *S. alternifolia*), has come to dominate Europe's indigenous *Spartina* spp. This plant is much better at stabilizing coastal mudflats, and so has caused quite significant changes in coastal accretion rates, and thus changes in the landscape (Elton, 1958: 26). Canadian pondweed (*Elodea canadensis*) became quite widespread in Europe during the nineteenth- and twentieth-centuries. The weed chokes streams and can thereby cause considerable changes in flooding and river erosion. There are many cases, in the Tropics and subtropics, of reservoirs and irrigation canals becoming overgrown with nuisance aquatic weeds. Such weed growth can damage turbines and boats and pollute water, and may also provide breeding sites for insects that carry diseases that debilitate the rural community. Where aquatic weeds choke irrigation supply systems, they can reduce flows and upset good management. Reduced water supplies may mean lost crops and possibly salt accumulation in the soil, and may increase waterlogging alongside channels. One of the most common problem species is the water hyacinth (*Eichhornia crassipes*).

Dutch elm disease fungus (*Certocystis ulmi*) was probably introduced into the UK by Man and spread by bark beetles of the *Scolytus* genus in the 1970s. The disease has had a marked effect on the landscape and on the wildlife dependent upon the elm (*Ulmus* spp.). An alien, the mequite shrub/tree (*Prosopis pallia*) now dominates much of Hawaii's lowland areas, in part because introduced livestock have helped spread it (Fosberg, 1972).

In Northern Australia, a shrub from Central America: prickly mimosa (*Mimosa pigra*) has become a problem. It is also a nuisance in Thailand. Introduced in the late 1970s, this mimosa is unpalatable to grazing animals and insects. Water buffalo (*Bubalus bubalis*), also introduced to Australia by Man and themselves causing considerable damage to wetlands and wildlife, aid the spread of the mimosa by creating damaged areas that the shrub colonizes. Once established, dense inpenetrable thickets are formed which make travel difficult and which exclude native shrubs like *Melaluca* spp. (Anon, 1988i; Lonsdale & Braithwaite, 1988). Ironically, an Australian *Melaluca* (*M. quinquenervia*): the *cajeput* has become a problem species in Florida where it displaces native plants, and tends to depress water-tables through transpiration, leading to the conversion of swampland to woodland (Mooney & Drake, 1987 (see Chapter 7). The Florida Everglades have serious drainage difficulties caused by growths of this species and a number of other introductions, notably *Casurina* spp., and Brazilian 'pepper' (*Schinus terebinthifolius*) (Maltby, 1986: 38). In drier parts of America, the tamarisk (*Tamarix* spp.) or 'salt cedar' has become a serious pest. Introduced from Eurasia, the plants choke streams, tends to lower groundwater and may deposit salts at the soil surface. The ice plant (*Mesembyanthemum crystallinium*) has been a problem in California and Australia where it can invade degraded pastures and, once established, concentrates salts at the soil surface (Mooney & Drake, 1986: 168).

Japanese knotweed (*Reynoutria japonica*, formerly *Polygonium cuspidatum*), has becoming a major nuisance in various parts of the UK over the last *c.* 20 years, mainly along river banks and where there is disturbed land. The plant is spread by floods and by soil shifted by landscaping operations or by fly-tipping, and can disturb buildings, drains and tarmac paving, embankment works, river flood-control schemes, etc. It also shades out other species and thus has deleterious effects on conservation areas and landscaping work. Common rhododendron (*Rhododendron ponticum*) is a problem in many areas of the UK and W. Europe. It shades out native woodland species, can poison livestock, may discourage some wildlife and is difficult to eradicate once established (Simons, 1988b).

In some savannas, there has been extensive ploughing of the native vegetation and replacement with 'improved pasture' species. In parts of Latin America, African grasses and legumes are being spread to improve the rangelands (Harris, 1980: 294).

Introduced or invading animals that have caused land degradation

There are numerous instances where introductions or invading species have caused problems. In the following section selected cases are described.

A recent invader of N. Ireland which could potentially cause serious changes to soil fertility is the flatworm *Artioposthia triangulata*, native to New Zealand. This preys on earthworms and has spread very fast. If unchecked *Artioposthia* might reduce earthworms enough to affect agriculture. (*New Scientist* 125 issue 1703 10/2/90: 27).

During the nineteenth-century, the American vine aphid (*Phylloxera vitifolia*) was introduced to Europe. Within a few years it had ruined most of the continent's vinyards. At huge cost, growers were forced to graft their vines on American rootstocks to resist the aphid. Had there not been American rootstock, alternative land use would have had to have been found for huge areas. The American Colorado beetle (*Leptinotarsus decemlineata*) has continued to threaten potato crops around the world. In 1936, a giant snail (*Achatina fulica*) was introduced to Hawaii, it is now a significant pest on Oahu Is., where it has destroyed native snails and does considerable damage to plants. In 1956, African honey bees (*Apis mellifera seutellata*) escaped from a breeding station in S. Brazil; they had interbred with Latin American bees on both sides of the Andes as far north as the USA borders by 1988. The cross-bred bees have largely replaced native colonies and are more aggressive and, according to some authorities, yield less honey (Kent, 1989).

The muskrat (*Ondatra zibethicus*) and the Coypu (*Myocastor coypus*) have been a problem in Europe, particularly in the eastern UK from the 1930s until quite recently. Escapees from fur farms colonized wetland and caused considerable damage to banks, dykes and crops through their grazing and trampling and digging (Taylor, 1979). The Chinese mitten crab (*Eriocheir sinensis*) probably reached Europe in the bottom tanks of ships, when ballast water was pumped out. The crab colonied a number of river systems where its burrowing causes severe bank damage (Elton, 1958).

The rabbit (*Oryctolagus cuniculatus*) was introduced to Australia by settlers in the eighteenth-century, with virtually no native carnivores to control them and with grazing habits different to the marsupials which plants had adapted to the damage was considerable in some areas, until the 1950s when the disease myxomatosis was introduced. But, by 1988, rabbits had made a recovery and were again causing severe damage, especially in South Australia by overgrazing perennial range plants and tree seedlings. The numbers appear to have increased after good rains in 1987 and they are now apparently much more immune to the disease that once controlled them – myxomatosis (*The Times*, 24/11/88: 8). In the South Atlantic, South Indian Ocean and subAntarctic: the Falkland Is., Macquarie Is., Ile St Paul, Iles Kerguelen, Iles Crozet, Auckland Is. have suffered severe damage from introduced rabbits, and, in some cases, sheep, reindeer and cattle (Holdgate, 1970; 928; Detwyler, 1971: 480). A recent invader of parts of Australia is the cane toad (*Bufo marinus*), which causes considerable damage to smaller marsupials and other wildlife. In N. America the spruce budworm (*Christoneura fumiferana*) has defoliated millions of hectares of conifers; if introduced to plantations or natural forest elsewhere it would cause havoc.

Because it happened relatively recently, the impacts of plant and animal introductions on oceanic islands, notably the Hawaiian Islands and New Zealand, have been well documented. Islands in the South Atlantic/Antarctic Ocean like Hawaii, have gained some plant species through introduction/accidental dispersal by Man. They have also lost a number of unique plants since the coming of humans (Glasby, 1986). One species which Man has dispersed to many new environments, including some of the Hawaiian Islands and New Zealand, which has acquired the reputation for causing land degradation is the goat. In the Galapagos Island Group, Is., Pinta had three goats released in 1959, between 1971 and 1977 over 40,000 were shot (Dunbar, 1984: 3). The pattern has been similar on islands like Juan Fernandez and Rodriguez (Pacific) (Gade, 1985). The Atlantic island of Saint Helena has suffered '. . . complete and catastrophic destruction . . .' of vegetation which is attributed to goats introduced in AD 1513. Today, there are virtually no native trees where once there appears to have been an extensive tree cover.

The pig (family *Suidae*) also has a bad reputation. Introduced to some of the Hawaiian Islands around AD 400, this is now a major threat to forest cover, wildlife and by (rooting and trampling) is a cause of soil erosion. It is not just larger organisms that cause problems, a number of ant species have been dispersed and are generating problems. For example, the Argentine ant (*Iridomyrmex humilis*) has virtually eliminated indigenous ants and many other insects from large areas of the Hawaiian Islands (Stone & Loope, 1987).

12 *Conclusion: conservation and preventative/remedial strategies*

CONSERVATION

CONSERVATION has a wide range of meanings. In general, though, it involves seeking one, or both, of two main goals: 1. To protect habitats. By means of: reduction of soil erosion/protection of watershed areas, control of avalanches, prevention of pollution protection of historically important features, etc. 2. To protect plants and animals. Plant and animal species may have very restricted ranges and very specific demands for survival. If these are upset a species may be lost for ever. There is not the degree of finality involved in the conservation of land; some degree of restoration may well be possible if degradation occurs. Restoration of an extinct species is impossible.

Conservation may involve wild species or domesticated species, the latter may be at risk if they have been superseded by newer varieties. There are three categories of arguments that have been put forward against allowing species extinction: utilitarian – the species may be of value to Man; ethical – Man has an obligation to protect, or, at least, not himself destroy lifeforms; ecological – maintaining species diversity ensures a more stable environment.

In spite of decades of experience in establishing watershed protection reserves/forests, there is still debate over their value in reducing erosion or in controlling streamflow. Groundcover of shrubs or grass but not tree cover might, in some circumstances, prevent erosion and conserve moisture better than forest reserves (Smiet, 1987).

There are a number of ways of conserving plant and animal species: (a) Areas may be protected as reserves or national parks. (b) Plant germplasm can be banked as: tissue cultures, dormant or deep-frozen seeds or bulbs, or as living/growing specimens in botanic gardens. (c) Animals can be conserved as: zoo specimens possibly with collections of frozen germplasm to reduce the chance of in-breeding given the limited numbers of individual creatures that can be kept caged. (d) It may be possible to provide small conservation areas or features which support wildlife in developed areas or have some other main use(s): for example, road verges can be seeded with wild plants, gardens and parks may have plots of wild plants, nest boxes can be provided for birds, bats, etc, in public areas or plantations.

Given the complexity of natural associations of animals and plants, only conservation areas offer a potentially 'total solution'. Other conservation involving selection of elements of flora or fauna for gene bank, zoo or botanic garden means the loss of what the collector misses or is forced to miss.

Out of its ecological 'context' a species may not be able to survive or reproduce in a conservation area, a gene bank may have limited value because stored material often has a fixed storage life, and, when revived to reproduce and restock the bank, it may either not germinate or, if it does, may then fail to reach maturity because some crucial environmental factor is missing. With limited storage life for 'banked' material, gene bank conservation can sometimes be temporary and therefore unsatisfactory.

Both conservation areas and genetic storage are vulnerable to disruption, a reserve may suffer a bushfire, encroachment by settlers or poachers or some other misfortune, a gene bank may be ruined by a failure in refrigeration, lack of adequate funding or a disease outbreak. As far as is possible, a number of separate and similar conservation areas or genetic material collections should be established to give insurance against loss. The International Board for Plant Genetic Resources plans to establish a germplasm store in a tunnel driven into permanently frozen ground in Spitzbergen, the idea being to offer all nations, including the poor ones facilities where plant (and possibly other genetic material) can be stored where there is no risk of defrosting, flooding, or, hopefully, any other disaster.

Conservation can be compatible with other land uses such as recreation and tourism, aesthetic landscape, watershed protection, etc. The spectrum is wide, compatibility depending on the land use(s) and the sensitivity of the environment and organisms. However, as a general rule, the more intense the land use, the less conservation.

The future value of vast numbers of wild plants and animals has not been appraised, some species could become vital crops or livestock, or may be ideal for stabilizing land undergoing erosion, or may have a role to play in pollution control. Present crops and livestock will require input of fresh genetic material from time to time to ensure vigour and ability to withstand new diseases or environmental change. If the pool of wild material is lost, Man's future range of actions to counter or avoid land degradation, and to sustain food and commodity production, will be restricted, perhaps catastrophically. It is probable that less than 1% of tropical forest species of higher plants have been subjected to even rough appraisal of their value, yet, in 1987, it was established that tropical plants, especially rainforest species, had provided, at least initially before commercial synthesis, about 25% of all the prescribed drugs used in the USA (Repetto & Gillis, 1988: 15). But two, of the many potentially useful species include: *Zea diploperennis*, likely to have value in maize breeding, and *Copaifera landsdorfii* the sap of which tree can be burnt in diesel engines with virtually no processing required.

Extinction is a natural process, there is always going to be some loss and, in the past, as at the end of the Cretaceous, there have been relatively sudden and catastrophic losses. Mankind from early in his history has caused extinctions, but, in the last few hundred years, the pace has accelerated far beyond the natural 'background level'. The rate of loss of 'biodiversity' is now frightening. Estimates vary a lot but it seems probable that, if present trends continue, without further deterioration, then 15 to 20% of all plants and animals now alive will probably be extinct by AD 2000 (Gradwohl & Greenberg, 1988: 51). Extinctions resulting from human activity are not a new problem, although the scale and pace are accelerating. The loss of over 100 genera of large mammals between *c.* 40,000 BP and the present corresponds to the established chronology and pattern of Man's spread in prehistoric to recent times (Brothwell, 1978; Joss *et al.*, 1986: 545; Freedman, 1989: 275). Some regions have already suffered severe losses: Peninsular

Malaysia logged much of its rich lowland dipterocarp forests between the mid 1950s and late 1980s; only about 10% of the Malagasy Republic's original forest is left, and there are many more examples.

Natural flora and fauna face the following threats:

• The reduction of total unspoilt area.
• The conversion of natural/unspoiled vegetation and fauna into altered forms, including monocultures or near monocultures.
• Fragmentation of existing natural vegetation or conservation areas into smaller and smaller plots.

Conservation areas

By 1985, there were over 3000 national parks or equivalent areas worldwide, more than 400 million ha in total (Harrison et al., 1982). There are countless smaller conservation areas, some deliberately created, some existing through accident. All of these areas vary greatly in the diversity they conserve and in their vulnerability. Year by year, new conservation opportunities arise, for example, in the UK: disused railway lines, old quarries and gravel pits, motorway verges and high-rise buildings now provide valuable conservation sites for some species.

Reliance on accident to create conservation areas would be grossly inadequate. Faced with accelerating species loss and habitat damage and probable climatic change conservation areas must be vigorously identified, demarcated and then well managed. In selecting conservation areas, there are four basic questions that have to be asked:

. What area(s) should be conserved?
. What shape or size should the conservation area be?
. What management strategy should be applied to the conservation area?
.. What management strategy should there be for the surrounding area?

To answer these questions requires an examination of the dynamics of species survival in conservation areas. It also demands an awareness of what pressures conservation areas face. Conservation areas are typically subject to pressures from settlers, poachers, fuelwood collectors, feral domestic animals, regional and local pollution, regional water-table changes and invasions by 'alien' (non-local) species. (Table 12.1 lists some important questions relating to conservation area selection/siting/management.) Given the pace of species loss and the lack of support for conservation and, so far, inadequacy of funds, conservation areas will, as often as not, be selected and maintained on a triage basis, i.e. the areas that are safe will get little more help, the hopeless cases will probably have to be abandoned and efforts will concentrate on areas that will best respond to management.

Conservation areas are often well separated from other similar plant and animal associations and they are often small. They have much in common with off-shore or oceanic islands. The latter are islands that are isolated by ocean expanses, and their species are more protected from arrival of new 'competitor' species' than off-shore islands. Most conservation areas are set in an 'ocean' of development: degraded natural vegetation, farmland, urban development, etc. This 'ocean' is often less of a barrier to the arrival of new species than the real ocean is for an oceanic island. Nevertheless, some insight may be gained into how species survive over the long term in restricted-extent conservation areas, and into the likely rates of change in species, through endogenous causes and, as a result of invasion by species

Table 12.1. *Some important questions relating to conservation areas.*

* What size should the conservation area be?
* Are a number of smaller conservation areas better than one or a few large ones?
* What shape should a conservation area be?
* How important is distance, not necessarily spatial distance (a barrier to species dispersal could be quite abrupt) between conservation areas?
* Is there an ideal pattern for distribution of conservation areas: clusters, linear strings, maximum dispersal?
* What is the difference if the conservation area is close to: extensive areas of natural habitat; a number of patches of natural habitat; no natural habitat; lies in an 'ocean' of degraded or completely altered, no longer natural, habitat or; is linked by 'corridors' or 'stepping-stones' to other conservation areas?
* What is the character of the conservation area, does it have little variety or a wide diversity of habitats? Are any niches vacant or potentially easy for a newly arrived species to occupy?
* What is the best land management for the region(s) surrounding the conservation area?

Note: In this chapter, conservation area/reserve/national park are used loosely and are deemed synonymous (here, there is no distinction made between conservation with some land use and conservation with no land use).

from outside the conservation area, by examining the findings of island biogeographers (Diamond, 1975; Miller, 1978). Although much of the theory still needs confirmation, island biogeography *may* help conservation area managers select the best areas for conservation and develop better strategies for management (Higgs, 1981).

What size should conservation areas be?

In an ideal world, the answer might be: as big as possible and safely bigger than adequate. Size is one important factor to be taken into account if forced into a triage approach to management of conservation. A reserve may be of a size that makes long-term conservation unlikely, in which case it may be better to divert scarce resources to areas that are believed to be viable. Much of the theory relating to size/viability of conservation areas comes from island biogeography. Although there have been some more practical, less theoretical studies, for example, studies of Barro Colorado Island in Lake Gatun (Panama Canal Zone), which has been isolated from surrounding forests since 1924, this has given useful indications about rates of species loss (Proctor, 1984).

How many plant/animal species an island/conservation area can hold depends on a complex of factors, which include:

- The time the island/conservation area has been available for species to live on it without major disruption.
- A number of environmental parameters (food supply, rainfall, temperature, exposure, altitude range, land area, terrain, etc).
- The dynamics of inter-specific competition.
- The isolation of the island/conservation area from source(s) of species. Barriers to dispersal need not be extensive; a narrow ditch or steep slope may be sufficient; also, a barrier to one species may be little hindrance to another with better or different dispersal capabilities.

An island or a reserve will tend to lose species over time, even if protected from all environmental change and arrival of new species that threaten the indigenous ones. In practice, even the most isolated island/reserve will gain new arrivals. The questions are: will extinctions be replaced by arrivals to keep a balance, or will it cause an imbalance and the loss of existing species? What proportion of the species will survive over the long term without extinction or drastic change?

There have been attempts to establish the natural 'background rate' of species loss. This has been found to be very roughly 1 species per year globally over the last 600 million years until about 70,000 BP, after that time losses have accelerated. Areas of lowland tropical rainforest, in, say, South East Asia or Amazonia are likley to have more species of organism per hectare than oceanic islands, but there may not be as much endemism, i.e. species unique to a limited area. One must therefore expect some extinction if extensive forest is converted into 'islands' and if island biogeographic laws come into play (Miller, 1978: 194).

Different species demand different habitats, of differing area, to maintain viable populations. Selection of sites deserving conservation, and estimates of minimum size of conservation area, should make allowance for environmental change. If possible, conservation area size and siting should ensure resilience enough to withstand climatic change, acid deposition, and so on. Experience shows that a newly created tropical forest reserve is likely to lose species after a while; reduced regeneration takes time to manifest, as has been discovered in Panama and New Zealand (Diamond, 1976: 36).

It is the tropical lowland forest environments which hold particularly rich and diverse populations of plants and animals, and which are being very rapidly lost. These environments thus demand special conservation efforts, they also present more conservation difficulties than might be the case in cooler and drier environments. This is largely because the diversity of flora and fauna results in very complex interdependence of species, commonly symbiotic relationships, and low densities of individual species, so it may be difficult to maintain a satisfactory reproduction/regeneration of species over the long term. There has been, and remains, wide disagreement over the minimum critical size of conservation areas in the Tropics. One author suggested the minimum size for a tropical forest reserve, if it is to continue to conserve anywhere near the original complement of species, would be 2500 km². Less than that area and there would be too few individual species to maintain a satisfactory reproduction. Tropical forest is diverse which means individuals of a species tend to be scattered (Simberloff & Abele, 1976; Barrett, 1980: 230; Lovejoy et al., 1983; Lewin, 1984).

In the Singapore Botanic Gardens, there is a 200 to 300 m² plot – the 'Garden Jungle' that was once dipterocarp forest. In spite of a high standard of conservation management over many decades, that plot had no dipterocarp species by the 1980s (Author, visit 1978; Caufield, 1982: 45). Careful monitoring is required even where a conservation area is well managed.

The minimum size of a conservation area matters most when that area is isolated from other areas of similar habitat. When that is the case, it must maintain its stocks from within; there will be no influx of genetic material to help reduce the risks of inbreeding, etc. 'Size' is a little misleading, a small area with a lot of diversity of terrain, moisture regime, etc, might be better than a much bigger area of uniform environment. Nevertheless, larger islands (oceanic and those closer to a continent) typically support more species (Higgs, 1981: 118), lose fewer species through 'genetic drift', and

probably better withstand losses caused when component habitats are struc
by localized storm, flood, volcanic eruption, etc. Larger reserves a
probably easier and cheaper to run than several small ones. Caufield (198
46) felt that, if well selected, only about 10% of the world's rainforests wou
probably provide adequate long-term conservation.

As conservation areas become surrounded by an 'ocean' of developmen
two problems are likely to arise: 1. The breeding population of some or a
species may be too small. 2. Local and regional changes in the surroundin
developed lands may upset the regional hydrology and climate, affecting th
conservation area. There are some measures which might help counter thes
problems: 1. The conservation area is managed so that the peripheral par
act as a buffer area for the interior. 2. Conservation areas are linked by linea
reserves or stepping-stone reserves to improve exchange of species. Belts c
woodland, hedges, ditches, riparian strips, railway and roadside verges ma
be sufficient for some species especially those that can move about usin
conservation areas as temporary refuges or breeding areas (Sanders &
Hobbs, 1989; Harris, 1984a, b).

What areas should be conserved?

Ideally, the answer to this question should be 'areas that have representativ
collections of plants and animals and scenery, each of which is capable c
maintaining itself without too much change over the long term with a goo
degree of security'. In practice, conservation areas have not always bee
demarcated by well-informed ecologists, rather they tend to be:

- Land that is too remote or inaccessible to have been exploited.
- Land which has been of little value.
- Once used, now derelict and recolonized land.
- Land undeveloped due to some risk: social unrest, weapons testing
  disease risk, flood risk, etc.
- Land held by a rich landowner who has not had to exploit and damag
  it.
- Land believed to be of religious or cultural importance.

Already much land has been lost or spoilt before the conservation nee
was apparent. Where there exists a community of rare organisms, wher
there exists a particularly well-developed example of an ecosystem or
population of one important organism, conservation may be desirable
Where such land is free of threats or can be managed to avoid threats, the
conservation makes sense. McClosky & Spalding (1989) produced
reconnaissance-level inventory of the areas of the Earth's land surfac
'. . .still predominantly influenced by forces of nature'. The findings of thi
study indicate that, one-third of the world's land surface (48,069,951 km²) i
still wilderness. About 41% of this wilderness is in Antarctica or the high
Arctic, about 20% is in temperate regions, 20% is warm desert, 11% is in th
Tropics, 4% is mountain/upland and 3% is cold winter desert. While no
particularly precise, the study showed that less than 20% of remainin
wilderness is protected by conservation areas.

With large areas of the rainforests of the Far East, Africa and Amazoni
already cleared and developed or scheduled for such treatment, selectin
conservation areas is becoming more and more a question of dealing wit
'left-overs'. However, it is important to try and get the best 'left-overs' an
those that offer best conservation chances. The concept of Pleistocen
refugia might help identify such areas, although there is some debate ove
the validity of the concept.

During the 'glacial periods' of the Pleistocene, it is believed by some, that, with drier, cooler conditions, the tropical forests retreated and survived in certain favourable localities known as 'refugia' (Prance & Lovejoy, 1985: 146; Freedman, 1989: 290). These have been mapped using present distribution of animal and plant species and palaeoecological evidence (Fig. 12.1(a) and 12.1(b)). If these 'refugia' now have the best diversity of organisms and have, in the past, offered more protection from environmental changes then they would be ideal conservation sites today. Caufield (1982: 45) suggested that, in Amazonia, it might be possible to save 75% of species on 5% of the land assuming the refugia were saved as conservation areas, and if these really are what it is claimed they are. Similar 'refugia' have been postulated for Africa's rainforests (Fig. 12.1(c)). In the Far East, there has been more human disturbance and the situation has been complicated by sea level change exposing and isolating a multitude of islands. Consequently refugia maps are not available. Some of the 'refugia' areas in Amazonia and elsewhere have already been degraded. While some researchers are doubtful that refugia are areas of greater resistance to environmental change, there seems less debate that they could be areas of greater species diversity and knowing this alone is useful for conservation (Colinvaux, 1989: *The Times*, 27/7/89: 13).

It may be necessary to design a conservation area to suit larger animals or animals that range widely without which plant species would fail to regenerate. A population of plants may survive for decades, but not reproduce if an animal vital to their reproduction, say a pollinator or seed disperser, dies out because the reserve area is too small to allow safe movement or migration. On Mauritius there is a good example: the tambalacoque tree (*Calvaria major*) was at risk of extinction because, although it shed seeds, they never germinated. On the assumption the tree was dependent upon the now extinct dodo (*Raphus cucullatus*) a botanist fed the seeds to a 'substitute dodo' (a turkey) and seedlings were recently produced for the first time since the 1860s (Janzen & Martin, 1982; Freedman, 1989: 282).

The People's Republic of China has conservation problems in spite of strong government support. In 1962, c. 60 Chinese plant and animal species were threatened with extinction. In 1989 the number had grown to c. 300 species (possibly better documentation explains some of this rise). By 1989, China had established more than 400 reserves covering about 2% of the total land area. This, together with recent legislation to protect wildlife, should have improved things, but clearly intent and law may not be enough when it comes to conservation.

Helping conservation areas conserve

Conservation areas could be divided into:

1. *Natural or near-natural environments* where conservation is virtually the only goal.
2. *Semi-natural environments* where conservation is the main goal, but where there may be some other activity or land use: collection of forest products, culling of excess game animals, tourism, sport-fishing, etc.
3. *Areas or locations which somehow help a species or species survive, but which are subjected to some use other than conservation*: e.g. flooded fields used by migrating birds as feeding grounds, houses on which housemartins or swallows nest, verges of motorways or railways, etc.

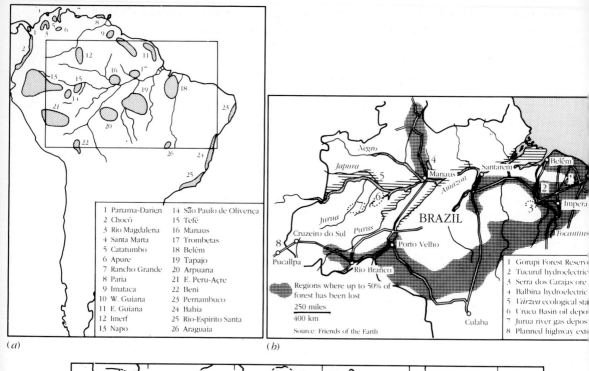

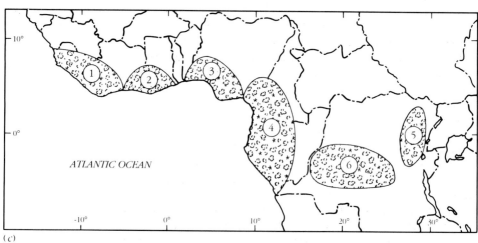

Fig. 12.1. Tropical lowland forest 'refugia'; (a) postulated for S. America; (b) extent of clearance and threats which may remove remaining refugia; (c) postulated for Africa.*

(a) *Areas of South America which it has been suggested are tropical forest 'refugia'.*

(b) *Extent of clearance and threats to forest and 'refugia'.*

(c) *Areas of lowland Africa which it has been suggested are tropical forest refugia: 1. Guinea refugia; 2. Gold Coast refugia; 3. Nigerian refugia; 4. Cameroon refugia; 5. N. and E. Congo refugia; 6. S.W. Congo refugia.*

*Note: *It is difficult to recognize and map refugia for S. Asia and S.E. Asia.*

Sources: *map (a) Pádua & Quintao (1982) Parks and biological reserves in the Brazilian Amazon. Ambio, XI(5), 309–14. Meggers et al. 1973: 81; Barrett (1980: 225); map (b) The Financial Times, 7/1/89: supplement; map (c) Laurent in Meggers et al. (1973: 259–69).*

In many cases, conservation is but one of a number of land uses. This can be a benefit, if it pays for the management of the land so that there is little or no degradation. Unfortunately, it is often the case that land uses conflict with conservation directly, e.g. farmers may use pesticide or shoot wildlife, or indirectly, e.g. the land user exploits the land, causes degradation and the wildlife suffers.

Conservation and avoidance of land degradation both require constant monitoring and policing. Legislation and accepted practices help a lot, but alone are not enough. For example, in Brazilian Amazonia, Law requires settlers keep half of their landholdings as unfelled forest. In practice, settlers commonly clear half the land and then sell the other half to someone who repeats the process.

In many parts of the world, the profits to be made from sales of protected plants or animals are huge by local standards and the authorities charged with enforcing conservation have inadequate resources. In this situation, a conservation area is unlikely to offer much protection unless the authorities can control and tap this trade themselves. There is a possibility the 'buyer' might be controlled. The Convention on International Trade in Endangered Species 1975 (CITES) was intended to effect such controls, unfortunately by 1980 it had been signed by only 80 of the world's nations. The loss of species and the degradation of land could be controlled by education of potential buyers and by controls on potential sellers of various natural products, often in cities and lands far away from the area threatened. Non-governmental bodies have realized this and have started to act.

A major problem is allocating responsibility for conservation (Schiotz, 1989). Conservation can involve a range of different interests such as: central government: state government/local government; local, possibly aboriginal, peoples; recent settlers; conservation group/department staff and there may be conflict of interest between them. Setting aside land for conservation without being aware of the needs and demands of these different groups will tend to end in difficulty (Anderson & Grove, 1987: 85).

Since the late 1980s, Colombia has granted control of more than 18 million ha of her Amazon territories to about 70,000 Indians. The policy has been to involve the Indians in conservation, basically by allowing them to follow their traditional ways on this land and encouraging them to 'police' it against the inroads of settlers and commercial agriculture (Bunyard, 1989).

Even when there is a willingness to prevent land degradation and species loss, without appropriate management, problems will arise. There may be a need for a buffer zone between conservation areas and other land uses or there may be problems caused by such buffer zones. A buffer zone surrounding a conservation area with a belt of semi-natural vegetation may be worse than one of developed farmland or plantation. This is because the semi-natural vegetation may support ruderal species: aggressive, invasive 'weeds' that could invade the reserve and cause problems (Kent, 1987: 99).

What have been termed 'edge effects' operate on the fringes of conservation areas, the influence of outside weather and drainage is felt, people may enter and graze livestock, remove wood or other products, and fire sweeping through surrounding coutryside may encroach. Reserve area managers commonly distinguish 'core areas' and edge effect areas; the latter may well be seen as a buffer zone for the former. Some plants and animals thrive in disturbed 'edge-effect' environments, but others require minimal disturbance conditions of core areas. The smaller the conservation area, the greater the proportion of land subjected to edge effects (see Fig. 12.3a). If the conservation area is too small to maintain a breeding population of plants or

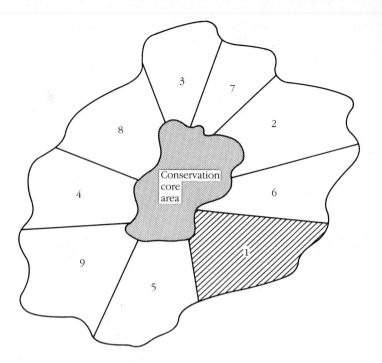

Fig. 12.2. *A small conservation area surrounded by a buffer zone with segments cleared over a long rotation to maximize the area of relatively mature forest in contact with it.*
Note: *Assume each segment is used for about 5 years after clearing. At start of the cycle, the whole is relatively natural land. After use, segment 1 would have 40 years to recover (longer if there are more segments). The segments close to any that has been cleared should have a reasonably mature cover to improve the chances of recolonizing the used area.*

animals in a 'core area' without in breeding, it may be possible to manage a buffer zone to ensure there is maximum area of 'back-up' forest which can provide organisms to interbreed with those in the inadequate 'core' (Fig. 12.2).

A problem in some regions is not so much lack of support from local people as a lack of a clear boundary to the conservation area. In such situations better boundary marking could help. In drier regions, there is a risk that bushfires will spread across conservation area boundaries. To counter such risk, Costa Rica's Santa Rosa National Park has experimented with cleared areas as barriers against fire and these have proved very successful (Cherfas, 1986).

Conservation of larger animal species can cause problems. Elephants may cause tremendous damage to the reserve, especially during droughts, if their numbers become too great. Elephants and other large game may also migrate or wander out of conservation areas and cause crop damage or be seen to 'compete' for grazing with livestock (for discussion of conflict between traditional pastoralists and conservation, see Sandford, 1983; Anderson & Grove, 1987: 111). It may be possible to counter problems by providing suitable migration tracks, or fencing and culling may be necessary to control numbers. Compensation of farmers for crop damage may help reduce hunting by those who lose crops. Game in various conservation areas have been culled in the belief that they harbour or spread livestock diseases, notably rinderpest or trypanosomiasis in Africa; in the UK, the badger has

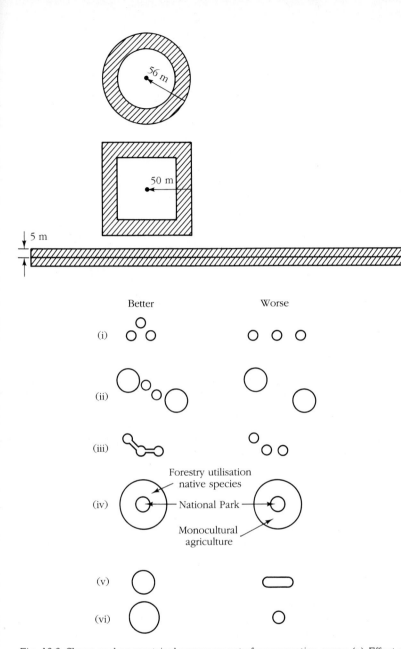

Fig. 12.3. Shape and geometrical arrangement of conservation areas. (a) *Effect of shape of conservation area (shaded 'edge effect') areas approx. equal.* Source: Author. (b) *Suggested geometrical principles for design of conservation areas derived from island biogeography. There may be lower species extinction in those on the left.* Sources: *Diamond, 1975; Barrett, 1980: 231 (Fig. 7); The Environmentalist, 5(1), p. 56 (Fig. 12.2) of 1985.*

often been culled as a measure to counter bovine tuberculosis. Such difficulties might be reduced by immunization of livestock or game species. Conservation has often been implemented without really considering local socio-economic issues; also conservation policies tend to be largely 'western' in outlook, and, having been designed, and possibly managed, by Europeans can be poorly adapted to meet vital local needs.

Paying for conservation

Even where there is no other land use, conservation still might be able to earn enough to pay its way, through sales of 'patents' or 'copyrights' on genetic material, tourism, or through debt swaps for conservation deals. Conservation areas can generate revenue if entry fees are charged to tourists; a service charge may be made if the area protects a catchment, large companies may support conservation for public relations reasons, or national and international bodies and governments may fund conservation (McNeely, 1989: 311). Often the problem is that poor people who need fuelwood, forest products or land encroach on conservation areas. Unless they receive aid, the conservation area will remain under threat; there are similar difficulties involved in the control of desertification (funding the control of desertification is discussed in Chapter 8).

The 'World Heritage Convention' (UNESCO Convention Concerning the Protection of the World Cultural and Natural Heritage), held in 1972, issued a protocol that had been signed by 102 nations by 1988. The agreement of signatories is that there are elements of the cultural and natural heritage of individual countries which are of such outstanding international value that their protection should be the concern and responsibility of the international community. Another positive move has been the setting up of the World Conservation Monitoring Centre by the International Union for the Conservation of Nature and Natural Resources (IUCN), World Wide Fund for Nature (WWF), and the United Nations Environment Programme (UNEP). Based in Cambridge (UK), the Centre aims to get a global overview of conservation data and to make data available to those involved in conservation at regional and local levels in developing countries.

Another promising, somewhat controversial development which has the potential to help reduce land degradation and to aid conservation of wildlife in even the poorest countries is the debt-for-conservation swap. These have been described as: '. . .a mutual face-saving option on debt, giving benefits to conservation. The first of these deals was probably in the Colombian Amazon in 1987. Typically, the swaps work as follows: commercial banks realize that they will probably never recoup the huge loans they have paid to developing countries, mainly in the 1970s (McNeely, 1989). Rather than write off the debts, they sell them at a large discount, i.e. the donor buys a debt in hard currency at a discount in the banking market and it is then cashed for the borrower's own currency, making the donor's money go further. In the case of Costa Rica's Guanacaste Conservation Project, in 1988, banks sold off each US$ 1.0 of debt for US$ 0.25, mainly to non-governmental organizations like the World Wildlife Fund – USA and the Nature Conservancy – USA. Costa Rica's Central Bank agreed to pay the remaining US$ 0.75 in local currency, provided the money was spent on conservation in Costa Rica. In effect, conservationists could triple their money and help reduce Costa Rica's debts, also conservation remained under Costa Rican control. In practice, Costa Rica spent about US$ 17 million on the Guanacaste National Park and, in so doing, paid off US$ 24 million of debt (Pearce, 1989b).

In 1987, Bolivia's proposals for the Beni Biological Reserve were frustrated for lack of funds. An American non-governmental organization, a private foundation – Conservation International – took over a large debt in return for which Bolivia set up a 1.4 million ha conservation area and provided a US$ 250,000 endowment to pay for managing the Reserve. Conservation International advise and Bolivian staff manage the Reserve.

Funding for debt-for-nature swaps has mainly come from the USA. However, the eastern bloc have also shown interest in such arrangments, Boyle & Archill (1989: 120) note the USSR has offered to write off some of the debts owed in return for nature conservation arrangements; the UK and the Netherlands have also made deals.

Ecuador has also used debt-for-conservation swap. According to recent press reports, the WWF have undertaken to buy US$ 10 million of Ecuador's US$ 11 billion debts owed to western banks. A New York bank has agreed to let WWF pay the loan of US$ 10 million off at a cheap rate and to use 3 million of it for conservation in Ecuador's Galapagos Islands. The rest of the loan is to be spent on conservation of parts of mainland Ecuador (*The Sunday Times*, 9/5/89: A3). In some of the debt-for-conservation swaps presently under way, American banks have been able to claim, as USA tax-deductable, any value given to a debtor country to allow it to pledge funds to a non-governmental organization for conservation (Cartwright, 1989: 124).

Not all countries have welcomed the debt-for-conservation swap. Some governments and NGOs see it as external interference in national conservation – a sort of 'greenmail' (*The Times*, 11/5/89: 10). The World Rainforest Movement is one international NGO which has voiced concern at the swaps (Pearce, 1989b).

In addition to debt-for-conservation swaps, the World Bank and some richer countries have begun to step up their support for conservation, for example, the UK's Overseas Development Administration announced £1.0 million support for the Korup National Park in the Cameroon (*The Times*, 15/2/89: 5).

PREVENTATIVE AND REMEDIAL STRATEGIES

Ten years ago, *The World Conservation Strategy* (IUCN, UNEP & WWF, 1980: 3) noted:

Living resources essential for human survival and sustainable development are increasingly being destroyed or depleted. At the same time human demands for these resources is growing fast . . . the predicament . . . [*is*] . . . caused by growing numbers of people demanding scarcer resources . . . exacerbated by the disproportionately high consumption rates of developed countries.

Little has changed, at the root of much of the land degradation problem lie the same causes.

Sometimes the process and sometimes the cause(s) of land degradation are obvious, but there are situations where apparently harmless actions trigger a more-or-less complex chain of causation leading to land degradation. During the last 40 years or so, we have gathered knowledge about the global environment (and about social processes), and we should be more alert to the risks. However, when a threat is recognized, it does not go away: in practice, there is much inadvertent change in the environment and much less intentional management (Botkin *et al.*, 1989: 32).

Prevention or remedial action requires five things:

1. *Satisfactory baseline data* – without information on the structure function and status of the environment, or on past, present and likely future demands upon it, it is impossible to arrive at satisfactory management strategies.
2. *Satisfactory monitoring* – monitoring is vital for updating baseline data and for recognizing the emergence of environmental problems.
3. *Satisfactory strategies for prevention/mitigation of land degradation* – somehow these have to be developed, tested and perfected.

4. *The willingness to take preventative/remedial action* – this may be hindered for many reasons, for example, because people involved must forego short-term benefits. Also, decision-makers, and the people they answer to, do not always perceive the need to act.

5. *The resources to take preventative/remedial action* – these include: skilled manpower, access to a satisfactory database, technology, funding.

In practice there may be a sixth factor: there may be little time available to counter/solve a land degradation problem before it gets out of control.

The UNEP has been establishing a database on the global environment which may help solve the problem of inadequate baseline data. The database, a sophisticated geographical information system, is known as the Global Resource Information Database (GRID). Much of the information fed into it has come from the UNEP Global Environment Monitoring System (GEMS). GRID, together with scientific expertise that the UNEP is assembling, should make possible better early warning of land degradation and better information access for strategies to counter the problem – poor nations should have easy access to these facilities. Interestingly, some of the funding for GRID has come from commercial, multinational corporation sources (Watts, 1990).

The easing of East–West tensions recently opens up opportunities for dialogue and the possibility that there may be diversion of some of the superpowers' military spending into combatting environmental problems (and to countering socioeconomic problems that often lie at the roots of land degradation). More important, for the first time in over 40 years, one of the greatest threats of land degradation: nuclear warfare, seems to be receding slightly.

There has been a tremendous growth in the 'green movement' and public interest in the environment, mainly in the developed nations and in the eastern bloc; the indications are that this will be sustained. Such developments are hopefully indicative of a shift in public attitudes towards more concern for environmental protection. There have also been international agreements, such as the Montreal Protocol, which illustrate that nations can subjugate sovereign interests in order to solve mutually threatening environmental problems. There have also been changes in the attitude of economic institutions, like the World Bank, towards greater integration of environment with economic development.

There seems to be a growth in concern for the environment; developing strategies to control degradation or to prevent it will not be quick or simple. *The World Conservation Strategy* noted: National and international capacities to conserve are ill-organized and fragmented – split up amongst sectors such as agriculture, forestry, fisheries and wildlife – with consequent duplication of effort, gaps in coverage, competition/for money and influence and conflict; and they have little influence on the development process, with the result that development, the principal means of tackling human problems, too often adds to them by destroying the living resource base of human welfare.'

That observation holds true ten years on, there is a need for better co-ordination of environmental management.

There are signs of a 'sea change' in economic thinking: with the 'Brundtland Report' (World Commission on Environment and Development, 1987) and, more recently, the 'Pearce Report' (Pearce *et al.*, 1989) there have been clear and influential statements. Economists are now asking: what constitutes sustainable development and what modifications does it require of economic–environmental interactions. There have been proposals for resource/environment accounting systems, and in a recent study by Pearce (in Botkin *et al.*, 1989: 313) it was suggested that the concept of Sustained Economic Development (SED) (which may be broadly viewed as a sustainable increase in per capita income over time) should be merged with the concept of Sustainable Use of Resources and Environment (SURE) (which may be defined as a rate of use of resources/environment that doesn't deplete the Earth's capital). The merging of these two concepts into SEDSURE would make it more likely that poor people would take part in environmental management.

To carry out a strategy, it is necessary to have a planning organization and an implementation body. There must be a suitable organizational and institutional structure if the management of strategy implementation is to be sustained and effective. Within such structures, it is necessary to have an overall view (the recruitment of personnel, mustering of resources and co-ordination will probably be on a global scale), yet, without local 'roots', little will be achieved. Cliché it may be, but a 'green movement' motto: 'think globally, act locally', might be the best advice to environmental managers. The environment is not static, it is prone to change, is constantly changing or is in some 'steady-state'. Management strategies must therefore be adaptive. Given the complex environmental/social/economic inter-relationships involved in land degradation, there is a need for a multidisci-plinary approach.

There are active governmental bodies, international agencies, charity bodies and other organizations involved in trying to prevent or mitigate land degradation. Where there are gaps and weaknesses, these need to be recognized and filled, overall co-ordination should be strengthened and the people involved in land degradation and countering it should be involved and motivated.

References

Adams, R., Adams, M., Willens, A. & Willens, A. (1978). *Dry Lands: man and plants*. London: The Architectural Press.

Adams, R. M., Rosenzweig, C., Peart, R. M., Ritchie, J. T., McCarl, B. A., Glyer, J. D., Curry, R. B., Jones, J. W., Boote, K. J. & Allen, L. H. Jr (1990). Global climate change and US Agriculture. *Nature, London*, **345(6276)**, 219–24.

Addiscot, T. (1988). Farmers, fertilizers and the nitrate flood. *New Scientist*, **120(1633)**, 50–3.

Adefolalu, D. O. (1983). Desertification of the Sahel. In *Natural Resources in Tropical Countries*, ed. Ooi Jin Bee, pp. 402–38. Singapore: Singapore University Press.

Adriawan, E. & Moniaga, S. (1986). The burning of a tropical forest: fire in East Kalimantan. What caused this catastrophe? *The Ecologist*, **16(6)**, 269–70.

Agarwal, B. (1986). *Cold Hearths and Barren Slopes: the woodfuel crsis in the Third World*, London: Zed Books.

Ahmad, Y. J. & Kassas, M. (1987). *Desertification: financial support for the biosphere*. London: Hodder and Stoughton.

Aiken, R. & Leigh, C. H. (1985). On the declining fauna of Peninsular Malaysia in the post-colonial period. *Ambio*, **XIV(1)**, 15–22.

Aiken, S. R. & Leigh, C. H. (1987). Queensland's Daintree Rainforest at risk, *Ambio*. **XVI(2–3)**, 131–41.

Alcamo, J., Amman, J. P., Hettelingh, M., Holmberg, Hordijk, L., Kämäri, J., Kauppi, L., Kauppi, P., Kornai, G. & Mäkelä, A. (1987). Acidification in Europe a simulation model for evaluating control strategies. *Ambio*, **XV(5)**, 232–45.

Allan, P. (1965). *The African Husbandman*. Edinburgh: Oliver and Boyd.

Allan, R. J. (1988). El Niño Southern Oscillation influences in the Australasian region. *Progress in Physical Geography*, **12(3)**, 313–48.

Allchin, B., Goudie, A. & Hegde, K. T. M. (1978). *The Prehistory and Palaeography of the Great Indian Desert*. London: Academic Press.

Allen, J. C. & Barnes, D. F. (1985). The cause of deforestation in developing countries. *Annals of the Association of American Geographers*. **75(2)**, 163–84.

Allen, N. J., Knapp, G. W. & Stadel, C. (eds.) (1988). *Human Impact on Mountains*. Totowa (NJ): Rowman and Littlefield.

Allsopp, R., Hall, D. & Jones, T. (1985). Fatal attraction for the tsetse fly. *New Scientist*, **108(1481)**, 40–3.

Anderson, I. (1989). The myth of sustainable logging: the case for a ban on tropical timber imports. *The Ecologist*, **19(5)**, 166–8.

Anderson, I. & Grove, R. (eds.) (1987). *Conservation in Africa: people, policies and practice*. Cambridge: Cambridge University Press.

Anon. (1982). *Development Forum*, **X(3)**, p. 5.

Anon. (1983). Irish advisors exploit African bogs. *New Scientist*, **97(1339)**, p. 24.

Anon. (19884). *Behind the Weather: an unnatural disaster – drought in North East Brazil*. Oxford: OXFAM Public Affairs Unit.

REFERENCES   Anon. (1985a). Long range air pollution: a threat to European forests. *Unasylva*, **34(149)**, 14–25.

Anon. (1985b). Deadly harvest (pesticides and the Third World). *South*, special issue: January, 1985.

Anon. (1986). The acid rain controversy in Europe and North America: a political analysis. *Ambio*, **XV(1)**, 47–51.

Anon. (1987a). The restless deserts continue to grow. *New Scientist*, **113(1549)**, p. 28.

Anon. (1987b). Sea temperatures predict African drought. *New Scientist*, **116(1580)**, p. 25.

Anon. (1987c). *Towards Sustainable Development* (14 case-studies prepared by African and Asian journalist for the Nordic Conference on Environment and Development, Sallsjöbaden, Stockholm, 8–10 May, 1987). London: The PANOS Institute.

Anon. (1987d). Icy clues to a carbon dioxide with climate connection. *New Scientist*, **119(1588)**, p. 34.

Anon. (1988a). Chopping down rainfall. *New Scientists*, **118(1612)**, p. 38.

Anon. (1988b). Soil erosion tops crisis list. *New Scientist*, **117(1600)**, p. 29.

Anon. (1988c). Melting in the greenhouse. *The Times Higher Education Supplement*, 9/9/89, p. 15.

Anon. (1988d). Scientist warns about costs of 'greenhouse effect'. *The Times*, 24/8/88: 6.

Anon. (1988e). Rising methane means falling ozone. *New Scientist*, **118(1605)**, p. 31.

Anon. (1988f). Importance of volcanic activity overestimated. *New Scientist*, **117(1597)**, p. 36.

Anon. (1988g). Volcanoes poised to blow another ozone hole. *New Scientist*, **119(1628)**, p. 42.

Anon. (1988h). Heathlands of England harbour cancer spores. *New Scientist*, **118(1608)**, p. 23.

Anon. (1988i). Australia tots up the buffalo bill. *New Scientist*, **118(1614)**, p. 35.

Anon. (1990). Texas finds fresh fibres for tomorrow's news. *New Scientist*. **125(1703)**, p. 35.

Arden-Clarke, C. & Hodges, D. (1987). Soil erosion: the answer lies in organic farming. *New Scientist*, **113(1547)**, 41–3.

Arianoutsou-Faraggitaki, M. (1985). Desertification by overgrazing in Greece: the case of Lesvos Island. *Journal of Arid Environments*, **9(3)**, 237–42.

Armstrong, S. (1988). Marooned on a mountain of manure. *New Scientist*, **120(1640)**, 51–5.

Arnold, J. E. M. (1987). Community forestry *Ambio*, **XVI(2–3)**, 122–8.

Arnon, I. (1981). *Modernizing Agriculture in Developing Countries: resources, potentials and problems*. Chichester: John Wiley and Sons.

Aubréville, A. M. (1987). *Climats, Forêts et Desertification de l'Afrique Troicale*. Paris: Société d'Editions Geographiques, Maritimes et Coloniales.

Aubréville, A. M. (1985). The disappearance of the tropical forests of Africa. *Unasylva*, **37(2)**, No. 148, 18–27.

Ayoade, J. O. (1988). *Tropical Hydrology and Water Resources*. London: Macmillan.

Bach, W. (1986). Nuclear war: the effects of smoke and dust on weather and climate. *Progress in Physical Geography*, **10(3)**, 315–63.

Baillie, M. G. (1989). Hekla 3: how big was it? *Endeavour. New Series*: **13(2)**, 78–82.

Bain, J. S. (1973). *Environmental Decay: economic causes and remedies*. Boston: Little Brown and Co.

Baker, R. (1984). Protecting the environment against the poor: the historical roots of the soil erosion orthodoxy in the Third World. *The Ecologist*, **14(2)**, 53–60.

Baker, A., Brooks, R. & Reeves, R. (1988). Growing for gold . . . and copper . . . and zinc. *New Scientist*, **117(1603)**, 44–5.

Bakker, R. (1988). *The Dinosaur Heresies*. Harmondsworth: Penguin Books.

Balek, J. (1977). *Hydrology and Water Resources in Tropical Africa*. Amsterdam: Elsevier.

Barbier, E. B. (1987). The concept of sustainable economic development. *Environmental Conservation*. **14(2)**, 101–10.

Barbier, E. B. (1989a). *Economics, Natural Resources Scarcity and Development: conventional and alternative views*. London: Earthscan Publications (IIED).

Barbier, E. B. (1989b). The global greenhouse effect: economic impacts and policy considerations. *Natural Resources Forum*, **13(1)**, 20–32.

Barnaby, F. (1982). The effects of a global nuclear war: the arsenals. *Ambio*, **XI(2–3)**, 76–83.

Barr, B. M. & Braden, K. (1988). *The Disappearing Russian Forest: a dilemma in Soviet resource management*. Totowa (NJ): Rowman and Littlefield.

Barrett, S. W. (1980). Conservation in Amazonia. *Biological Conservation*, **18**, 209–35.

Barrow, C. J. (1985). The development of the *várzeas* (floodlands) of Brazilian Amazonia. In *Change In The Amazon Basin, vol. 1: man's impact on forests and rivers*, ed. J. Hemming, pp. 108–28. Manchester: Manchester University Press.

Barrow, C. J. (1987a). *Water Resources and Agricultural Development in the Tropics*. Harlow: Longman.

Barrow, C. J. (1987b). The impact of hydroelectric development on the Amazonian environment, with particular reference to the Tucuruí Project. *Journal of Biogeography*, **15(1)**, 67–78.

Bartelmus, P. (1986). *Environment and Development*. London: Allen and Unwin.

Battistini, R. & Richard-Vindard, G. (eds.) (1972). *Biogeography and Ecology in Madagascar*, The Hague: Dr W. Junk.

Bayfield, N. G. (1971). Some effects of walking and skiing on vegetation at Cairngorm. In *The Scientific Management of Animal and Plant Communities and Conservation*, eds. E. Duffey & A. S. Watt, pp. 469–485. Oxford: Blackwell Scientific Publications.

Beard, J. (1989). Gravity puts the squeeze on sewage. *New Scientist*, **122(1667)**, p. 34.

Beaumont, P. (1989). *Environmental Management and Development in Drylands*. London: Routledge.

Bell, R. H. (1987). Conservation with a human face: conflict and reconciliation African land use planning. In *Conservation in Africa: people, policies and practice*, eds. D. Anderson & R. Grove, p. 79–101. Cambridge: Cambridge University Press.

Beudot, F. (1987). *Elements for a Bibliography on the Sahelian Countries*. Paris: OECD Development Centre.

Bird, E. C. (1985). *Coastal Changes a Global Review*. Chichester: John Wiley and Sons.

Blaikie, P. (1985). *The Political Economy of Soil Erosion in Developing Countries*. Harlow: Longman.

Blaikie, P. (1989). Explanation and policy in land degradation and rehabilitation for developing countries. *Land Degradation & Rehabilitation*, **1(1)**, 23–37.

Blaikie, P. & Brookfield, H. (1987). *Land Degradation and Society*. London: Methuen.

Bliss, L. C., Heal, O. W. & Moore, J. J. (eds.) (1981). *Tundra Ecosystems: a comparative analysis*. Cambridge: Cambridge University Press.

Board na Mona. (1985). *Fuel Peat in Developing Countries* (World Bank Technical Paper, 41 # BK0537). Washington DC: World Bank.

Boels, D., Davies, D. B. & Johnston, A. E. (1982). *Soil Degradation*. Rotterdam: A. A. Balkema.

Bokhari, S. M. (1980). Case study on waterlogging and salinity problems in Pakistan. *Water Supply and Management*, **4(2)**, 171–92.

Bolin, b., Döös., Bo, R., Jäger, J. & Warrick, R. A. (eds.) (1986). *The Greenhouse Effect, Climatic Changes and the Ecosystem* (SCOPE 29). Chichester: John Wiley and Sons.

Bondictti, E. Λ. (1982). Effects on agriculture. *Ambio*, **XI(2–3)**, 138–42.

Bonnett, P. J., Leeks, G. J. & Cambray, R. S. (1989). Transport processes for Chernobyl-labelled sediments: preliminary evidence from upland mid-Wales. *Land Degradation & Rehabilitation*, **1(1)**, 39–50.

Bonnifield, P. (1979). *The Dust Bowl: men, dirt and depression*. Albuquerque: University of New Mexico Press.

Boserüp, E. (1965). *The Conditions of Agricultural Growth: the economics of agrarian change under population pressure*. London: George Allen and Unwin.

REFERENCES   Botkin, D. B., Caswell, M. F., Estes, J. E. & Orio, A. A. (eds.) (1989). *Changing the Global Environment*. Boston: Academic Press.

Bourke, G. (1987). Forests in the Ivory Coast face extinction. *New Scientist*, **114(1564)**, p. 22.

Boutier, F. (1983). *Tropical Savannas* (Ecosystems of the World No. 13). Amsterdam: Elsevier.

Bouwman, A. F. (1990). Land use related sources of greenhouse gases. *Land Use Policy*, **7(2)**, 154–65.

Bowander, B. (1987). Environmental problems in developing countries. *Progress in Physical Geography*, **11(2)**, 246–59.

Boyle, S. & Ardill, J. (1989). *The Greenhouse Effect: a practical guide to the world's changing climate*. London: Hodder and Stoughton.

Bradshaw, A. D. & Chadwick, M. J. (1980). *The Restoration of Land: the ecology and reclamation of derelict and degraded land*. Oxford: Blackwell.

Branford, S. (1988). Choking the Amazon. *New Scientist*, **116(1581)**, 67–68.

Branford, S. & Glock, O. (1985). *The Last Frontier: fighting over land in the Amazon*. London: Zed Books.

Bridges, E. M. (1978). *World Soils* (2nd edn). Cambridge University Press: Cambridge.

Briggs, D. J. & Courtney, F. M. (1985). *Agriculture and Environment: the physical geography of temperate agriculture*. London: Longman.

Brookes, C. E. (1926). *Climate Through the Ages: a study of climatic factors and their variations*. London: Earnest Benn.

Brothwell, D. (1978). On the complex nature of man–animal relationships from the Pleistocene to early agricultural societies. In *Conservation and Global Extinction Patterns*, ed. J. D. Hawkes, pp. 45–59. London: Duckworth.

Brown, L. R. (1977). *Redefining National Security* (Worldwatch Paper No. 14). Washington DC: Worldwatch Institute.

Brown, L. R. (1978). *The Worldwide Loss of Cropland* (Worldwatch Papers No. 24). Washington DC: Worldwatch Institute.

Brown, L. R., Chandler, W., Flavin, C., Postel, S., Starke, L. & Wolfe, E. (1984). *State of the World: a Worldwatch Institute report on progress towards a sustainable society*. New York: W. W. Norton.

Brubaker, S. (1972). *To Live on Earth: man and his environment in perspective*, Baltimore: Resources for the Future and Johns Hopkins University Press.

Bruenig, E. F. (1987). The forest ecosystem: tropical and boreal. *Ambio*, **XVI(2–3)**, 68–85.

Brush, S. B. (1987). Diversity and change in Andean agriculture. In *Lands at Risk in the Third World: local-level perspectives*, eds. P. D. Little & M. M. Horowitz, pp. 271–89. Boulder: Westview Press.

Bryson, R. A. (1967). Possibilities of major climatic modification and their implications: Northwest India. *Bulletin of the American Meteorological Society*, **48**, 136–42.

Bryson, R. A. (1989). Will there be a global 'greenhouse' warming? *Environmental Conservation*, **16(2)**, 97–9.

Bryson, R. A. & Murray, T. J. (1977). *Climate of Hunger: mankind and the world's changing weather*. Madison (Wisconsin): University of Wisconsin Press.

Buckman, R. E. (1987). Strengthening forestry institutions in the developing world. *Ambio*, **XVI(2–3)**, 120–1.

Buckocke, A. (1988). Famine spectre as crops fail in Sudan. *The Times*, 6/2/88, p. 6.

Bull, D. (1982). *A Growing Problem: pesticides and the Third World*. London: OXFAM.

Bunney, S. (1990). Prehistoric farming caused 'devastating' soil erosion. *New Scientist*, **125(1705)**, p. 29.

Bunyard, P. (1989). Guardians of the Amazon. *New Scientist*, **124(1695)**, 38–41.

Burbridge, P. R. (1988). Coastal and marine resource management in the Straits of Malacca. *Ambio*, **XVII(3)**, 170–7.

Calabri, G. (1983). Fighting fires in Mediterranean forests. *Unasylva*, **35(141)**, 14–21.

Caldecott, J. (1988). Climbing towards extinction. *New Scientist*, **118(1616)**, 62–6.

Caldwell, J. C. (1977). Demographic aspects of drought: an examination of the African drought of 1970–74. In *Drought in Africa 2* (revised edn), eds. D. Dalby, R. H. Harrison-Church & F. Bezzaz, pp. 93–100. London: International African Institute.

Caldwell, L. K. (1984). Political aspects of ecologically sustainable development. *Environmental Conservation.* **11(4)**, 299–308.

Caldwell, M. (1977). *The Wealth of Some Nations.* London: Zed Press.

Campbell, A. (1990). The greening of Australia. *Our Planet* (UNEP), *(1)*. 7–8.

Canter, L. W. (1986). *Environmental Impacts of Agricultural Production Activities.* Chelsea (Michigan): Lewis Publishers.

Carlstein, T. (1982). *Time, Resources, Society and Ecology: on the capacity for human interaction in space and time (vol. 1. Pre-industrial societies).* London: George Allen and Unwin.

Carson, R. (1962). *Silent Spring.* New York: Houghton Mifflin.

Cartwright, J. (1989). Conserving nature, decreasing debt. *Third World Quarterly,* **11(2)**, 114–27.

Caufield, C. (1982). *Tropical Moist Forest: the resource, the people, the threat,* London: Earthscan Publications (IIED).

Caufield, C. (1985). *In the Rainforest.* London: Pan Books.

Chadwick, M. J. & Goodman, G. T. (eds.) (1975). *The Ecology of Resource Degradation and Renewal.* Oxford: Blackwell Scientific.

Chambers, R., Longhurst, R. & Pacey, A. (1981). *Seasonal Dimensions to Rural Poverty.* London: Frances Pinter.

Chapman, V. J. (1975). *Mangrove Vegetation.* Vaduz: J. Cramer.

Charles, D. C. (1989). Will these lands ne'er be clean? *New Scientist,* **122(1670)**, 36–7.

Charney, J. G. (1975). Dynamics of deserts and drought in the Sahel. *Quarterly Journal of the Royal Meteorological Society,* **101**, 193–202.

Charney, J. G., Stone, P. H. & Quirk, W. J. (1975). Drought in the Sahara: a biophysical feedback mechanism. *Science,* **187(4175)**, 434–5.

Cherfas, J. (1986). How to grow a tropical forest. *New Scientist,* **112 (1531)**, 26–7.

Chisholm, A. & Dumsday, R. (eds.) (1987). *Land Degradation: problems and policies.* London: Cambridge University Press.

Chi Jung Jim. (1987). Trampling impacts of recreationists on picnic sites in a Hong Kong country park. *Environmental Conservation,* **14(4)**, 117–27.

Chown, M. (1986). The red island is bleeding to death. *New Scientist,* **111(1524)**, 57–8.

Christiansson, C. (1988). Degradation and rehabilitation of agropastoral land perspectives on environmental damage in semiarid Tanzania. *Ambio,* **17(2)**, 144–52.

Clark, S. S. & McLoughlan, L. C. (1986). Historical and biological evidence for fire regimes in the Sydney region prior to the arrival of Europeans: implications for future bushland management. *Australian Geographer,* **17(2)**, 101–12.

Clark, W. C. & Munn, R. E. (eds.) (1986). *Sustainable Development of the Biosphere.* Cambridge: Cambridge University Press.

Clements, F. E. (1916). *Plant Succession.* Washington DC: Carneigi Institute of Washington, Publication No. 242.

Cloudsley-Thompson, J. L. (1975). *Terrestrial Environments.* London: Croom Helm.

Clover, C. (1988). Hole in ozone layer 'goes for a walk'. *The Daily Telegraph,* 23/11/88, p. 10.

Coblentz, B. E. (1978). The effects of feral goats (*Campra hircus*) on island ecosystems. *Biological Conservation,* **13**, 279–86.

Cole, M. M. (1986). *The Savannas: biogeography and geobotany.* London: Academic Press.

Colinvaux, P. A. (1989). The past and future Amazon. *Scientific American,* **260(5)**, 68–74.

Commoner, B. (1972). *The Closing Circle: confronting the environmental crisis.* London: Cape.

Conway, G. R. (ed.) (1985). *Agricultural Systems Research for Developing Countries.* Canberra: International Agricultural Research.

REFERENCES   Conway, G. R. (1988). Rainbow over Wollo. *New Scientist*, **118(1611)**, p. 70.

Cooper, C. F. (1974). The ecology of fire. In *Ecology, Evolution and Population Biology*, ed. Scientific American, pp. 294–302. San Francisco: Freeman and Co. (Scientific American Publications).

Cottrell, A. (1978). *Environmental Economics: an introduction for students of the resource and environmental sciences*. London: Edward Arnold.

Council on Environmental Quality. & Department of State. (1982). *The Global 2000 Report to the President: entering the twenty-first century*. Harmondsworth: Penguin Books.

Cowling, E. B. (1989). Recent changes in chemical climate and related effects on forests in N. America and Europe. *Ambio*, **XVIII(3)**, 167–71.

Cross, M. (1983). Last chance to save Africa's topsoil. *New Scientist*, **199(1368)**, 288–93.

Cross, M. (1988). Spare the tree and spoil the forest. *New Scientist*, **120(1640)**, 24–5.

Dalby, D., Harrison Church, R. J. & Bezzaz, F. (eds.) (1977). *Drought in Africa 2* (revised edn). London: (210 High Holborn) International African Institute.

Darkoh, M. B. (1987). Socio-economic and institutional factors behind desertification in Southern Africa. *Area*, **19(1)**, 25–33.

Dasman, R. F. (1985). Achieving the sustainable use of species and ecosystems. *Landscape Planning*, **12(4)**, 211–19.

Davenport, P. & Young, J. (1988). Can we stop Britain drowning? *The Times*, 21/10/88, p. 14.

Davidson, J., Tho Yow Pong. & Bijleveld, M. (eds.) (1985). *The Future of Tropical Rainforests in South East Asia* (Proceedings of a Symposium, Kepong, Malaysia 1–2 Sept., 1983 – IUCN Commission on Ecology Papers No. 10). Gland: IUCN.

Dawnay, I. (1989). Forester without honour. *The Financial Times*, 7/2/89: p. 7.

Dawson, J. A. & Doornkamp, J. C. (eds.) (1973). *Evaluating the Human Environment: essays in applied geography*. London: Edward Arnold.

Dayton, S. (1988). Canadians confirm ozone hole in Arctic. *New Scientist*, **118(1616)**, p. 47.

DeBooysen, P. & Tainton, N. M. (eds.) (1984). *Ecological Effects of Fire in S. African Ecosystems*. Berlin: Springer-Verlag.

DeGroot, P. (1990). Are we missing the grass for the trees? *New Scientist*, **125(1698)**, 29–30.

DeLaune, R. D., Patrick, W. H. & Peceshki, S. R. (1987). Forseeable flooding and death of coastal wetland forests. *Environmental Conservation*, **XIV(2)**, 129–33.

Detwyler, T. R. (ed.) (1971). *Man's Impact on Environment*. New York: McGraw-Hill.

DeVos, A. (1975). *Africa, The Devastated Continent: man's impact on the ecology of Africa*. The Hague: Dr W. Junk Publishers.

Diamond, J. M. (1975). The island dilemma: lessons of modern biogeographic studies for the design of nature reserves. *Biological Conservation*, **7**, 129–46.

Diamond, J. M. (1976). Critical areas for maintaining viable populations of species. In *The Breakdown and Restoration of Ecosystems*, eds. M. W. Holdgate & M. J. Woodman, pp. 27–40. New York: Plenum Press.

Dianwu Zhao. & Bozen Sun. (1986). Air pollution and acid rain in China. *Ambio*, **XV(1)**, 2–5.

Dimbleby, G. W. (1975). Archaeological evidence of environmental change. *Nature*, **256(5516)**, 265–8.

Dixon, J. A., James, D. E. & Sherman, P. B. (1989). *The Economics of Dryland Management*. London: Earthscan (IIED).

Dixon, J. A., James, D. E. & Sherman, P. B. (eds.) (1990). *Dryland Management: economic case studies*. London: Earthscan Publications (IIED).

Dorner, P. & El-Shafie, M. (eds.) (1980). *Resources and Development: natural resource policies and economic development in an interdependent world*. London: Croom Helm.

Doubleday, G. P. (1974). The reclamation of land after coal mining. *Outlook on Agriculture*, **8(3)**, 156–62.

Douglas, I. G. (1981). Soil conservation measures in river basin planning. In

River Basin Planning: theory and practice. eds. S. K. Saha & C. J. Barrow, pp. 49–73. Chichester: John Wiley and Sons.

Douglas, I. G. & Spencer, T. S. (eds.) (1985). *Environmental Change and Tropical Geomorphology*. London: George Allen and Unwin.

Down, C. G. & Stocks, J. (1977). *Environmental Impact of Mining*. London: Applied Science Publishers.

Doxiadis, C. A. (1977). *Ecology and Ekistics*. London: Paul Elek.

Drake, J. A. (ed.) (1989). *The Ecology of Biological Invasions* (SCOPE No. 37). Chichester: John Wiley and Sons.

Dregne, H. E. (1983). *Desertification of Arid Lands*. Chur: Harwood Academic Publishers.

Dregne, H. E. (1984). Combating desertification: evaluation of progress. *Environmental Conservation*, **11(2)**, 115–21.

Dregne, H. E. (1985). Aridity and land degradation: guarded optimism for the future of arid lands. *Environment*, **27(8)**, 16–33.

Dregne, H. E. (1987). Soil erosion: cause and effect. *Land Use Policy*, **4(4)**, 412–18.

Dudley, W. & Min Lee. (1988). *Tsunami!* Honolulu: University of Hawaii Press.

Dunbar, R. (1984). Scapegoat for a thousand deserts. *New Scientist*, **104(1430)**, 30.

Dütsch, H. U. (1987). The Antarctic ozone hole and its possible global consequences. *Environmental Conservation*. **14(2)**, 95–6.

Eastwood, D. A. & Pollard, H. J. (1987). Lowland colonization or coca production: Bolivia's irreconcilable policies. *Singapore Journal of Tropical Geography*, **8(1)**, 15–25.

Eckholm, E. P. (1976). *Losing Ground: environmental stress and world food prospects*. Oxford: Pergamon Press.

Eckholm, E. P. (1979). *Planning for the Future: forestry for human needs*. (Worldwatch Paper No. 26). Washington DC: Worldwatch Institute.

Eckholm, E. P. & Brown, L. R. (1977). *Spreading Deserts – the hand of Man* (Worldwatch Papers No. 13). Washington DC: Worldwatch Institute.

Eckolm, E. P., Foley, G., Barnard, G. & Timberlake, L. (1984). *Fuelwood: the energy crisis that won't go away*. London: Earthscan Publications (IIED).

Ehrlich, P. R., Ehrlich, A. H. & Holdren, J. P. (1970). *Ecoscience: population, resources, environment*. San Francisco: W. H. Freeman.

El-Ashry, M. T. (1985). Study shows mountain ecosystems may be especially sensitive to acid deposition. *Ambio*, **XIV(3)**, 179–80.

El-Hinnawi, E. & Hashmi, M. (eds.) (1982). *Global Environmental Issues (UNEP)*. Dublin: Tycooly International Publishing.

El-Moghraby, A. I., Ali, O. M. & El-Seed, M. T. (1987). Desertification in Western Sudan and strategies for rehabilitation. *Environmental Conservation*, **14(3)**, 227–31.

El-Swaify, S. A., Moldenhauer, W. C. & Lo, A. (eds.) (1985). *Soil Erosion and Conservation*. Akeny (Iowa): Soil Conservation Society of America.

Elsworth, S. (1984). *Acid Rain*. London: Pluto Press.

Elton, C. S. (1958). *The Ecology of Invasions of Animals and Plants*. London: Chapman and Hall.

Etherington, J. R. (1983). *Wetland Ecology*. London: Edward Arnold.

Ewin, P. J. & Bazeley, D. R. (1989). Jungle law in Thailand's forests. *New Scientist*, **124(1691)**, 42–6.

Eyles, G. O. (1987). *Soil Erosion in the South Pacific* (Environmental Studies Report No. 37, Institute of Natural Resources, University of the South Pacific). Palmerston North: New Zealand Ministry of Private Works and Development.

Eyre, L. A. (1987). Jamaica: test case for tropical deforestation? *Ambio*, **XVI(6)**, 338–43.

Eyre, S. (1978). *The Real Wealth of Nations*. London: Edward Arnold.

Ezealor, A. U. (1987). New threats to Nigeria's savanna woodlands. *Environmental Conservation*, **14(3)**, 262–4.

Falloux, F. & Murkundi, A. (eds.) (1988). *Desertification Control and Renewable Resource Management in the Sahelian and Sudanian Zones of West Africa* (World Bank Technical Paper No. 70). Washington DC: World Bank.

REFERENCES   Fantechi, R. & Margaris, N. S. (eds.) (1986). *Desertification in Europe* (Proceedings of the International Symposium on the EEC Programme on Climatology, Mytilene, Greece, 15–18 April, 1984), Dordrecht: D. Reidel Publishing.

FAO. (1981). *Eucalyptus for Planting* (2nd edn). FAO Forestry series 11, Rome: FAO.

Farman, J. (1987). What hope for the ozone layer now? *New Scientist*, **116(1586)**, 49–54.

Farman, J. C., Gardiner, B. G. & Shanklin, J. D. (1985). Large losses of total ozone in Antarctica reveal seasonal ClO_x/NO_x interactions. *Nature*, London, **315(6016)**, 205–10.

Farvar, M. T. & Milton, J. P. (eds.) (1972). *The Careless Technology: ecology and international development*. Garden City (New York): Natural History Press.

Fearnside, P. M. (1989). Deforestation in Brazilian Amazonia: the rates and causes of forest destruction. *The Ecologist*, **9(6)**, 214–24.

Ferguson, J. (1988). Desert in the making. *New Scientist*, **118(1613)**, p. 68.

Fernandes, W., Menon, G. & Viegas, P. (1988). *Forests, Environment and Tribal Economy: deforestation, impoverishment and marginalization in Orissa*. New Delhi: Indian Social Institute (New Delhi 110003).

Fernando, V. (1989). The problem of shifting cultivation. *IUCN Bulletin*, **20(1–3)**, p. 18.

Fifield, R. (1988). Frozen assets of the ice cores, *New Scientist*, **118(1608)**, 28–9.

Flenley, J. R. (1982). The evidence for ecological change in the tropics. *The Geographical Journal*, **148(1)**, 11–15.

Flenley, J. R. & King, S. M. (1984). Late Quaternary pollen records from Easter Island. *Nature*, London, **307(5949)**, 47–50.

Foley, G. & Bernard, G. (1984). *Farm and Community Forestry*. (IIED Technical Report No. 3 – Energy Information Programme). London: Earthscan Publications (IIED).

Foley, G., Moss, P. & Timberlake, L. (1984). *Stoves and Trees – how much wood would a woodstove save if a woodstove could save wood?* London: Earthscan Publications (IIED).

Ford, J. (1971). *The Role of Trypanosomiasis in African Ecology*. Oxford: Oxford University Press.

Forestier, K. (1989). The degreening of China. *New Scientist*, **123(1671)**, 52–8.

Forrester, J. (1971). *World Dynamics*. Cambridge: Wright-Allen Press.

Forse, B. (1989). The myth of the marching desert. *New Scientist*, **121(1650)**, 31–2.

Fosberg, F. R. (1972). Man's effect on island ecosystems. In *The Careless Technology: ecology and international development*, eds. M. T. Farvar & J. P. Milton, pp. 869–79. Garden City (New York): Natural History Press.

Forster, L. J. (ed.) (1986). *Agricultural Development in Drought-Prone Africa*. London: Overseas Development Institute.

Fortes, M. D. (1988). Mangroves and seagrass beds of East Asia: habitats under stress. *Ambio*, **XVII(3)**, 207–13.

Franke, R. W. & Chasin, B. H. (1980). *Seeds of Famine: ecological destruction and the development dilemma in the West African Sahel*. Montclair (New Jersey): Allanheld, Osmun.

Freedman, B. (1989). *Environmental Ecology: the impacts of pollution and other stresses on ecosystem structure and function*. London: Academic Press.

Friedman, R. (1989). Grazing cattle can change local climate. *New Scientist*, **123(1680)**, p. 30.

Furley, P. & Newey, N. W. (1983). *Geography of the Biosphere: an introduction to the nature, distribution and evolution of the world's life zones*. London: Butterworth.

Futures. (1988). vol. **20(6)**, issue on sustainable development.

Gade, D. W. (1985). Man and nature on Rodrigues, tragedy of an island commons. *Environmental Conservation*, **12(3)**, 207–16.

Gall, C. (ed.) (1981). *Goat Production*. London: Academic Press.

Gamlin, L. (1988). Sweden's factory forests. *New Scientist*, **117(1597)**, 41–7.

Garlick, J. P. & Keay, R. W. (eds.) (1970). *Human Ecology in the Tropics*. Oxford: Pergamon Press.

Gaye, S. (1987). Glaciers of the desert. *Ambio*, **16(6)**, 351–6.

Gee, H. (1988a). High methane. *The Times*, 9/4/88, p. 8.

Gee, H. (1988b). Alarm bells on the forest fire front. *The Times*, 22/7/88, p. 11.

Geertz, C. (1963). *Agricultural Involution: the process of change in Indonesia*. Berkeley (California): University of California Press.

Geojournal. (1988). **17(2)**, special issue: 'Forests of the World'.

Gerasimov, I. P., Armand, D. L. & Yefron, K. M. (eds.) (1971). *Natural Resources in the Soviet Union: their use and renewal* (translation from 1963 Russian original by J. I. Romanowski). San Francisco: W. H. Freeman.

Gerrard, A. J. (1988). *Mountain Environments: an examination of the physical geography of mountains*. London: Bellhaven Press.

Ghatak, S. & Turner, R. K. (1978). Pesticide use in less developed countries: economic and environmental considerations. *Food Policy*, **3(2)**, 136–46.

Ghosh, P. K. (ed.) (1984). *Population, Environment and Resources, and Third World Development*. Westport (Conn.): Greenwood Press.

Gilbert, F. S. (1980). The equilibrium theory of island biogeography: fact or fiction? *Journal of Biogeography*, **7(3)**, 209–35.

Gillen, K. & McGrath, S. (1989). Muck, metals and minerals. *New Scientist*, **124(1689)**, 31–2.

Ginzberg, A. S. (1989). Some atmospheric and climatic effects of nuclear war. *Ambio*, **XVIII(7)**, 384–90.

Glantz, M. H. (ed.) (1976). *The Politics of Natural Disaster: the case of the Sahel drought*. New York: Praeger Publishers.

Glantz, M. H. (ed.) (1977). *Desertification. Environmental degradation in and around arid lands*. Boulder: Westview Press.

Glantz, M. H. (ed.) (1987). *Drought and Hunger in Africa: denying famine a future*. Cambridge: Cambridge University Press.

Glantz, M. H. & Katz, R. W. (1985). Drought as a constraint in sub-Saharan Africa. *Ambio*, **XIV(6)**, 334–9.

Glasby, G. P. (1986). Modification of the environment in New Zealand. *Ambio*, **XV(5)**, 266–71.

Gleick, P. H. (1989). Climate change and international politics: problems facing developing countries. *Ambio*, **XVIII(6)**, 333–9.

Glenny, M. (1987). Czechs act over pollution in Bohemia. *New Scientist*, **114(1564)**, p. 22.

Godwin, P. (1986). Plague of locusts puts Africa under threat. *The Times*, 24/8/86, p. 14.

Goldberg, E. D. (1985). *Black Carbon in the Environment: properties and distribution*. New York: Wiley-Interscience.

Goldsmith, E. (1989). Gaia and evolution. *The Ecologist*, **19(4)**, 147–53.

Goodall, D. W. & Perry, R. A. (eds.) (1981). *Arid Land Ecosystems: structure, functioning and management* (vol. 2). Cambridge: Cambridge University Press.

Goodland, R. J. & Irwin, H. S. (1975). *Amazon Jungle: green hell to red desert*. Amsterdam: Elsevier Scientific.

Goodman, G. T. & Bray, S. A. (1975). *Ecological Aspects of the Reclamation of Derelict Land*. Norwich: GeoAbstracts.

Gorham, E. (1989). Scientific understanding of ecosystem acidification: a historical review. *Ambio*, **XVIII(3)**, 150–4.

Gorman, M. L. (1979). *Island Ecology*. London: Chapman and Hall.

Gorse, J. (1985). Desertification in the Sahelian and Sudanic Zones of West Africa. *Unasylva*, **37(No. 150)**, 2–18.

Gorse, J. E. & Steeds, D. R. (1987). *Desertification in the Sahelian and Sudanian Zones of West Africa*, (World Bank Technical Paper No. 61). Washington DC: World Bank.

Goudie, A. S. (1973). *Duricrusts in Tropical and Subtropical Landscapes*. Oxford: Clarendon Press.

Goudie, A. S. (1977). *Environmental Change*. Oxford: Oxford University Press.

Goudie, A. S. (1981). *The Human Impact: man's role in environmental change*. Oxford: Basil Blackwell.

Gradus, Y. (ed.) (1985). *Desert Development: man and technology in sparselands*. Dordrecht: D. Reidel Publishing.

Gradwohl, J. & Greenberg, R. (1988). *Saving the Tropical Forests*, London: Earthscan Publications (IIED).

REFERENCES   Grainger, A. (1982). *Desertification: how people make deserts, how people can stop and why they don't*. London Earthscan Publications (IIED).

Grainger, A. (1990). *The Threatening Desert: controlling desertification*. London: Earthscan Publications (IIED).

Greene, O., Percival, I. & Ridge, I. (1985). *Nuclear Winter*. London: Blackwell.

Greenland, D. J. & Lal, R. (eds.) (1977). *Soil Conservation and Management in the Humid Tropics*. Chichester: John Wiley and Sons.

Gregory, S. (ed.) (1988). *Recent Climatic Changes*. London: Bellhaven Press.

Gribbin, J. (1979). Disappearing threat to ozone. *New Scientist*, **81(1142)**, 474–6.

Gribbin, J. (1985). The drying of the Sahel. *New Scientist*, 105(1447), p. 8.

Gribbin, J. (1986). Global warming is linked to Sahel drought. *New Scientist*, **110(1505)**, p. 24.

Gribbin, J. (1988a). Natural oscillations explain El Niño. *New Scientist*, **118(1618)**, p. 44.

Gribbin, J. (1988b). An atmosphere in convulsions. *New Scientist*, **116(1588)**, 30–1.

Gribbin, J. (1988c). Britain shivers in the global greenhouse effect. *New Scientist*, **118(1616)**, 42–3.

Gribbin, J. (1988d). The ozone layer. *New Scientist*, **118(1611)**, special supplement (Inside Science No. 9).

Gribbin, J. (1988e). *The Hole in the Sky: man's threat to the ozone layer*. London: Corgi Books.

Gribbin, J. (1988f). The greenhouse effect. *New Scientist*, **120(1635)**, special supplement (Inside Science No. 13).

Griffiths, I. L. & Binns, J. A. (1988). Hunger, help and hypocrisy: crisis and response to crisis in Africa. *Geography*, **73(1)**, 48–54.

Grout-Smith, T. (1989). Profits and Loess from China's silt. *New Scientist*, **123(1681)**, 60–2.

Grove, A. T. (ed.) (1985). *The Niger and its Neighbours: environmental history and hydrology, human use and health hazard of the major West African rivers*. Rotterdam: A. A. Balkema.

Grove, R. (1990). The origins of environmentalism. *Nature, London*, **345(6270)**, 11–14.

Gupta, I. C. (1979). *Use of Saline Water in Agriculture: in semi-arid zones of India*. New Delhi: Oxford and IBH Publishing.

Hadley, M. & Lanly, J. P. (1983). Tropical forest ecosystems: identifying differences, seeking similarities. *Nature and Resources*, **XIX(1)**, 2–19.

Hall, A. E., Cannel, G. H. & Lawton, H. W. (eds.) (1979). *Agriculture in Semi-arid Environments*. Berlin: Springer-Verlag.

Hall, A. L. (1978). *Drought and Irrigation in North East Brazil*. Cambridge: Cambridge University Press.

Hardin, B. H. (1968). The tragedy of the commons. *Science*, **162(3859)**, 1243–8.

Hare, F. K. (1977a). Connections between climate and desertification. *Environmental Conservation*, **4(2)**, 81–90.

Hare, F. K. (1977b). Climate and desertification. In *Desertification: its causes and consequences*, ed. UN, pp. 63–167. Oxford: Pergamon Press.

Hare, F. K. (1979). Climatic variation and variability: empirical evidence from meteorological and sources. In *Proceedings of the World Climatic Conference, Geneva, 12–23 February, 1979* (WMO Publication 537). ed. WMO, pp. 51–87. Geneva: World Meteorological Organization.

Harlin, J. M. & Berardi, G. M. (eds.) (1987). *Agricultural Soil, Loss: processes, policies and prospects*. Boulder: Westview Press.

Harris, D. R. (ed.) (1980). *Human Ecology in Savanna Environments*. London: Academic Press.

Harris, L. D. (1984a). *The Fragmented Forest: island biogeographic theory and the preservation of biotic diversity*. Chicago: University of Chicago Press.

Harris, L. D. (1984b). The fragmented forest. Island biogeography: fact or fiction? *Journal of Biogeography*, **7(3)**, 209–35.

Harrison, J., Miller, K. & McNeely, J. (1982). The world coverage of protected areas: development goals and environmental needs. *Ambio*, **XI(5)**, 238–45.

Harrison, P. (1987a). *The Greening of Africa: breaking through in the battle for land and food*. London: Paladin Grafton Books.

Harrison, P. (1987b). A tale of two stoves. *New Scientist*, **114(1562)**, 40–3.

Harrison, P. (1987c). Trees for Africa. *New Scientist*, **114(1560)**, 54–7.

Harwell, M. A. & Hutchinson, T. C. (1985). *Environmental Consequences of Nuclear War, volume II: ecological and agricultural effects*. SCOPE 28. Chichester: John Wiley and Sons.

Hawkes, J. G. (ed.) (1978). *Conservation and Agriculture*. London: Duckworth.

Heathcote, R. L. (1980). *Perception of Desertification*. Tokyo: UN University.

Heathcote, R. L. (1983). *The Arid Lands: their use and abuse*, London: Longman.

Hecht, J. (1988). America in peril from the sea. *New Scientist*, **118(1616)**, 54–9.

Hecht, S. B. (1985). Environment, development and politics: capital accumulation and the livestock sector in Eastern Amazonia. *World Development*, **13(6)**, 663–84.

Heckman, J. (1985). Culture and the environment on the Cape Verde Islands. *Environmental Management*, **9(2)**, 141–50.

Hekstra, G. P. (1986). Will climatic change flood the Netherlands? Effects on agriculture, land use and well-being. *Ambio*, **XV(6)**, 316–26.

Hekstra, G. P. (1989). Global warming and rising sea levels: the policy implications. *The Ecologist*, **19(1)**, 4–15.

Hicks, B. B. (ed.) (1984). *Deposition Both Wet and Dry* (Acid Precipitation Series, vol. 4). Oxford: Butterworth.

Higgins, G. M., *et al.* (1982). *Potential Population Supporting Capacities of Lands in the Developing World*. Rome: FAO.

Higgins, G. M. (1988). *Soil Degradation and its Control in Africa*. Paper to First All-African Soil Science Conference, Kampala, Uganda 5–10 December, 1988 (15 pp.). Kampala: University of Kampala (mimeo.).

Higgins, R. (1980). *The Seventh Enemy: the human factor in the global crisis*. London: Pan Books.

Higgs, A. J. (1981). Island biogeography theory and nature reserve design. *Journal of Biogeography*, **8(1)**, 17–24.

Hill, A. R. (1987). Ecosystem stability: some recent perspectives. *Progress in Physical Geography*, **11(3)**, 315–33.

Hilton, K. J. (ed.) (1967). *The Lower Swansea Valley Project*. London: Longman.

Hindley, K. (1987). How mountains of sand carry the Sahara south. *The Times*, 24/11/87, p. 16.

Hinrichsen, D. (1986). Multiple pollutants and forest decline. *Ambio*, **XV(5)**, 258–65.

Hirsch, P. (1987). Deforestation and development in Thailand. *Singapore Journal of Tropical Geography*, **8(2)**, 128–38.

Holdgate, M. W. (1970). *Antarctic Ecology*, vol. 2. London: Academic Press.

Holdgate, M. W., Kassas, M. & White, G. F. (eds.) (1982). *The World Environment 1972–82*. (UNEP Report). Dublin: Tycooly International.

Holdgate, M. W. & Woodman, M. J. (1976). *The Breakdown and Restoration of Ecosystems*. New York: Plenum Press.

Holland, P. G. (1986). Mallee vegetation: steady state or successional? *Australian Geographer*, **1792**, 113–20.

Holland, P. G. & Olson, S. (1989). Introduced versus native plants in austral forests. *Progress in Physical Geography*, **13(2)**, 260–94.

Holling, C. C. (1973). Resilience and stability of ecological systems. *Annual Review of Ecology and Systematics*, **4**, 1–23.

Holmes, J. W. & Talsma, T. (eds.) (1981). *Land and Stream Salinity* Developments in Agricultural Engineering vol. 2). Amsterdam: Elsevier.

Homewood, K. & Rodgers, W. A. (1987). Pastoralism, conservation and the overgrazing controversy. In *Conservation in Africa: people, policies and practice*, eds. D. Anderson & R. Grove, pp. 111–28. Cambridge: Cambridge University Press.

Horowitz, M. M. & Little, P. D. (1987). African pastoralism and poverty: some implications for drought and famine. In *Drought and Hunger in Africa: denying famine a future*, ed. M. H. Glantz, pp. 59–82. London: Cambridge University Press.

Houghton, R. A. & Woodell, G. M. (1989). Global climatic change. *Scientific American*, **260(4)**, 18–26.

Howell, P., Lock, M. & Cobb, S. (1988). *The Jonglei Canal: impacts and opportunities*. Cambridge: Cambridge University Press.

Hudson, N. (1981). *Soil Conservation*. London: Batsford.

Hudson, N. (1987a). Limiting degradation caused by soil erosion. In *Land Transformation in Agriculture*, eds. M. G. Wolman & F. G. Fournier, pp. 153–70. Chichester: John Wiley and Sons.

Hudson, N. (1987b). The art of conservation. *SPLASH: Newsletter for SADCC Soil and Water Conservation and Land Utilization Programme (Lesotho)*, **3(3)**, pp. 4, 22–3.

Huggett, R. J. (1988). Terrestrial catastrophism, causes and effects. *Progress in Physical Geography*, **12(4)**, 509–32.

Huggett, R. J. (1989). Superwaves and superfloods: the bombardment hypothesis and geomorphology. *Earth Surface Processes & Landforms*, **14(5)**, 433–42.

Hulme, M. (1989). Is environmental degradation causing drought in the Sahel? An assessment from recent empirical research. *Geography*, **74(1)**, 38–46.

Huntington, E. (1915). *Civilization and Climate*. New Haven: Yale University Press.

Hurst, P. (1989). *Rainforest Politics: the destruction of forests in South East Asia*. London: Zed Press.

Hutchings, P. & Saenger, P. (1987). *Ecology of Mangroves*. St. Lucia (Australia): University of Queensland Press.

Hutchinson, T. C. & Meema, K. M. (eds.) (1987). *Effects of Atmospheric Pollutants on Forests, Wetlands and Agricultural Ecosystems*, Berlin: Springer-Verlag.

Hutnik, R. & Davis, G. (eds.) (1973). *Ecology and Reclamation of Degraded Land*, vols. 1 and 2. New York: Gordon and Breach.

Hyndman, D. (1988). Ok Tedi: New Guinea's disaster mine. *The Ecologist*, **18(1)**, 24–9.

Ichikawa, M. (1983). Desertification in the Brazilian Northeast. *Special Publication, University of Hiroshima Research and Sources Unit for Regional Geography*, **14**, 133–44.

Idso, S. B. (1985). The search for global CO_2 etc. Greenhouse effects. *Environmental Conservation*, **12(1)**, 29–35.

IIASA. (1989). *IIASA Options*, Sept., 1989. Laxenberg: International Institute for Applied Systems Analysis.

Immler, H. (1986). How Adam Smith valued nature. *Development: seeds of change*, **3**, 45–9.

Independent Commission on International Development Issues. (1980). *North–South: a programme for survival* (the 'Brandt Report'). London: Pan Books.

Independent Commission on International Humanitarian Issues. (1986a). *The Encroaching Desert: the consequences of human failure*. London: Zed Books.

Independent Commission on International Humanitarian Issues. (1986b). *The Vanishing Forest: the human consequences of deforestation*. London: Zed Books.

International Society of Soil Science., Association Internationale de là Science ou Sol., International Bodenkundliche Gesellschaft. & Sociedad International de la Ciencia del Suelo. (1988). *Proceedings of the First Regional Workshop on a Global Soils and Terrain Digital Database and Global Assessment of Soil Degradation (SOTER Report 3), 20–25 March, 1988, Montivideo (Uruguay)*. Wageningen (Netherlands): ISSS.

IUCN. (1975a). *Ecological Guidelines for Development in the American Humid Tropics* (Proceedings of an International Meeting, Caracas, Venezuela, 20–22 Feb., 1974: IUCN Publications New Series No. 31). Morges (Switzerland): IUCN.

IUCN. (1975b). *The Use of Ecological Guidelines for Development in the Tropical Forest Areas of South East Asia*. (Proceedings of a Meeting held at Bandung, Indonesia 29th May – 1st June, 1974 – IUCN Publications New Series No. 32). Morges (Switzerland): IUCN.

IUCN. (1986). *The IUCN Sahel Report: a long-term strategy for environmental rehabilitation* (Report of the IUCN Task Force on the Sahel and other drought-affected regions of Africa). Gland (Switzerland): International Union for the Conservation of Nature and Natural Resources.

IUCN. (1989). Special report: wetlands. *IUCN Bulletin*, **20(4–6)**, 9–20.

IUCN, UNEP. & WWF. (1980). *World Conservation Strategy: living resource conservation for sustainable development*. Gland: International Union for Conservation of Nature and Natural Resources.

Ives, J. D. & Messerli, B. (1989). *The Himalayan Dilemma: reconciling development and conservation*. London: Routledge.

Ives, J. D. & Pitt, D. C. (eds.) (1988). *Deforestation: social dynamics in watersheds and mountain ecosystems*. Routledge: London.

Jackson, W., Berry, W. & Colman, B. (eds.) (1984). *Meeting the Expectations of the Land: essays in sustainable agriculture and stewardship*. San Francisco: North Point Press.

Jago, N. (1987). The return of the eighth plague. *New Scientist* **114(1565)**, 47–51.

James, A. L. (1966). Stabilizing mine dumps with vegetation. *Endeavour*, **25(96)**, 154–7.

James, B. (1989). A harvest from the rain forest. *The Times*, 15/2/89, p. 12.

Jansen, E. & VanDobben, H. F. (1987). Is decline of *Cantharellus cibarius* in the Netherlands due to air pollution? *Ambio*, **XVI(4)**, 211–13.

Janzen, D. H. & Martin, P. S. (1982). Neotropical anachronisms: the fruits the Gomphotheres ate. *Science*, **215(4528)**, 19–27.

Johnson, A. (1987). Emergency action by the EEC to counter locust invasion. *The Times*, 5/11/87, p. 7.

Johnson, B. F. & Cowrie, J. (1969). The seed-fertilizer revolution and labour force absorption. *American Economic Review*, **LIX(4)**, p. 574.

Johnston, R. J. & Taylor, P. J. (ed.) (1986). *A World Crisis? Geographical perspectives*. Oxford: Basil Blackwell.

Johnstone, B. (1987). Japan saps the world's rain forests. *New Scientist*, **114(1554)**, p. 18.

Jones, A. K. (1990). Social Symbiosis: a Gaian critique of contemporary social theory. *The Ecologist*, **20(3)**, 108–13.

Jones, M. (1988). In search of the safe CFCs. *New Scientist*, **118(1614)**, 56–60.

Jordan, W. R. III., Gilpin, M. E. & Aber, J. D. (eds.) (1988). *Restoration Ecology: a synthetic approach*. Cambridge: Cambridge University Press.

Joss, P. J., Lynch, P. W. & Williams, O. B. (1986). *Rangelands: a resource under siege*. Cambridge: Cambridge University Press.

Journal of Bioscience (1985). **35(9)**: issue on the aftermath of nuclear war.

Joyce, C. (1988a). The tree that caused a riot. *New Scientist*, **117(1600)**, 454–9.

Joyce, C. (1988b). The Earth's lungs have an acid breath. *New Scientist*, **118(1617)**, p. 42.

Kardell, L., Steen, E. & Fabaio, A. (1986). Eucalyptus in Portugal – a threat or a promise? *Ambio*, **XV(1)**, 6–13.

Kartawinata, K., Adsoemarto, S., Riswan, S. & Vadya, A. P. (1981). The impact of man on tropical forest in Indonesia. *Ambio*, **X(2–3)**, 115–19.

Kassas, M. (1987). Drought and desertification. *Land Use Policy*, **4(4)**, 389–400.

Kayasseh, M. & Schenck, C. (1989). Reclamation of saline soils using calcium sulphate from the titanium industry. *Ambio*, **XVIII(2)**, 124–7.

Kebbede, G. & Jacob, M. J. (1988). Drought, famine and the political economy of environmental degradation in Ethiopia. *Geography*, **73(1)**, 65–70.

Kemf, E. (1988). The re-greening of Vietnam. *New Scientist*, **118(1618)**, 53–7.

Kent, M. (1987). Island biogeography and habitat conservation. *Progress in Physical Geography*, **11(1)**, 91–102.

Kent, R. B. (1989). The African honeybees in Peru: an insect invader and its impact on bee keeping. *Applied Geography*, **9(4)**, 237–57.

Kirkby, M. J. & Morgan, R. P. (eds.) (1980). *Soil Erosion*. Chichester: John Wiley and Sons.

Kirmse, R. D. & Norton, B. E. (1984). The potential of *Acacia albida* for desertification control and increased productivity in Chad. *Biological Conservation*, **29(2)**, 121–41.

Klein, R. M. & Perkins, T. D. (1987). Cascades of causes and effects in forest decline. *Ambio*, **XVI(2–3)**, 86–93.

Kovda, V. A. (1980). *Land Aridization and Drought control*. Boulder: Westview Press.

Kovda, V. A. (1982). To prevent aridization, combat salinity. *Environmental Conservation*, **9(3)**, 323–7.

Kovda, V. A. (1983). Loss of productive land due to salinization. *Ambio*, **XII(2)**, 91–3.

Kozlowski, T. T. & Ahlgren, C. E. (eds.) (1974). *Fire and Ecosystems*, New York: Academic Press.

Kunstadter, P., Bird, E. C. & Sabhasri, S. (eds.) (1986). *Man in the Mangroves: the socioeconomic situation of human settlement in mangrove forests.* Tokyo: UN University (E.86.111.A7).

Kuusela, K. (1987). Forest products – world situation. *Ambio*, **XVI(2–3)**, 80–5.

Lacaux, J. P., Servant, J. & Baudet, J. G. (1987). Acid rain in the tropical forests of West Africa. In *Acid Rain: scientific and technical advances*, eds. R. Perry, R. M. Harrison, J. N. Bell & J. N. Lester, pp. 264–9. London: Selper.

Laidler, K. (1989). A whole lot of mining going on. *New Scientist*, **123(1679)**, 49–51.

Lal, D. & Russel, E. W. (eds.) (1981). *Tropical Agricultural Hydrology: watershed management and landuse.* Chichester: John Wiley and Sons.

Lal, R., Hall, G. F. & Miller, F. P. (1989). Soil degradation: 1. basic processes. *Land Degradation & Rehabilitation*, **1(1)**, 51–69.

Lal, R., Sanchez, P. A. & Cummings, R. W. Jr. (eds.) (1986). *Land Clearing and Development in the Tropics.* Rotterdam: A. A. Balkema.

Lamb, H. H. (1982). *Climate, History and the Modern World*, London: Methuen.

Land, T. (1982). El Niño hold the key to long range forecsting. *The Times*, 26/11/87, p. 14.

Lateef, N. V. (1980). *Crisis in the Sahel: a case study in development cooperation.* Boulder: Westview Press.

Leach, G. & Mearns, R. (1989). *Beyond the Woodfuel Crisis: people, land and trees in Africa.* London: Earthscan Publications (IIED).

Leblond, B. & Guérin, L. (1988). *Soil Conservation: project design and implementation using labour-intensive techniques* (2nd edn). Geneva: International Labour Organization.

Lenihan, J. & Fletcher, W. W. (eds.) (1976). *Reclamation* (Environment and Man vol. 9: the biological environment). Glasgow: Blackie.

Lewin, R. (1984). Parks: how big is big enough? *Science*, **255(4662)**, 611–12.

Lewis, L. A. & Berry, L. (1988). *African Environments and Resources.* London: Allen and Unwin.

Lewis, L. A. & Coffey, W. J. (1985). The continuing deforestation of Haiti. *Ambio*, **XIV(3)**, 150–60.

Lewis, R. R. III. (1982). *Creation and Restoration of Coastal Plant Communities.* Boca Raton: CRC Press.

Lighttowlers, P. (1988). A poisoned landscape gathers no moss. *New Scientist*, **118(1611)**, 53–8.

Lindén, O. & Jernelöv, A. (1980). The mangrove swamps – an ecosystem in danger. *Ambio*, **IX(2)**, 81–8.

Linear, M. (1982). Gift of poison: the unacceptable face of development. *Ambio*, **XI(1)**, 2–8.

Linear, M. (1985). *Zapping the Third World: the disaster of development aid.* London: Zed Press.

Little, P. D. & Horowitz, M. M. (eds.) (1987). *Lands at Risk in the Third World: local perspectives.* Boulder: Westview Press.

Lloyd, P. (1988). The ice man drilleth. *The Times*, 13/4/88, p. 12.

Lockwood, J. G. (1984). The Southern Oscillation and El Niño. *Progress in Physical Geography*, **8(2)**, 102–10.

Lockwood, J. G. (1986). The causes of drought with particular reference to the Sahel. *Progress in Physical Geography*, **10(2)**, 111–19.

Lohmann, L. (1990). Commercial tree plantations in Thailand: deforestation by any other name. *The Ecologist*, **20(1)**, 9–17.

Lonsdale, M. & Braithwaite, R. (1988). The shrub that conquered the bush. *New Scientist*, **120(1634)**, 52–5.

Lovejoy, T., Bierregarrd, R. O., Rankin, J. & Schubart, H. O. (1983). Ecological dynamics of tropical forest fragments. In *Tropical Rain Forest: ecology and management*, eds. S. L. Sutton, T. C. Whitmore & A. C. Chadwick, pp. 377–84. Oxford: Basil Blackwell.

Lovelock, J. E. (1979). *Gaia: a new look at life on Earth.* Oxford: Oxford University Press.

Lovelock, J. E. (1990). Hands up for the Gaia hypothesis. *Nature, London*, **344(6262)**, 100–2.

Lovelock, J. E. & Whitfield, M. (1982). The lifespan of the biosphere. *Nature, London,* **296(5857),** 561–3.

Lowe, J. & Lewis, D. (1980). *The Economics of Environmental Management.* Oxford: Philip Allen Publishers.

Lowe, P., Cox, G., MacEwen, M., O'Riordan, T. & Winter, M. (1986). *Countryside conflicts: the politics of farming, forestry and conservation.* Aldershot: Gower Publishing.

Ludwig, J. A. (1987). Primary productivity in arid lands: myth and realities. *Journal of Arid Environments,* **13(1),** 1–7.

Mabbutt, J. A. (1984). A new global assessment of the status and trends of desertification. *Environmental Conservation,* **11(2),** 103–13.

Mabbutt, J. A. (1987). Implementation of the Plan of Action to Combat Desertification: progress since UNNCOD. *Land Use Policy,* **4(4),** 371–88.

Mabbutt, J. A. & Wilson, A. W. (1980). *Social and Environmental Aspects of Desertification.* Tokyo: United Nations University.

Macarthur, R. H. & Wilson, E. O. (1967). *The Theory of Island Biogeography.* Princetown (NJ): Princetown University Press.

Macdonald, I. A., Ortiz, L., Lawesson, J. E. & Bosconowak, J. (1988). The invasion of highlands in Galápagos by the red quinine-tree. *Chinchona succirubra. Environmental Conservation,* **15(3),** 215–20.

MacKenzie, D. (1984). Anybody want to save the ozone layer? *New Scientist,* **104(1430),** 10–11.

MacKenzie, D. (1987a). Can Ethiopia be saved? *New Scientist,* **115(1579),** 54–8.

MacKenzie, D. (1987b). Ethiopia's hand to the plough. *New Scientist,* **116(1579),** 52–5.

MacKenzie, D. (1988a). Uphill battle to save Filipino trees. *New Scientist,* **118(1619),** 42–3.

MacKenzie, D. (1988b). Coming soon: the next ozone hole. *New Scientist,* **119(1628),** 38–9.

MacKenzie, D. (1988c). Call to unleash dieldrin on locust plague. *New Scientist,* **119(1630),** p. 26.

MacNeill, J. (1989). Strategies for sustainable economic development. *Scientific American,* **261(3),** 105–11.

Mahaney, W. C. (1986). Environmental impact in the alpine and subalpine belts of Mount Kenya, East Africa. *Mountain Research and Development,* **6(3),** 247–60.

Mahar, D. J., Muscat, R., Kirchner, J. W., Ledec, G., Goodland, R. J. & Drake, J. M. (eds.) (1985). *Population Growth and Human Carrying Capacity: two perspectives* (World Bank Staff Working Papers No. 690). Washington DC: World Bank.

Malingreau, J. P., Stephens, G. & Fellows, L. (1985). Remote sensing of forest fires: Kalimantan and North Borneo in 1982–3. *Ambio,* **XIV(6),** 314–21.

Malingreau, J. P. & Tucker, C. J. (1988). Large-scale deforestation in the southeastern Amazon basin of Brazil. *Ambio,* **XVII(1),** 49–55.

Maltby, E. (1986). *Waterlogged Wealth: why waste the world's wet places?* London: Earthscan Publications (IIED).

Mani, M. S. & Giddings, L. E. (1980) *Ecology of Highlands* (Monographiae Biologicae, vol. 40). The Hague: Dr W. Junk.

Mann, R. (1987). Development and the Sahel disaster: the case of the Gambia. *The Ecologist,* **17(2),** 84–90.

Margaris, N. S. (1987). Desertification in the Aegean Islands. *Ekistics,* **323/324,** 132–6.

Markham, S. F. (1944). *Climate and Energy of Nations.* London: Oxford University Press.

Marsh, G. P. (1864). *Man and Nature: or physical geography as modified by human action.* New York: Charles Scribner.

Martin, R. B. & R. G. Klein. (1984). *Quaternary Extinctions.* Tucson: University of Arizona Press.

Mather, A. S. (1987). Global trends in forest resources. *Geography,* **72(1),** 1–15.

Matlock, W. G. (1981). *Realistic Planning for Arid Lands: natural resource limitations to agricultural development.* Chur: Harwood Academic Publishers.

McClosky, J. M. & Spalding, H. (1989). A reconnaissance-level inventory of the amount of wilderness remaining in the world. *Ambio,* **XVIII(4),** 221–7.

McCormick, J. (1988). *Acid Earth: the global threat of acid pollution.* London Earthscan Publications (IIED).

McNeely, J. A. (1989). How to pay for conserving biological diversity. *Ambio*, **XVIII(6)**, 303–18.

Meadows, D. H., Meadows, D. L., Randers, J. & Behrens, W. W. III. (1972). *The Limits to Growth: a report for the Club of Rome's project on the predicament of mankind.* London: Pan Books.

Meggers, B. J., Ayensu, E. S. & Duckworth, W. D. (eds.) (1973). *Tropical Forest Ecosystems in Africa and South America: a comparative review.* Washington DC: Smithsonian Institution Press.

Meigs, P. (1953). World distribution of arid and semi-arid homoclimates. In *Reviews of Research on Arid Zone Hydrology* (Arid Zone Programme 1), ed. UNESCO, pp. 203–10. Paris: UNESCO.

Middleton, N. (1988). *Atlas of Environmental Issues.* Oxford: Oxford University Press.

Milas, S. (1984). Population crisis and desertification in the Sudano-Sahelian region. *Environmental Conservation*, **11(2)**, 168–9.

Miller, R. I. (1978). Applying island biogeographic theory to an East African reserve. *Environmental Conservation*, **5(3)**, 191–5.

Milliman, J. D., Broadus, J. M. & Gable, F. (1989). Environmental and economic implications of rising sea-level and subsiding deltas: the Nile and Bengal examples. *Ambio*, **XVIII(6)**, 340–5.

Milne, A. (1988a). *Our Drowning World: population, pollution and future weather.* Bridport (UK): Avery Publishing Group.

Milne, R. (1988b). Corrosive clouds choke Britain's forests. *New Scientist*, **117(1604)**, p. 27.

Milne, R. (1989). Toxic time bomb ticks away beneath modern homes. *New Scientist*, **122(1670)**, p. 34.

Mitchell, B. (1979). *Geography and Resource Analysis.* London: Longman.

Mitsch, W. J. & Gosselink, J. G. (1986). *Wetlands.* New York: Van Nostrand Reinhold.

Mohnen, V. A. (1988). The challenge of acid rain. *Scientific American*, **259(2)**, 14–22.

Molion, L. C. (1989). The Amazonian forests and climatic stability. *The Ecologist*, **9(6)**, 211–13.

Mooley, D. A. & Pant, G. B. (1981). Droughts in India over the last 200 years, their socio-economic impacts and remedial measures for them. In *Climate and History*, eds. T. M. L. Wigley, *et al.*, pp. 465–78. Cambridge: Cambridge University Press.

Mooney, H. A. & Drake, J. A. (eds.) (1986). *Ecology of Biological Invasions of N. America and Hawaii.* Berlin: Springer-Verlag.

Mooney, H. A. & Drake, J. A. (1987). The ecology of biological invasions. *Environment*, **29(5)**, 10–15, 34–7.

Moore, P. D. (1975). Origin of blanket mires. *Nature*, **256(5516)**, p. 267.

Moore, P. D. & Bellamy, D. J. (1974). *Peatlands.* London: Elek Science.

Moran, E. F. (1987). Monitoring fertility degradation of agricultural lands in the lowland tropics. In *Lands at Risk in the Third World: local-level perspectives*, eds. P. D. Little & M. M. Horowitz (with A. E. Nyerges), pp. 69–91. Boulder: Westview.

Morgan, W. B. & Moss, R. P. (1988). *Fuelwood and Rural Energy Production in the Humid Tropics.* London: Tycooly International Publications.

Mortimore, M. J. (1988). Desertification and resilience in semi-arid West Africa. *Geography*, **73(1)**, 61–4.

Mortimore, M. J. (1989). *Adapting to Drought: farmers, famines and desertification in West Africa.* Cambridge: Cambridge University Press.

Moser, P. & Moser, W. (1986). Reflections on the MAB–6 Obergurgl Project and tourism in an alpine environment. *Mountain Research and Development*, **6(2)**, 101–18.

Mosiman, T. (1985). Geo-ecological impacts of ski piste contruction in the Swiss Alps. *Applied Geography*, **5(1)**, 29–37.

Moss, R. P. & Morgan, W. B. (1981). *Fuelwood and Rural Energy: production and supply in the humid tropics.* Dublin: Tycooly International Publications.

Mould, R. F. (1988). *Chernobyl: the real story*. Oxford: Pergamon Press.

Müller-Hohenstein, K. (ed.) (1975). *International Workshop on the Development of Mountain Environments: an interdisciplinary approach for future strategy* (German Foundation for International Development). Munich: Food and Agriculture Development Centre.

Munn, R. E. (1988). Towards sustainable development: an environmental perspective. Paper presented to Conference on Environment and Development, Milan, 24–26 March, 1988 (mimeo.).

Munslow, B., Katerere, Y., Ferf, A. & O'Keefe, P. (1988). *The Fuelwood Trap: a study of the SADCC region*. London: Earthscan Publications (IIED).

Myers, N. (1980). *Conservation of Tropical Moist Forest (Report for Committee on Research Priorities in Tropical Biology of the National Research Council)*. Washington DC: National Academy of Sciences.

Myers, N. (1985a). *The Gaia Atlas of Planet Management: For today's caretakers of tomorrow's world*. London: Pan Books.

Myers, N. (1985b). *The Primary Source: tropical forests and our future*. London: Norton Publishers.

Myers, N. (1986a). Economics and ecology in the international arena: the phenomenon of 'linked linkages'. *Ambio*, **XV(5)**, 296–300.

Myers, N. (1986b). The environmental basis of sustainable development. *The Annals of Regional Science*, **21** (special edition), 33–4.

Myers, N. (1987a). Book review: Tropical Forest Agriculture. *Forest Ecology and Management*, **20**, 321–4.

Myers, N. (1987b). Seeing the wood for the trees. *Nature*, **330(6145)**, p. 286.

Myers, N. (1987c). Emergent aspects of environment: a creative challenge. *The Environmentalist*, **7(3)**, 163–74.

Myers, N. (1988). Tropical deforestation and remote sensing. *Forest Ecology and Management*, **23**, 215–25.

Nicholson, S. (1983). The chronology of sub-Saharan Africa. In *Environmental Change in the West African Sahel*. ed. National Academy of Sciences, pp. 71–92. Washington DC: National Academy of Sciences.

Nortcliff, S. (1986). Soil loss estimation. *Progress in Physical Geography*, **10(3)**, 249–55.

Nour, J., Press, M., Stewart, G. & Tuohy, J. (1986) Africa in the grip of witchweed. *New Scientist*, **109(1490)**, 44–8.

Nye, P. H. & Greenland, D. J. (1960). *Soil Under Shifting Cultivation*. Harpenden: Commonwealth Agricultural Bureau.

OECD. (1977). *Strategy and Programme for Drought Control and Development in the Sahel*. Paris: OECD.

Olson, S. (1987). Red destinies: the landscape of environmental risk in Madagascar. *Human Ecology*, **15(1)**, 67–89.

Olsson, K. (1984). Long-term changes in the woody vegetation in N. Kordofan, the Sudan. A study with the emphasis on *Acacia senegal. Lunds Universitets Natur Geographiska Institution, rapporter och notiser, 60,* Lund: University of Lund.

Olsson, L. (1983). Desertification or climate? Investigation regarding the relationship between land degradation and climate in the Central Sudan. *Lund Studies in Geography Series A. Physical Geography, No. 60*, Lund: University of Lund.

O'Neill, B. (1989). Nuclear safety after Chernobyl. *New Scientist*, **122(1670)**, 59–65.

Ong, Jin Eong. (1982). Mangroves and aquaculture in Malaysia. *Ambio*, **XI(5)**, 252–7.

Onimode, B. (1988). *A Policital Economy of the African Crisis*. London: Zed Press.

Onyeanusi, A. E. (1986). Measurement of impact of tourist off-road driving on grasslands in Masi Mara National Reserve, Kenya: a simulation approach. *Environmental Conservation*, **13(4)**, 325-9.

O'Riordin, T. (1976). *Environmentalism*. London: Pion.

Otterman, L. (1974). Baring high-albedo soils by overgrazing a hypothesized desertification mechanism. *Science*, **186(4163)**, 531–53.

Oxenham, J. R. (1966). *Reclaiming Derelict Land*. London: Faber and Faber.

Pádua, M. T. & Quintáo, A. T. (1982). Parks and biological reserves in the Brazilian Amazon. *Ambio*, **XI(5)**, 309–14.

Pain, S. (1987). Funding uncertainties threaten wetlands pact. *New Scientist*, **114(1652)**, p. 24.

Pain, S. (1988). No escape from the global greenhouse. *New Scientist*. **120(1638)**, 38–43.

Pain, S. (1990). Coral reefs will thrive in the greenhouse. *New Scientist*, **125(1706)**, p. 30.

Parikh, J. K. (ed.) (1988). *Sustainable Development in Agriculture*. Dordrecht: Martinus Nijhoff.

Park, C. C. (1980). *Ecology and Environmental Management*. Boulder: Westview Press.

Park, C. C. (1987). *Acid Rain: rhetoric and reality*. London: Methuen.

Parry, M. L., Carter, T. R. & Konijn, N. T. (eds.) (1988a). *The Impact of Climatic Variations on Agriculture (vol. 1 Assessments in Cool Temperate and Cold Regions)*. Dordrecht: Kluwer Academic Publishers.

Parry, M. L., Carter, T. R. & Konijn, N. T. (eds.) (1988b). *The Impact of Climatic Variations on Agriculture (vol. 2 Assessments in Semi Arid Regions)*. Dordrecht: Kluwer Academic Publishers.

Parsons, J. P. (1975). The changing nature of New World tropical forests since European colonization. In *Ecological Guidelines for Development in the American Humid Tropics*, ed. IUCN, pp. 28–37. Morges: IUCN.

Parsons, P. A. (1989) Conservation and global warming: a problem in biological adaption to stress. *Ambio*, **XVIII(6)**, 322–5.

Pearce, D., Markandya, A. & Barbier, E. B. (1989). *Blueprint for a Green Economy*. London: Earthscan Publications (IIED).

Pearce, F. (1986a). *Acid Rain*. Harmondsworth: Penguin.

Pearce, F. (1986b). Are cows killing Britain's trees? *New Scientist*, **112(1531)**, p. 20.

Pearce. F. (1987a). Banishing the salt of the Earth. *New Scientist*. **114(1564)**, 53–6.

Pearce. F. (1987b). Acid Rain. *New Scientist*, **116(1585)**, supplement.

Pearce. F. (1988a). Gaia: a revolution comes of age. *New Scientist*, **117(1604)**, 32–3.

Pearce, F. (1988b). Ozone threat spreads from the Arctic. *New Scientist*, **118(1605)**, 22–3.

Pearce, F. (1989a). How economic growth can be greenhouse-friendly. *New Scientist*, **123(1672)**, p. 34.

Pearce, F. (1989b). Kill or cure? remedies for the rainforest. *New Scientist*, **123(1682)**, 40–3.

Pearce, F. (1989c). Methane: the hidden greenhouse gas. *New Scientist*, **122(1663)**, 37–41.

Pearce, F. (1989d). Methane locked in permafrost may hold the key to global warming. *New Scientist*, **121(1654)**, p. 28.

Pearce, F. & Anderson, I. (1989). Is there an ozone hole over the North Pole? *New Scientist*, **121(1653)**, 32–3.

Pecsi, M. (1987). International Loess Symposium in China, Xian, Shaanzi Province, October 5–16, 1985. *Geojournal*, **14(4)**, 435–45.

Pereira, H. C. (1973). *Land Use and Water Resources*. Cambridge: Cambridge University Press.

Pereira, J. & Thomas, A. (1985). This horrible natural experiment. *New Scientist*, **106(1452)**, 34–8.

Perry, R., Harrison, R. M., Bell, J. N. & Lester, J. N. (eds.) (1987). *Acid Rain: scientific and technical advances*. London: Selper.

Pimm, S. L. (1984). The complexity and stability of ecosystems. *Nature*, **307(5949)**, 321–6.

Pollard, E., Hooper, M. D. & Moore, N. W. (1974). *Hedges*, London: Collins.

Porritt, J. (1988). Education for life on Earth. *Geography*, **73(1)**, 1–8.

Prance, G. T. & Lovejoy, T. E. (eds.) (1985). *Key Environments: Amazonia*. Oxford: Pergamon Press (for IUCN).

Pratt, C. (1965). Chemical fertilizers. *Scientific American*, **212(1)**, 67–72.

Price, M. F. (1985). Impacts of recreational activities on alpine vegetation in Western North America. *Mountain Research and Development*, **5(3)**, 263–77.

Price, M. F. (1987). Tourism and forestry in the Swiss Alps: parasitism or symbiosis? *Mountain Research and Development*, **7(1)**, 1–12.

Prior, J. & Tuohy, J. (1987). Fuel for Africa's fires. *New Scientist*, **115 (1571)**, 48–51.

Proctor, J. (1984). Tropical forest conservation. *Progress in Physical Geography*, **8(3)**, 433–449.

Pye, K. (1984) Loess. *Progress in Physical Geography*, **8(3)**, 176–217.

Ramade, F. (1984). *Ecology of Natural Resources* (translated from the French by W. J. Duffin). Chichester: John Wiley and Sons.

Rambler, M. B., Margulis, L. & Fester, R. (eds.) (1989). *Global Ecology: towards a science of the biosphere*. London: Academic Press.

Randrianarijaona, P. (1983). The erosion of Madagascar. *Ambio*, **XII(6)**, 308–11.

Rapp, A. (1976). Needs of environmental monitoring for desert encroachment control. In *Can Desert Encroachment be Stopped? a study with emphasis on Africa* (Ecological Bulletins, No. 24). eds. A. Rapp., H. N. Le Houérou, & B. Lundholm, pp. 231-6. Stockholm: Swedish Natural Research Council.

Rapp, A., Le Houérou, H. N. & Lundholm, B. (eds.) (1976). *Can Desert Encroachment be Stopped?: a study with the emphasis on Africa*, (Ecological Bulletins No. 24). Stockholm: Swedish Natural Sciences Coucil.

Redclift, M. (1984). *Development and the Environmental Crisis: red or green alternatives?*. London: Methuen.

Redclift, M. (1987). *Sustainable Development: exploring the contradictions*. London: Methuen.

Rees, J. (1985). *Natural Resources: allocation, economics and policy*. London: Methuen.

Rees, W. E. (1990). The ecology of sustainable development. *The Ecologist*, **20(1)**, 18–24.

Reganold, J. (1989). Farming's organic future. *New Scientist*, **122(1668)**, 49–52.

Reining, P. (ed.) (1978). *Handbook on Desertification Indicators* (based on the Science Association's 1976 Nairobi Seminar on Desertification). Washington DC: American Association for the Advancement of Science.

Repetto, R. (1986). Soil loss and population pressure in Java. *Ambio*, **XV(1)**, 14–18.

Repetto, R. (1987). Creating incentives for sustainable forest development. *Ambio*, **XVII(1)**, 49–55.

Repetto, R. & Gillis, M. (1988). *Public Policies and the Misuse of Forest Resources*. Cambridge: Cambridge University Press.

Reynolds, E. R. & Thompson, F. B. (eds.) (1989). *Forests, Climate and Hydrology. Regional impacts*. Tokyo: United Nations University.

Richards, K. (1989). All gas and garbage. *New Scientist*, **122(1667)**, 38–41.

Richards, P. W. (1973). The tropical rain forest. *Scientific American*, **229(6)**, 58–67.

Richards, P. W. (1984). The forests of South Vietnam in 1971–72: a personal account. *Environmental Conservation*, **11(2)**, 147–53.

Riddell, R. (1981). *Ecodevelopment: economics, ecology and development: an alternative to growth imperative models*. Farnborough: Gower Publishing.

Rind, D. (1984). Global climatic change in the 21st century. *Ambio*, **XIII(3)**, 148–51.

Roan, S. (1989). *Ozone Crisis: the 15 year evolution of a sudden global emergency*. Chichester: John Wiley and Sons.

Roberts, B. (1987). Australian land degradation and its control. *Ambio*, **XVI(5)**, 272–6.

Roberts, L. (1989). Global warming: blaming the sun. *Science*, **240(4933)**, 992–3.

Roberts, N. (1989). *The Holocene: an environmental history*. Oxford: Basil Blackwell.

Rodhe, H. (1989). Acidification in a global perspective. *Ambio*, **XVIII(3)**, 155–60.

Rodhe, H. & Herrera, R. (eds.) (1988). *Acidification in Tropical Countries* (SCOPE 36). Chichester: John Wiley and Sons.

Rosenberg, D. B. & Freedman, S. M. (1984). Application of a model of ecological succession to conservation and land-use management. *Environmental Conservation*, **11(4)**, 323–30.

Rosenberg, N. J. (ed.) (1978). *North American Droughts* (AAAS Selected Symposia Series No. 15). Boulder: Westview Press.

Rowland, F. S. (1988). Chloroflourocarbons, stratospheric ozone, and the Antarctic 'ozone hole'. *Environmental Conservation*, **15(2)**, 101–15.

REFERENCES   Ruddle, K. (1987). The impact of wetland reclamation. In *Land Transformation i*
Agriculture (SCOPE 32), eds. M. G. Wolman & F G. Fournier, pp. 171–202
Chichester: John Wiley and Sons.

Ruddle, K. & Manshard, W. (1981). *Renewable Natural Resources and th*
Environment: pressing problems in the developing world. Dublin: Tycooly Intern
ational Publishing.

Russel, N. (1988). Dust gets in your eyes: comparisons between the America
Drought and the Dust Bowl of the 1930s are misleading. *New Scientist*
119(1625), p. 61.

Russel Jones, R. & Wigley, T. (1989). *Ozone Depletion: health and environmenta*
consequences. Chichester: John Wiley and Sons.

Saarinen, T. F. (1966). *Perception of the Drought Hazard on the Great Plains*
Department of Geography Research Paper No. 106p. Chicago: University o
Chicago.

Sage, B (1979a). New Zealand forests in danger. *New Scientist*, **82(1149)**, 31–3

Sage, B. (1979b). Hawaii – paradise lost? *New Scientist*, **84(1185)**, 682–5.

Salatti, E., Lovejoy, T. E. & Vose, P. B. (1983). Precipitation and water cyclin
in tropical rain forests with special reference to the Amazon Basin. *Th*
Environmentalist, **39(1)**, 67–72.

Sanbach, F. (1980). *Environment Ideology and Policy.* Oxford: Blackwell.

Sanders, D. & Hobbs, R. (1989). Corridors for conservation. *New Scientist*
121(1649), 63–7.

Sandford, S. (1983). *Managing Pastoral Development in the Third World.* Chichester
John Wiley and Sons.

San Pietro, A. (ed.) (1982). *Biosaline Research: a look at the future.* New York
Plenum Press.

Sattaur, O. (1987). Trees for the people. *New Scientist*, **115(1577)**, 58–62.

Sayer, J. & McNeely, J. (1984). IUCN, WWF and wetlands. *IUCN Bulletin*
15(4–6), p. 46.

Schiotz, A. (1989). Conserving biological diversity: who is responsible? *Ambio*
XVIII(8), 454–7.

Schneider, S. (1989). *Global Warming: are we entering the greenhouse century?* London
Random House (for Sierra Club).

Schove, D. J. (1977). African droughts and the specturm of time. In *Drought i*
Africa 2, eds. D. Dalby., R. J. Harrison-Church & F. Bezzaz, pp. 38–53.
London: International African Institute.

Schumacher, E. F. (1974). *Small is Beautiful: a study of economics as if people mattered.*
London: Sphere Books.

SCOPE. (1983). *The Role of Fire in Northern Circumpolar Ecosystems.* (SCOPE
Report No. 18). Chichester: John Wiley and Sons.

Seneviratne, G. (1979). Salvation for salty soils. *Development Forum*, **VII(2)**, p. 5

Shiva, V. & Bandyopadhyay, J. (1986). The evolution, structure, and impact of
the Chipko Movement. *Mountain Research and Development*, **6(2)**, 133–142.

Shiva, V. & Bandyopadhyay, J. (1988). The Chipko Movement. In *Deforestation:*
social dynamics in watershed and mountain ecosystems. eds. J. Ives & D. C. Pitt.,
pp. 224–41. London: Routledge.

Shyamsunder, S. & Parameswarappa, S. (1987). Forestry in India - the foresters
view. *Ambio*, **XVI(6)**, 332–7.

Silverman, K. (ed.) (1986). *Benjamin Franklin – autobiography and other writings.*
Harmondsworth: Penguin Books.

Simberloff, D. S. & Abele, L. G. (1976). Island biogeography theory and
conservation practice. *Science*, **191(4224)**, 285–6.

Simmons, I. G. (1974). *The Ecology of Natural Resources.* London: Edward
Arnold.

Simon, J. L. (1981). *The Ultimate Resource.* Oxford: Martin Robertson.

Simon, J. L. & Kahn, H. (eds.) (1984). *The Resourceful Earth: a response to Global*
2000, Oxford: Blackwell.

Simons, P. (1988a). Costa Rica's forests are reborn. *New Scientist*, **120(1635)**
43–7.

Simons, P. (1988b). The day of the rhododendron. *New Scientist*, **119(1620)**,
50–5.

Simons, P. (1988c). Après ski le deluge. *New Scientist*, **119(1605)**, 49–52.

Simons, P. (1989). Nobody loves a canal with no water. *New Scientist*, **124(1685)**,
  48–52.

Sinclair, A. R. & Fryxell, J. M. (1985). The Sahel of Africa: ecology of a disaster.
  Canadian Journal of Zoology, **63(5)**, 987–94.

Sinclair, L. (1985). International Task Force plans to reverse tropical deforestation. *Ambio*, **XIV(6)**, 352–3.

Singh, G., Joshi, J. D., Chapra, S. K. & Singh, A. B. (1974). Late Quaternary
  history of vegetation and climate of the Rajasthan desert, India. *Philosophical
  Transactions of the Royal Society*, B., **267**, 467–501.

Singh, S. P., Ralhan, P. K. & Tenari, J. C. (1985). Stability of Himalayan climax
  oak forests in view of resilience hypothesis. *Environmental Conservation*, **12(1)**,
  73–5.

Sjörs, H. (1980). Peat on Earth: multiple use or conservation? *Ambio*, **IX(6)**,
  303–8.

Skarby, L. & Seldon, G. (1984) The effects of ozone on crops and forests. *Ambio*,
  XIII(2), 68–72.

Skiba, U. & Cresser, M. (1988). The ecological significance of increasing
  atmospheric carbon dioxide. *Endeavour*, new series. **2(3)**, 143–7.

Smiet, F. (1987). Tropical watershed forestry under attack. *Ambio*, **XVI(2–3)**,
  156–8.

Smil, V. (1984). *The Bad Earth: environmental degradation in China*. London: Zed
  Books.

Smith, B. & Baillie, C. (1985). Erosion in the savannas. *Geographical Magazine*,
  LVII(3), 137–41.

Smith, C. W. & Best, S. (1989). *Electromagnetic Man: health and hazard in the
  electrical environment*. London: J. M. Dent and Sons.

Spooner, B. (1986). The significance of desertification. In *Global Aspects of Food
  Production*. eds. M. S. Swaminathan & S. K. Sinha, pp. 337–57. London:
  Tycooly International Publishing.

Spooner, B. & Mann, H. S. (eds.) (1982). *Desertification and Development: dryland
  ecology in social perspective*. London: Academic Press.

Stanford Biology Study Group. (1971). Destruction of Indochina. In *Global
  Ecology: readings towards a rational strategy for man*, eds. J. P. Holdren & P. R.
  Ehrlich, pp. 146–54 New York: Harcourt Brace Jovanovich.

Stanton, W. (1989). Bleak prospects for limestone. *New Scientist*, **122(1664)**,
  56–60.

Stebbing, E. P. (1935). The encroaching Sahara: the threat to the West African
  colonies. *The Geographical Journal*, **85(4)**, 506–24.

Steinlin, H. J. (1982). Monitoring the world's tropical forests. *Unasylva*,
  34(No.137), 2–8.

Stevenson, G. G. (1989). The production, distribution and consumption of
  fuelwood in Haiti. *The Journal of Developing Areas*, **24(1)**, 59–76.

Stoddart, D. R. & Pethick, J. S. (1984). Environmental hazard and coastal
  reclamation problems and prospects in Bangladesh. In *Understanding Green
  Revolutions: agrarian change and development planning in South Asia*, eds. T. P.
  Bayliss-Smith & Sudhir Wanmali, pp. 339–61. Cambridge: Cambridge
  University Press.

Stone, C. P. & Loope, L. L. (1987). Reducing negative effects of introduced
  animals on native biotas in Hawaii: what is being done, what needs doing, and
  the role of national parks. *Environmental Conservation*, **14(3)**, 245–58.

Stonehouse, B. (1989). *Polar Ecology*. Oxford: Blackwell.

Street, P. (1987). Introduction. *Land Use Policy*, (special issue), **4(4)**, p. 362.

Svobida, L. (1986). *Farming the Dust Bowl: a first-hand account from Kansas* (first
  published as 'An Empire of Dust' in 1940 by Caxton Printers, USA). Kansas:
  University Press of Kansas.

Swift, J. (1977). Sahelian pastoralists: underdevelopment, desertification and
  famine. *Annual Review of Anthropology*, **6**, 457–78.

Sykes, M. (1987). Bracken: friend or foe? *The Ecologist*, **17(6)**, 241–2.

Szabolcs, I. (ed.) (1971). *European Solonetz Soils and their Reclamation*. Budapest:
  Akadémiai Kiadó.

Szabolcs, I. (1974). *Salt Affected Soils in Europe*. Budapest: Martinus Nijhoff (the
  Hague) and the Research Institute for Soil Science and Agricultural
  Chemistry of the Hungarian Academy of Sciences.

Szabolcs, I. (1988). The salinization potential of European soils. Paper presented to IIASA Workshop on Land Use Changes in Europe. Warsaw, 5–9 Sept. 1988. (mimeo.), 15 pp. Laxenberg: IIASA.

Tabatabai, A. M. (1985). Effects of acid rain on soils. *CRC Critical Reviews i Environmental Control*, **15**, 65–75.

Tansley, A. G. (1920). The classification of vegetation and the concept o development. *Journal of Ecology*, **8(2)**, 118–49.

Tawney, R. H. (1954). *Religion and the Base of Capitalism*. New York: Mento Books.

Taylor, J. (1979). The introduction of exotic plant and animal species into Britain. *The Biologist*, **26(5)**, 229–36.

Taylor, J. & Smith, R. (1980). Power in the peatlands. *New Scientist*, **88(1230)** 644–6.

Templet, P. H. & Meyer-Arendt, K. J. (1988). Louisiana wetland loss: a regiona water management approach to the problem. *Environmental Management* **12(2)**, 181–92.

The Economist, 6/12/86: 93–4.

The Environmentalist (1985). vol. 5(10) supplement issue on tropical forests.

Thirgood, J. V. (1981). *Man and the Mediterranean Forest: a history of resourc depletion*. London: Academic Press.

Thomas, W. L. Jr. *et al.* (1956). *Man's Role in Changing the Face of the Earth* Chicago: University of Chicago Press.

Thornes, J. B. (1985). The ecology of erosion. *Geography*, **70(3)**, 222–35.

Thornes, J. B. (1989). Solution to soil erosion. *New Scientist*, **122(1667)**, 45–9

Timberlake, L. (1985). *Africa in Crisis: the causes, the cures of environmenta bankruptcy*. London: Earthscan Publications (IIED).

Timberlake, L. (1988). Sustained hope for development. *New Scientist* **119(1620)**, 60–3.

Timmerman, P. (1986). Mythology and surprise in the sustainable developmen of the biosphere. In *Sustainable Development of the Biosphere*, eds. W. C. Clark & R. E. Munn, pp. 435–44. Cambridge: Cambridge University Press.

Tisdell, C. (1988). Sustainable development: differing perspectives of ecologists and economists, and relevance to LDCs. *World Development*, **16(3)**, 373–84

Titus, J. G. (1990). Greenhouse effect, sea level rise and land use. *Land Use Policy* **7(2)**, 138–54.

Todaro, M. P. (1981). *Economic Development in the Third World* (2nd edn.) London: Longman.

Tolba, M. K. (1982). *Development Without Destruction: evolving environmenta perceptions*. Dublin: Tycooly International Publishing.

Tolba, M. K. (1984). Harvest of dust. *Desertification Control Bulletin*, No. 10 (May 1984), p. 2, Nairobi: UNEP.

Tolba, M. K. (1987a). Ten years after UNCOD. *Land Use Policy*, **4(4)**, 363–70

Tolba, M. K. (1987b). *Sustainable Development: constraints and opportunities* London: Butterworths.

Tooley, M. J. (1987). Sea-levels. *Progress in Physical Geography*, **11(3)**, 292–9

Tooley, M. J. & Shennan, I. (eds.) (1987). *Sea-level Changes* (IBG Special Publications No. 20) Oxford: Basil Blackwell.

Troumbis, A. Y. (1987). Disturbance in Mediterranean islands: a demographic approach to changes in insular ecosystems. *Ekistics*, **323/324**, 127–31.

Turco, R. P., Toon, O. B., Ackerman, T. P., Pollack, J. B. & Sagan, C. (1983). Nuclear winter: global consequences of multiple nuclear explosions. *Science* **222(4630)**, 1283–92.

Tyler, G. (1984). The impact of heavy metal pollution on forests: a case study of Gusum, Sweden. *Ambio*, **XIII(1)**, 18–24.

UN. (ed.) (1977). *Desertification: its causes and consequences* (Compiled and edited by the Secretariat of the UN Conference on Desertification, Nairobi). Oxford: Pergamon Press.

UN Center on Transnational Corporations. (1985). *Environmental Aspects of the Activities of Transnational Corporations: a survey*. New York: UNCTC.

UNEP. (1987). *Environmental Data Report 1987*. Oxford: Blackwell.

UNEP. & Commonwealth of Australia. (1987). *Drylands Dilemma: a solution to the problem*. Canberra: Australian Government Publishing Service.

UNEP. & IUCN. (1988). *Coral Reefs of the World* (3 vols.). Cambridge: IUCN
Conservation Monitoring Centre.

UNESCO. (1975). *The Sahel: ecological approaches to land use*. (MAB Technical Notes), Paris: UNESCO.

UNESCO. (1977). *Development of Arid and Semi-Arid Lands: obstacles and prospects*. MAB Technical Note 6. Paris: UNESCO.

Usher, M. B. & Thompson, D. B. (eds.) (1988). *Ecological Change in the Uplands* (Special Publication No. 7 of the British Ecological Society). Oxford: Blackwell Scientific.

VanApeldoorn, G. J. (1981). *Perspectives on Drought and Famine in Nigeria*. London: George, Allen and Unwin.

Vannucci, M. (1988). The UNDP/UNESCO Mangrove Programme in Asia and the Pacific. *Ambio*, **XVII(3)**, 214–17.

Verstraete, M. M. (1983). Another look at desertification. In *Origin and Evolution of Deserts*, eds. S. G. Wells & D. R. Haragen, pp. 213–28. Albuquerque: University of New Mexico Press.

Vietmeyer, N. D. (1979). Tropical tree legumes: a front line against deforestation. *Ceres*, **12 (No. 5)**, 38–41.

Vines, B. (1987). Fire in the bush. *New Scientist*, **113(1549)**, 49–52.

Walker, B. H. (ed.) (1979). *The Management of Semi-Arid Ecosystems*. Amsterdam: Elsevier.

Walls, J. (1982). Desertification: toward a solution. *IUCN Bulletin* (April/May/June issue), p. 38.

Wallwork, K. L. (1974). *Derelict Land*. Newton Abbot: David and Charles.

Ward, B. & Dubos, R. (1972). *Only One Earth: the care and maintenance of a small planet*. Harmondsworth: Pelican Books.

Warren, A. (1986). Productivity, variability and sustainability as criteria of desertification. In *Desertification in Europe*, eds. R. Fantechi & N. S. Margaris, pp. 83–94. Dordrecht: D. Reidel Publishing.

Warren, A. & Maizels, J. (1977). Ecological change and desertification. In *Desertification: its causes and consequences*, ed. UN, pp. 169–260. Oxford: Pergamon Press.

Warrick, R. A. (1988). Carbon dioxide, climatic change and agriculture. *The Geographical Journal*, **154(2)**, 221–33.

Watts, D. (1966). *Man's Influence on the Vegetation of Barbados 1627 to 1800* (Occasional Papers in Geography No. 4). Hull: University of Hull.

Watts, D. (1987). *The West Indies: patterns of development, culture and environmental change since 1492*. Cambridge: Cambridge University Press.

Watts, M. J. (1989). The agrarian crisis in Africa: debating the crisis. *Progress in Human Geography*, **13(1)**, 1–41.

Watts, S. (1990). UN agency launches environmental warning system. *New Scientist*, **125(1707)**, p. 28.

Weber, F. R. & Stoney, C. (1989). *Reforestation in Arid Lands*. Arlington: Volunteers in Technical Assistance (1815 North Lynn Street, Arlington, Virginia 2209).

Weber, M. (1958). *The Protestant Ethic and the Spirit of Capitalism*. (English translation by Talbott Parsons). New York: Charles Scribner.

Webster, C. C. & Wilson, P. N. (1966). *Agriculture in the Tropics*. London: Longman.

Wellburn, A. (1988). *Air Pollution and Acid Rain: the global threat of acid pollution*. London: Earthscan Publications (IIED).

Wells, S. & Edwards, A. (1989). Gone with the waves. *New Scientist*, **124(1690)**, 47–51.

Wells, S. & Haragan, D. R. (eds.) (1983). *Origin and Evolution of Deserts*. Albuquerque: University of New Mexico Press.

Westing, A. H. (1984a). The remnants of war. *Ambio*, **XIII(1)**, 14–17.

Westing, A. H. (ed.) (1984b). *Environmental Warfare: a technological, legal and policy appraisal*. London: Taylor and Francis.

Westing, A. H. (1987). The ecological dimension of nuclear war. *Environmental Conservation*, **14(4)**, 293–306.

Westman, W. W. (1985). *Ecology, Impact Assessment and Environmental Planning*. New York: John Wiley and Sons.

REFERENCES   Westoby, J. (1987). *The Purpose of Forests: follies of development*. Oxford: Basil Blackwell.

Whitney, J. B. (1987). Impact of fuelwood use on environmental degradation in the Sudan. In *Lands at Risk in the Third World: local level perspectives*, eds. P. D. Little & M. M. Horrowitz, pp. 115–43. Boulder: Westview.

Wijkman, A. & Timberlake, L. (1985). Is the African drought an act of God or of man? *The Ecologist*, **15(2)**, 9–18.

Wilkie, T. (1988). Re-greening of the rainforests. *The Independent*, 8/8/88, p. 15.

Williams, M. (1989). Deforestation: past and present. *Progress in Human Geography*, **13(2)**, 176–208.

Williams, W. D. (1987). Salinization of rivers and streams: an important environmental hazard. *Ambio*, **XVI(5)**, 180–5.

Wilson, A., Bayfield, N. G. & Moyes, S. (1970). Research on human pressures on Scottish mountain tundra, soils, and animals. In *Productivity and Conservation in Northern Circumpolar Lands*, eds. W. J. Fuller & P. G. Kevan, pp. 256–66. Morges (Switzerland): International Union for the Conservation of Nature and Natural Resources.

Winkler, M. G. (1985). Environmental impacts of peat mining in the United States: documentation for wetland conservation. *Environmental Conservation*, **XII(4)**, 317–30.

Winstanley, D. (1983). Desert locust plagues. In *Origin and Evolution of Deserts*, eds. S. G. Wells & D. R. Harrigan, pp. 195–211. Albuquerque: University of New Mexico Press.

Winterbottom, R. & Hazlewood, P. T. (1987). Agroforestry and sustainable development: making the connection. *Ambio*, **XVI(2–3)**, 100–10.

Wischmeier, W. H. (1976). Use and misuse of the universal soil loss equation. *Journal of Soil and Water Conservation*, **31(1)**, 5–9.

Wischmeier, W. H. & Smith, D. D. (1960). A universal soil loss equation to guide conservation farm planning. *Transactions of 7th International Congress of Soil Science*, **1**, 418–25.

Wiseman, R. (1989). Quick purge puts salty land into production. *New Scientist*, **124(1686)**, p. 36.

WMO. (1986). *WMO Report on Drought and Countries Affected by Drought*, Geneva: World Meteorological Organization.

Woddis, J. (1967). *Introduction to Neo Colonialism*. London: Lawrence and Wishart.

Wolman, M. G. & Fournier, F. G. (eds.) (1987). *Land Transformation in Agriculture*. Chichester: John Wiley and Sons.

Wood, C. A. (1977). A preliminary ecology of Ethiopian droughts. In *Drought in Africa 2*, eds. D. Dalby, R. J. Harrison-Church & F. Bezzaz, pp. 68–73. London: International African Institute.

World Bank. (1985). *Desertification in the Sahelian and Sudanian Zones of West Africa*, World Bank, 60 pp.

World Bank. (1988). *Forestry Action Plan*. Washington DC: World Bank.

World Commission on Environment and Development. (1987a). *Our Common Future: report of the World Commission on Environment and Development*. (the 'Brundtland Report'). Oxford: Oxford University Press.

World Commission on Environment and Development. (1987b). *Food 2000: global policies for sustainable agriculture* (Report of the Advisory Panel on Food Security, Agriculture, Forestry and Environment to the World Commission on Environment and Development). London: Zed Books.

World Resources Institute, World Bank & UNDP. (1985). *Tropical Forests: a call for action*. (3 parts: I *The Plan*, 47 pp., II *Case Studies* 55pp., III *Country Investment Profiles*, 22 pp.). Washington DC: World Resources Institute (1735 New York Ave., N.W. Washington DC 20006).

World Resources Institute, International Institute for Environment and Development & UNEP (1987). *World Resources 1987–88: an assessment of the resource base that supports the global economy*, New York: Basic Books.

World Resources Institute, International Institute for Environment and Development & UNEP (1988). *World Resources 1988–89: an assessment of the resource base that supports the global economy*. New York: Basic Books.

Worster, D. (1979). *Dust Bowl: the Southern Plains in the 1930s.* New York: Oxford University Press (USA).

Zachar, D. (1982). *Soil Erosion* (Developments in Soil Science 10). Amsterdam: Elsevier Scientific.

Index

biodiversity
  see also species diversity 246
biofuel 239
biogas 115, 239
biological control of pests 194
biological weapons 226
biomass 22, 36, 45, 64, 94, 117, 181
biomass energy 48, 106
biosphere 5
birch 96
bison 173
bituminous coal 60
Black Death
  see plague
blackfly
  see also *Simulium* 155
Black Forest 62
Blake, William 6
blanket peats 64, 118, 125
blind staggers 236
blueberries 127
Bolivia 84, 131–5, 161, 256
bomb cratering 224
Bonnin Is. 139
Boreal forests 95–7
borehole sinking 167, 232
Borneo 85
boron 183, 191, 237
Botswana 119, 168
Bouhinia spp. 89
bovine tuberculosis 254
Brachystegia spp. 89
bracken 92, 240
Bragantina Zone 79
'Brandt Report' 8
Brazil 53, 60, 74–5, 77, 80–1, 85, 89,
  101–2, 104, 106, 119, 158, 170, 213,
  217, 230, 232, 239, 240, 242
Brazil nut 83, 100
brick making 229
brick pits 229
British Colombia 97
broad-leaved trees 62–3, 96
Bromeliad spp. 61
bromine 50
Brousse tigree ('tiger stripes') 148, 152
Brundtland Commission ('Bruntland
  Report') 8, 29, 258
buffalo 159, 241
buffer zones 105, 250, 254
buffering acidity 64
Buffo marinus 242
Bulgaria 134
bunds 215
burialgrounds 236
Burkina Faso 115, 160, 165, 176
Burma 78, 79, 82, 104
burning
  see also fires 34, 127, 240
burrowing animals 201
Burundi 126, 132
bush fallow 95
bush rotation agriculture
  see also shifting cultivation 156
bushfires
  see also fires 89, 91, 127, 155, 171–2,
  175, 224, 254
Butryospermum spp. 165
by-products 66, 233

C_3/C_4 photosynthesis 44–5
Caatinga 89
cable-logging 99
cacodylic acid 225
cadmium 235
Caesalpina spp. 83
Cairngorms 135
Caithness Flow Country area 127
cajeput 241
calcium 186
Caledonian Forest 96
Caliche 182
California 92, 123, 162, 171, 182, 184,
  188, 191, 230–2, 241
Calvaria spp. 251
Camargue 119
cambisols 64
Cameron Highlands
  see also hill stations 133, 135
Cameroon 257
Canada 68, 97, 123, 127, 129, 173, 175,
  188, 228, 237
Canadian pondweed 240
Canary Is. 184
cancer
  see also anti-cancer drugs/carcinogens
Cane toads 242
Cape Verde 166, 176
capybara 119
carbon dioxide 31–35, 97, 99
carbon loss
  see soil carbon
carbon monoxide 36
carbon sinks 32, 34, 48, 99, 128
carbon tax 67
carbon tetrachloride 50
carbonates 34
carbonic acid 54
carcinogens
  see also mutagenesis 92, 240
Caribbean 77
carrying capacity 17, 23, 25–6, 157, 166
cash cropping 160, 161
cash crops 110, 165
cassava 81, 239
Casurina spp. 241
catalytic converter 66–67, 69
catastrophes 13, 180
Catastrophe Theory 23–4
catchment management
  see also watershed management 130
cataracts of the eye 52
Catharanthus sp. 84
cattle 156, 158
cedar 75
cellulose production 239
Centrosema sp. 217
cement production 229
cereal production 98
cereals 171, 172
Cerrado 89, 170, 217
CFCs 15, 32–3, 36, 50, 52–3
Chad 165, 176
Chad L. 163
Chaga's Disease 100
chain dragging to clear bush 95
chain-of-causation 2, 13, 61, 73, 79, 146,
  257

channelization 120, 123
Chaporral 91
charcoal 81, 86, 94, 108, 115, 122, 171
check-dams 216
chemical amendment 191
Chenopodium spp. 133
Chernobyl Disaster 57, 127, 129, 237
Chicago 175
chicle 83
Chico Mendes 114
Chile 59, 91, 97, 106, 131, 134, 171
China
  see Peoples' Republic of China
Chinese mitten crab 242
Chinampas 226
Chinchona spp. 137
Chihicahuan Desert 173
chipboard production 122
Chipko Movement 113
Chitamene 95
chlorine 49–50, 225
chlorofluorocarbons
  see CFCs
Chortiocetes spp. 152
Christmas Is. 227
CILSS 176
CITES 253
civil unrest 152
clearcutting 122
clear felling 82
climate change 47
climax 23–4
cloud forest 130
clover 155, 183
Club du Sahel 176
coal 3, 34, 53–4, 57, 66, 96, 129, 229
coal-fired power stations 68
coal mines 229
coastal accretion 240
cobalt 231, 235
coca 81, 133, 226
cocaine 81
coco 81–2
Code of Conduct for Tropical Timber
  Traders 114
coffee 81, 133
Colisses 219
Colombia 74, 76, 79, 82, 104, 130, 132,
  227, 253, 256
colonialism 15
colonization by species 137
Colorado 134–5, 173, 232
Colorado beetle 241
Colorado R. 43, 191
commercialization 157, 209
Commiphora spp. 89
common resources 7–8, 18, 157
community forestry 101
compaction 180, 182, 186
Confucianism 5
conifers 62, 74–5, 86, 95, 97, 104, 138,
  242
Connecticut 101
conservation
  see also energy conservation 102, 113,
  136, 248
conservation areas 43, 247–50
conservation funding 256
constancy 22

São Paulo 55
Sarawak 82
Sardinia 171
Saskatchewan 188
Saudi Arabia 154
Scandinavia 95–6, 129
SCARP 191
Schinus spp. 241
Schistosomiasis 46, 153, 194
SCOPE 98
scrubbing 67
sea level change 34, 38–9, 85
seasonal debilitation 46
seasonal hunger/poverty 20
seasonal labour shortage 216
seasonally dry forest 89
sedentarization 158, 160
Sedgemoor 127
SED 259
selective logging 104
selenium 183, 231
semi-arid 23, 142
Senegal 152, 163, 165
Sequoiadendron spp. 92
Serra Pelada Mine 232
serotinus vegetation 92
Sertão 89, 170
settlers 79–80, 84, 108
sewage 36, 41, 122, 127, 195, 217, 234–5
shea butter 95, 165
sheet erosion (sheetwash) 134, 182, 200
shell craters 224
shelter-belts 217–18
shifting cultivation 80, 82, 84–5, 112,
    149, 151, 161, 168–9, 208
Shorea spp. 82
ship-building 96
shrinkage on drainage 181–2, 197
Siberia 128–9, 170
Sicily 171
Sierra-Club 6
Sierra Nevada (Spain) 134
Sierra Nevada (USA) 92
silage effluent 195
siltation 206
silting-up of reservoirs 206
Simulium damnosum 155
Singapore 122, 249
sitka spruce 44
ski impacts 128–9, 133, 209
skid trails 99
skidoos 12, 209
slash-and-burn
    see also shifting cultivation 95
Sleeping Sickness
    see Trypanosomiasis 154
slurry lagoons 195
smallholders 80, 86
Smallpox 226
Smith, Adam 3
smog 53, 55
Snowy Mountains 135
social differentiation 161
social forestry 102
sodication 187
sodification 187
sodium 186
sodium bicarbonate 187
sodium chloride 187, 231

sodium hydroxide 187, 231
sodium sulphate 187
sodium sulphide 187
soil acidification
    see acidification of soil
soil accumulation 200
soil carbon 34, 97, 128, 211, 213, 215,
    217
soil conditioners 215–16
Soil Conservation Service USA 175, 221
soil degradation 179
soil erosion 199
soil formation rate 205
soil loss 12
soil loss rate 203
soil structure changes 179
solar radiation 38
solifuxion 128, 200
solodization 187
Solonetz 187
Solontchak 187
solution 201
Somalia 87, 165
Somerset Levels 127
Sonneratia spp. 122
Sonoran Desert 173
soot 47, 68
sorghum 156, 239
South Africa 60, 171
South Georgia 138
sovereignty 101, 258
soya 45, 52, 212
Spain 142, 171
Spartina spp. 240
species diversity 22, 73–5, 86
species invasion 71, 79
species loss 82, 98, 136, 148, 246, 249
species retention 136
Sphagnum spp. 64, 125, 127
Spitzbergen 129, 246
spoil heap combustion 230
spoil heaps 230, 233
spruce budworm 242
squatters 79, 81, 133
Sri Lanka 78, 106, 131, 133
St. Anton 134
St. Francis of Assissi 5
stability 29
stall feeding 93, 132
steady-state
    see also equilibrium/Equilibrium Theory
    50, 91, 199, 209, 259
Steinbeck, John 4
steppelands 170
Stipa spp. 169
stock resources 13
Stockholm Conference on the Human
    Environment 8, 10, 54
stocking rates 27
stone lines 215
storms 39–41
stoves
    see also Jiko stove 115
Stratosphere 31–2
Stratospheric ozone
    see also ozone 31–2, 47, 49, 151, 238
straw burning 181, 208
straw as a raw material 116
Striga spp. 155, 181

strip mining 229, 230
St. Vincent 154
stubble burning
    see straw burning
SubAntarctic 129, 242
SubSaharan Africa 11
subsidence 195, 230, 232
subsurface erosion 200–1
succession 24
Sudan 19, 94, 104, 112, 153, 201
Sudano-Sahelian Zone 89, 151, 156, 159,
    161–3, 166–7, 176
Sudbury Smelter 54, 61
Sudd 119, 120
Suez Canal 172
suffosion 182, 186, 200
sugar bagasse 217
sugar cane 81, 166, 170, 208, 239
Sukhovei wind 170, 202
Sulawesi 85
sulphides 196
sulphur 54–5, 65
sulphur dioxide 36, 46, 54
sulphonic acid 50
sulphuric acid 55, 192
SST 50, 238
Sumatra 75, 85
Sundarbans 119, 122
sunflowers/sunflower oil 45, 239
Sungai Besi Tin Mines 231
SURE 259
Surinam 104, 154
sustainable development 28–9, 102, 212,
    258
sustainable growth 259
sustainable yield 28–9, 75
Sutherland 127
swamps 127
Swansea Valley 235
Sweden 54, 60, 68, 106, 134, 237
Swetonia spp. 82
Switzerland 60, 132
symbiotic 193, 249
synergistic
    see cumulative causation 193
Syria 91, 171

taboos 107–8
Taiga 129
tailings 230
Tamarix spp. 108, 155, 188, 241
Tamerugo sp. 108
Tambora Volcanic Eruption 37
tan bark 122
Tanzania 89, 160, 168
Tasmania 79, 97–8
Tatras Mtns. 134
Taungya 110
Tavy 168
taxes 81, 86, 102, 158, 168, 220
Taxodium spp. 118
TCDD 225
tea 81, 133
teak 79, 104, 107, 110, 204
technology transfer 19, 180
Tectonia spp. 79
TELMA 129
tenure 18, 188
Terminalia spp. 89